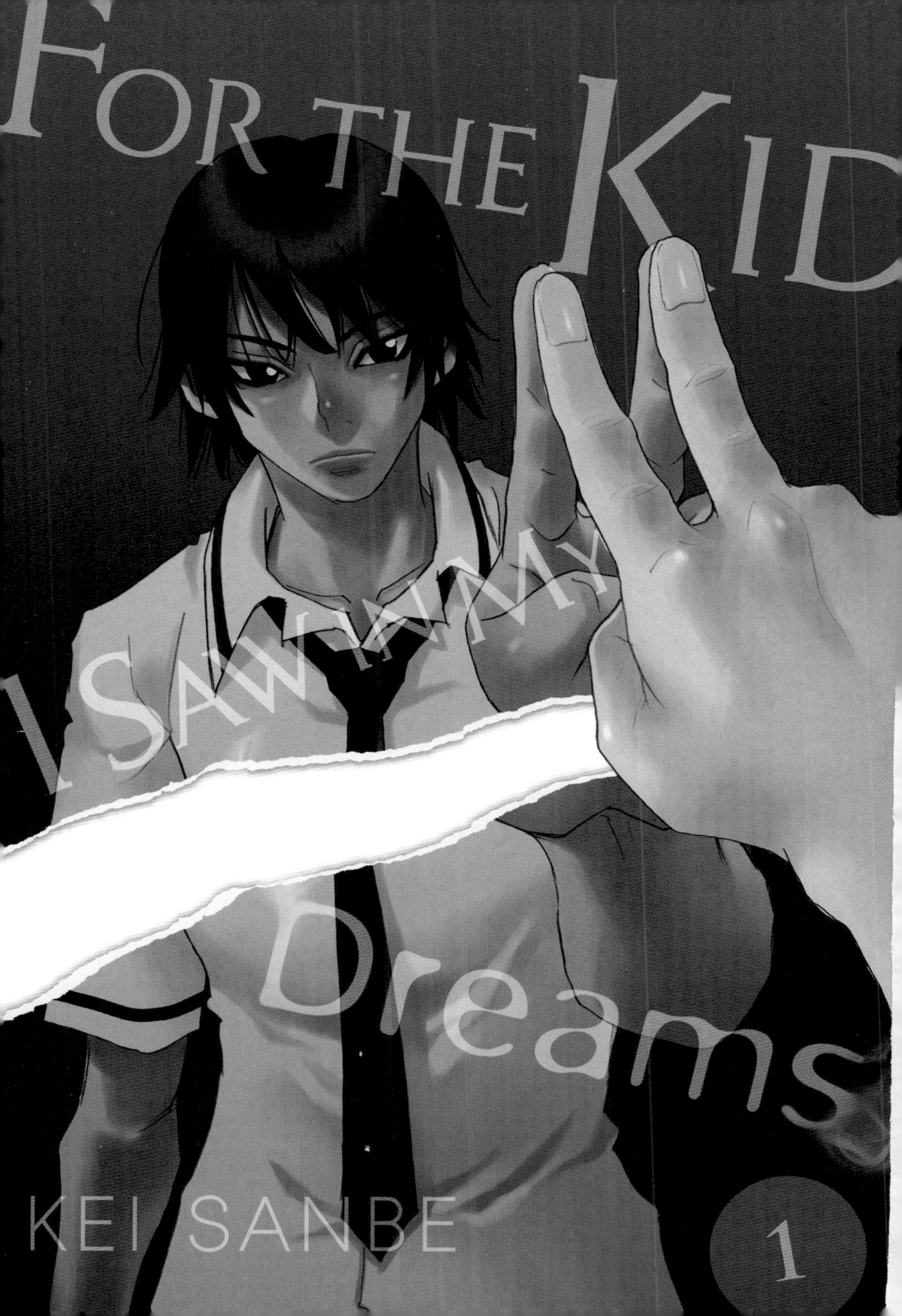
For the Kid
I Saw in My Dreams
KEI SANBE
1

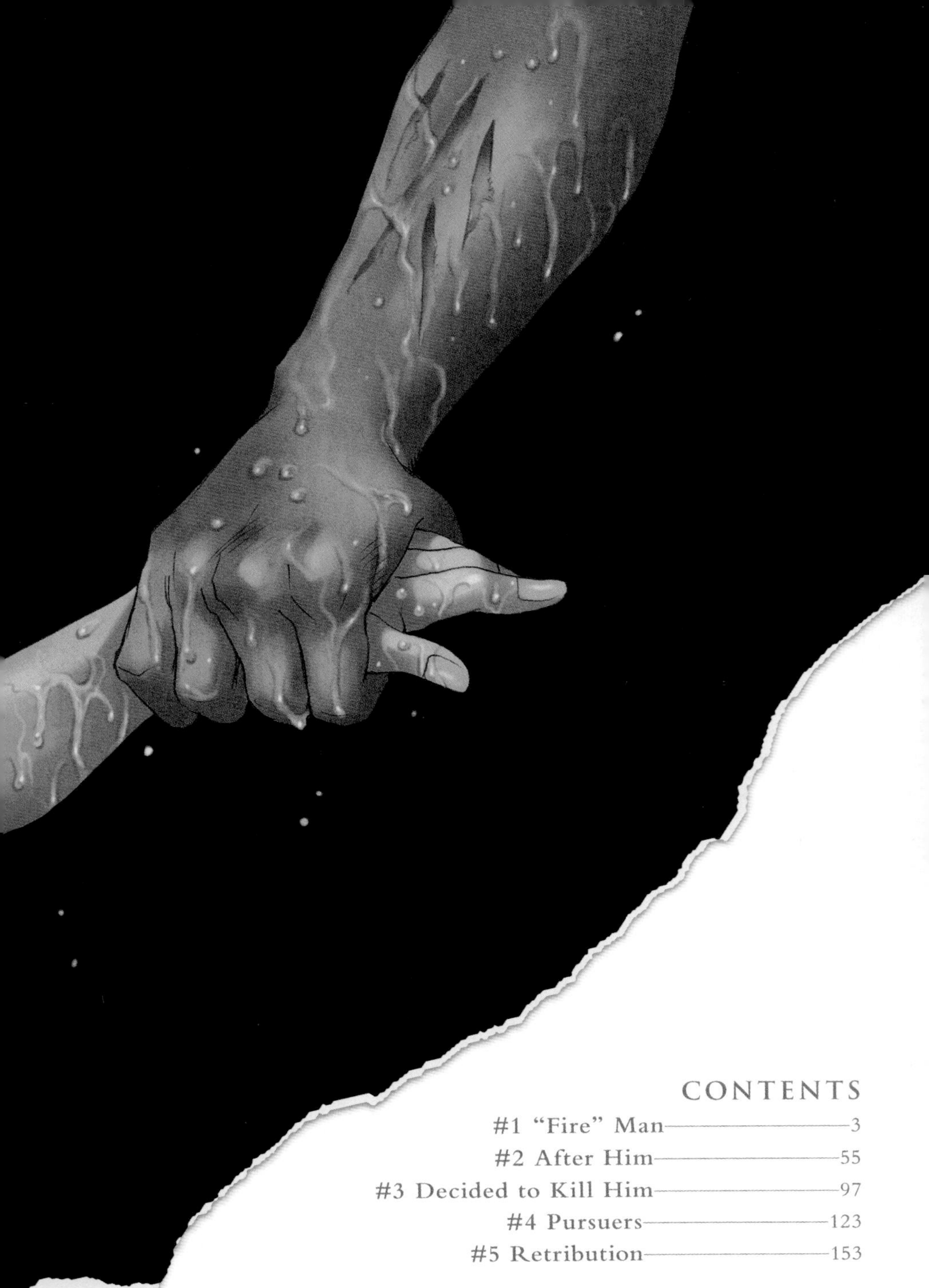

CONTENTS

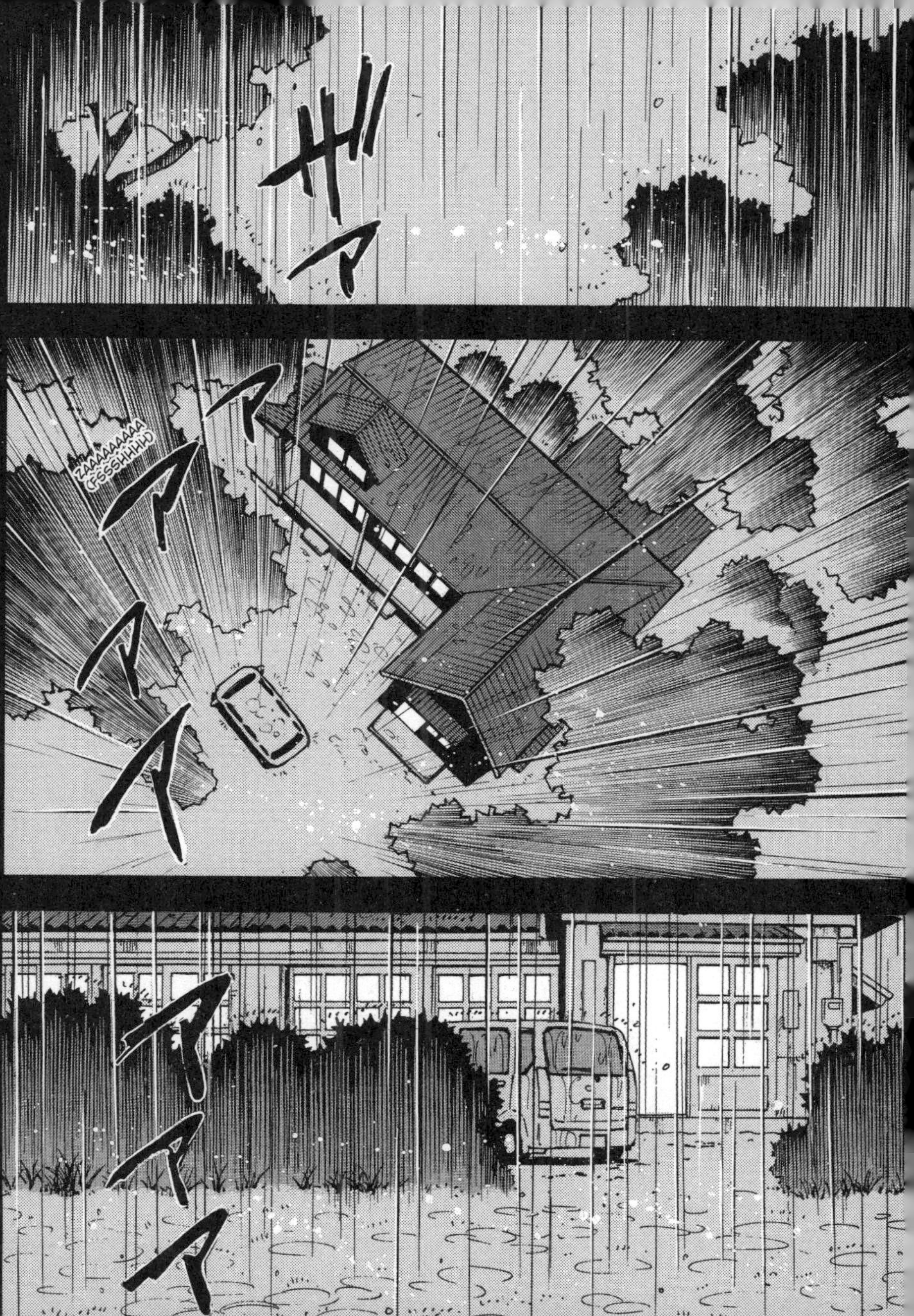
ザァ
ZAAAAAAAAA (FSSSHHHH)

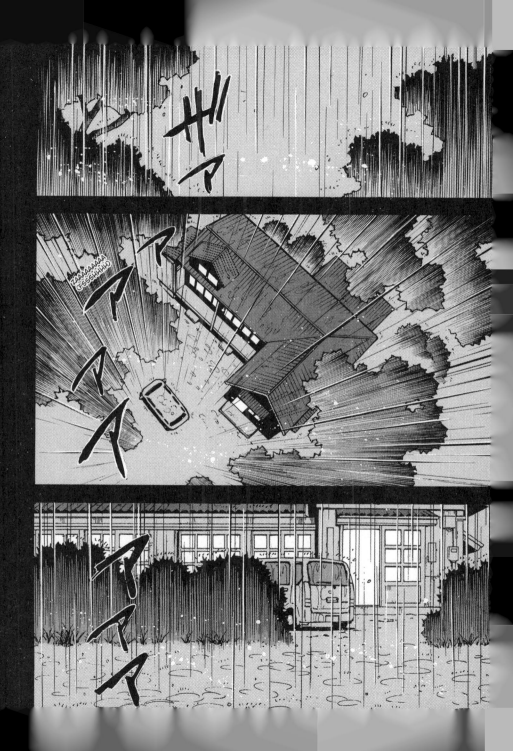

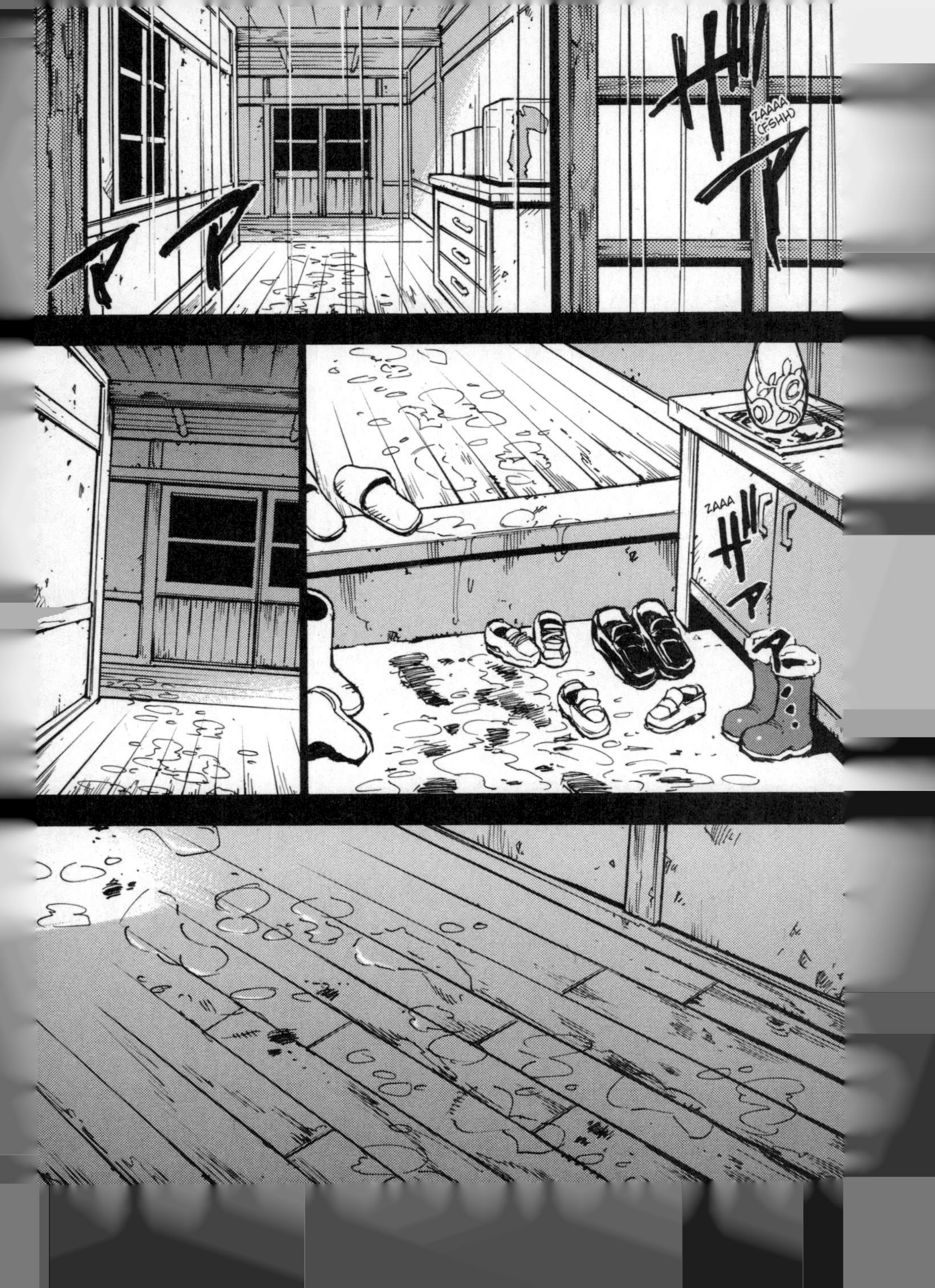
ZAAAA (FSHH)
ZAAA

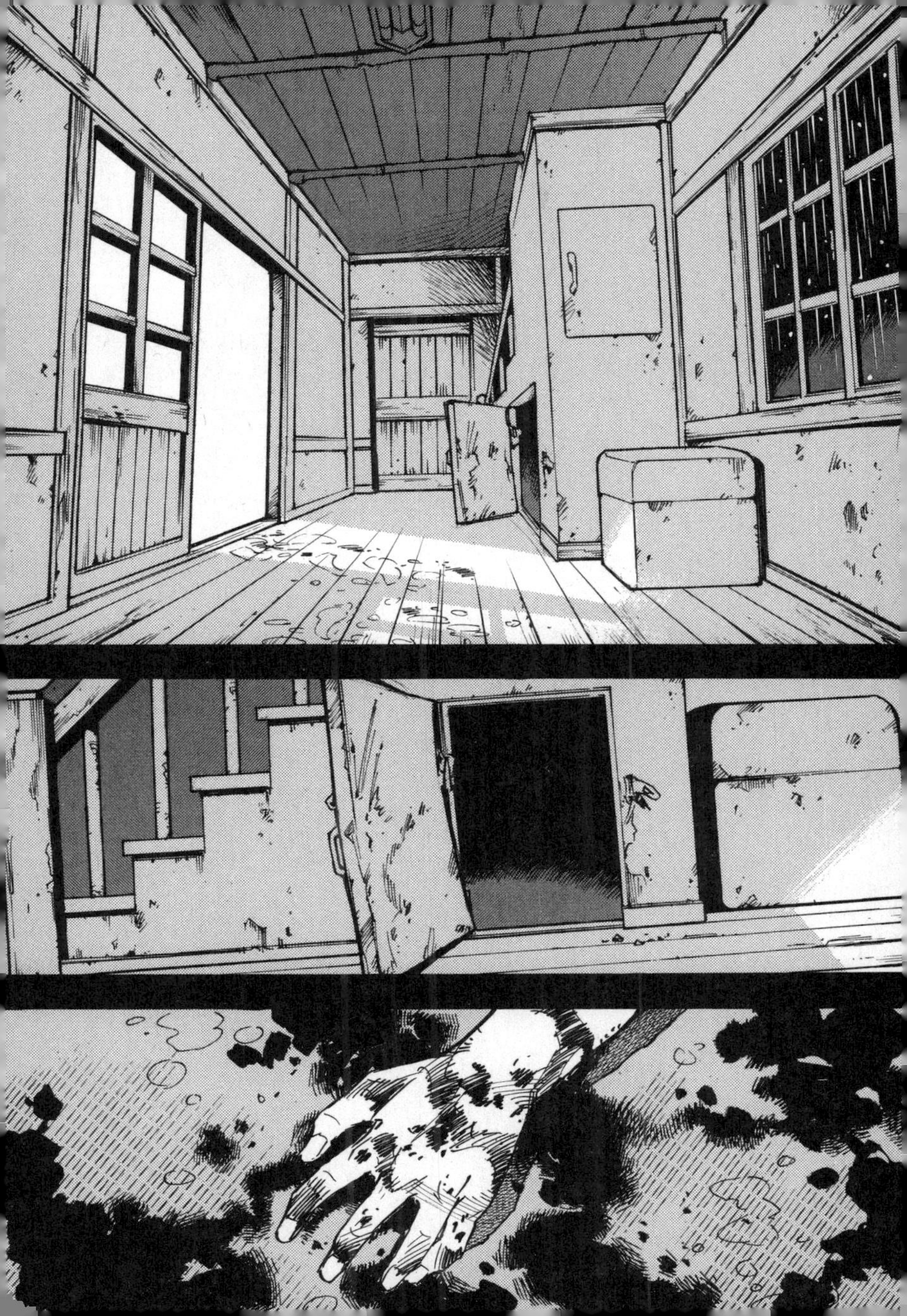

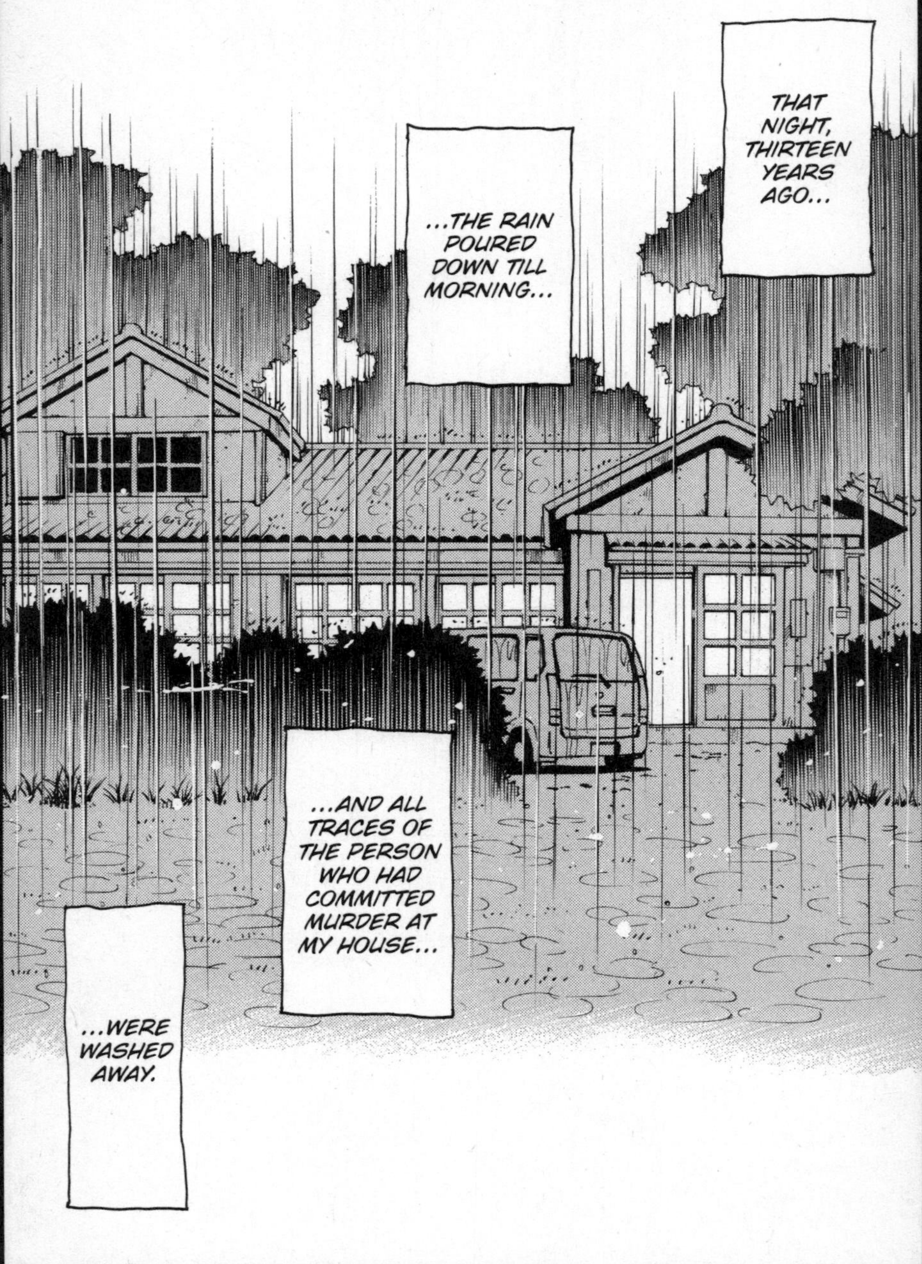
THAT NIGHT, THIRTEEN YEARS AGO...
...THE RAIN POURED DOWN TILL MORNING...
...AND ALL TRACES OF THE PERSON WHO HAD COMMITTED MURDER AT MY HOUSE...
...WERE WASHED AWAY.

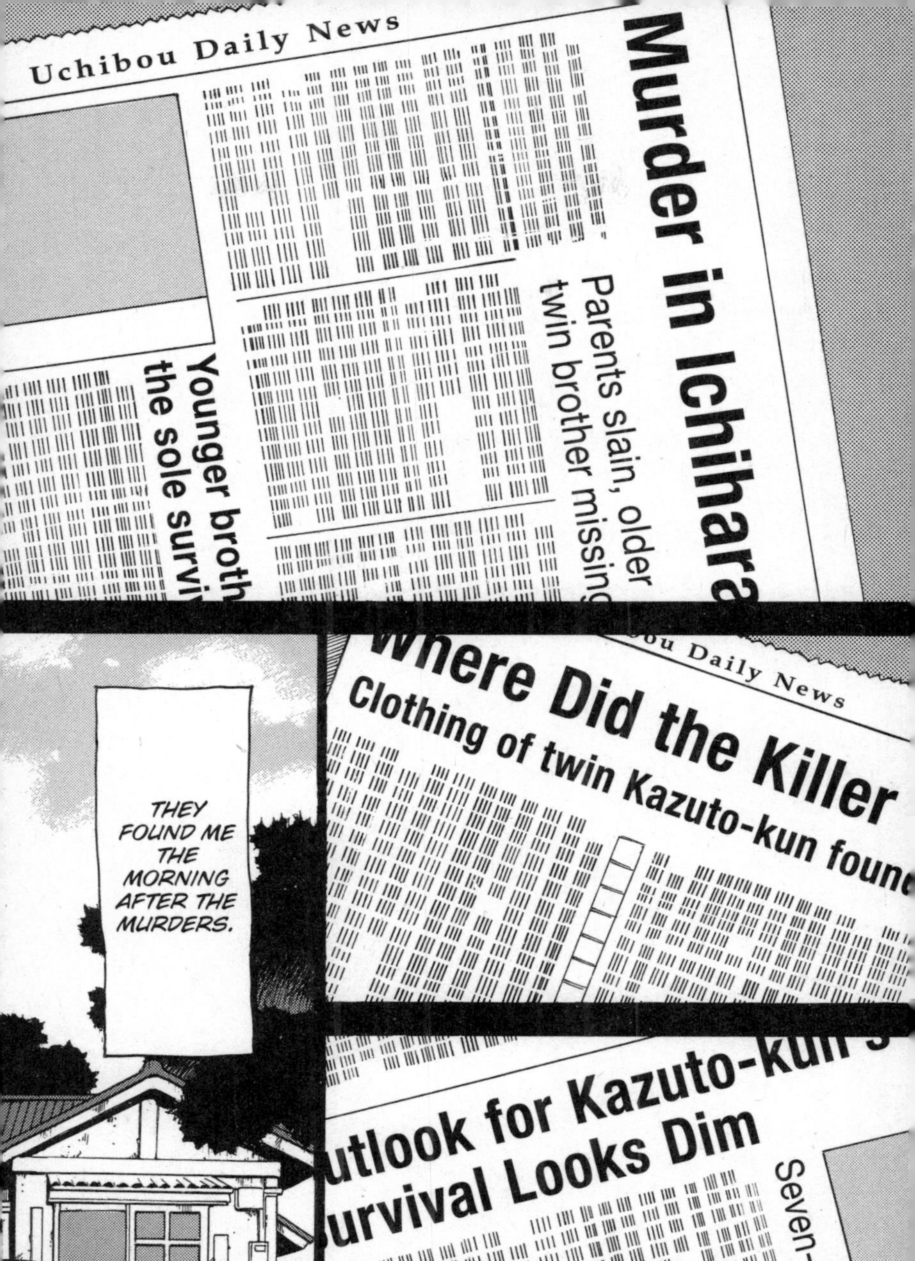
Uchibou Daily News
Murder in Ichihara
Parents slain, older twin brother missin
Younger broth
the sole survi
ou Daily News
Where Did the Killer
Clothing of twin Kazuto-kun foun
utlook for Kazuto-kun's
urvival Looks Dim
Seven-day
THEY FOUND ME THE MORNING AFTER THE MURDERS.

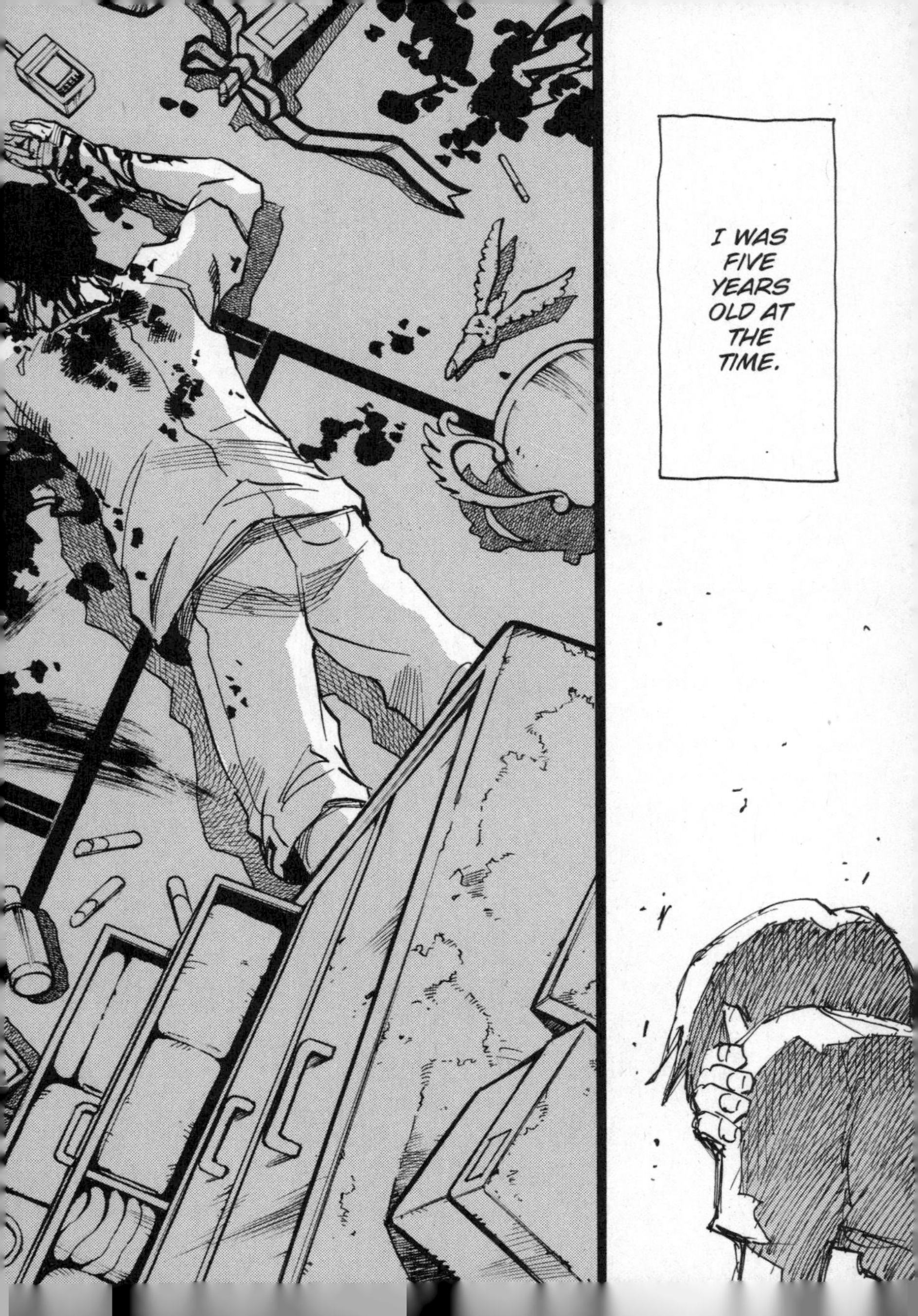
I WAS FIVE YEARS OLD AT THE TIME.

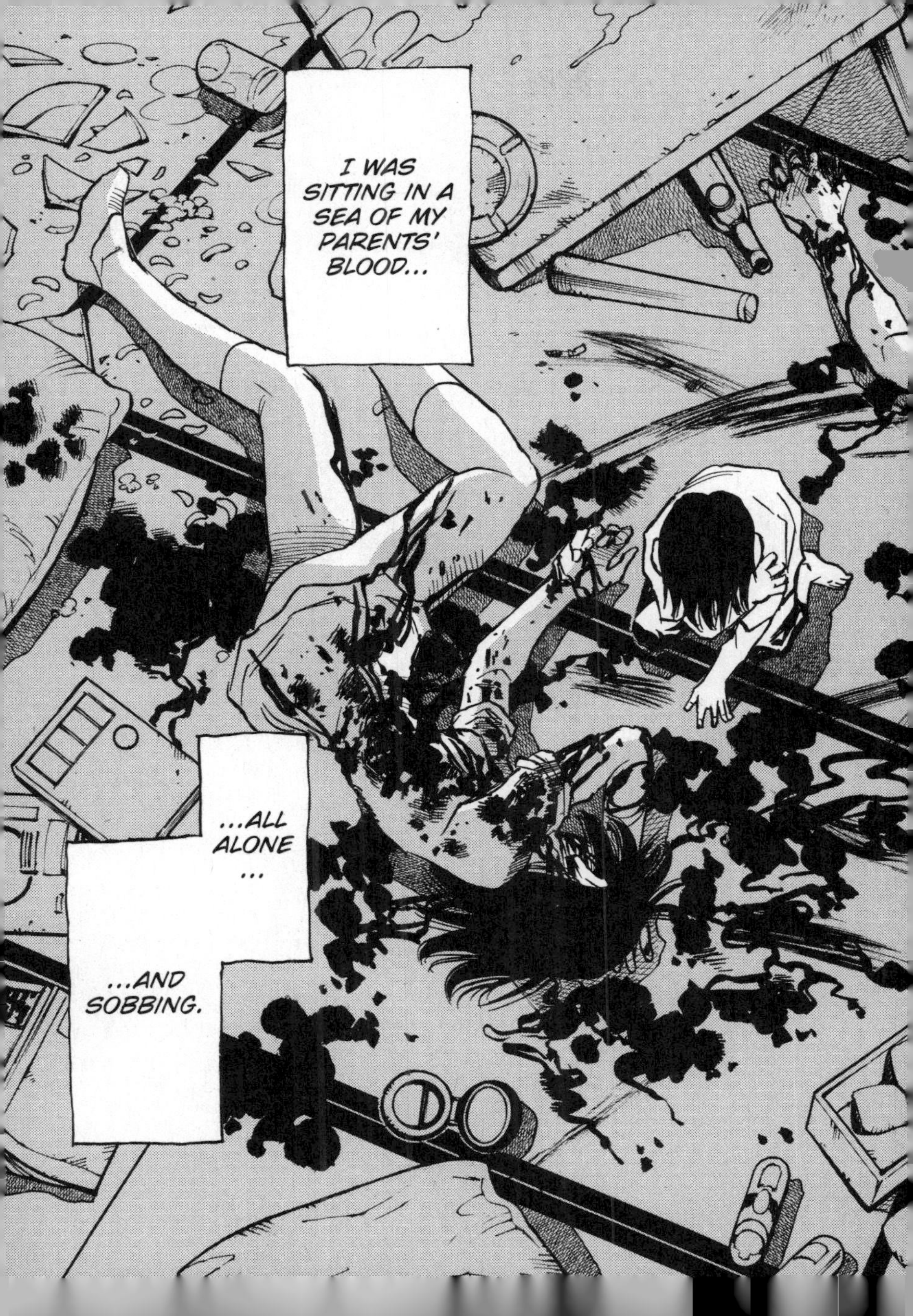
I WAS SITTING IN A SEA OF MY PARENTS' BLOOD...
...ALL ALONE ...
...AND SOBBING.

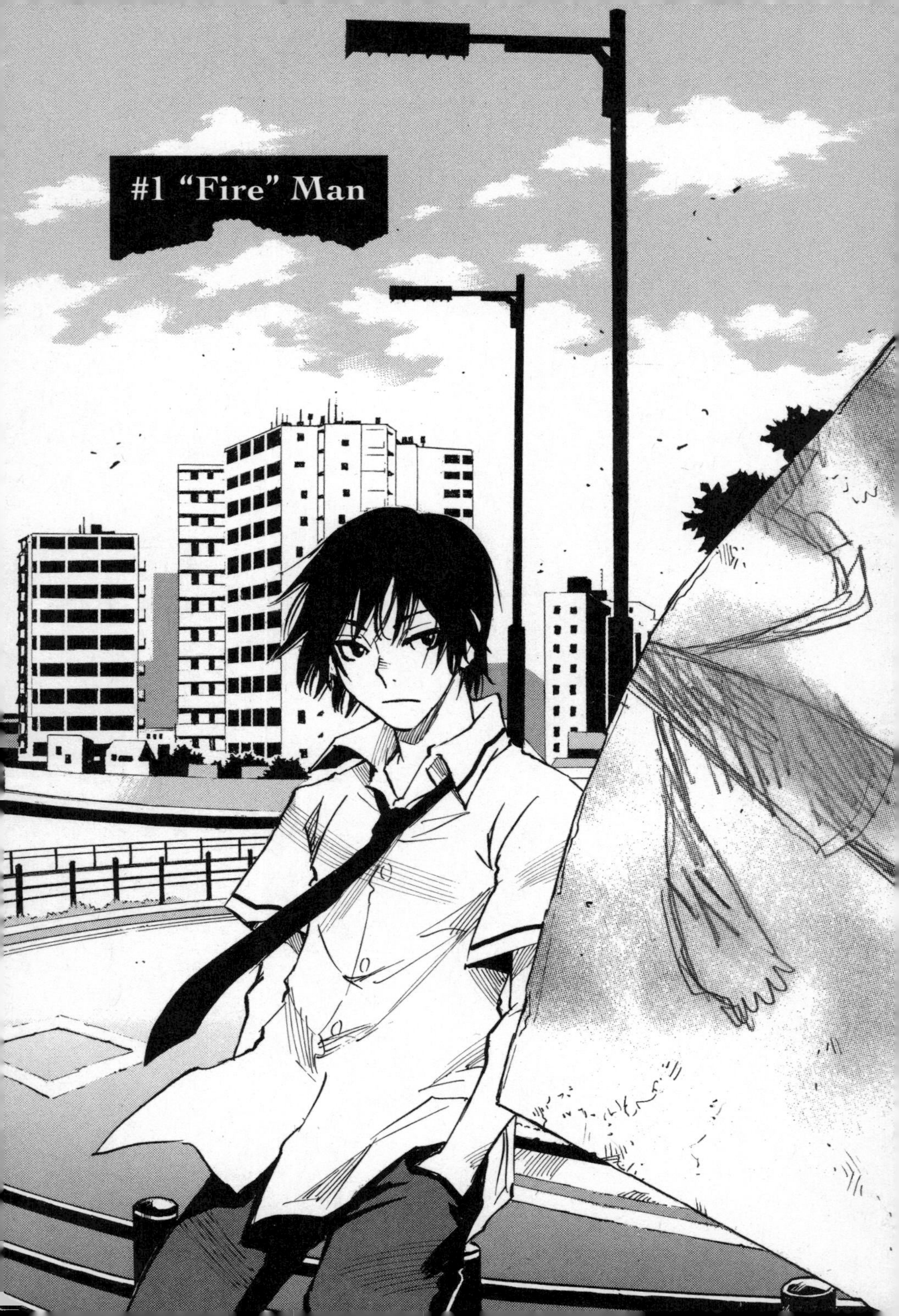
#1 "Fire" Man

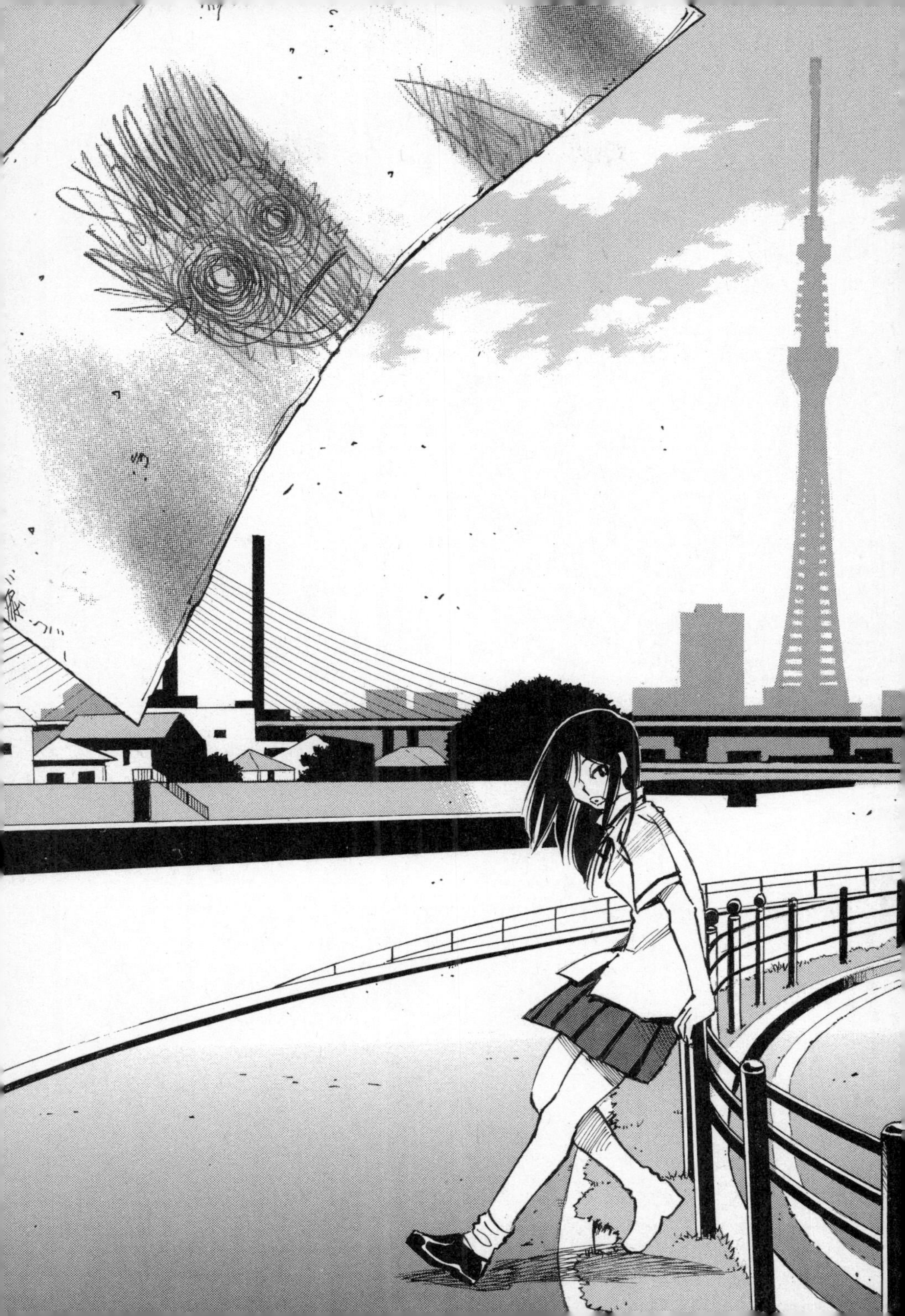

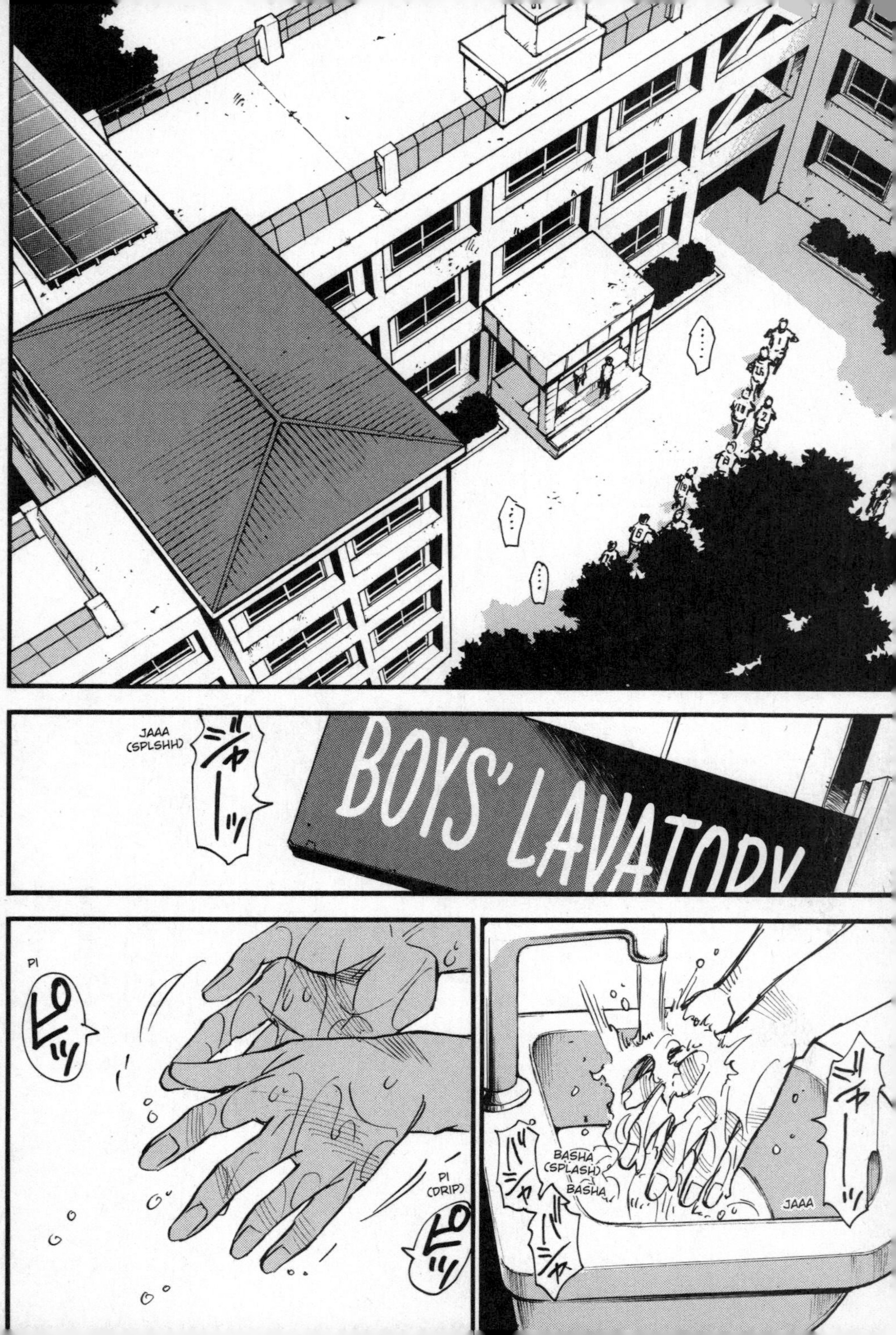
.....
.....
.....
JAAA (SPLSHH)
ジャーッ
BOYS' LAVAT
BASHA (SPLASH)
BASHA
バシャ
バシャ
JAAA
ジャーッ
PI
ピッ
PI (DRIP)
ピッ

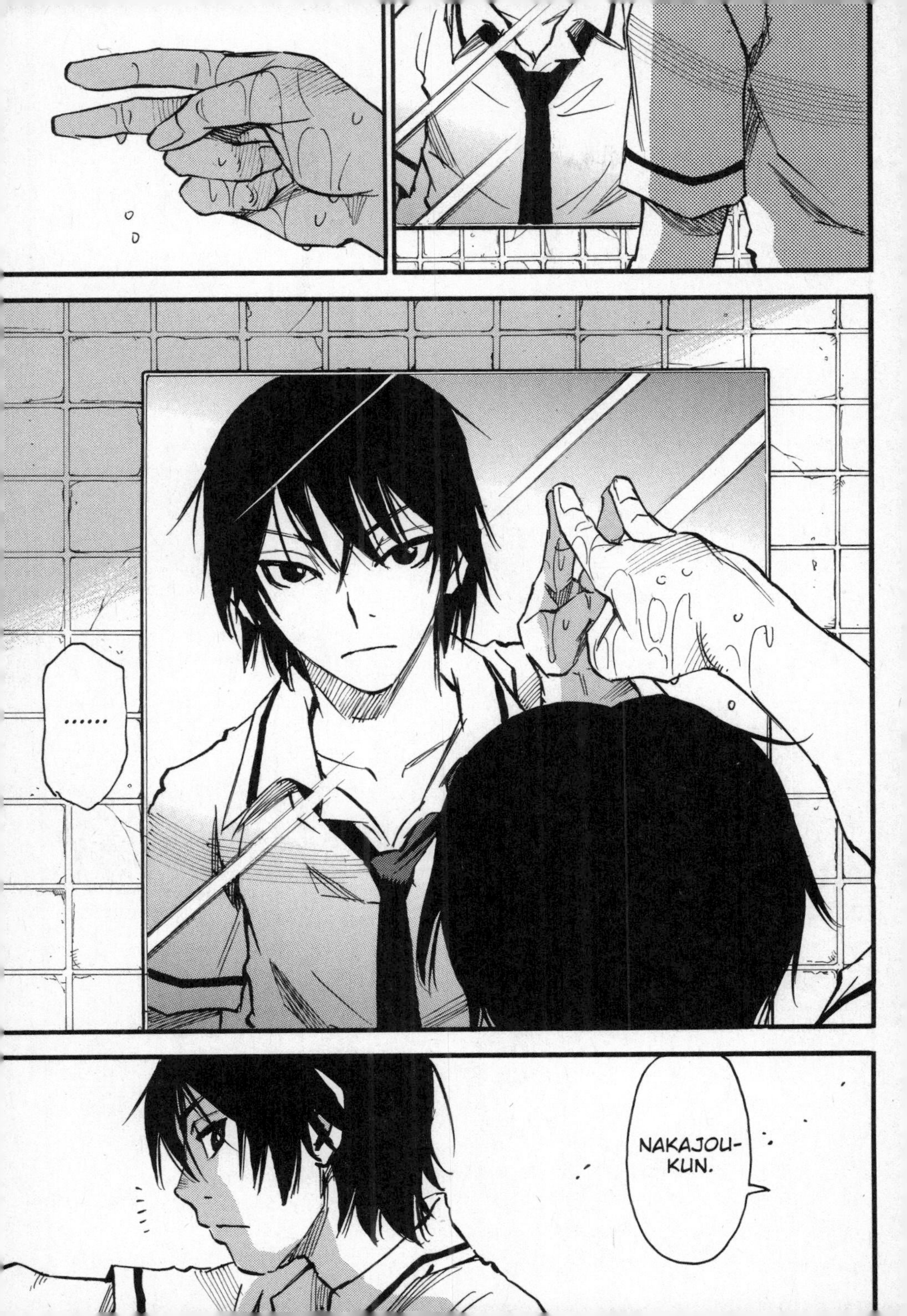
......
NAKAJOU-KUN.

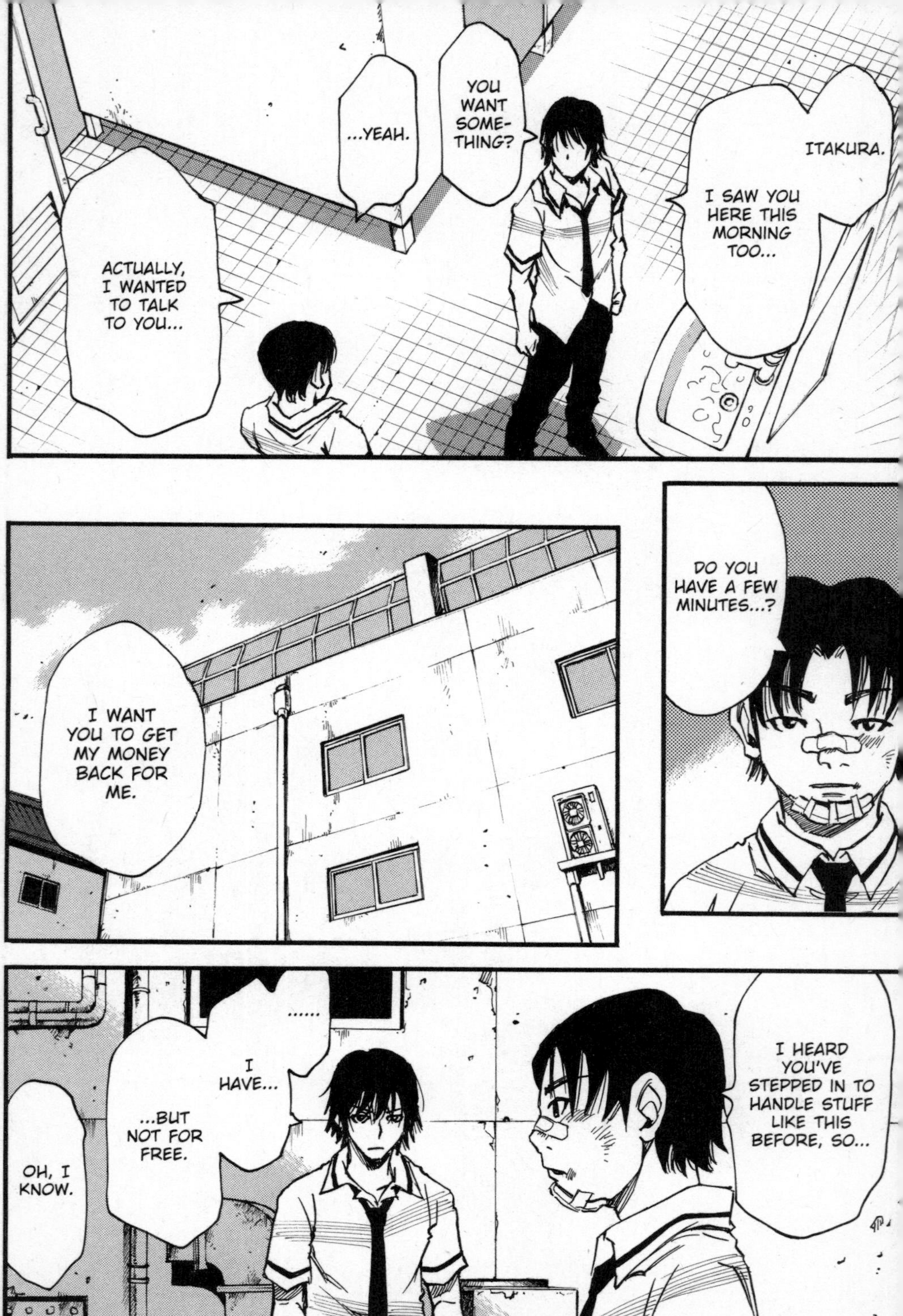
ITAKURA.
I SAW YOU HERE THIS MORNING TOO...
YOU WANT SOME-THING?
...YEAH.
ACTUALLY, I WANTED TO TALK TO YOU...
DO YOU HAVE A FEW MINUTES...?
I WANT YOU TO GET MY MONEY BACK FOR ME.
I HEARD YOU'VE STEPPED IN TO HANDLE STUFF LIKE THIS BEFORE, SO...
......
I HAVE...
...BUT NOT FOR FREE.
OH, I KNOW.

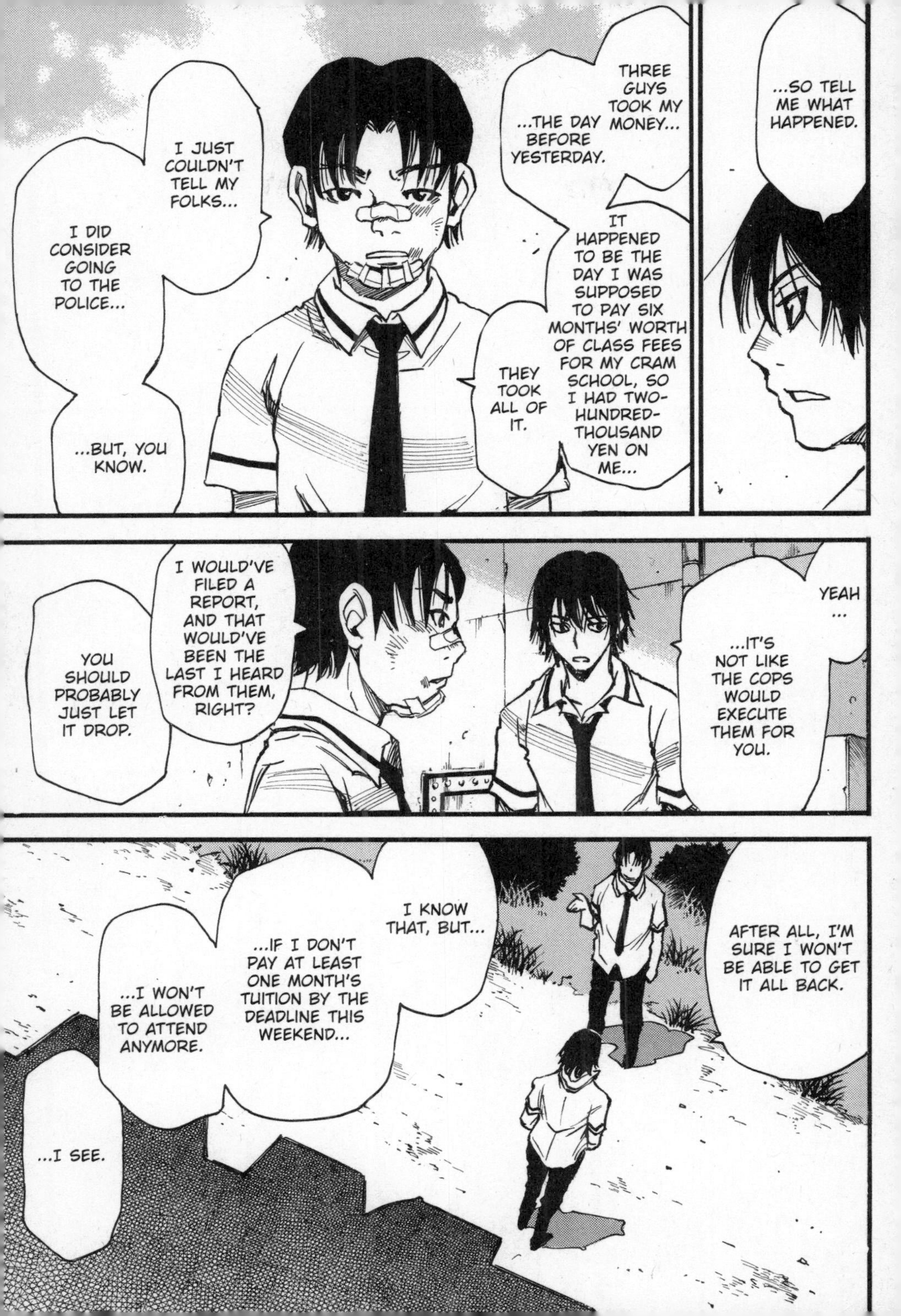
...SO TELL ME WHAT HAPPENED.
THREE GUYS TOOK MY MONEY...
...THE DAY BEFORE YESTERDAY.
IT HAPPENED TO BE THE DAY I WAS SUPPOSED TO PAY SIX MONTHS' WORTH OF CLASS FEES FOR MY CRAM SCHOOL, SO I HAD TWO-HUNDRED-THOUSAND YEN ON ME...
THEY TOOK ALL OF IT.
I JUST COULDN'T TELL MY FOLKS...
I DID CONSIDER GOING TO THE POLICE...
...BUT, YOU KNOW.
YEAH ...
...IT'S NOT LIKE THE COPS WOULD EXECUTE THEM FOR YOU.
I WOULD'VE FILED A REPORT, AND THAT WOULD'VE BEEN THE LAST I HEARD FROM THEM, RIGHT?
YOU SHOULD PROBABLY JUST LET IT DROP.
AFTER ALL, I'M SURE I WON'T BE ABLE TO GET IT ALL BACK.
I KNOW THAT, BUT...
...IF I DON'T PAY AT LEAST ONE MONTH'S TUITION BY THE DEADLINE THIS WEEKEND...
...I WON'T BE ALLOWED TO ATTEND ANYMORE.
...I SEE.

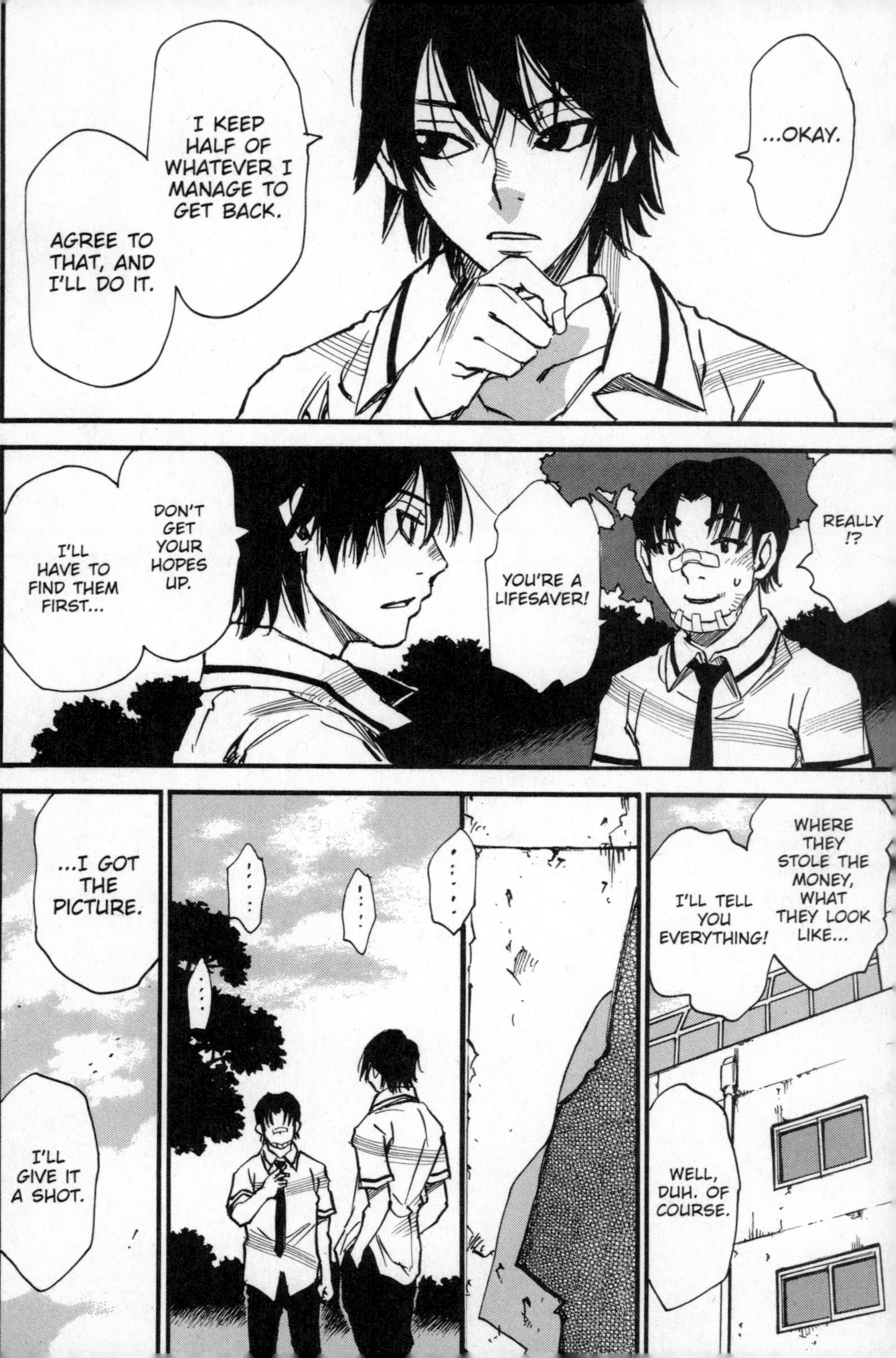
...OKAY.
I KEEP HALF OF WHATEVER I MANAGE TO GET BACK.
AGREE TO THAT, AND I'LL DO IT.
REALLY!?
YOU'RE A LIFESAVER!
DON'T GET YOUR HOPES UP.
I'LL HAVE TO FIND THEM FIRST...
WHERE THEY STOLE THE MONEY, WHAT THEY LOOK LIKE...
I'LL TELL YOU EVERYTHING!
WELL, DUH. OF COURSE.
...I GOT THE PICTURE.
I'LL GIVE IT A SHOT.

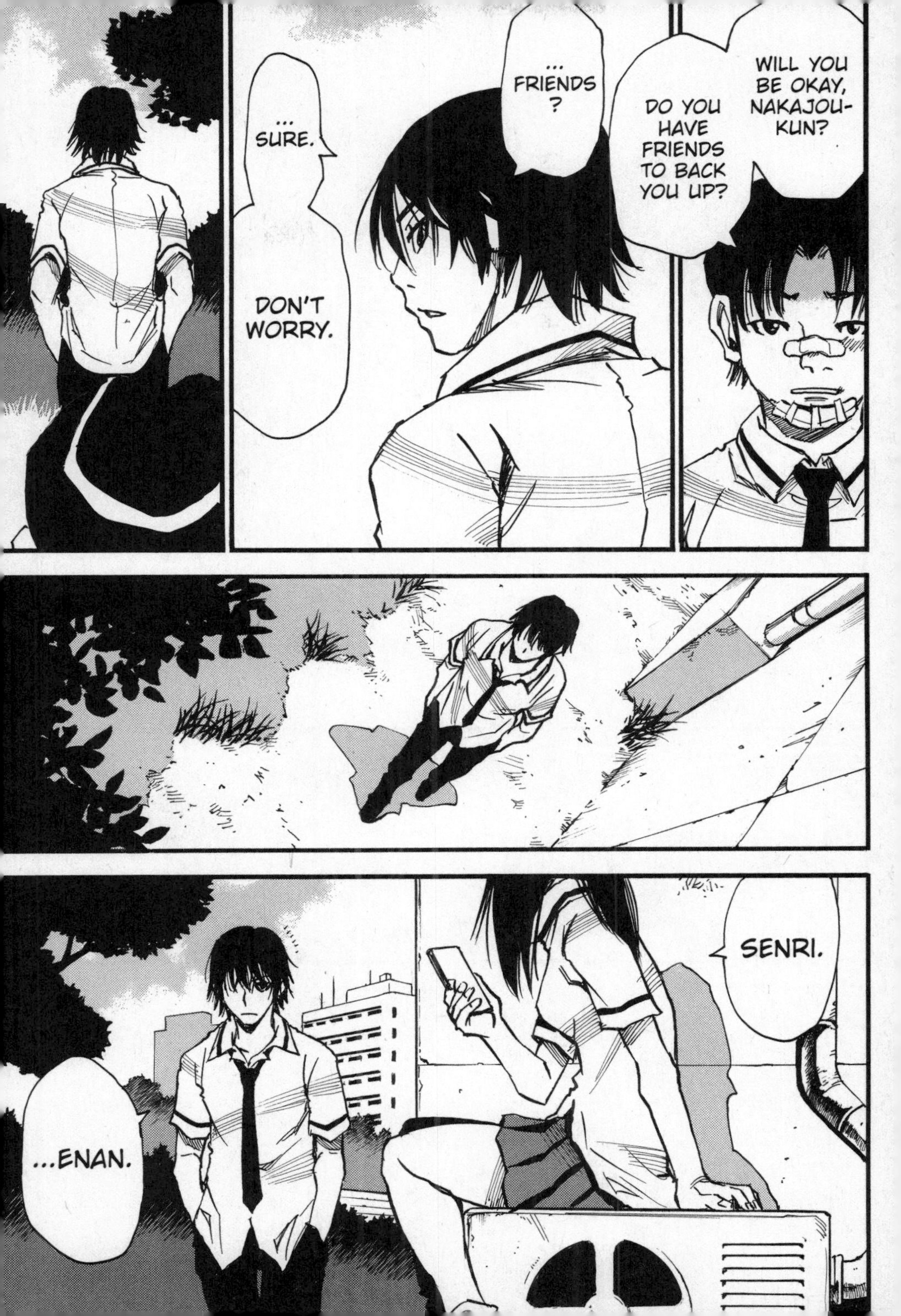
WILL YOU BE OKAY, NAKAJOU-KUN?
DO YOU HAVE FRIENDS TO BACK YOU UP?
... FRIENDS ?
... SURE.
DON'T WORRY.
SENRI.
...ENAN.

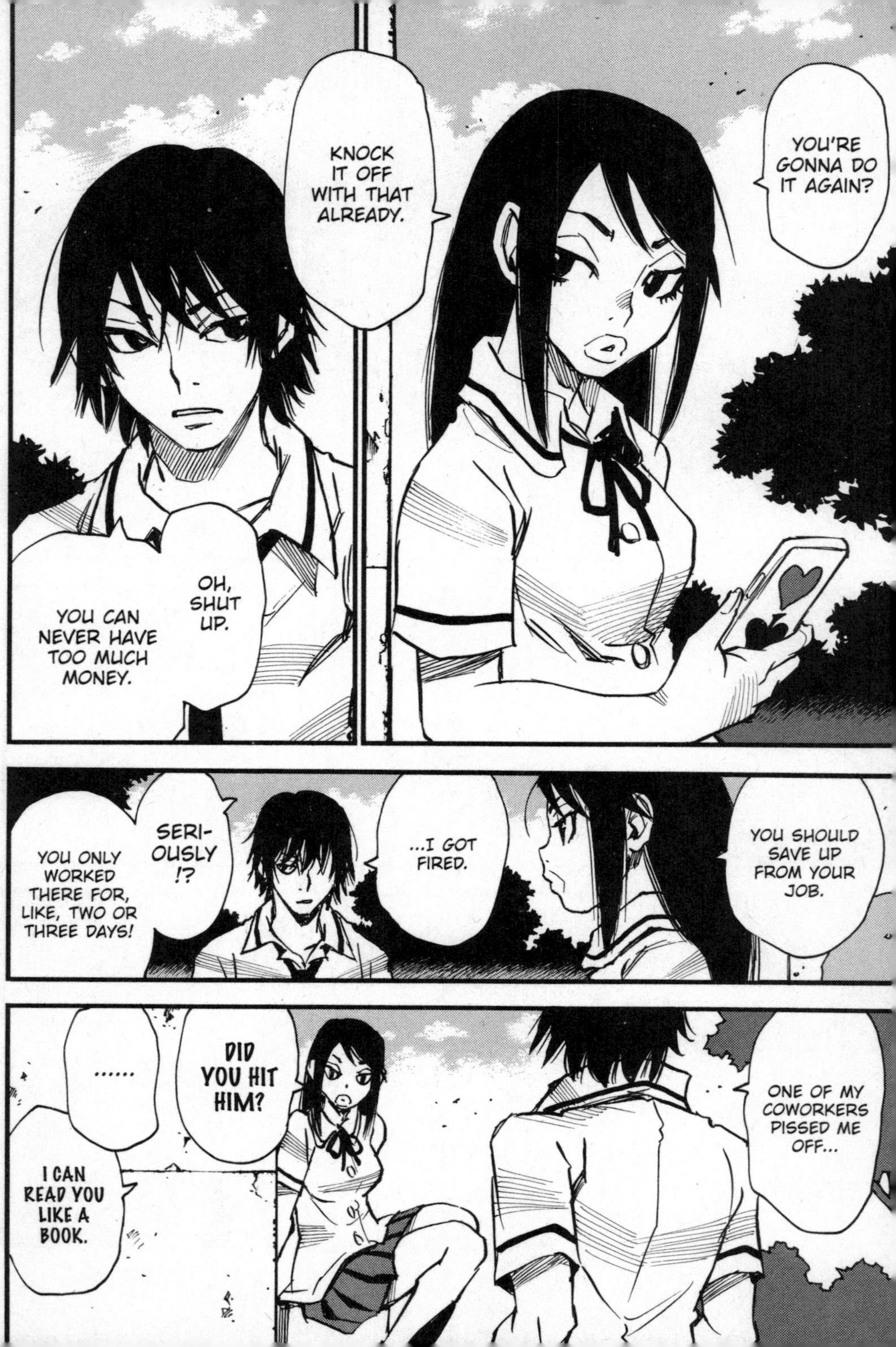
YOU'RE GONNA DO IT AGAIN?
KNOCK IT OFF WITH THAT ALREADY.
OH, SHUT UP.
YOU CAN NEVER HAVE TOO MUCH MONEY.
YOU SHOULD SAVE UP FROM YOUR JOB.
...I GOT FIRED.
SERI-OUSLY!?
YOU ONLY WORKED THERE FOR, LIKE, TWO OR THREE DAYS!
ONE OF MY COWORKERS PISSED ME OFF...
DID YOU HIT HIM?
......
I CAN READ YOU LIKE A BOOK.

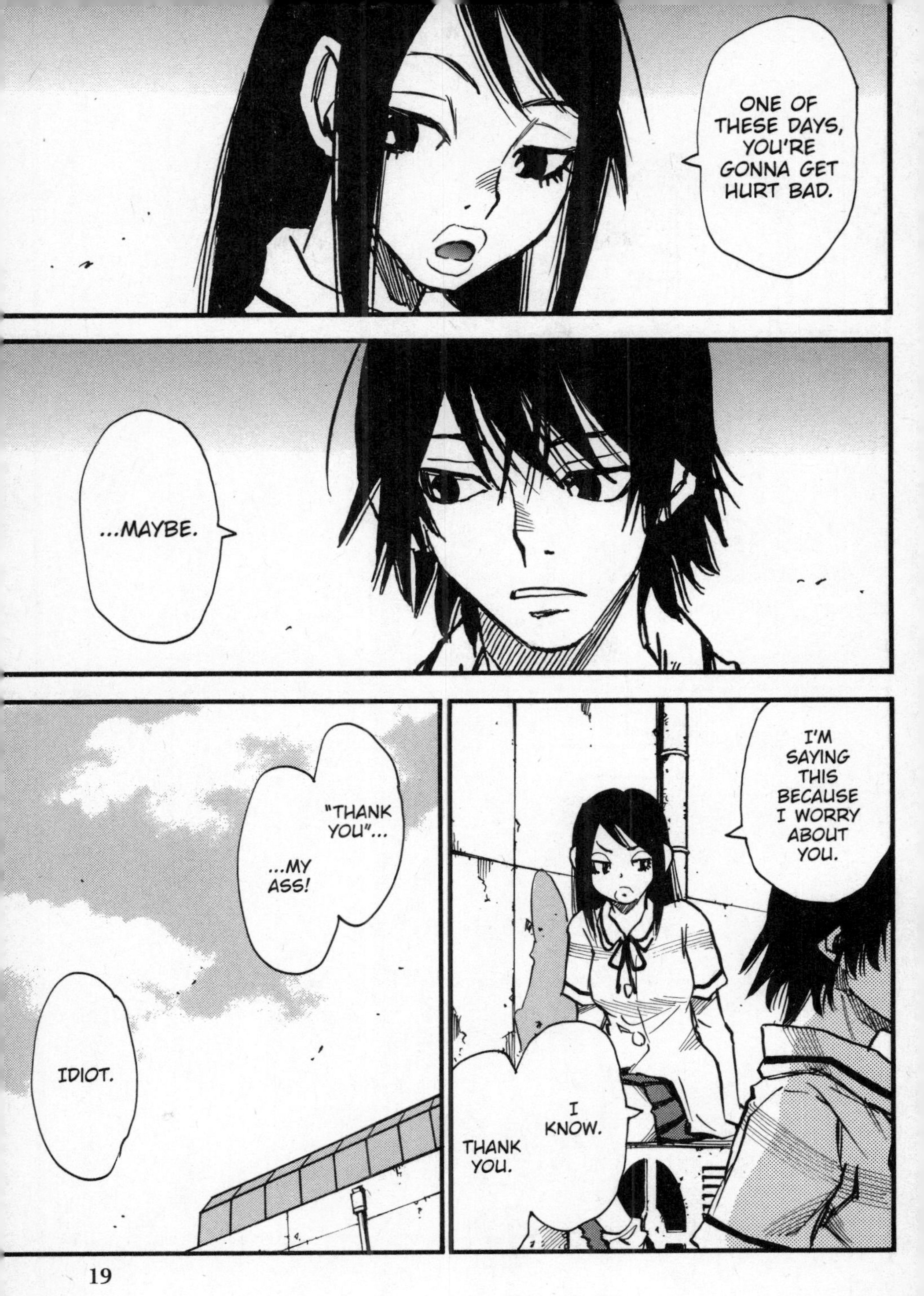
ONE OF THESE DAYS, YOU'RE GONNA GET HURT BAD.
...MAYBE.
I'M SAYING THIS BECAUSE I WORRY ABOUT YOU.
I KNOW.
THANK YOU.
"THANK YOU"...
...MY ASS!
IDIOT.

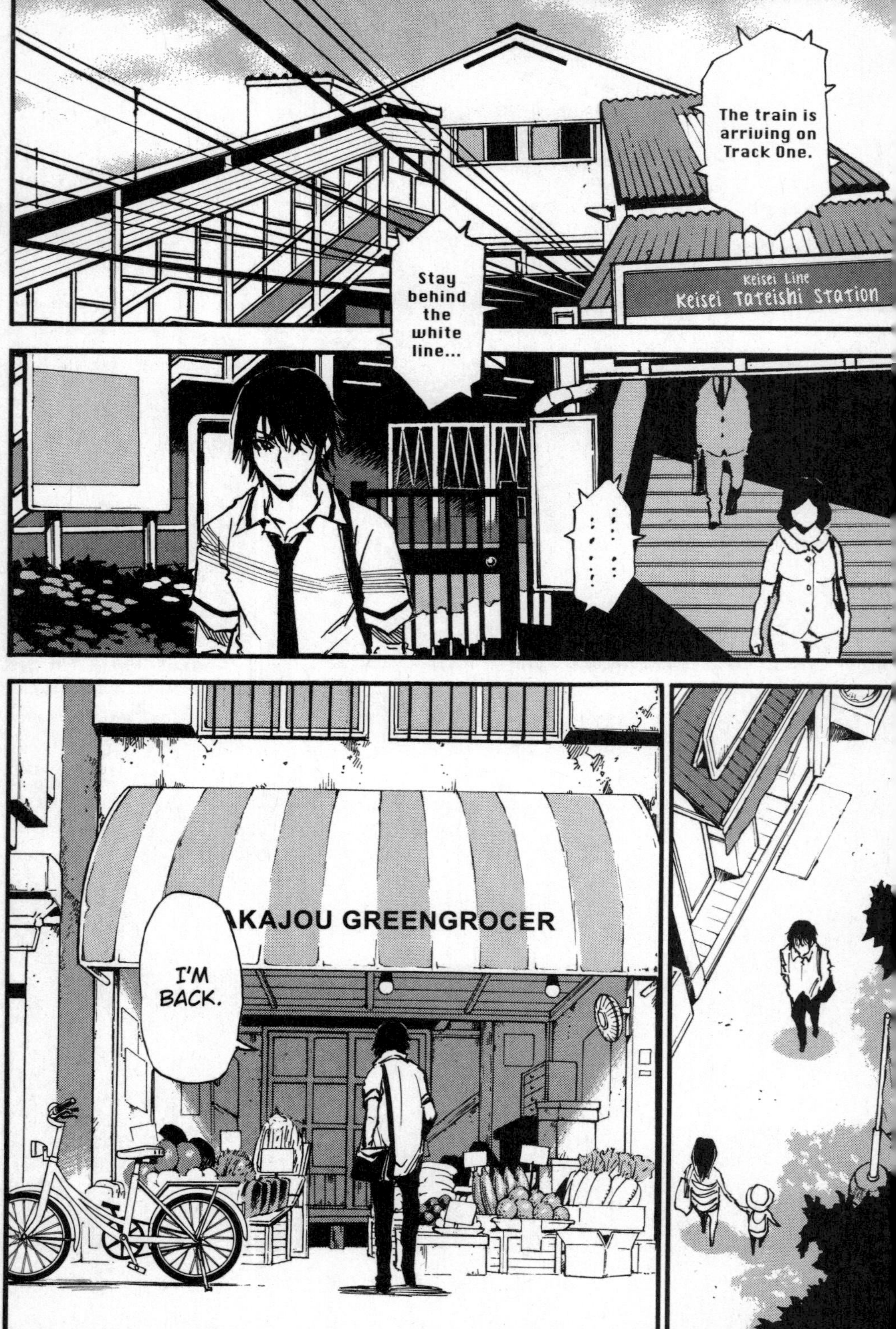
The train is arriving on Track One.
Stay behind the white line...
Keisei Line
Keisei Tateishi Station
......
AKAJOU GREENGROCER
I'M BACK.

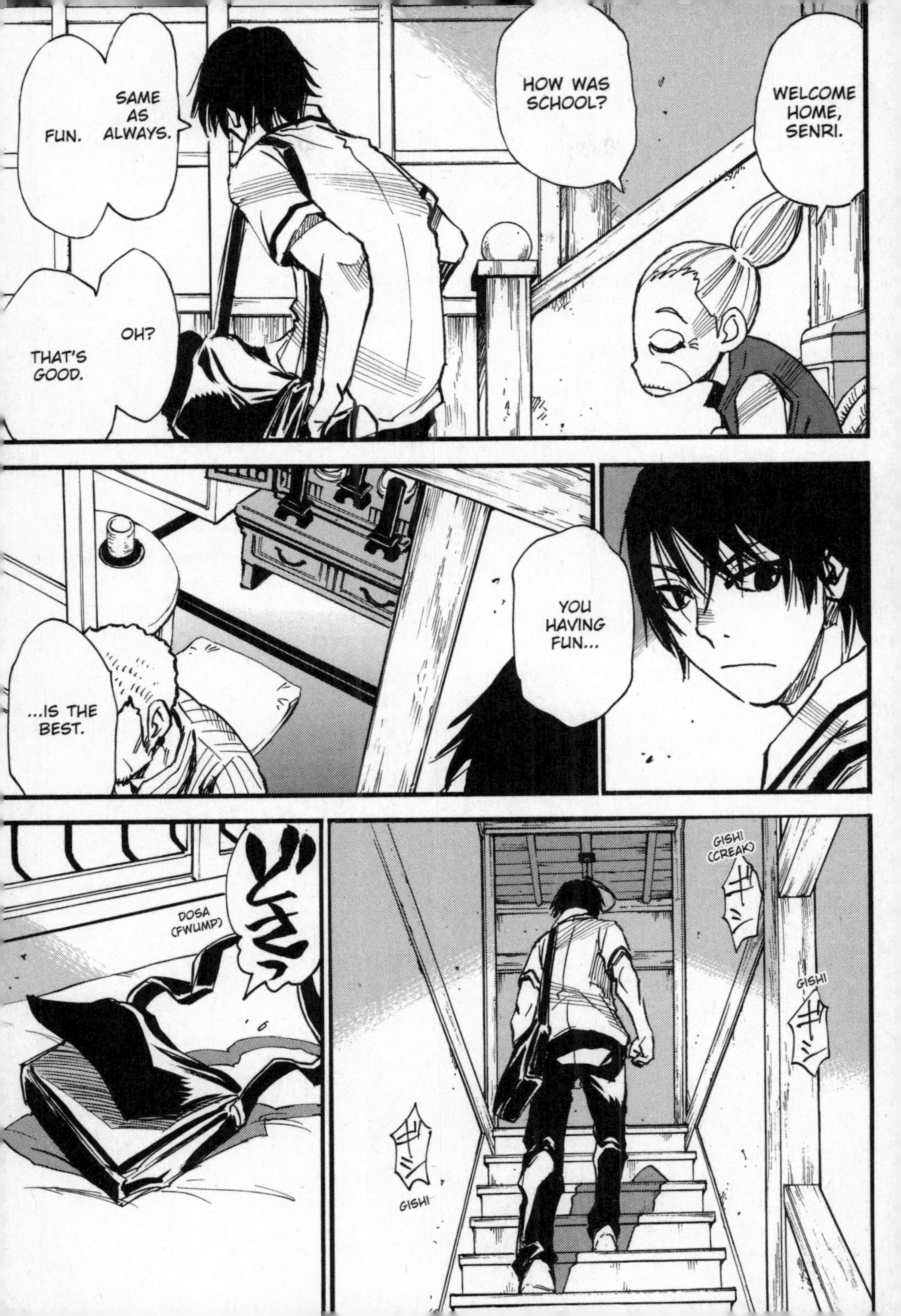
WELCOME HOME, SENRI.
HOW WAS SCHOOL?
SAME AS ALWAYS.
FUN.
OH?
THAT'S GOOD.
YOU HAVING FUN...
...IS THE BEST.
GISHI (CREAK)
GISHI
GISHI
DOSA (FWUMP)

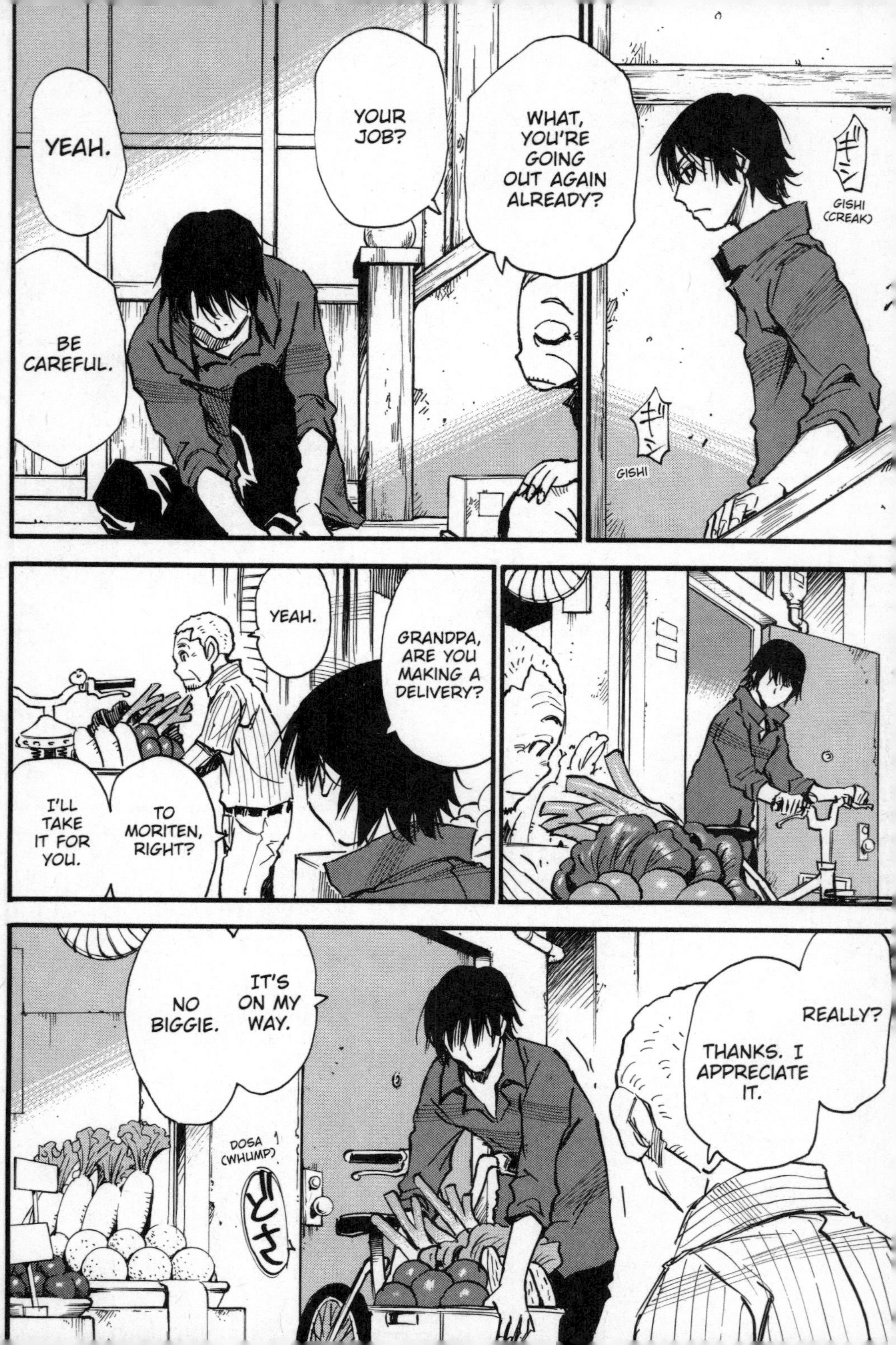
ギシ
GISHI (CREAK)
ギシ
GISHI
WHAT, YOU'RE GOING OUT AGAIN ALREADY?
YOUR JOB?
YEAH.
BE CAREFUL.
GRANDPA, ARE YOU MAKING A DELIVERY?
YEAH.
TO MORITEN, RIGHT?
I'LL TAKE IT FOR YOU.
REALLY?
THANKS. I APPRECIATE IT.
どさ
DOSA (WHUMP)
IT'S ON MY WAY.
NO BIGGIE.

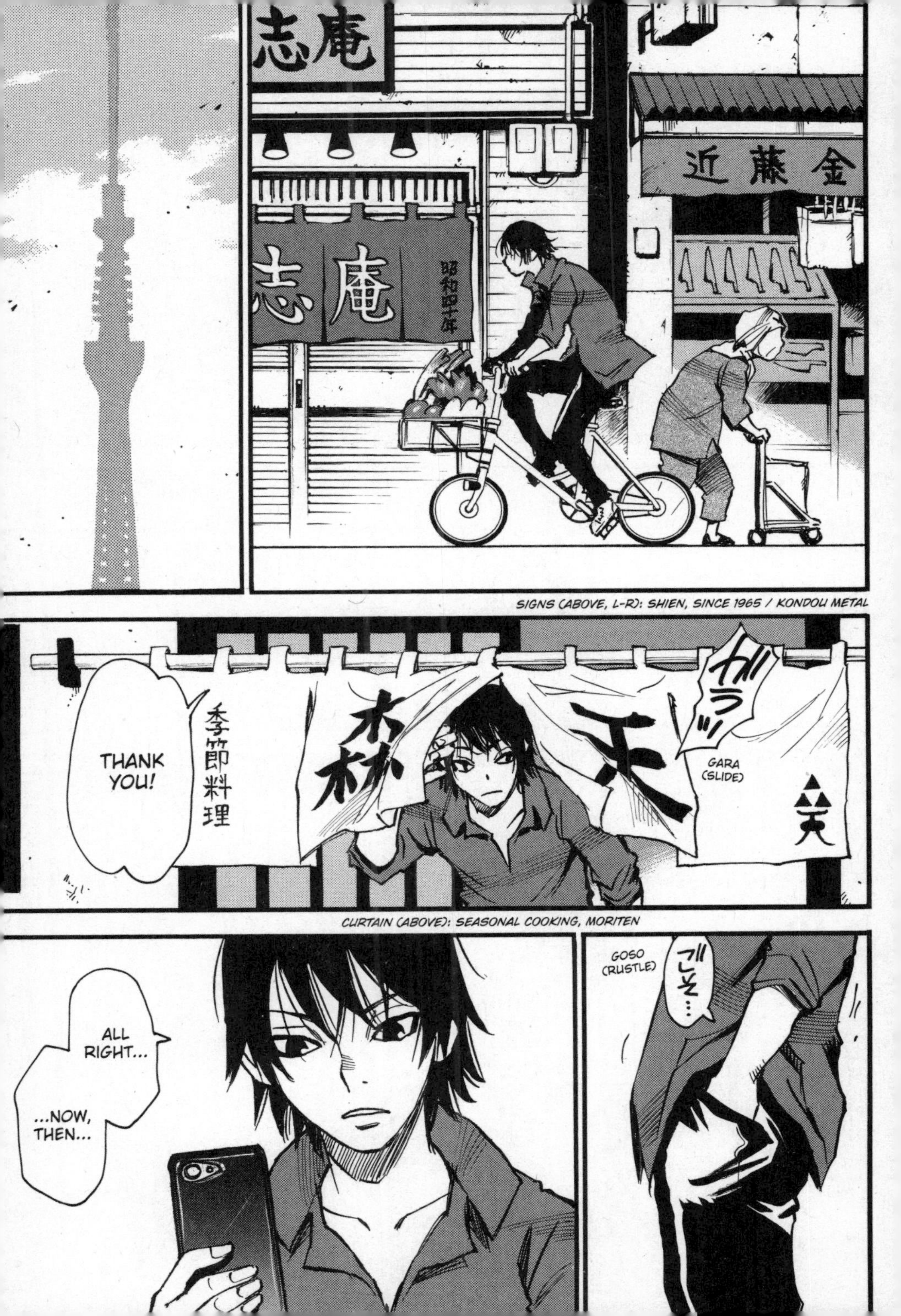
志庵
近藤金
志庵
昭和四十年
SIGNS (ABOVE, L-R): SHIEN, SINCE 1965 / KONDOU METAL
ガラッ
GARA (SLIDE)
THANK YOU!
季節料理
CURTAIN (ABOVE): SEASONAL COOKING, MORITEN
GOSO (RUSTLE)
ごそ…
ALL RIGHT...
...NOW, THEN...

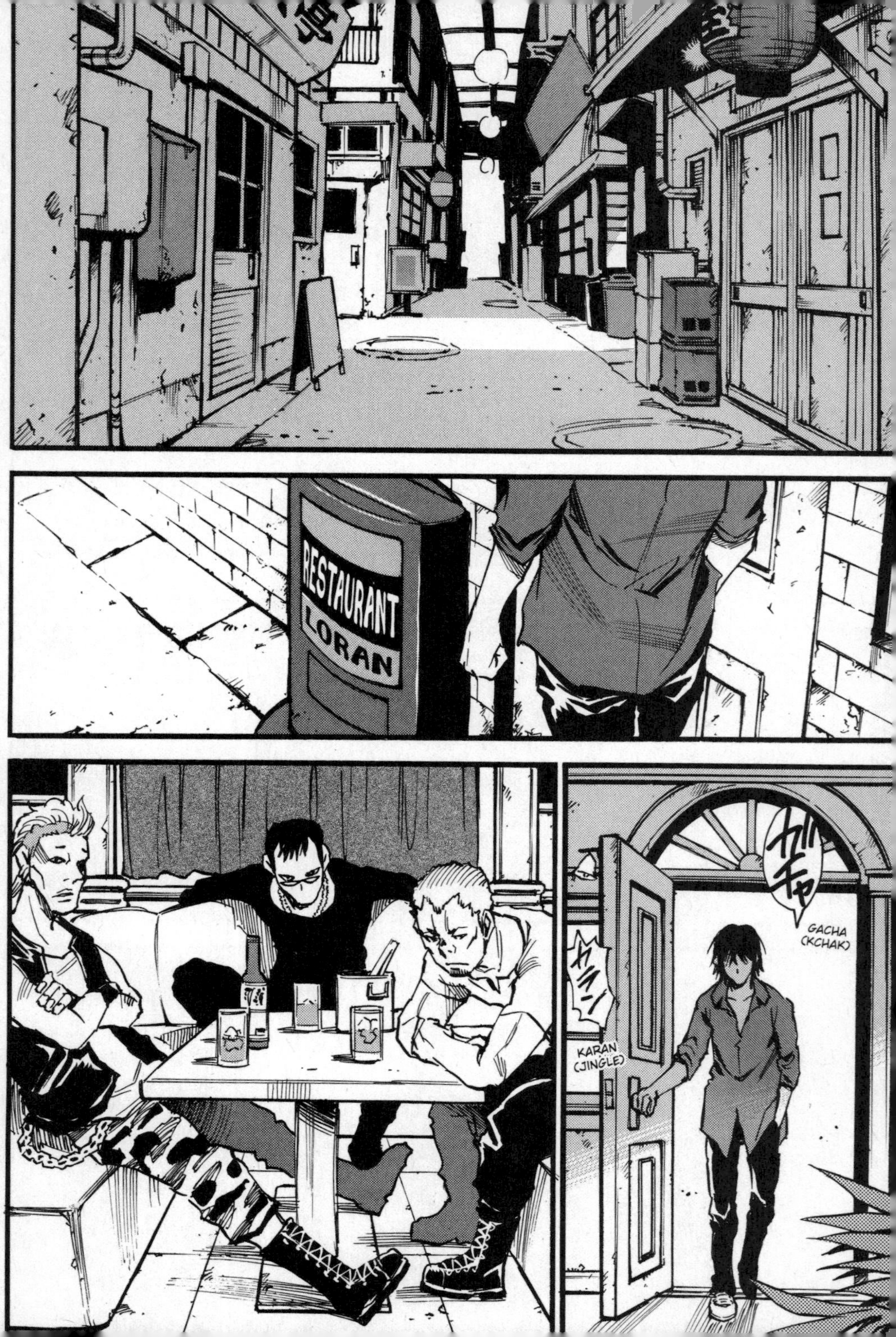
RESTAURANT
LORAN
ガチャ
GACHA (KCHAK)
カラン
KARAN (JINGLE)

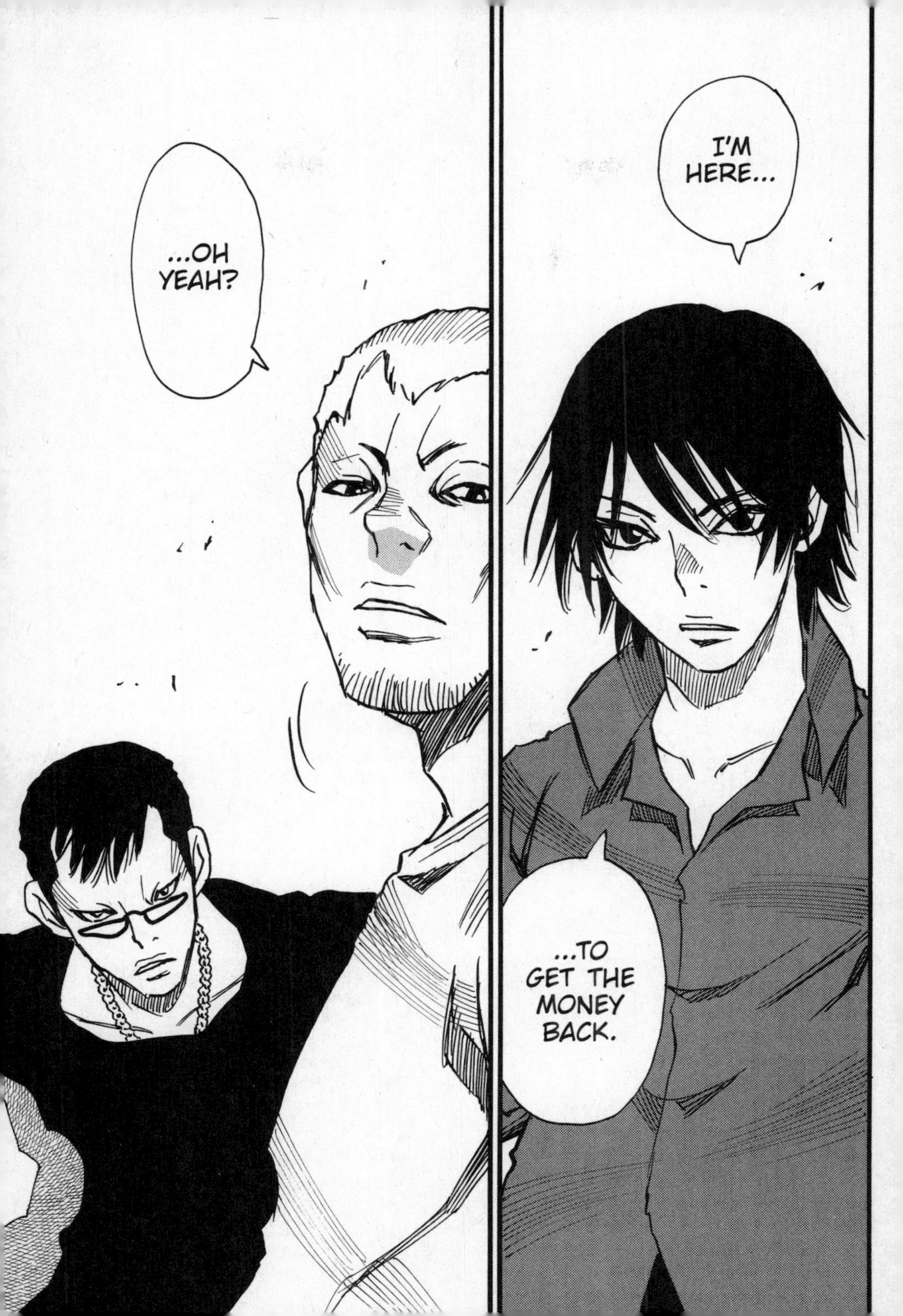
I'M HERE...
...TO GET THE MONEY BACK.
...OH YEAH?

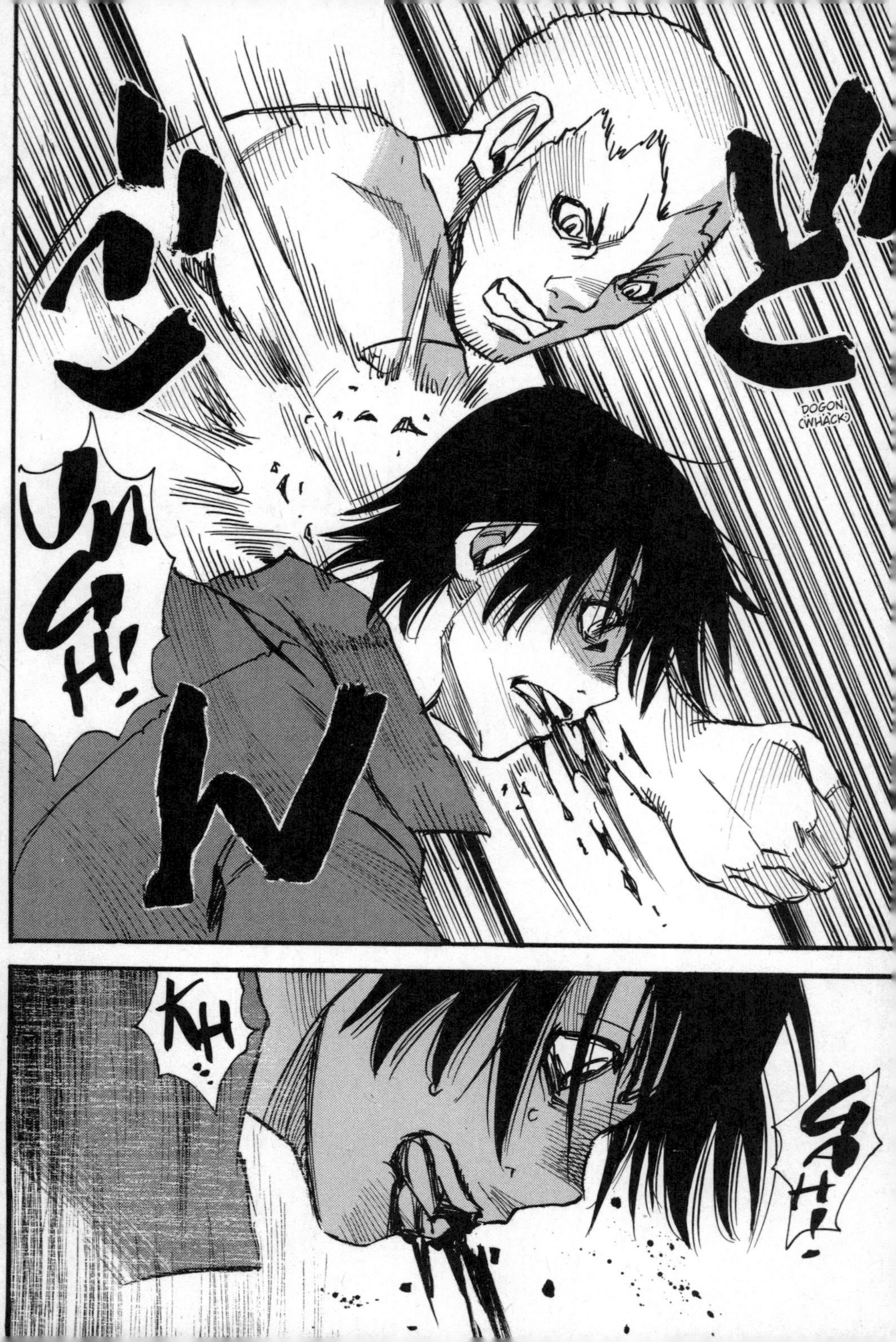
DOGON (WHACK)
UNGH!
GAH!
KH...

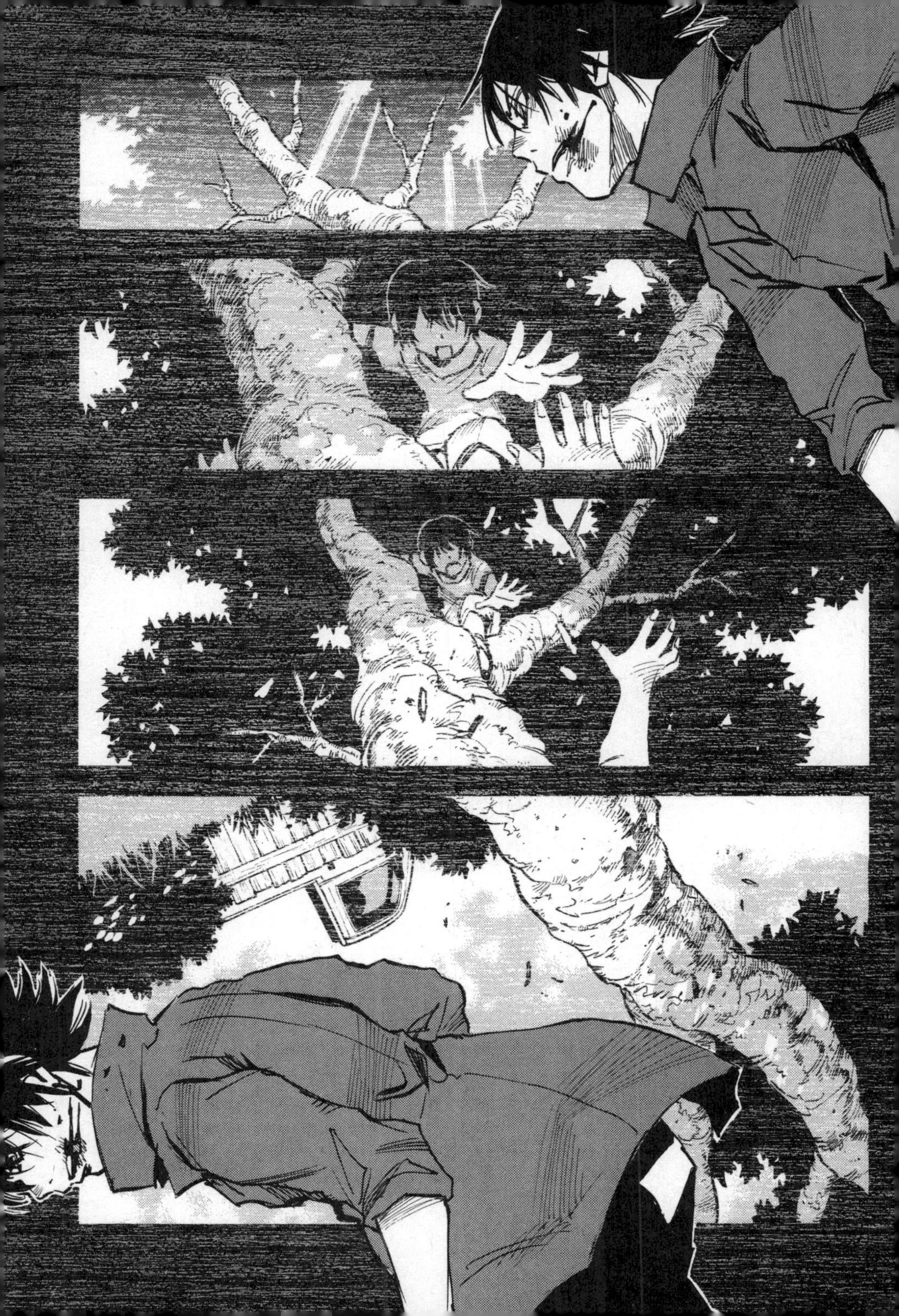

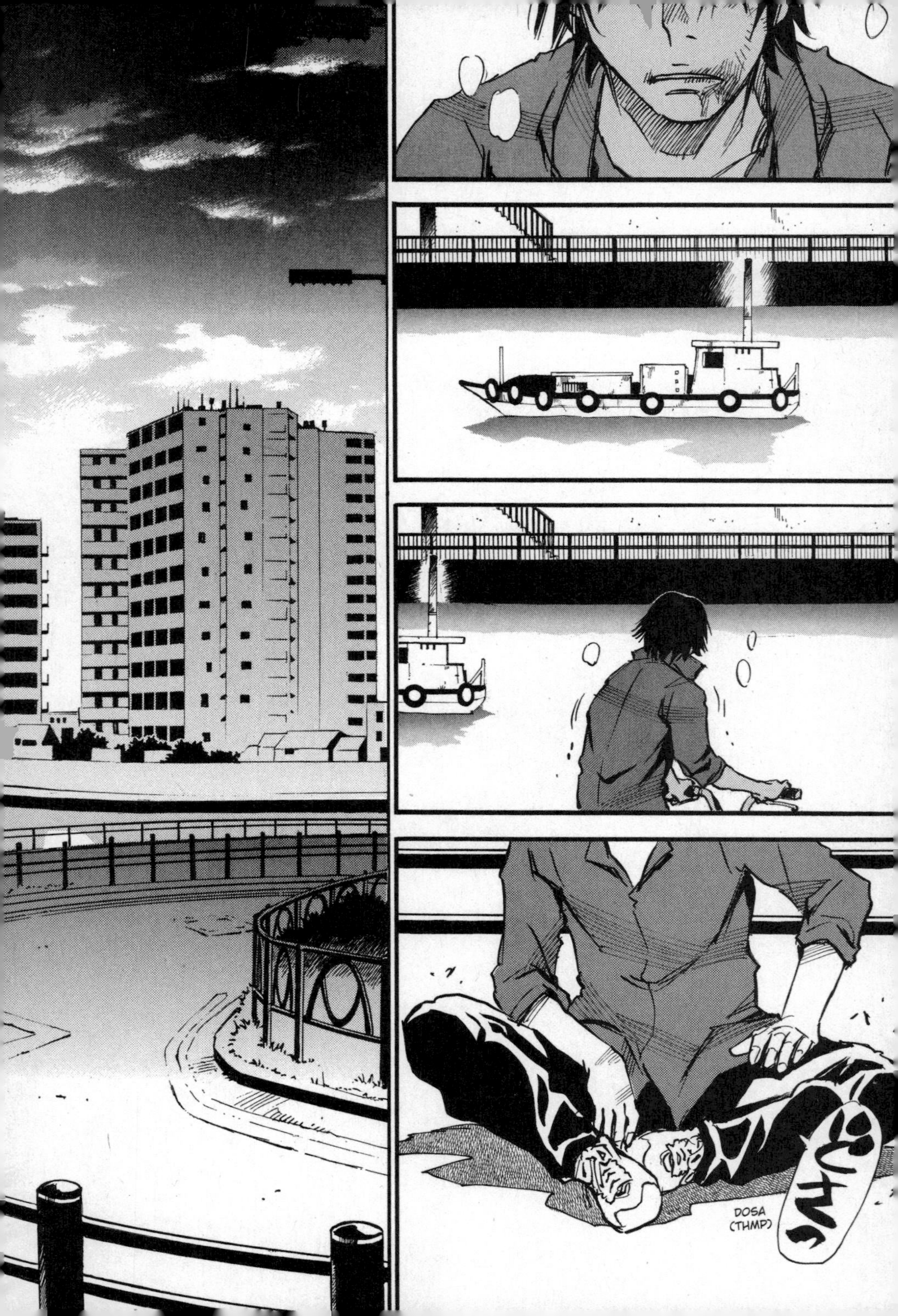
ドサ
DOSA
(THMP)

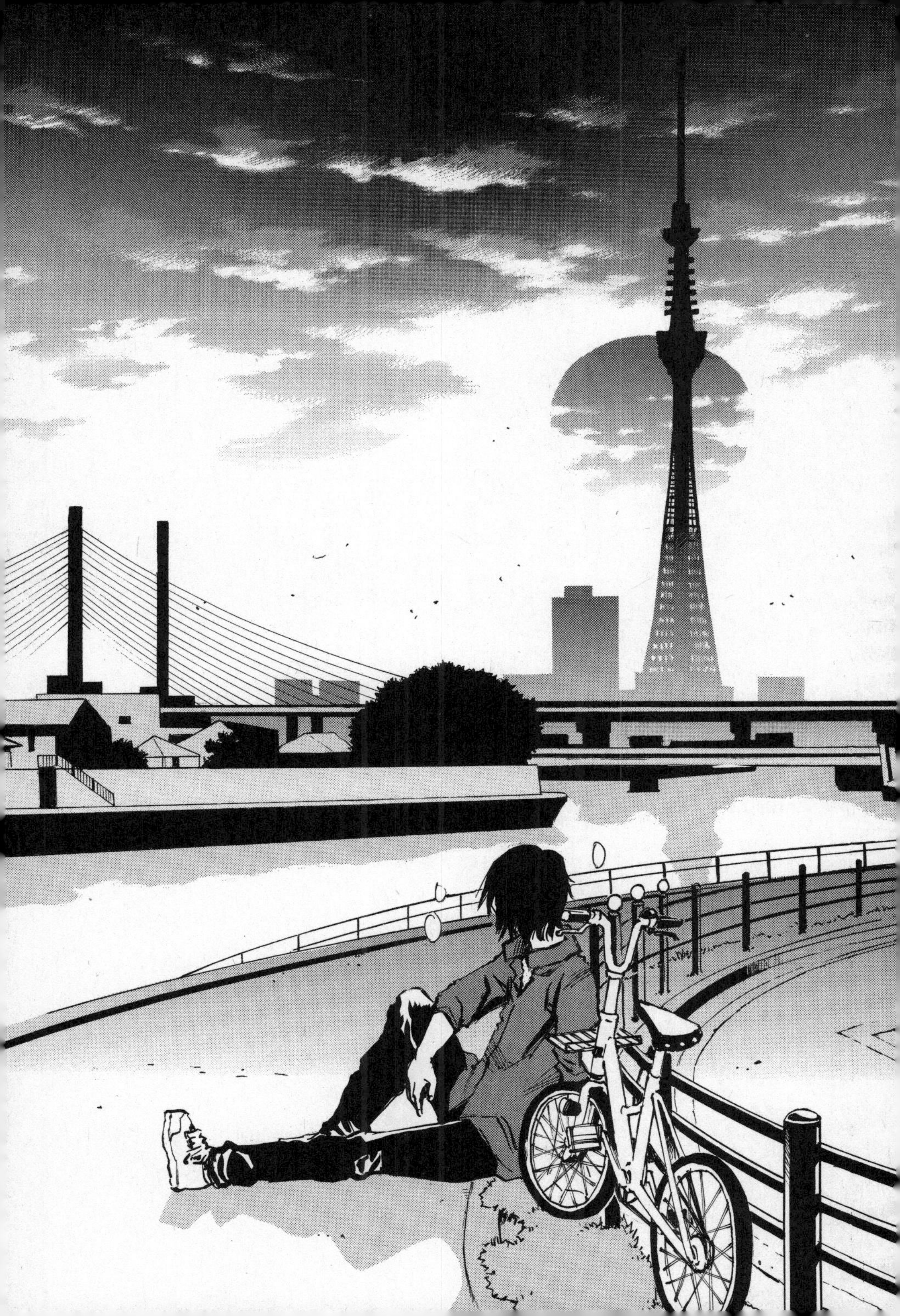

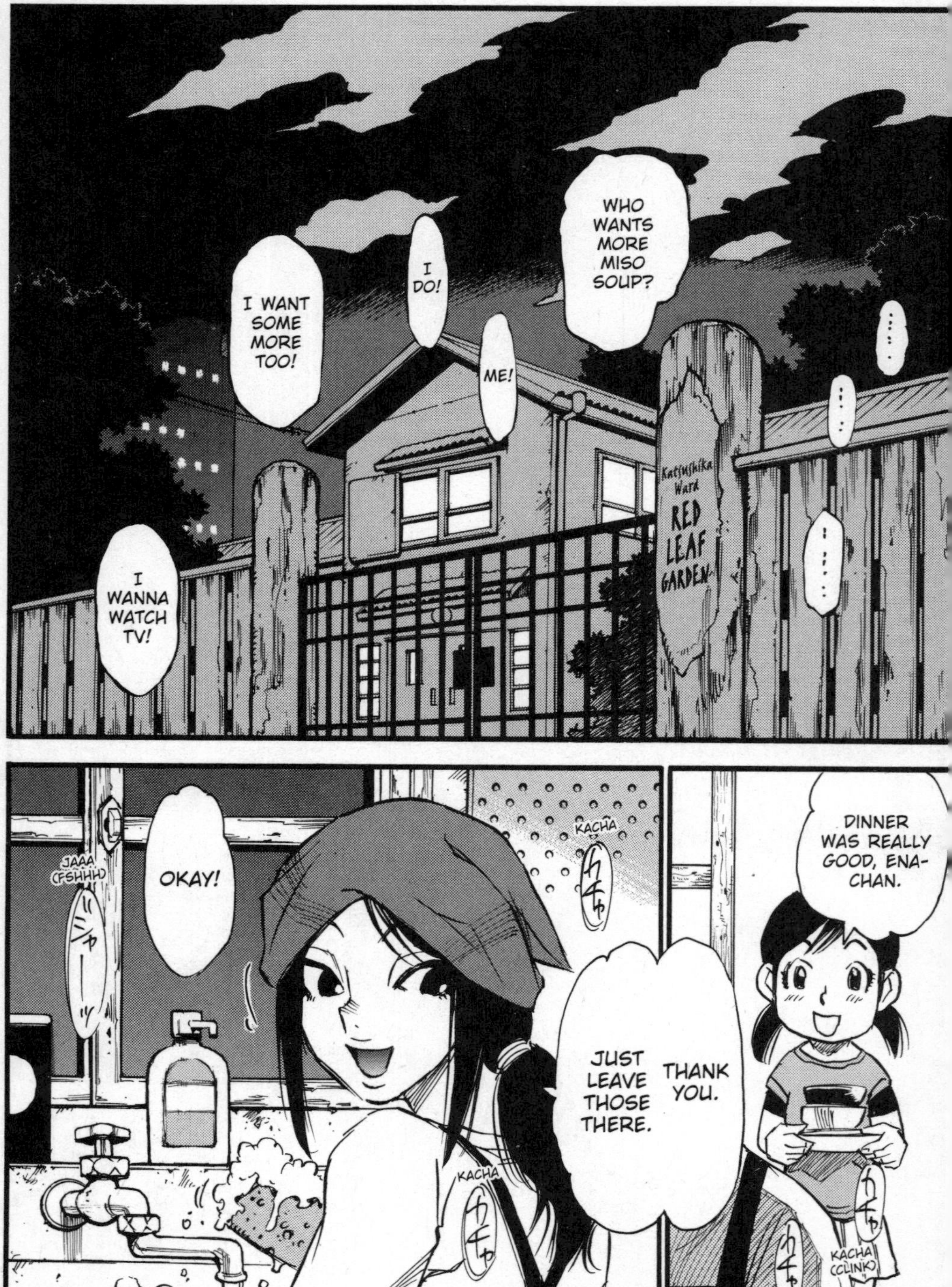
.....
....
....
WHO WANTS MORE MISO SOUP?
Katsushika Ward
RED LEAF GARDEN
I DO!
ME!
I WANT SOME MORE TOO!
I WANNA WATCH TV!
DINNER WAS REALLY GOOD, ENA-CHAN.
KACHA (CLINK)
KACHA
THANK YOU.
JUST LEAVE THOSE THERE.
KACHA
KACHA
OKAY!
JAAA (FSHHH)

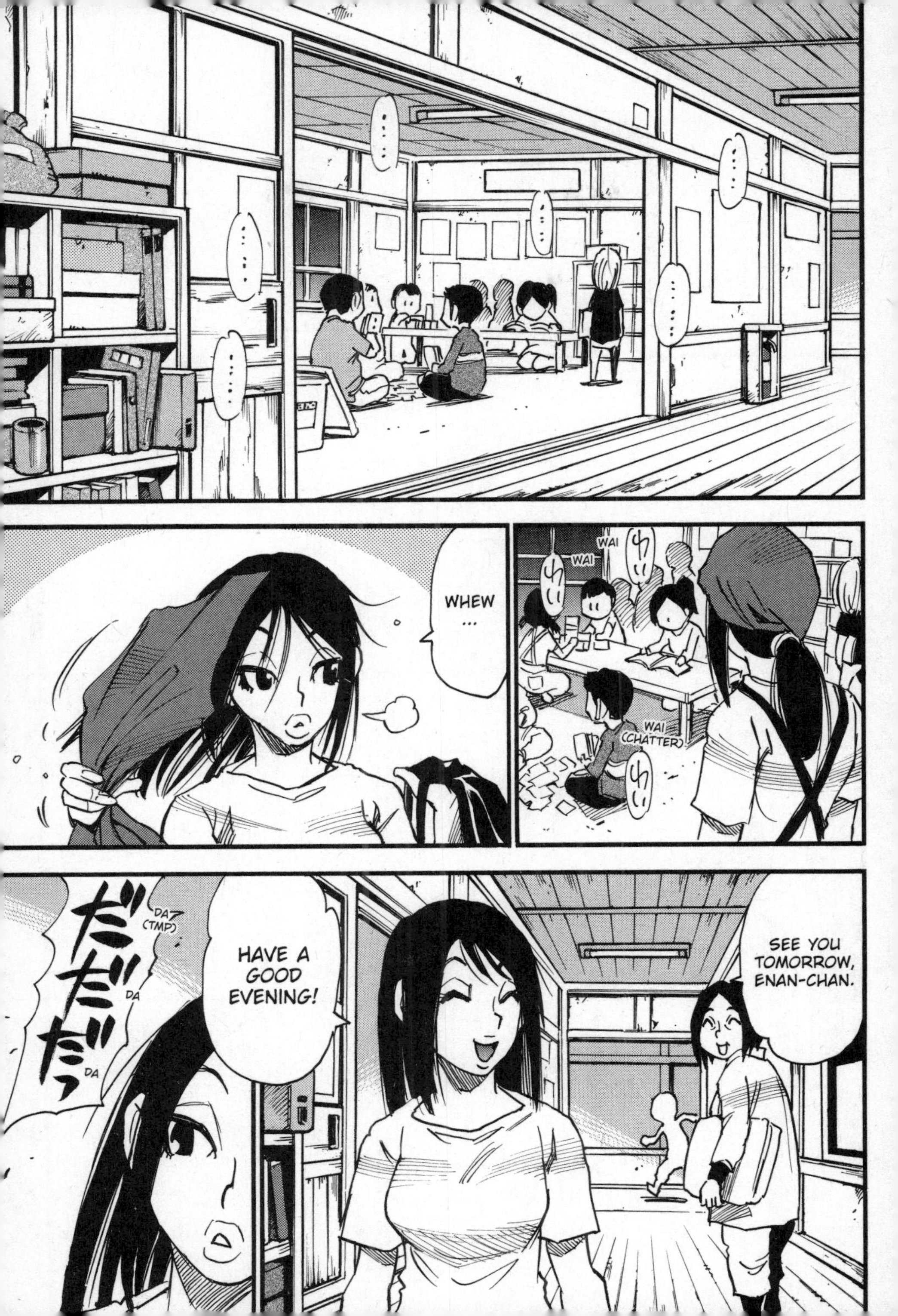
....
....
....
....
....
....
WAI
わい
WAI
わい
WAI (CHATTER)
わい
WHEW ...
SEE YOU TOMORROW, ENAN-CHAN.
HAVE A GOOD EVENING!
だだだっ
DA (TMP)
DA
DA

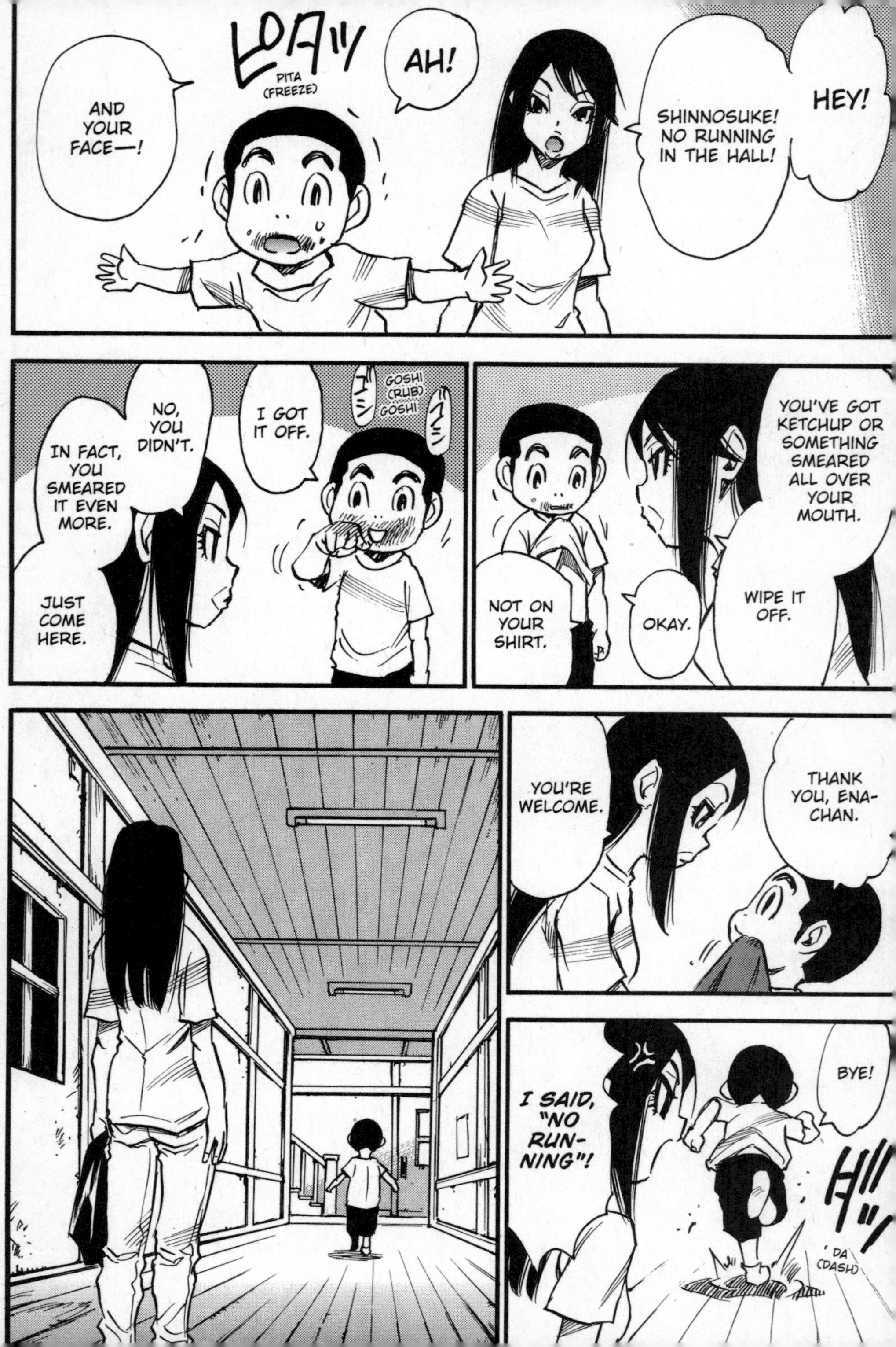
HEY!
SHINNOSUKE! NO RUNNING IN THE HALL!
AH!
PITA (FREEZE)
AND YOUR FACE—!
YOU'VE GOT KETCHUP OR SOMETHING SMEARED ALL OVER YOUR MOUTH.
WIPE IT OFF.
OKAY.
NOT ON YOUR SHIRT.
GOSHI (RUB) GOSHI
I GOT IT OFF.
NO, YOU DIDN'T.
IN FACT, YOU SMEARED IT EVEN MORE.
JUST COME HERE.
THANK YOU, ENA-CHAN.
YOU'RE WELCOME.
BYE!
I SAID, "NO RUN-NING"!
DA (DASH)

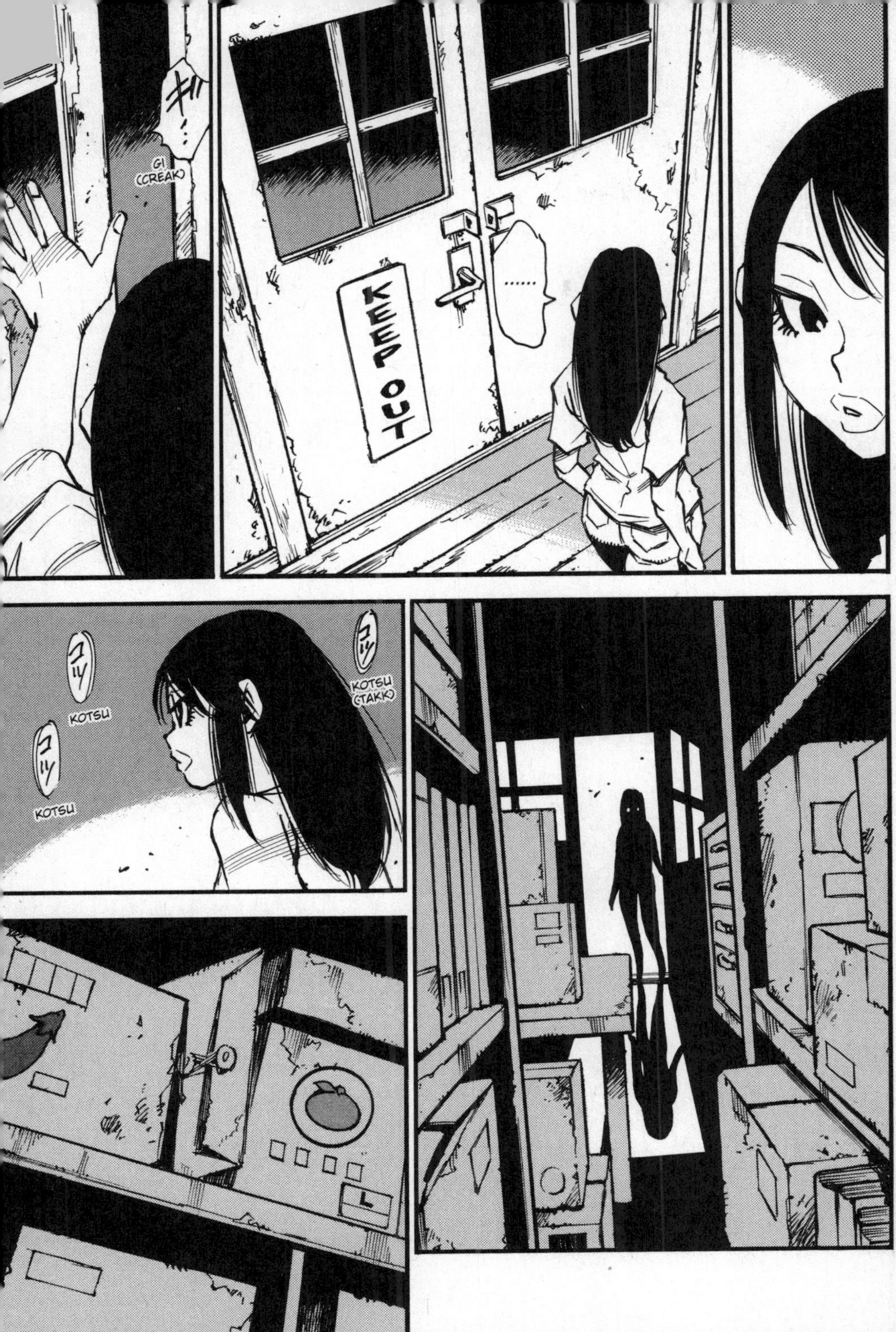

......
KEEP OUT
ギ
GI (CREAK)
コツ
KOTSU (TAKK)
コツ
KOTSU
コツ
KOTSU

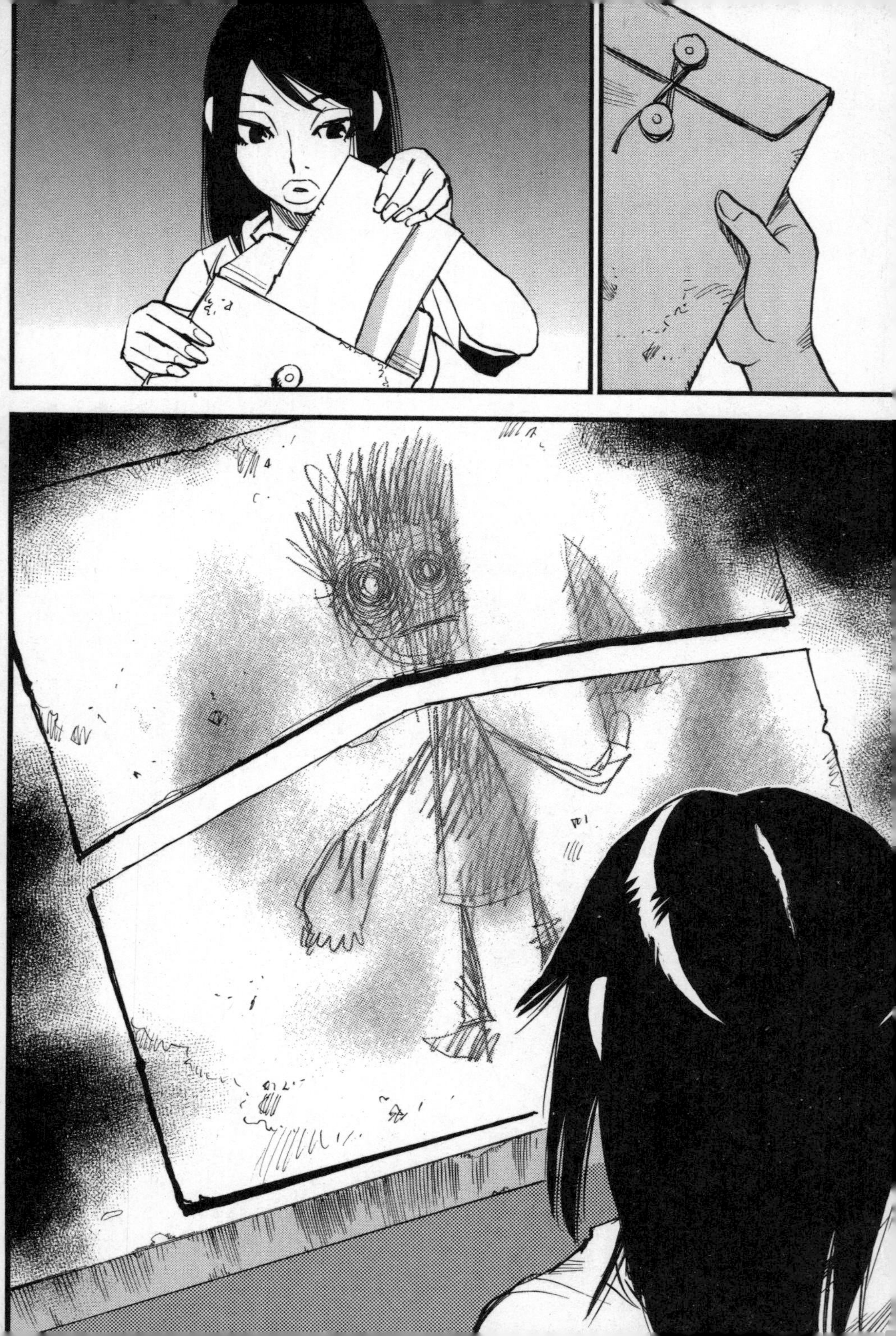

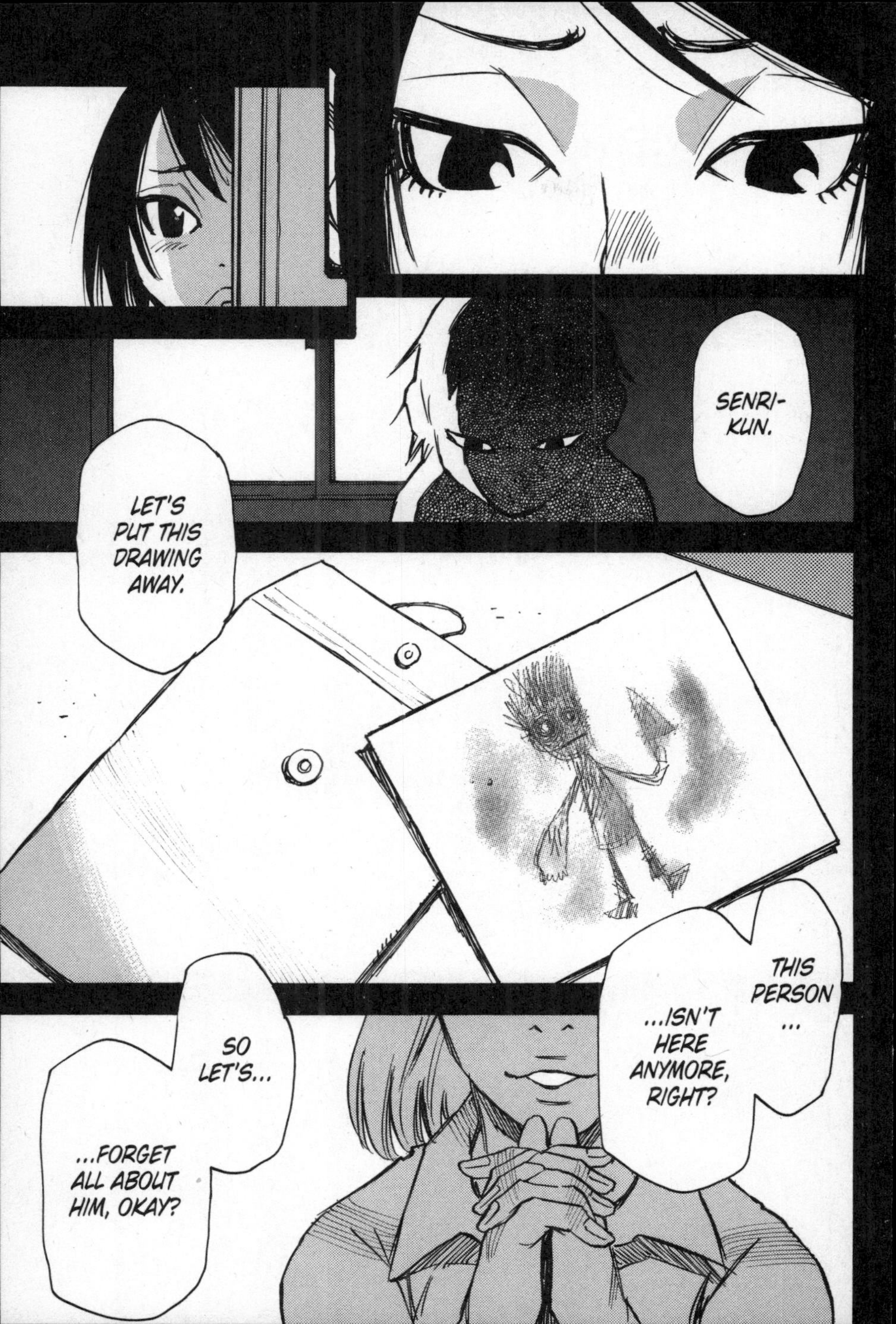
SENRI-KUN.
LET'S PUT THIS DRAWING AWAY.
THIS PERSON ...
...ISN'T HERE ANYMORE, RIGHT?
SO LET'S...
...FORGET ALL ABOUT HIM, OKAY?

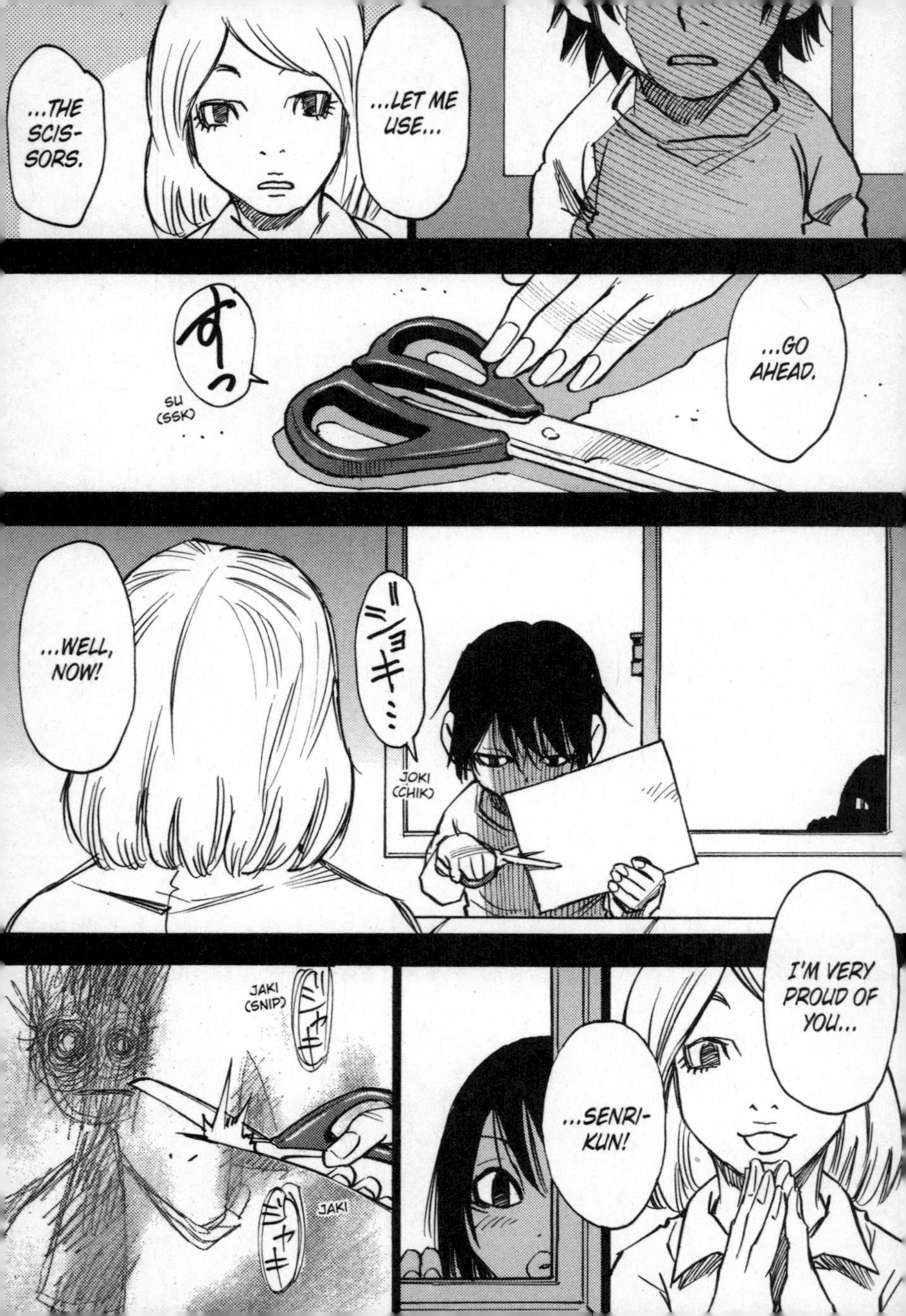
...LET ME USE...
...THE SCIS-SORS.
...GO AHEAD.
すっ
SU (SSK)
ジョキ…
JOKI (CHIK)
...WELL, NOW!
I'M VERY PROUD OF YOU...
...SENRI-KUN!
ジャキ
JAKI (SNIP)
ジャキ
JAKI

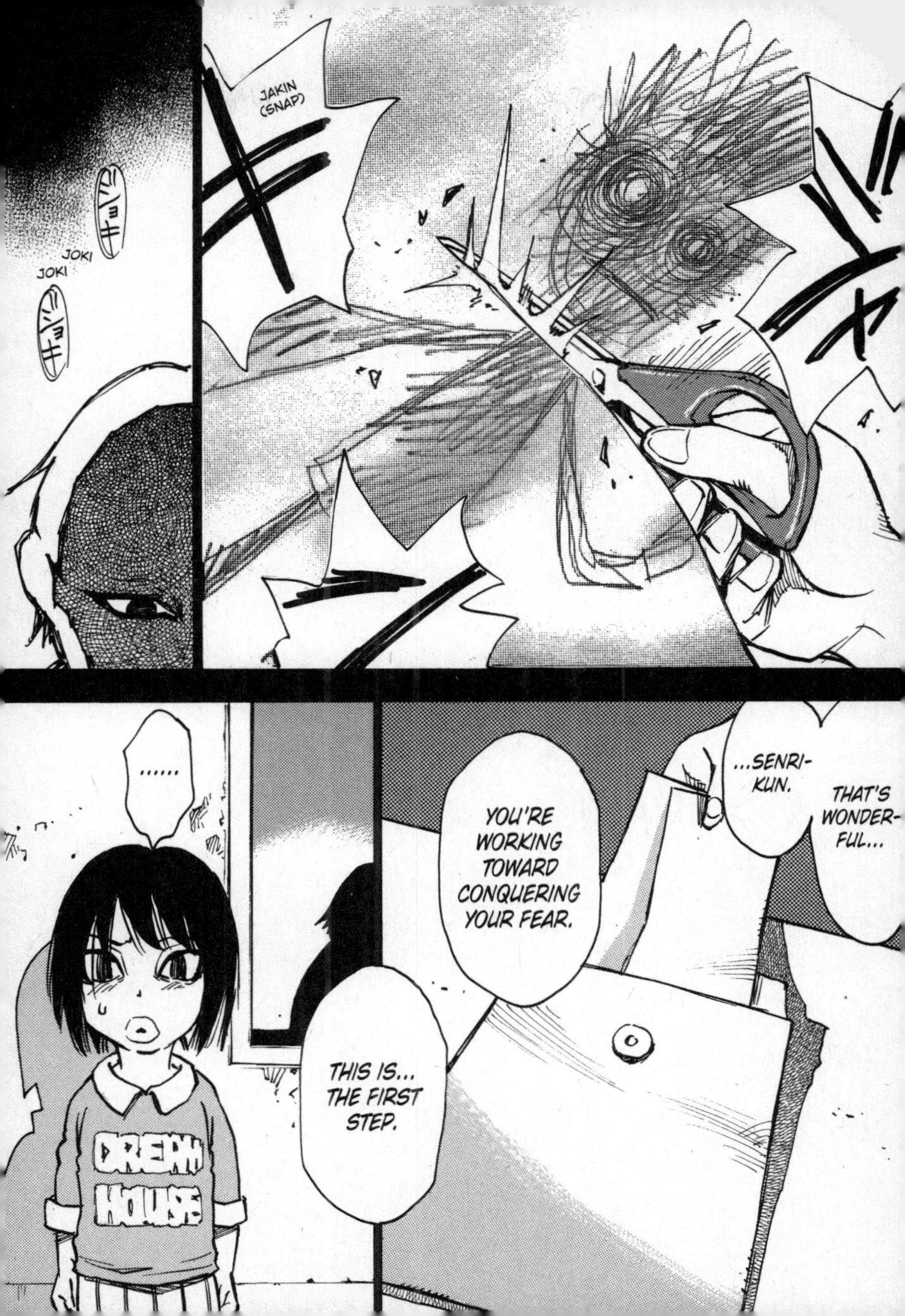
JAKIN (SNAP)
JOKI
JOKI
...SENRI-KUN.
THAT'S WONDER-FUL...
YOU'RE WORKING TOWARD CONQUERING YOUR FEAR.
THIS IS... THE FIRST STEP.
......

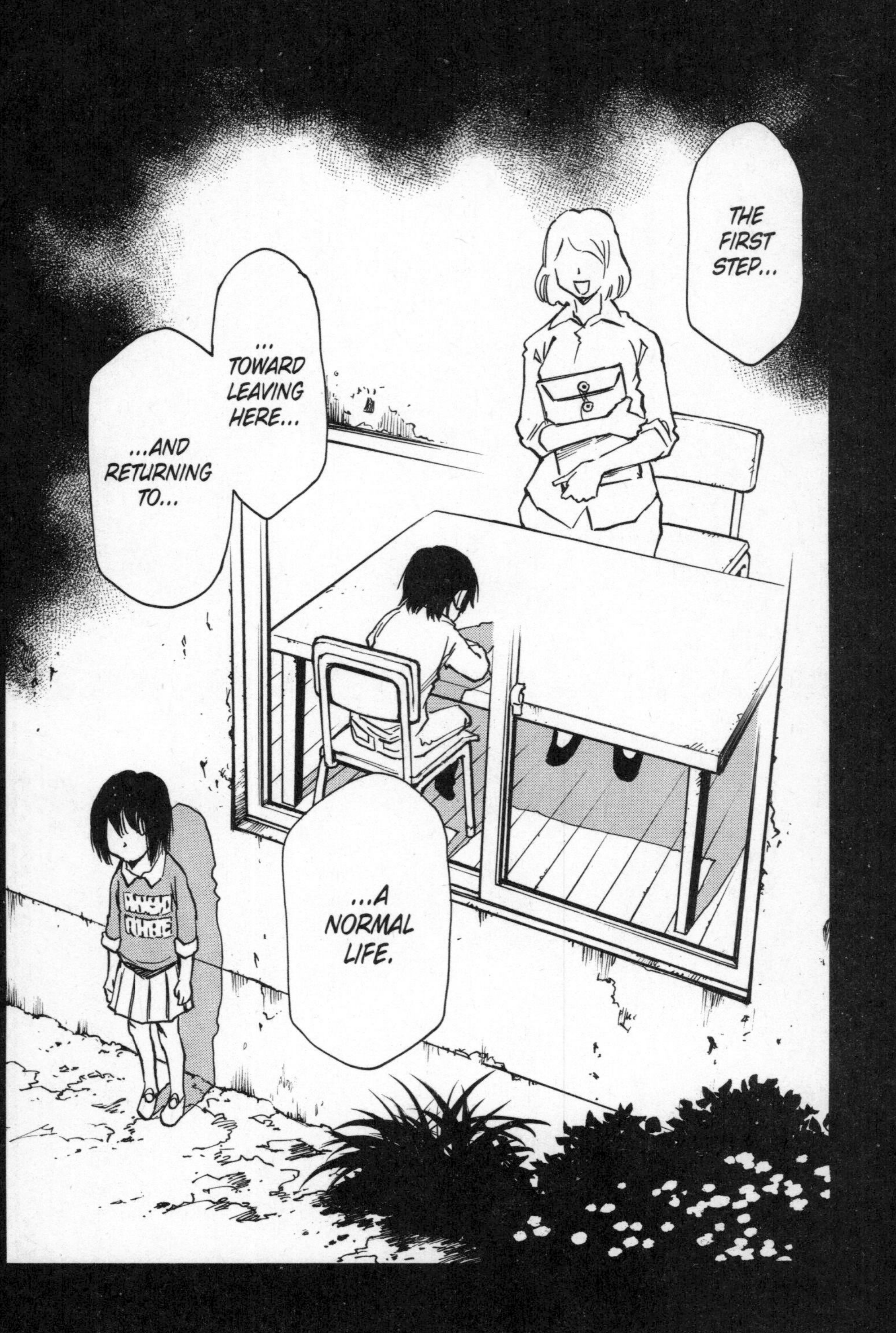
THE FIRST STEP...
... TOWARD LEAVING HERE...
...AND RETURNING TO...
...A NORMAL LIFE.

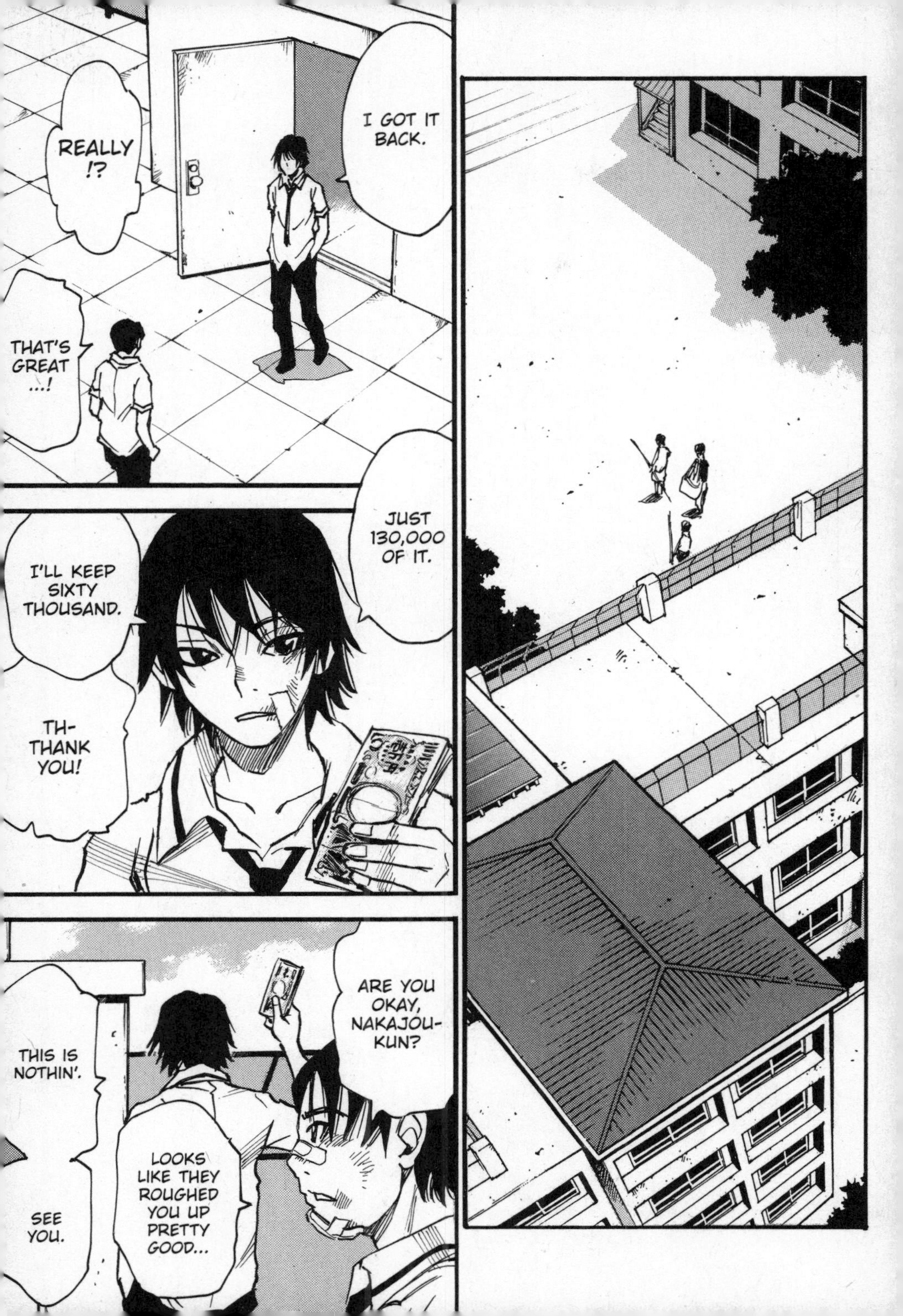
I GOT IT BACK.
REALLY !?
THAT'S GREAT ....!
JUST 130,000 OF IT.
I'LL KEEP SIXTY THOUSAND.
TH-THANK YOU!
ARE YOU OKAY, NAKAJOU-KUN?
THIS IS NOTHIN'.
LOOKS LIKE THEY ROUGHED YOU UP PRETTY GOOD...
SEE YOU.

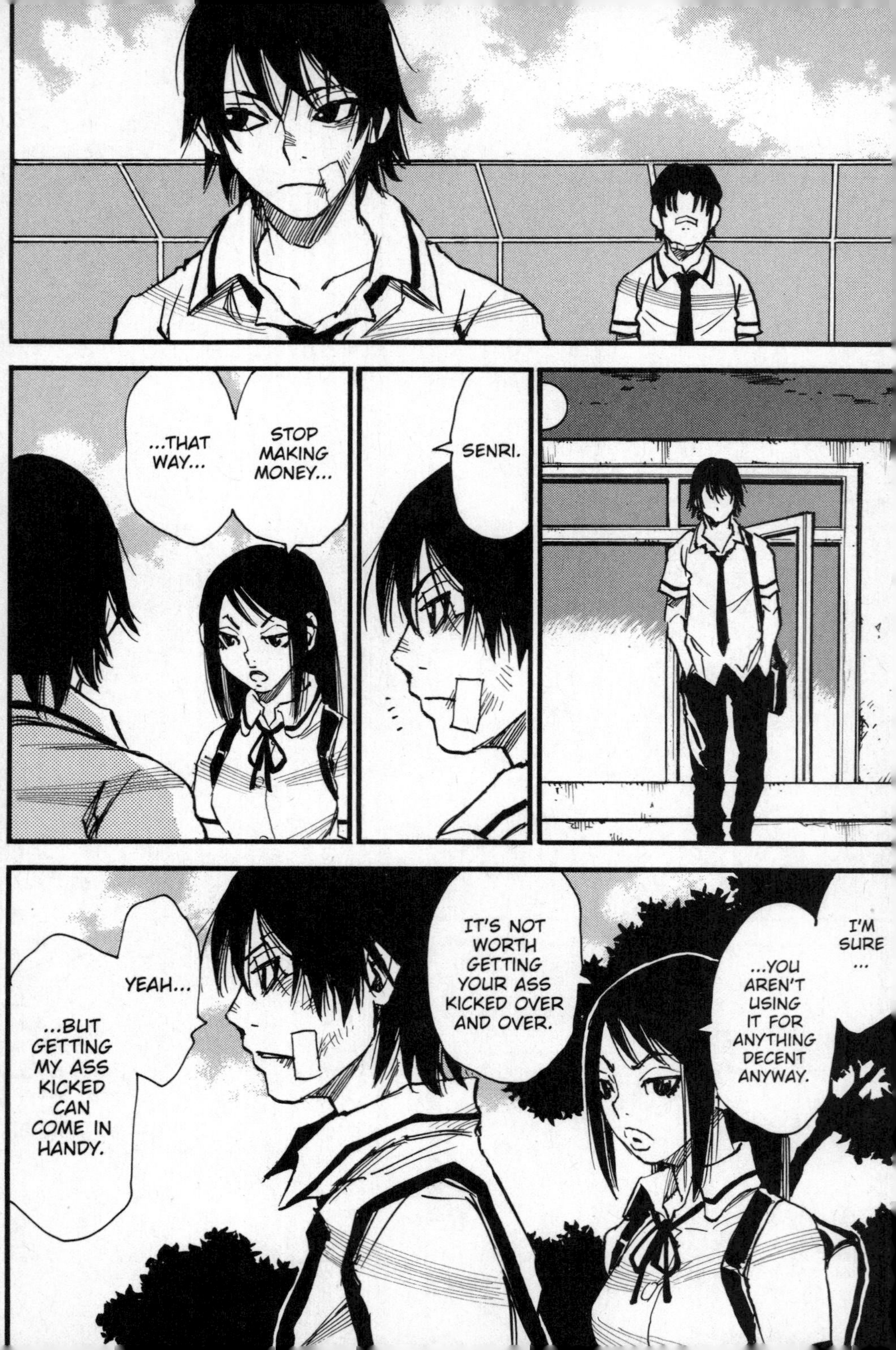
SENRI.
STOP MAKING MONEY...
...THAT WAY...
I'M SURE ...
...YOU AREN'T USING IT FOR ANYTHING DECENT ANYWAY.
IT'S NOT WORTH GETTING YOUR ASS KICKED OVER AND OVER.
YEAH...
...BUT GETTING MY ASS KICKED CAN COME IN HANDY.

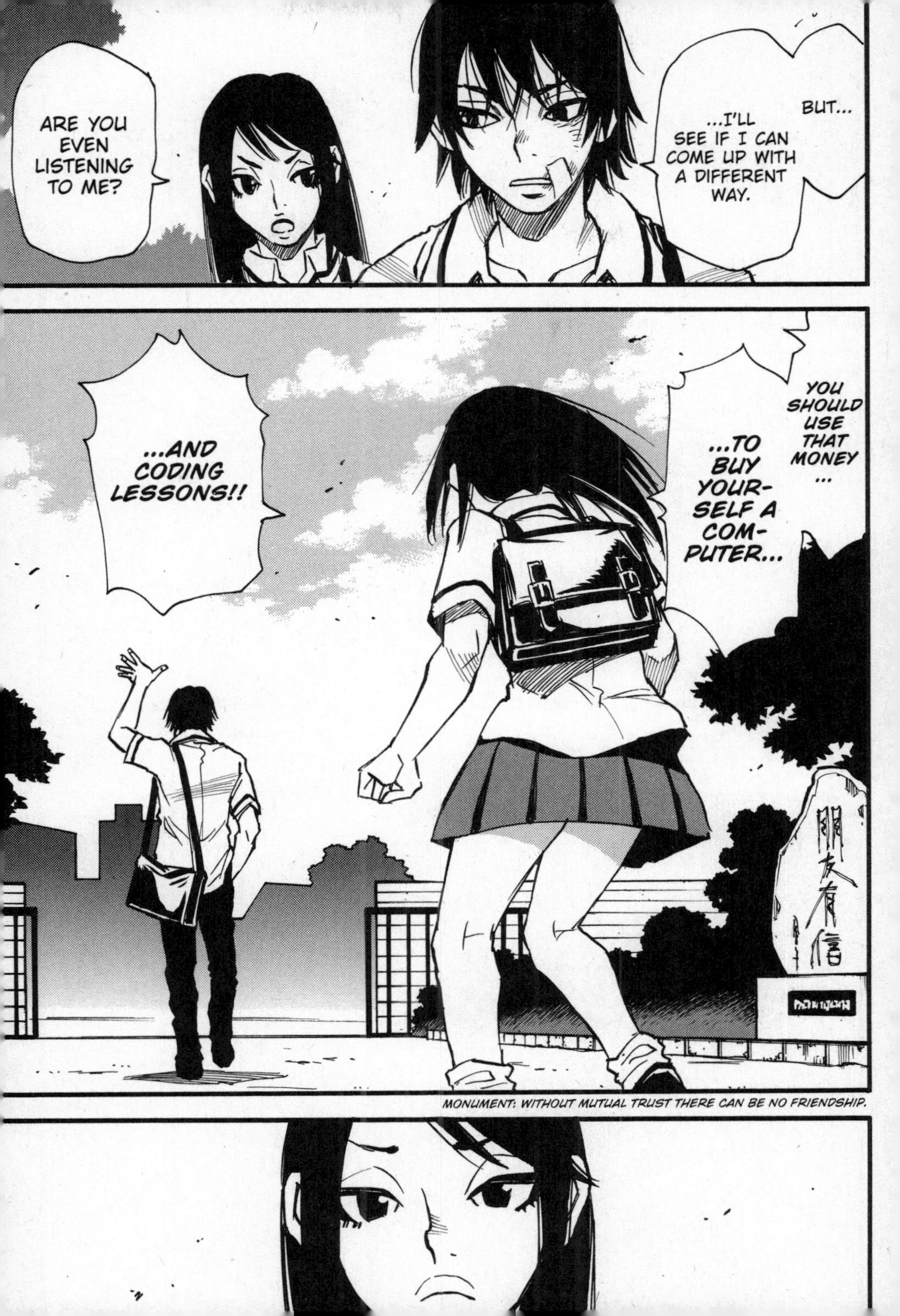
BUT...
...I'LL SEE IF I CAN COME UP WITH A DIFFERENT WAY.
ARE YOU EVEN LISTENING TO ME?
YOU SHOULD USE THAT MONEY ...
...TO BUY YOURSELF A COMPUTER...
...AND CODING LESSONS!!
朋友有信
MONUMENT: WITHOUT MUTUAL TRUST THERE CAN BE NO FRIENDSHIP.

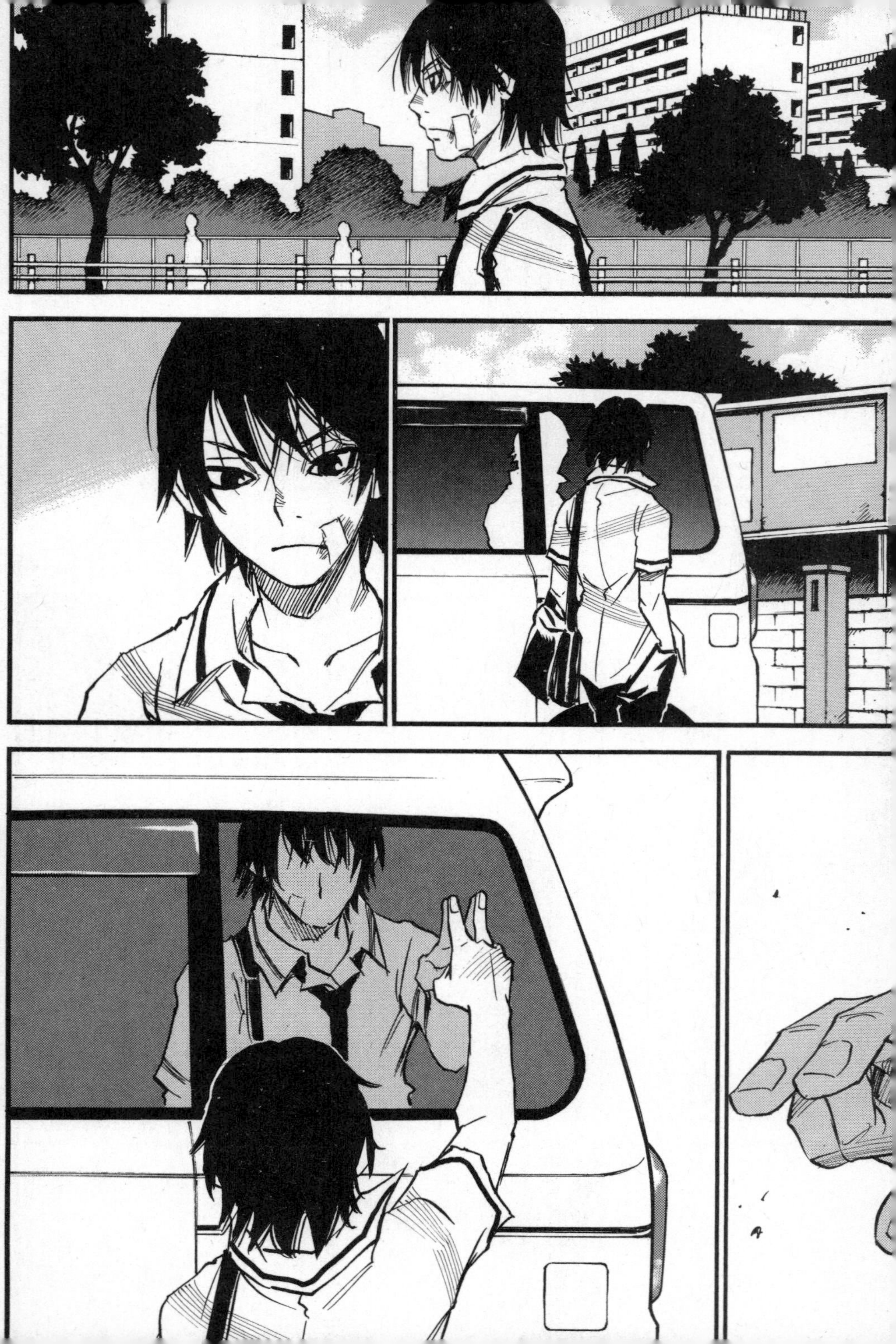

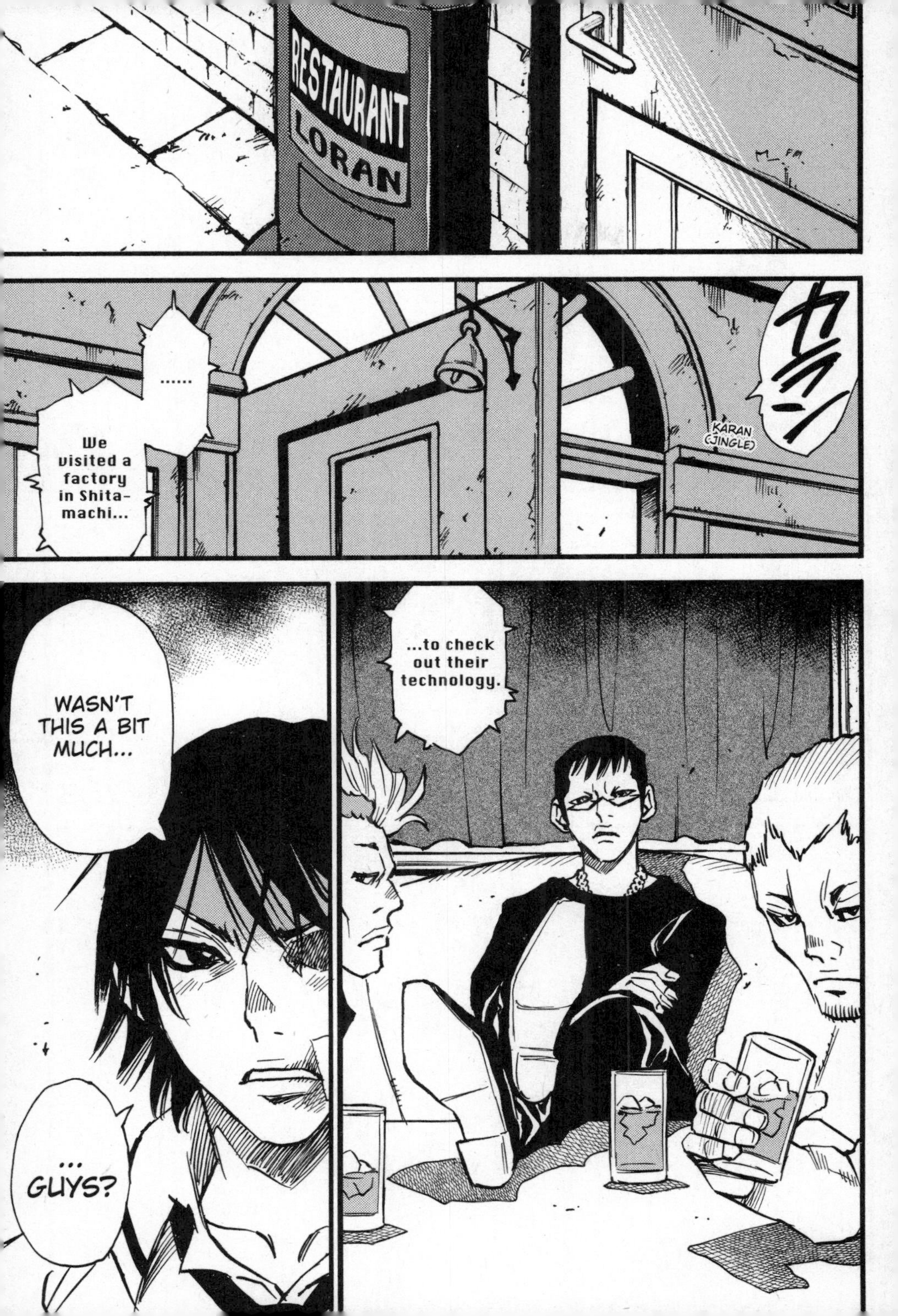
RESTAURANT
LORAN
カラン
KARAN (JINGLE)
......
We visited a factory in Shita-machi...
...to check out their technology.
WASN'T THIS A BIT MUCH...
... GUYS?

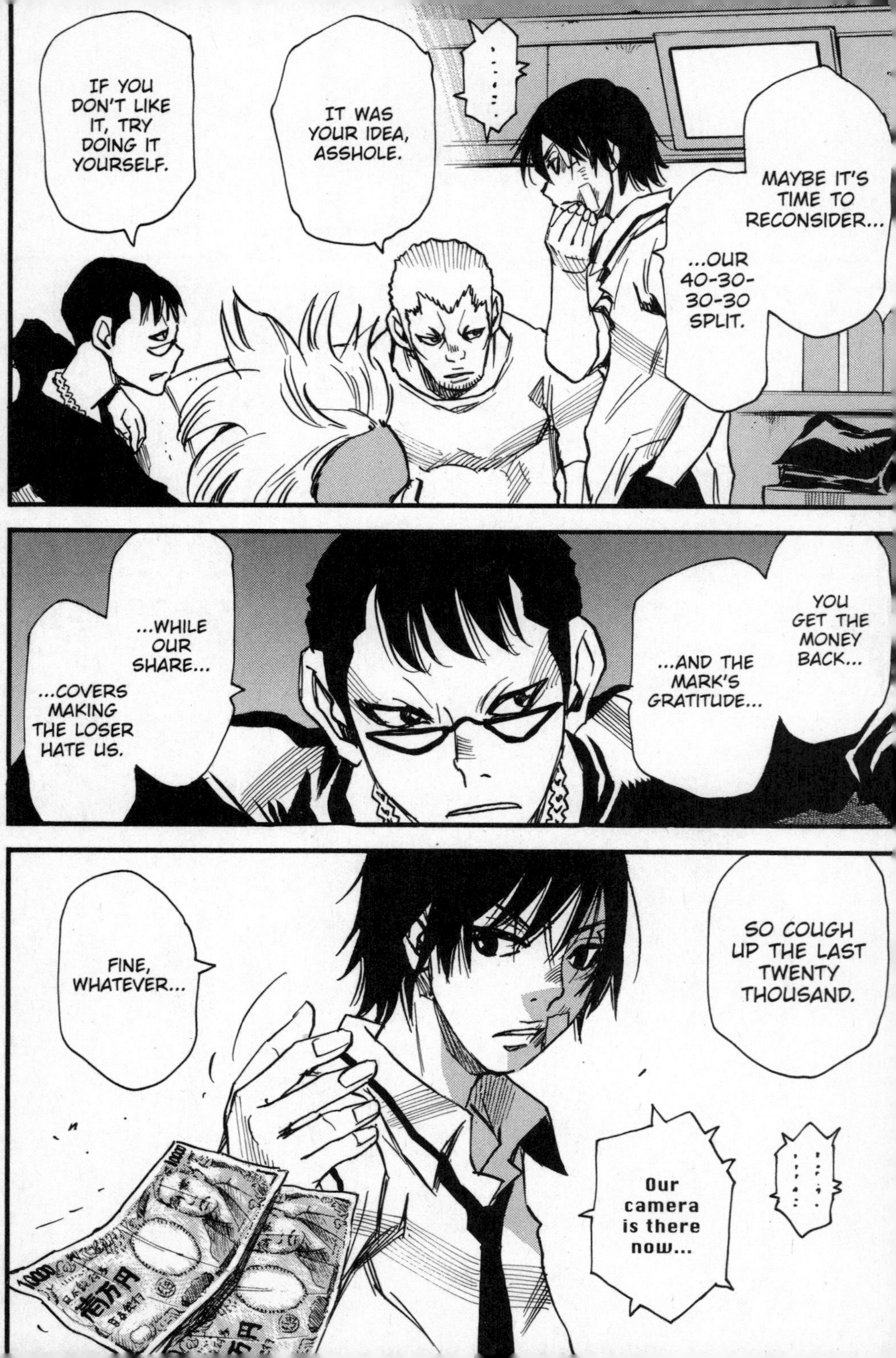

MAYBE IT'S TIME TO RECONSIDER...
...OUR 40-30-30-30 SPLIT.
IT WAS YOUR IDEA, ASSHOLE.
IF YOU DON'T LIKE IT, TRY DOING IT YOURSELF.
YOU GET THE MONEY BACK...
...AND THE MARK'S GRATITUDE...
...WHILE OUR SHARE...
...COVERS MAKING THE LOSER HATE US.
SO COUGH UP THE LAST TWENTY THOUSAND.
FINE, WHATEVER...
Our camera is there now...

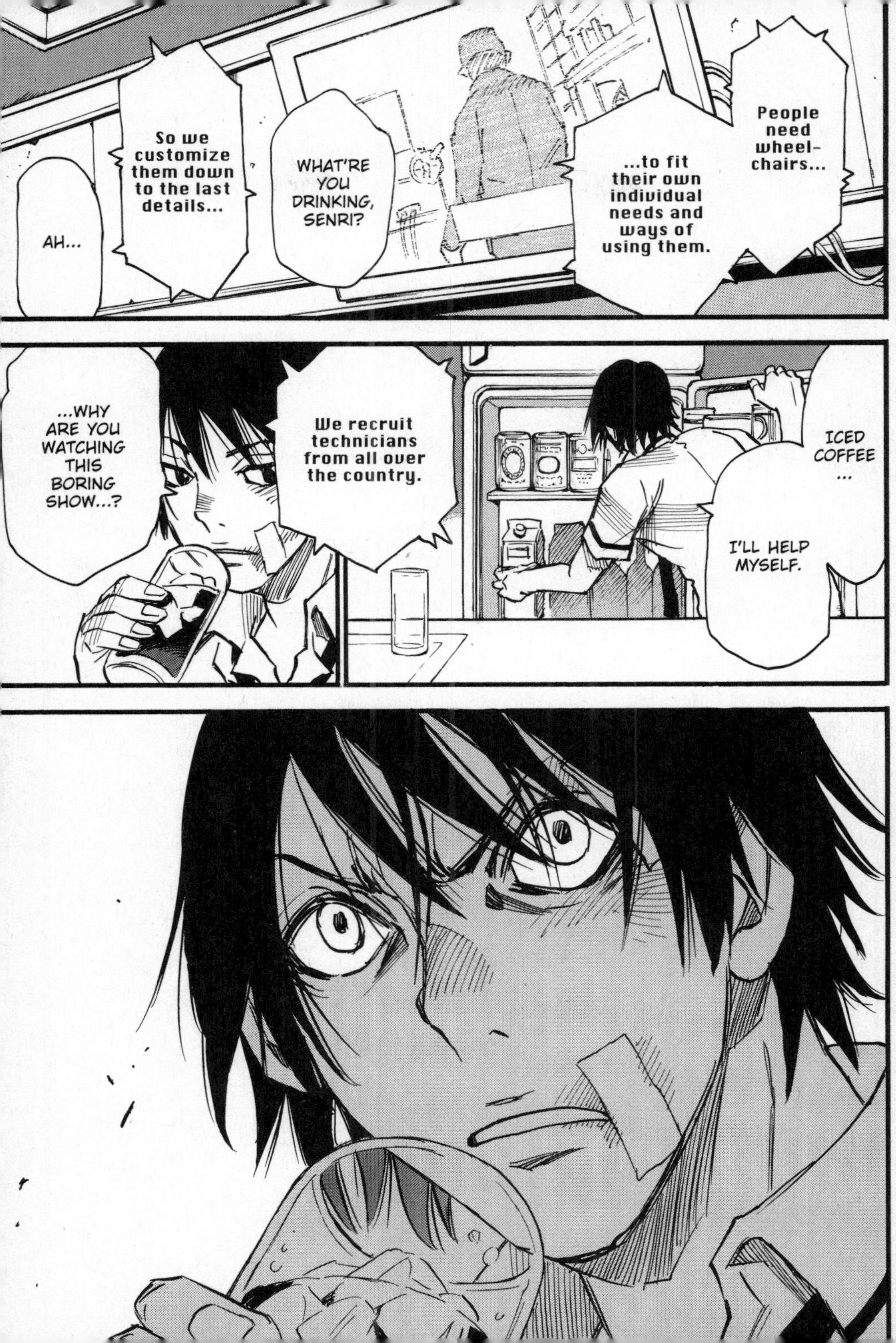
People need wheel-chairs...
...to fit their own individual needs and ways of using them.
WHAT'RE YOU DRINKING, SENRI?
So we customize them down to the last details...
AH...
ICED COFFEE ...
I'LL HELP MYSELF.
We recruit technicians from all over the country.
...WHY ARE YOU WATCHING THIS BORING SHOW...?

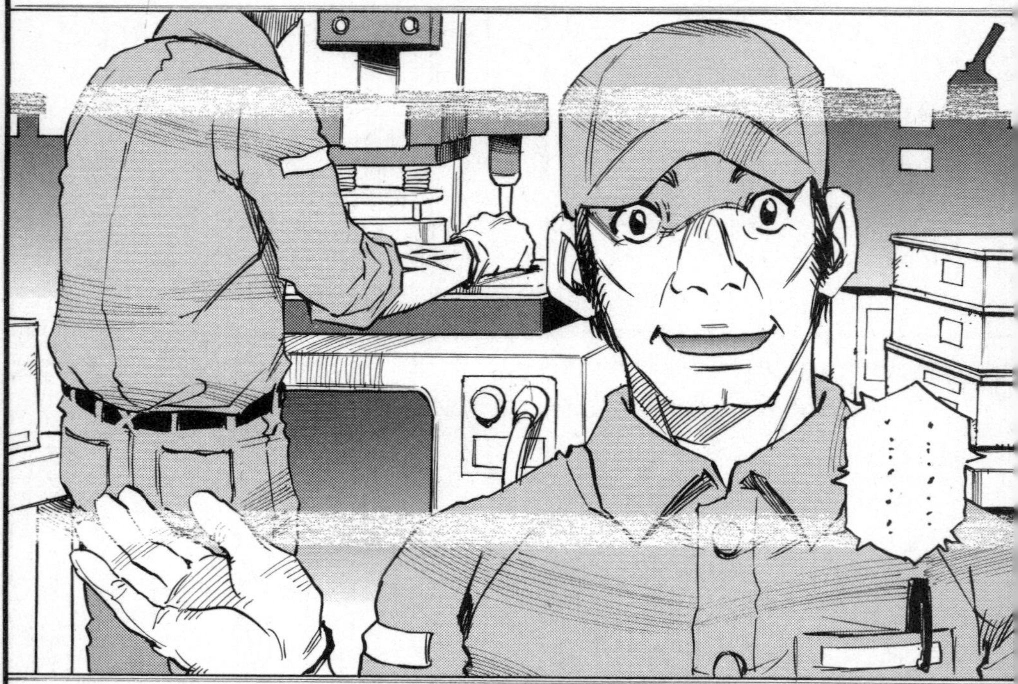
……
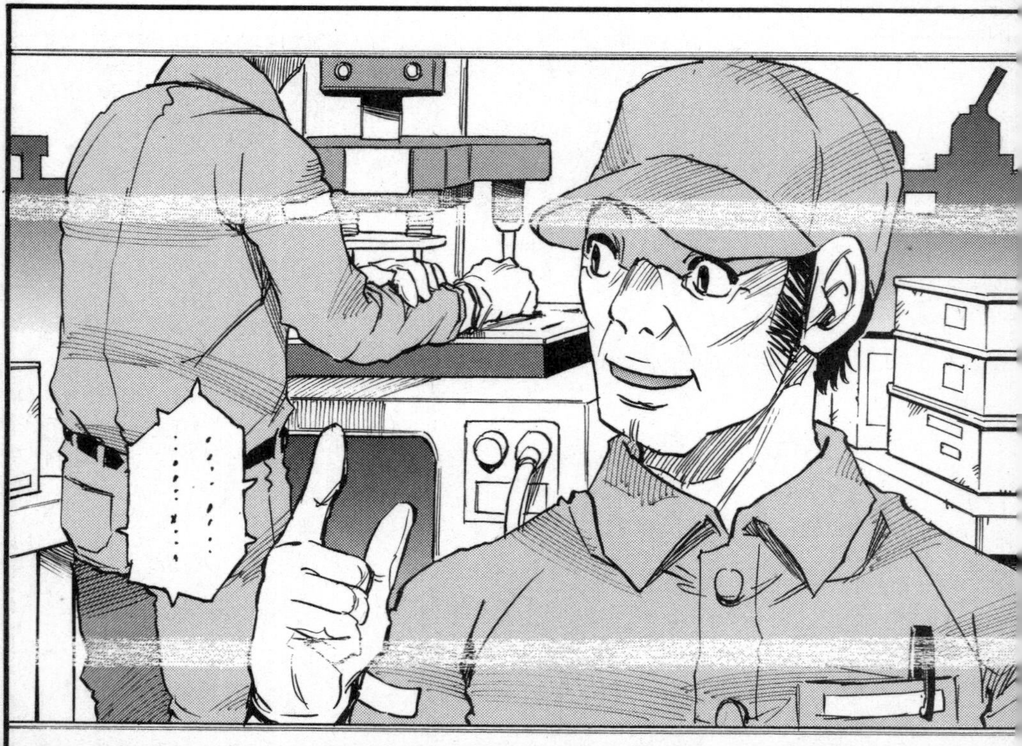
……

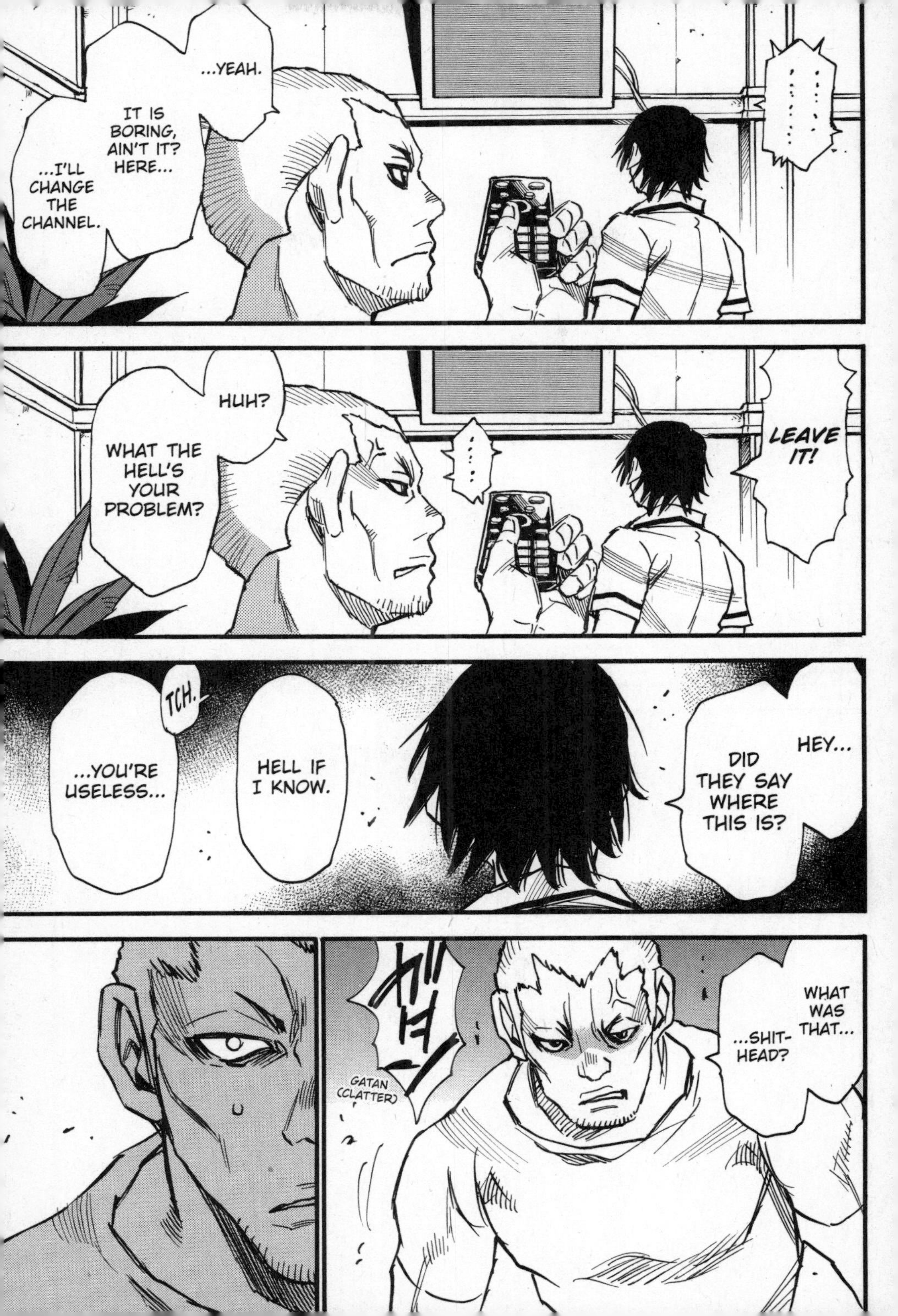
......
...YEAH.
IT IS BORING, AIN'T IT? HERE...
...I'LL CHANGE THE CHANNEL.
LEAVE IT!
......
HUH?
WHAT THE HELL'S YOUR PROBLEM?
HEY... DID THEY SAY WHERE THIS IS?
HELL IF I KNOW.
TCH.
...YOU'RE USELESS...
WHAT WAS THAT... ...SHIT-HEAD?
GATAN (CLATTER)

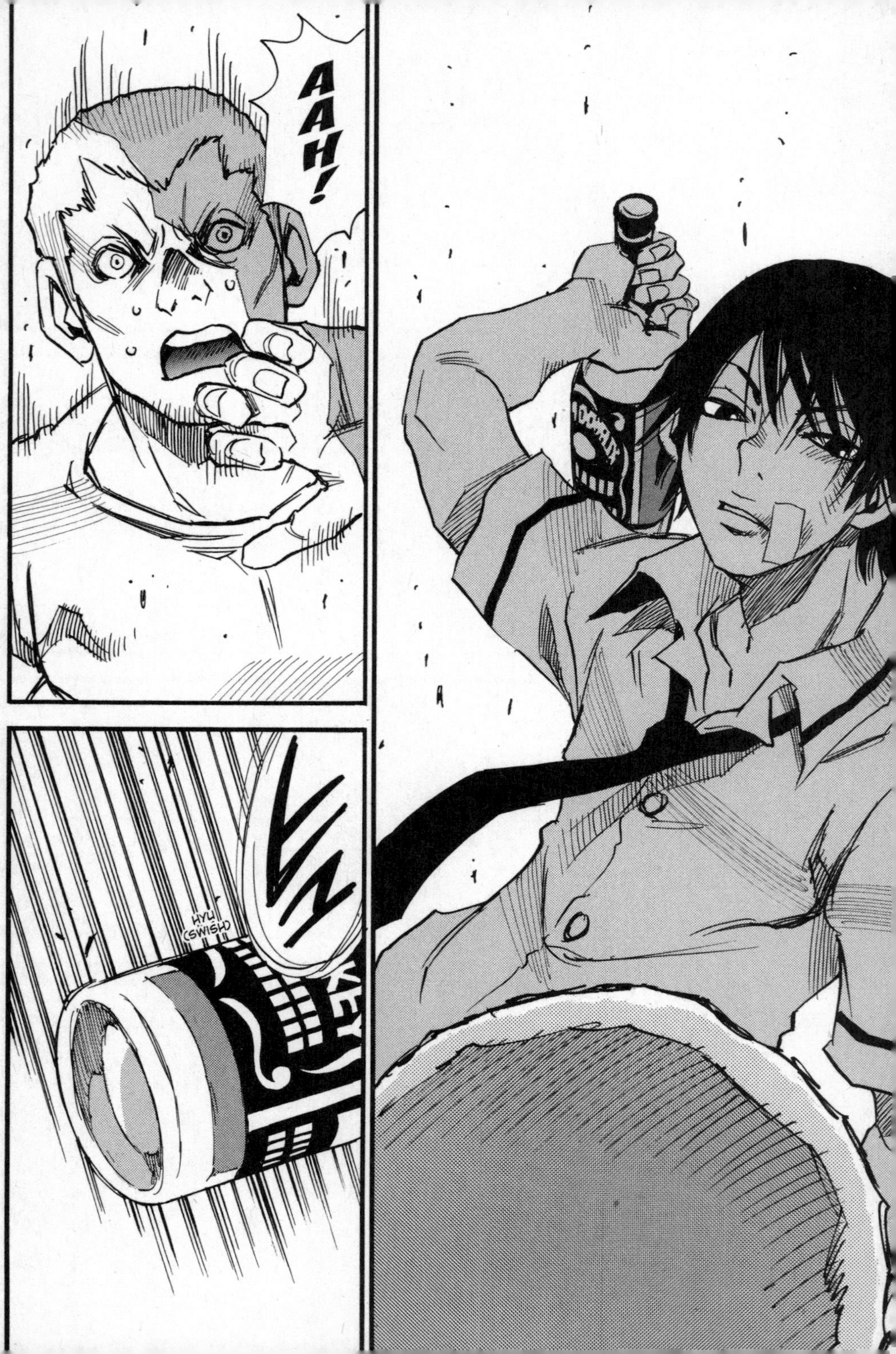
AAH!
HYU (SWISH)

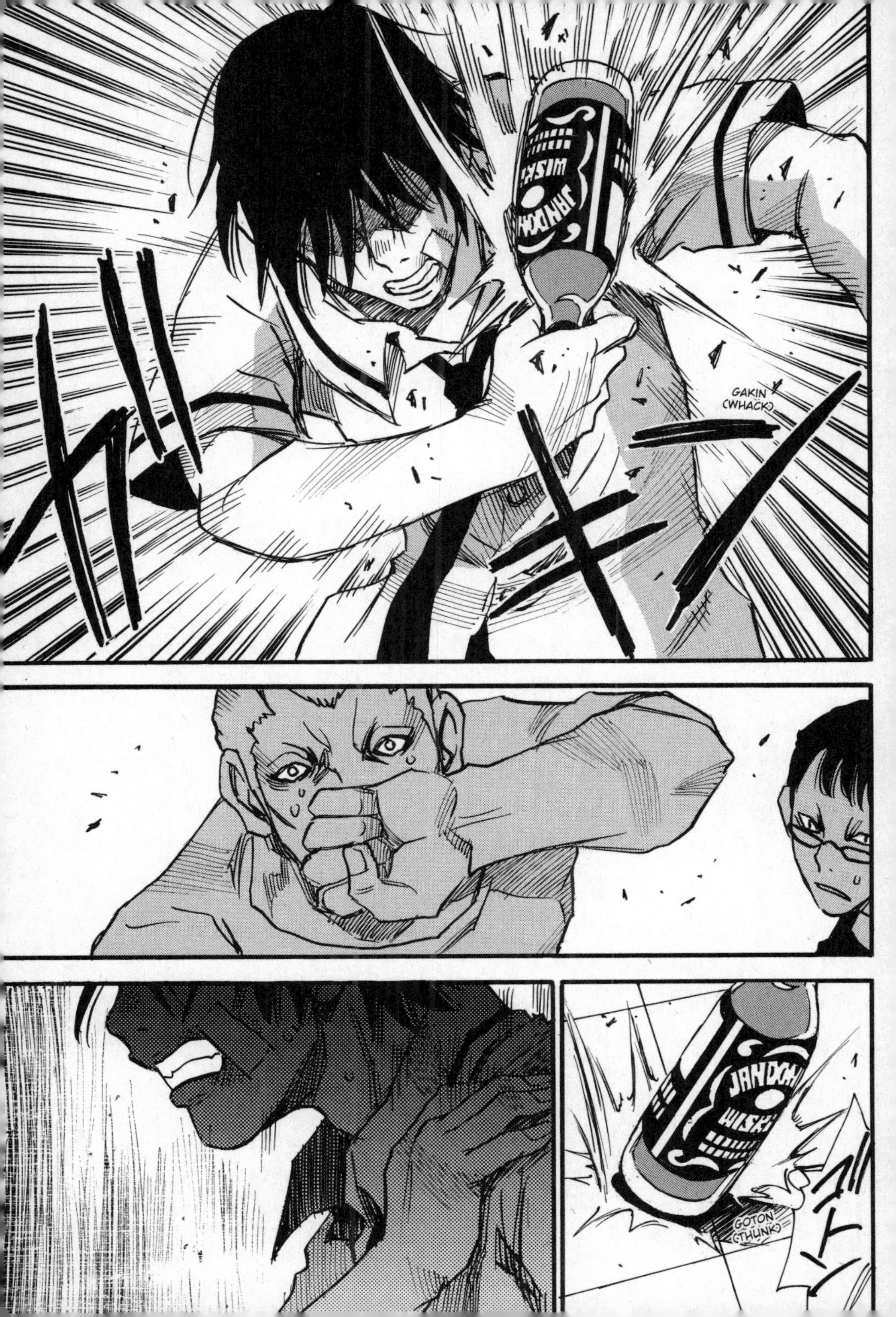
GAKIN (WHACK)
GOTON (THUNK)

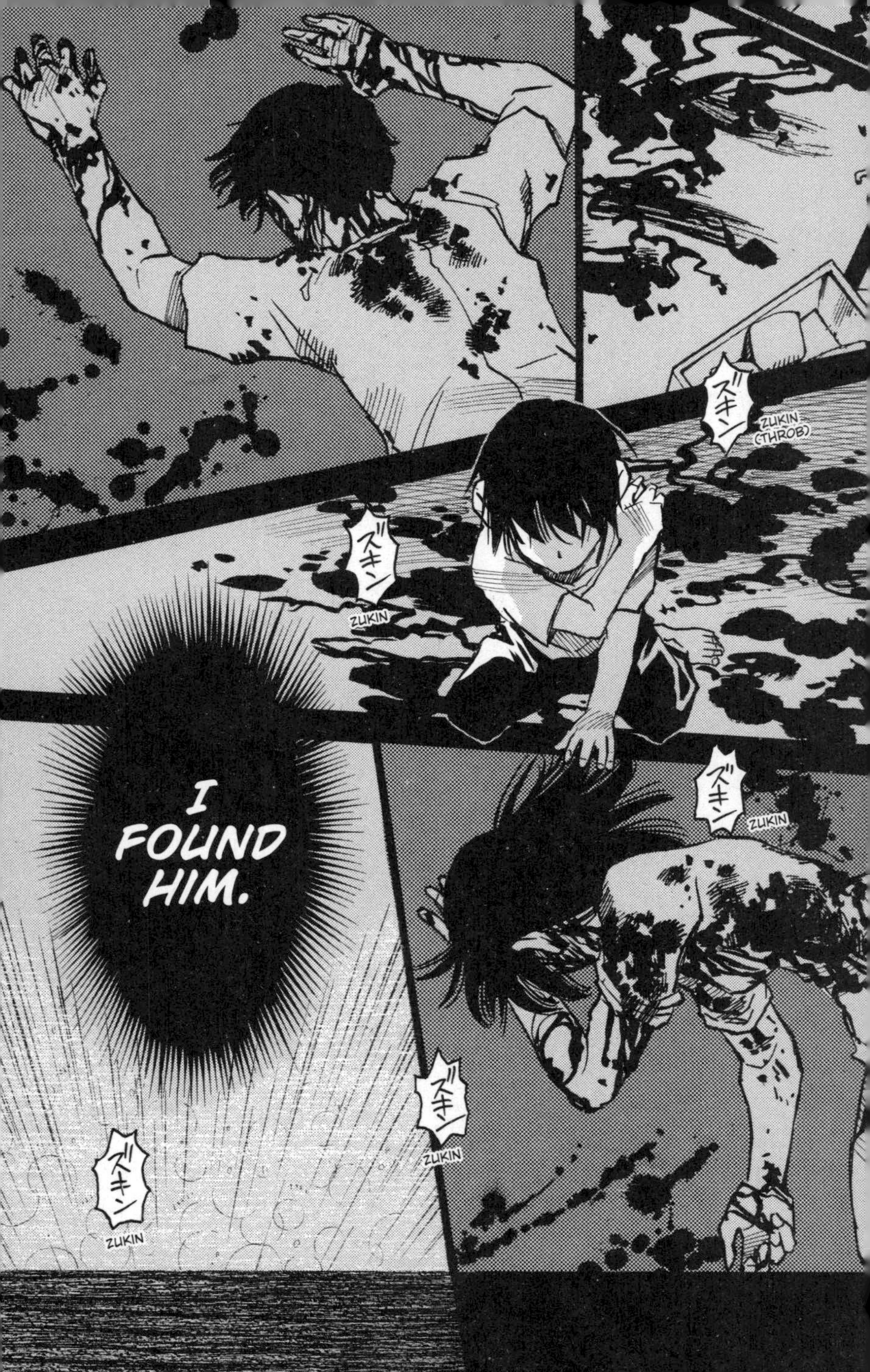
ズキン
ZUKIN (THROB)
ズキン
ZUKIN
ズキン
ZUKIN
ズキン
ZUKIN
I FOUND HIM.
ズキン
ZUKIN

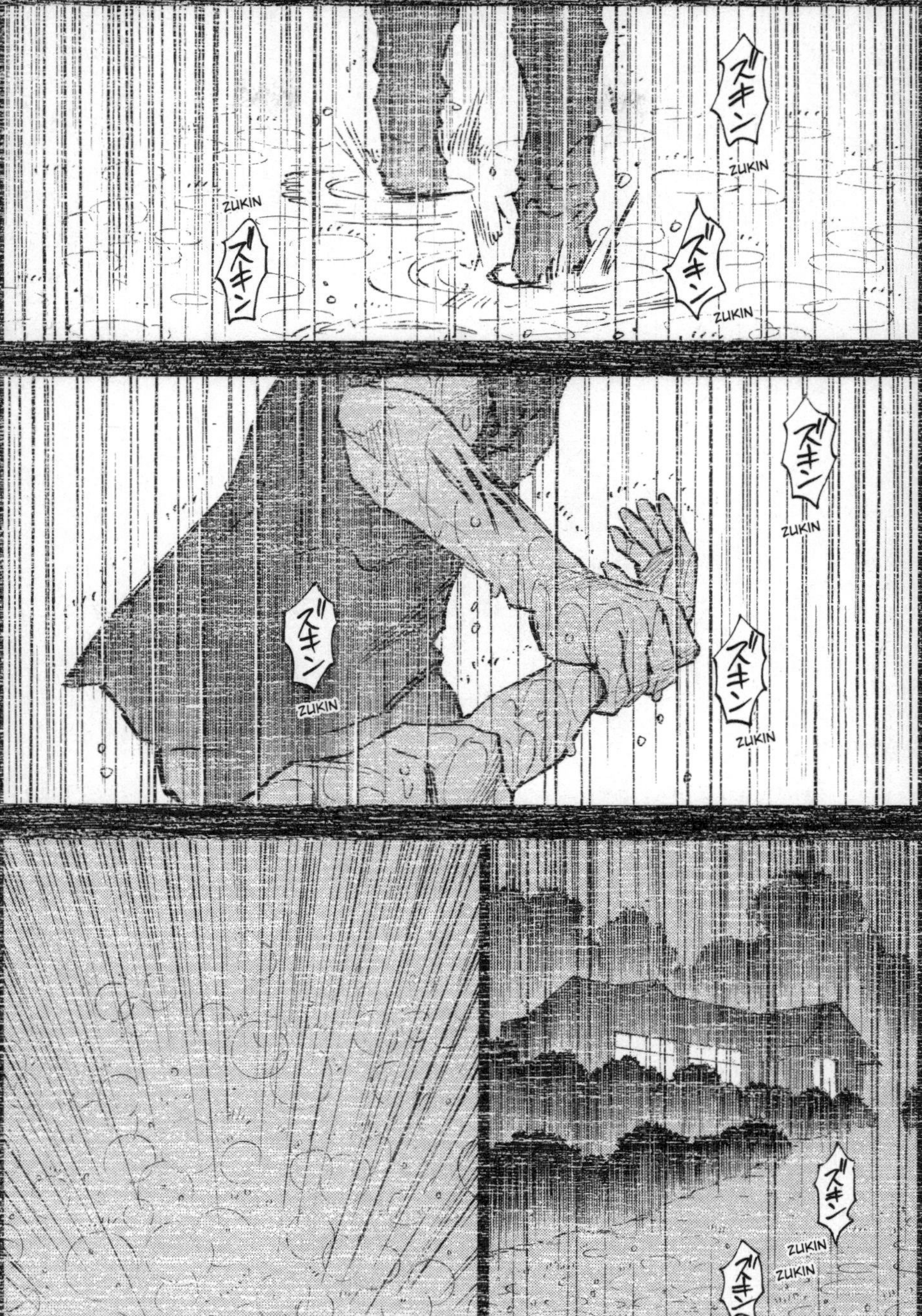
ズキン ZUKIN
ズキン ZUKIN
ZUKIN ズキン
ズキン ZUKIN
ズキン ZUKIN
ズキン ZUKIN
ズキン ZUKIN
ズキン ZUKIN

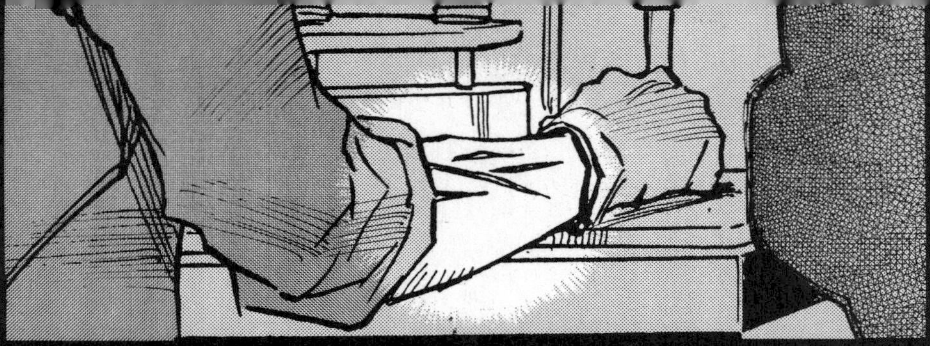

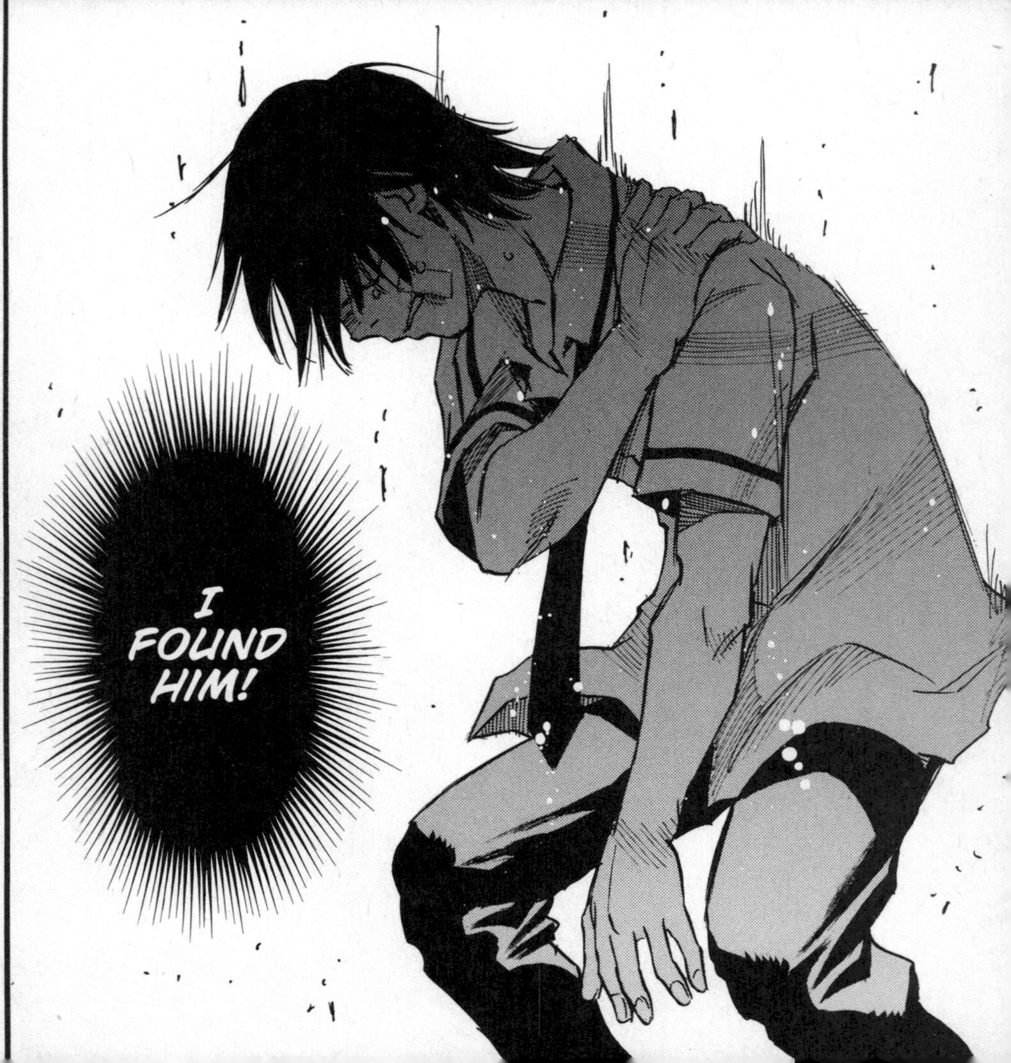
I FOUND HIM!

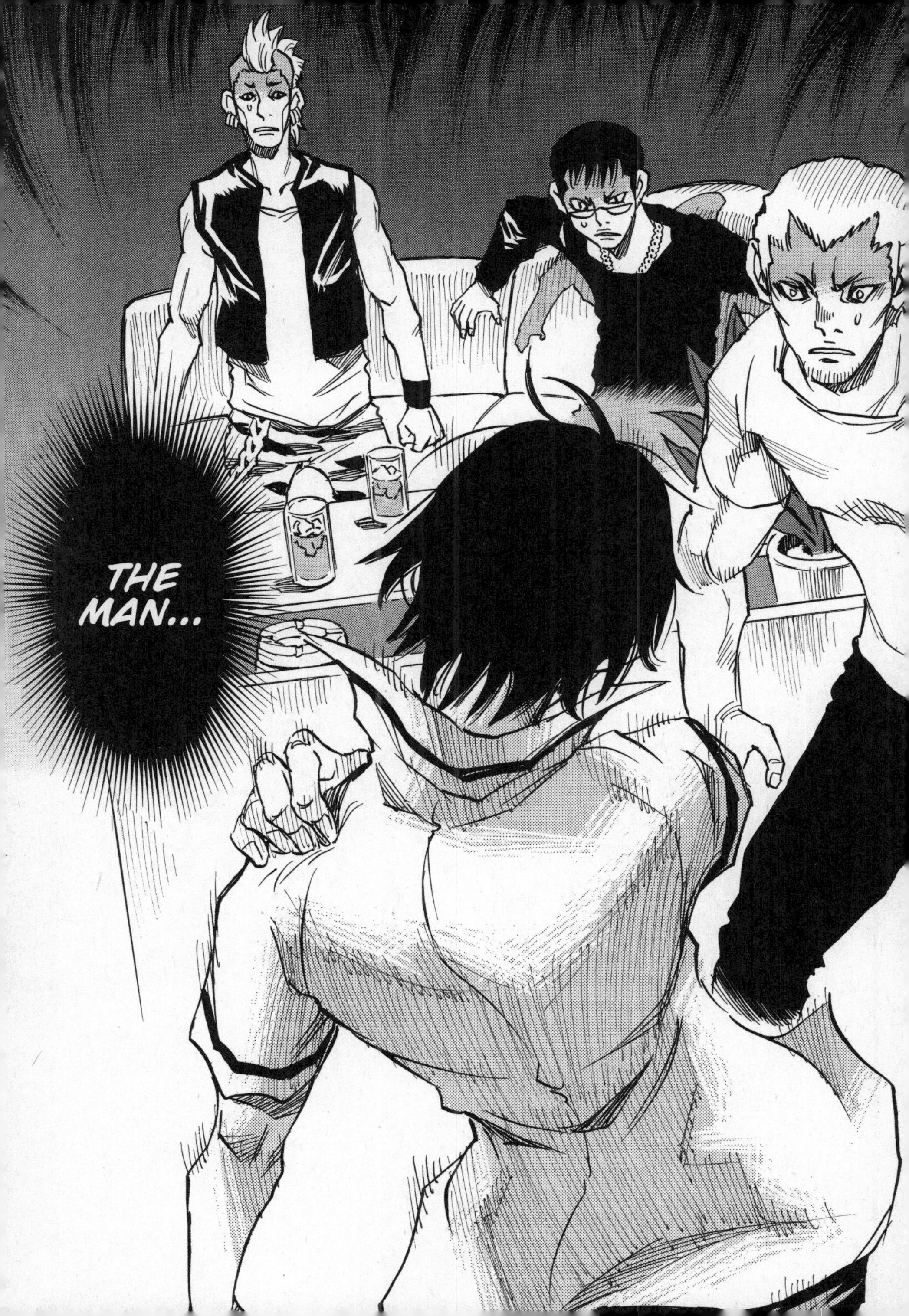
THE MAN...

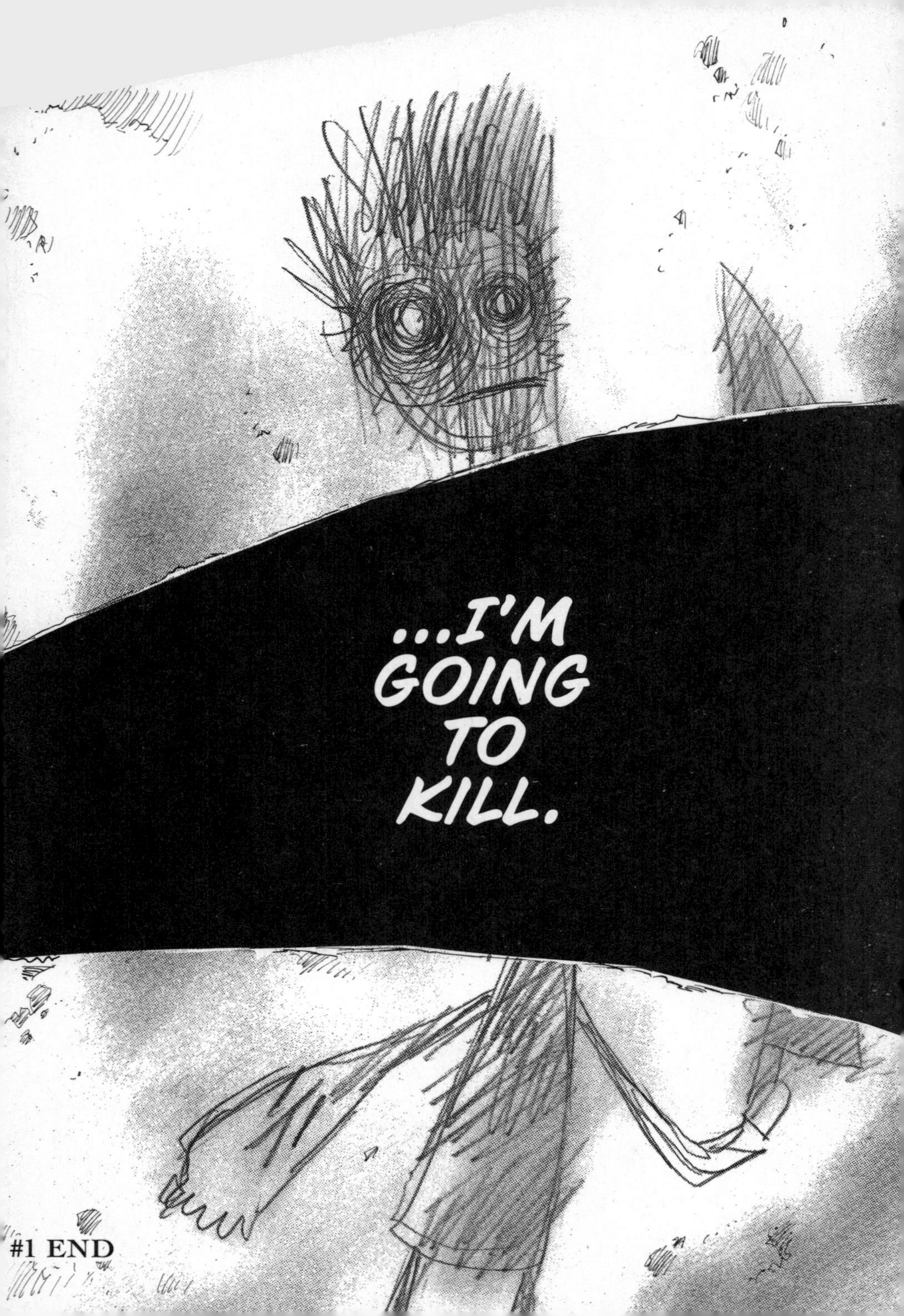
...I'M GOING TO KILL.
#1 END

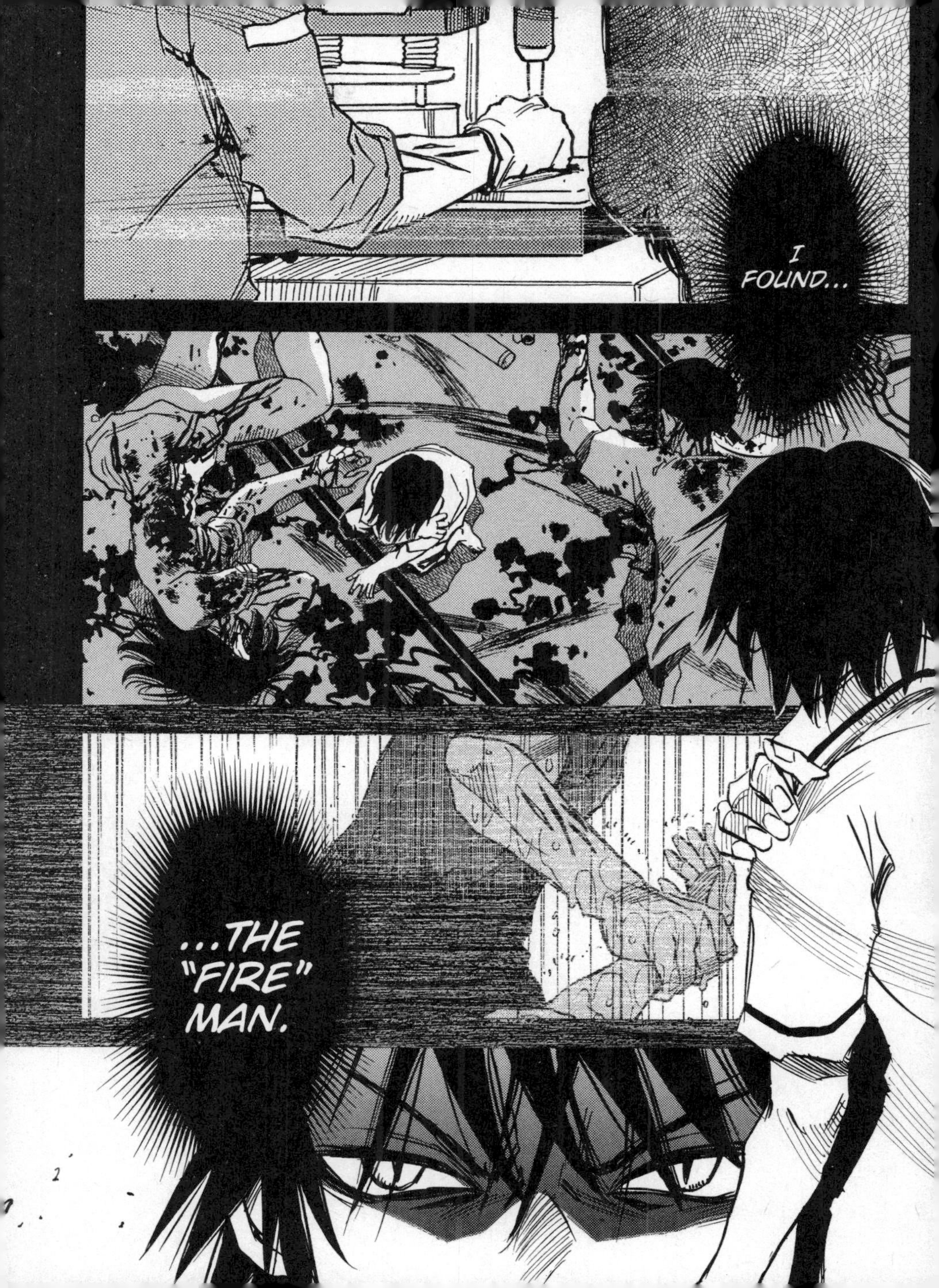
I FOUND...
...THE "FIRE" MAN.

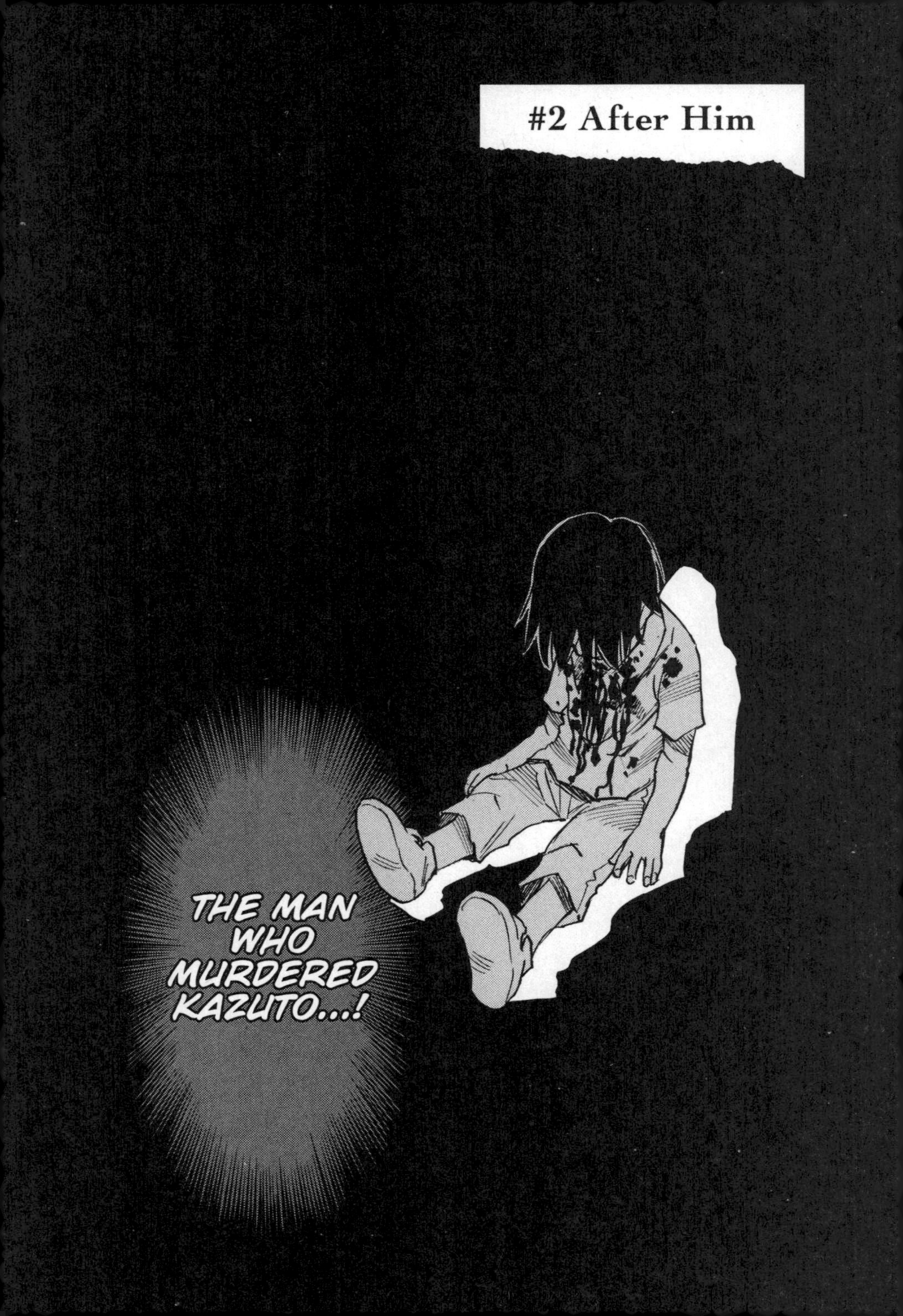
#2 After Him
THE MAN WHO MURDERED KAZUTO...!

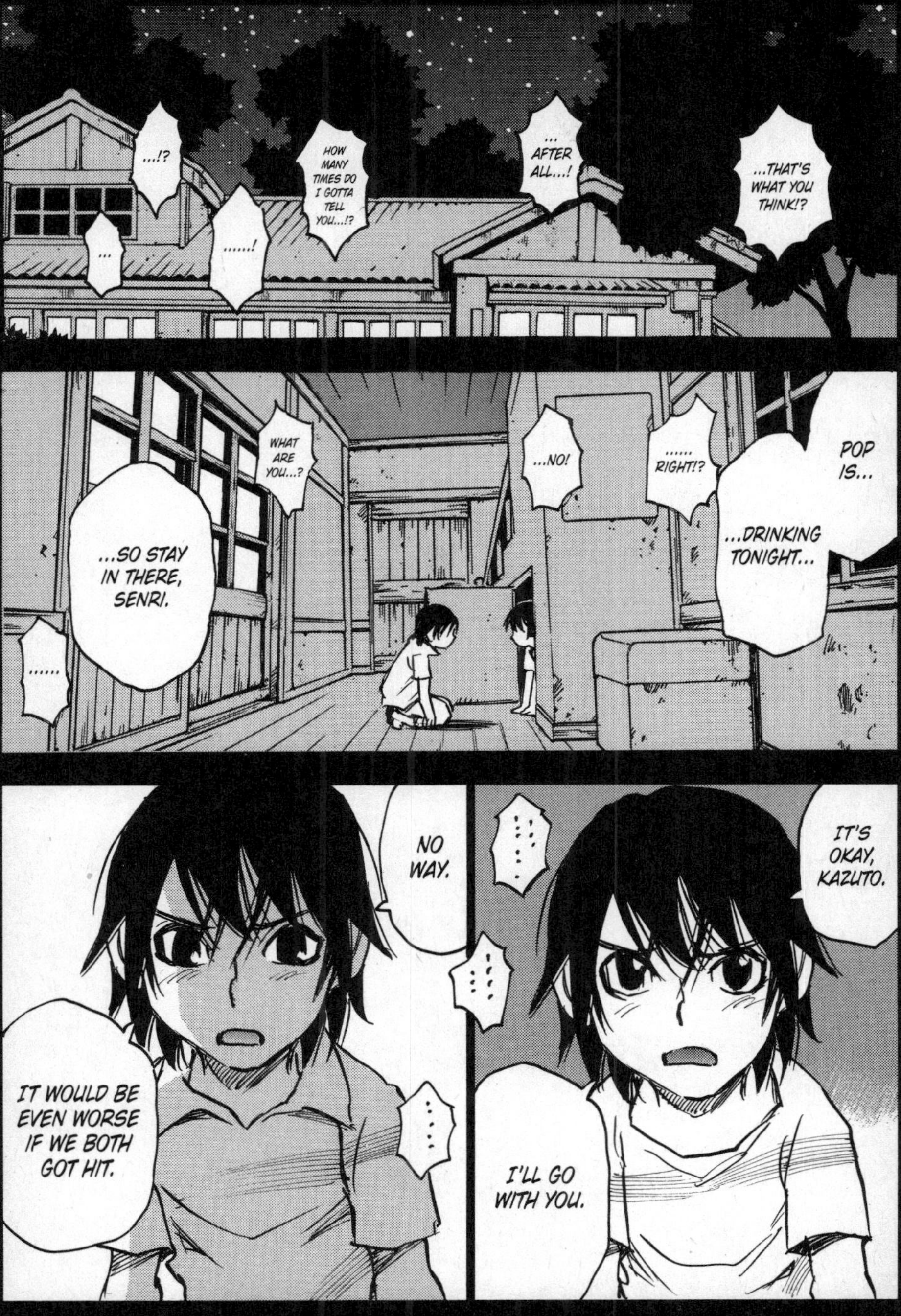
...THAT'S WHAT YOU THINK!?
... AFTER ALL...!
HOW MANY TIMES DO I GOTTA TELL YOU...!?
......!
...!?
...
POP IS...
...DRINKING TONIGHT...
...... RIGHT!?
...NO!
WHAT ARE YOU...?
...SO STAY IN THERE, SENRI.
......
IT'S OKAY, KAZUTO.
......
......
I'LL GO WITH YOU.
NO WAY.
......
IT WOULD BE EVEN WORSE IF WE BOTH GOT HIT.

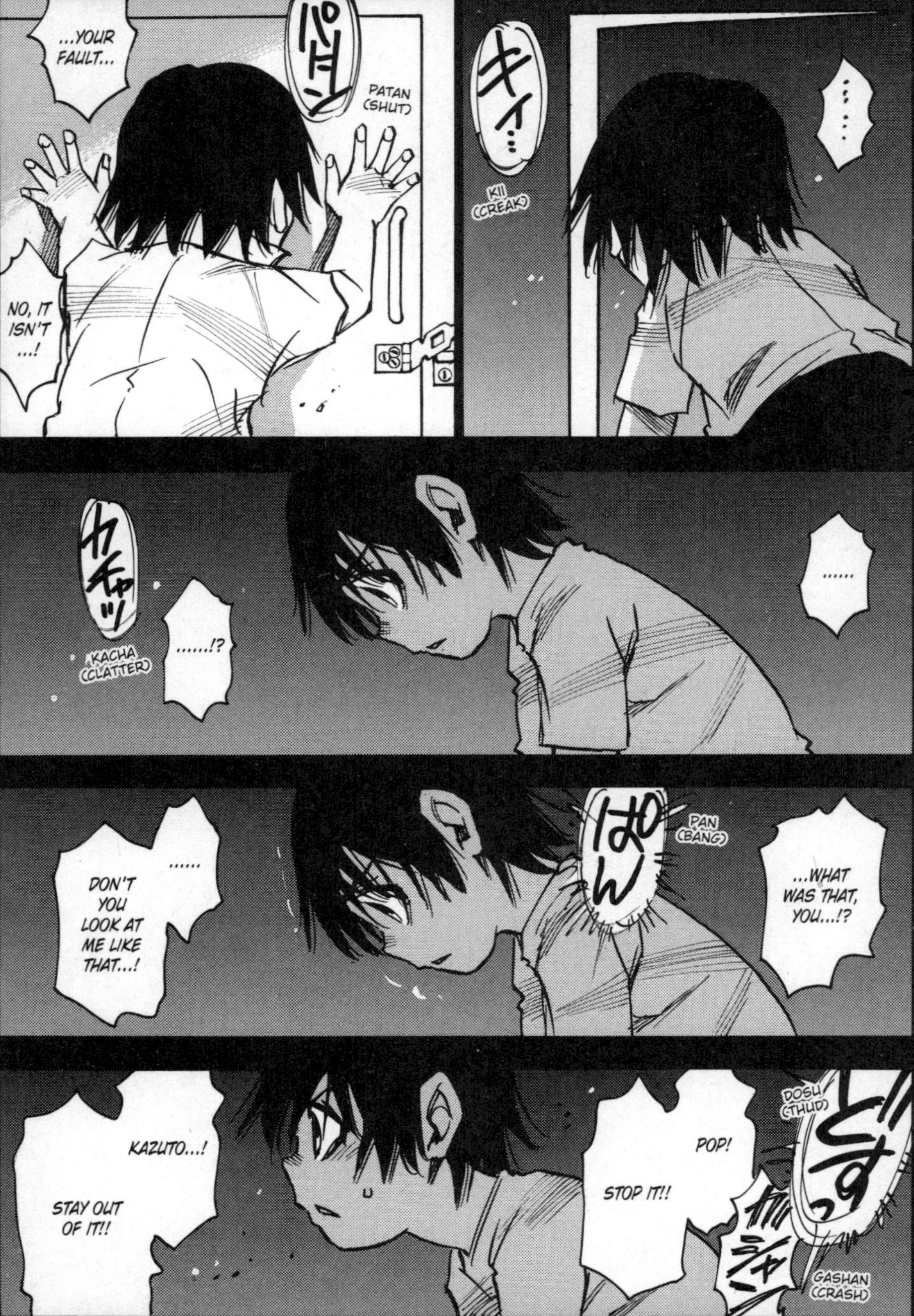
……
キィ…
KII (CREAK)
パタン
PATAN (SHUT)
...YOUR FAULT...
NO, IT ISN'T ...!
......
カチャッ
KACHA (CLATTER)
......!?
...WHAT WAS THAT, YOU...!?
ぱん
PAN (BANG)
......
DON'T YOU LOOK AT ME LIKE THAT...!
どすっ
DOSU (THUD)
POP!
STOP IT!!
GASHAN (CRASH)
KAZUTO...!
STAY OUT OF IT!!

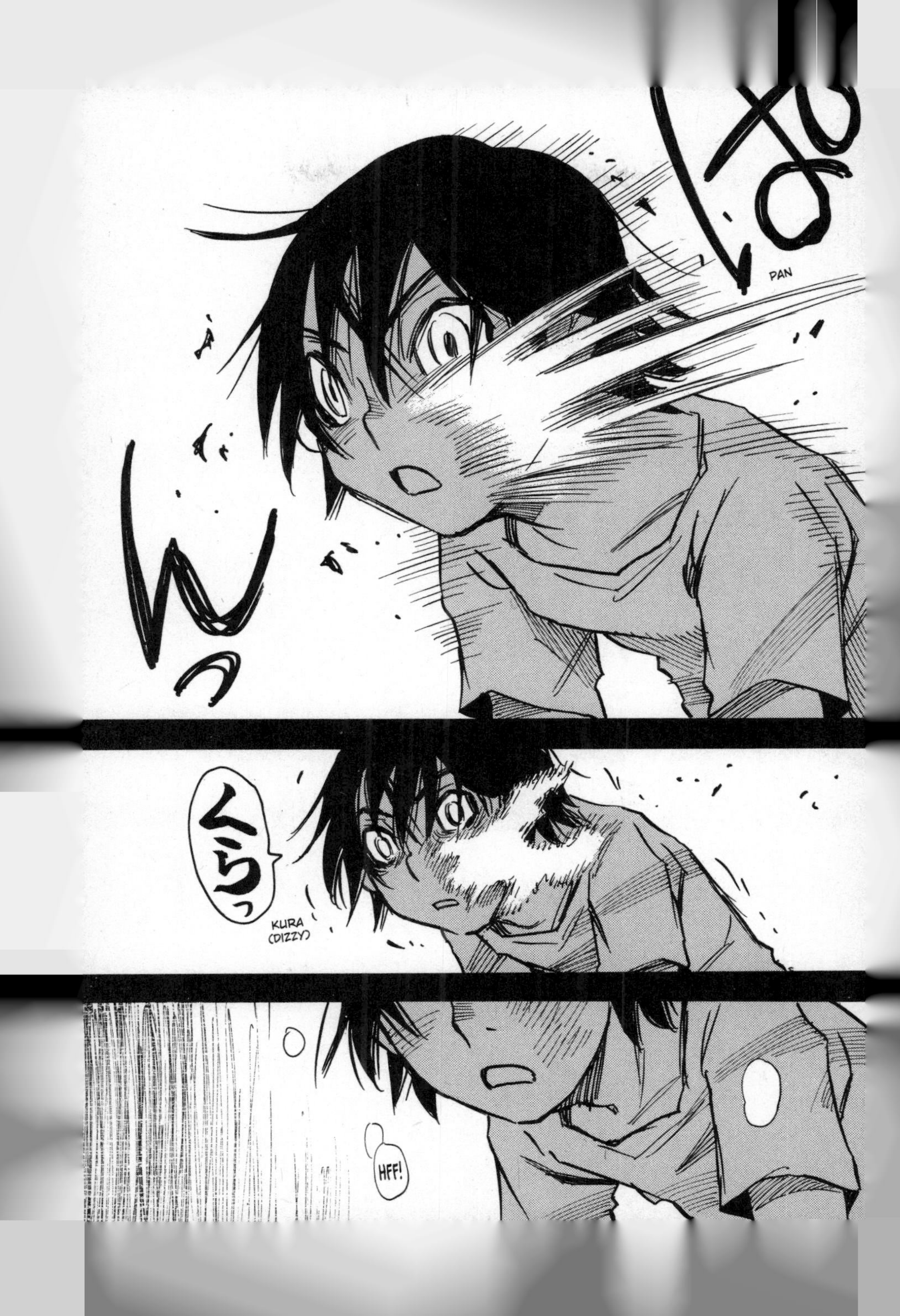
PAN
くらっ
KURA (DIZZY)
HFF!

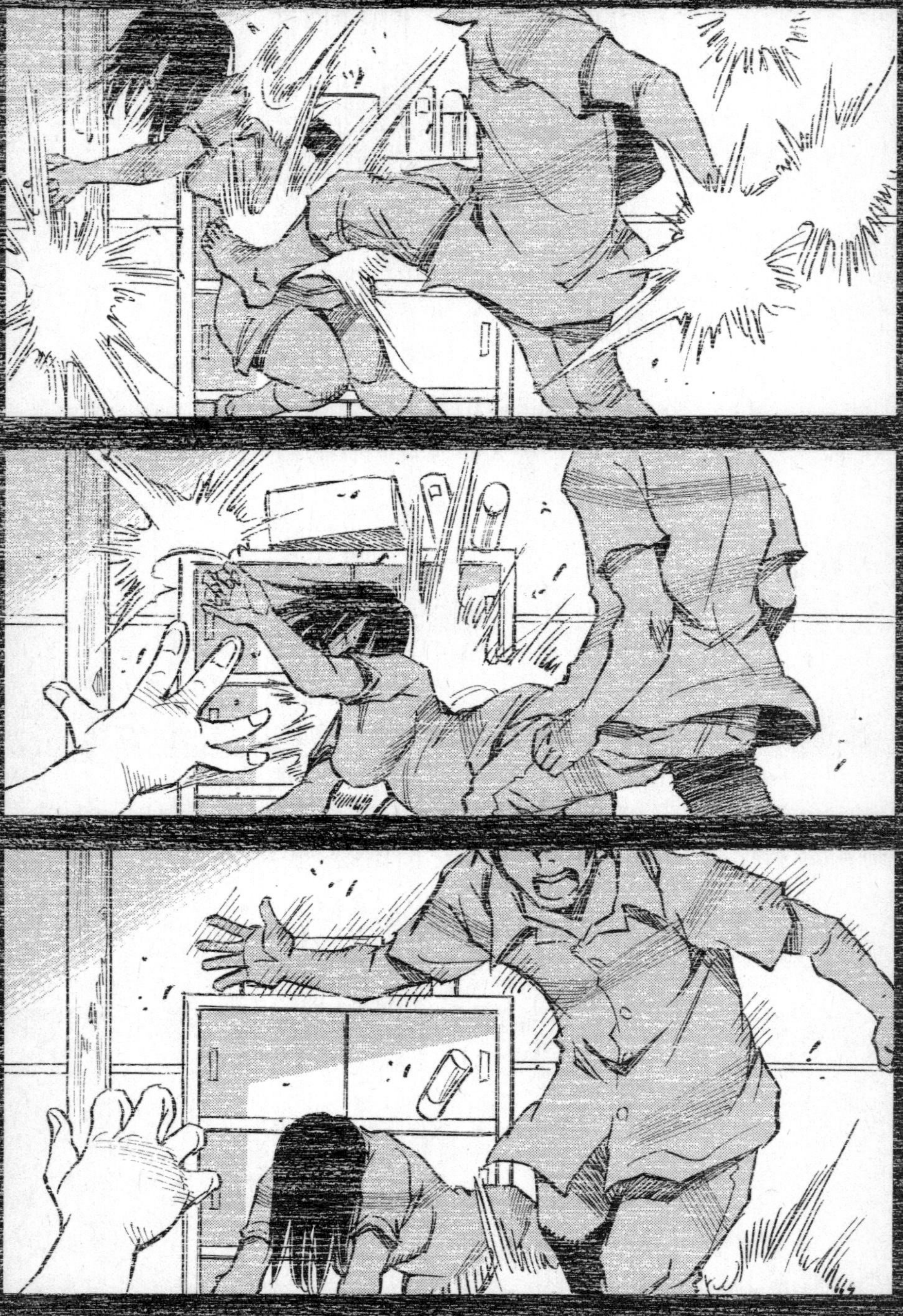

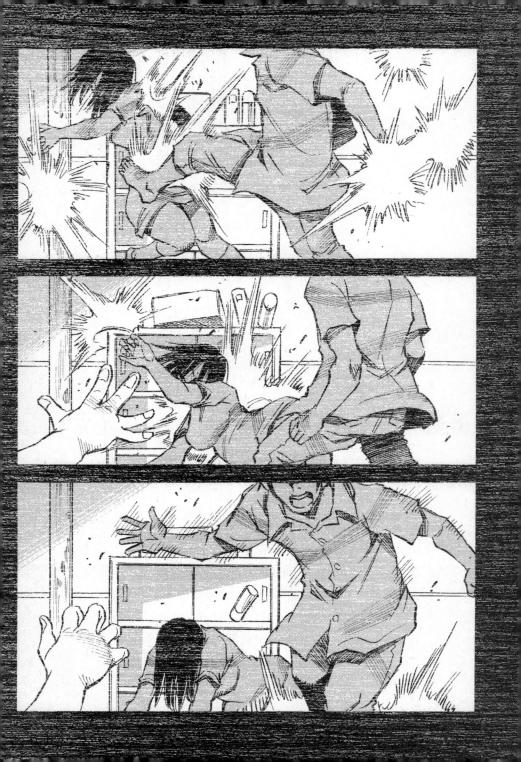

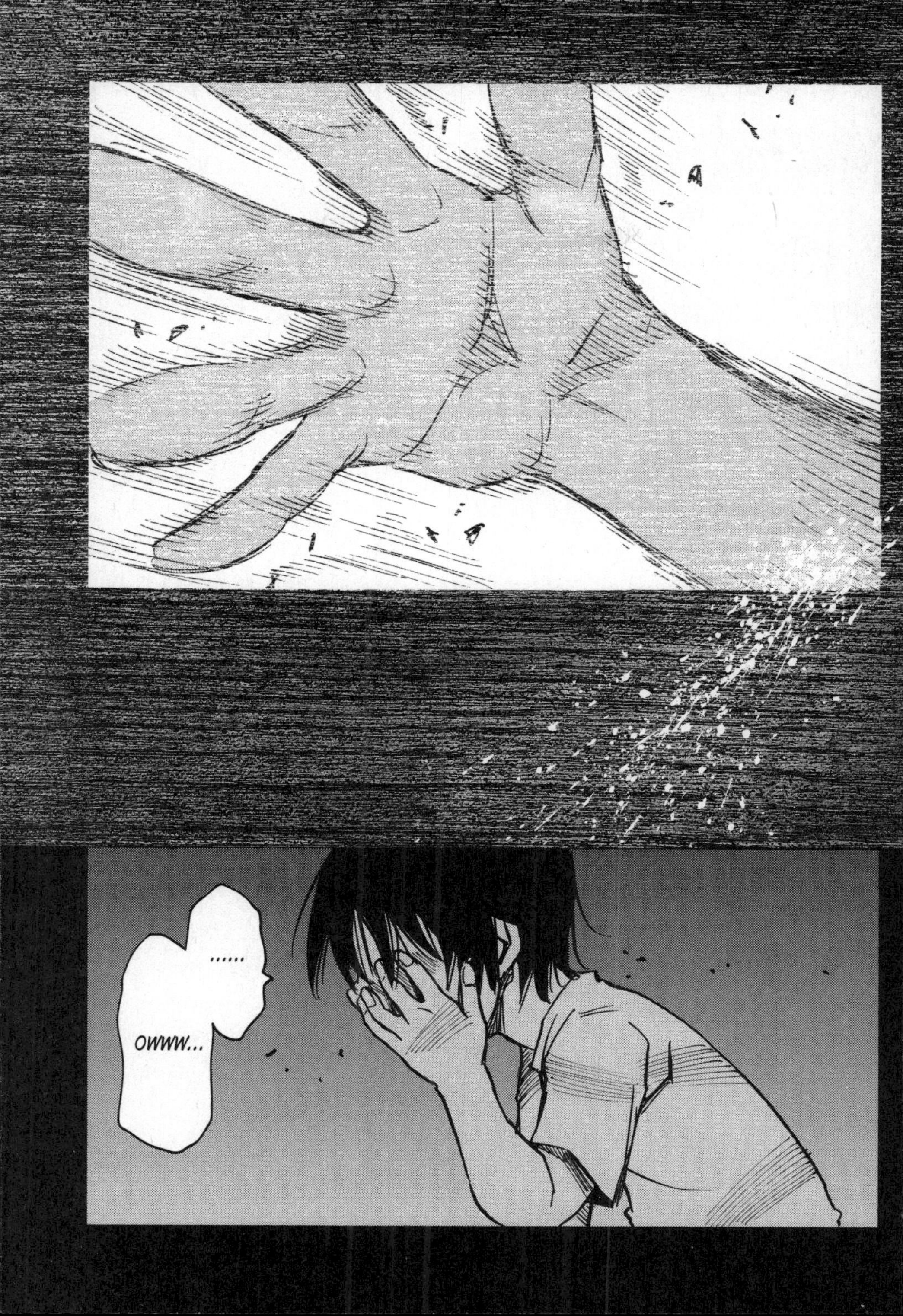
......
OWWW...

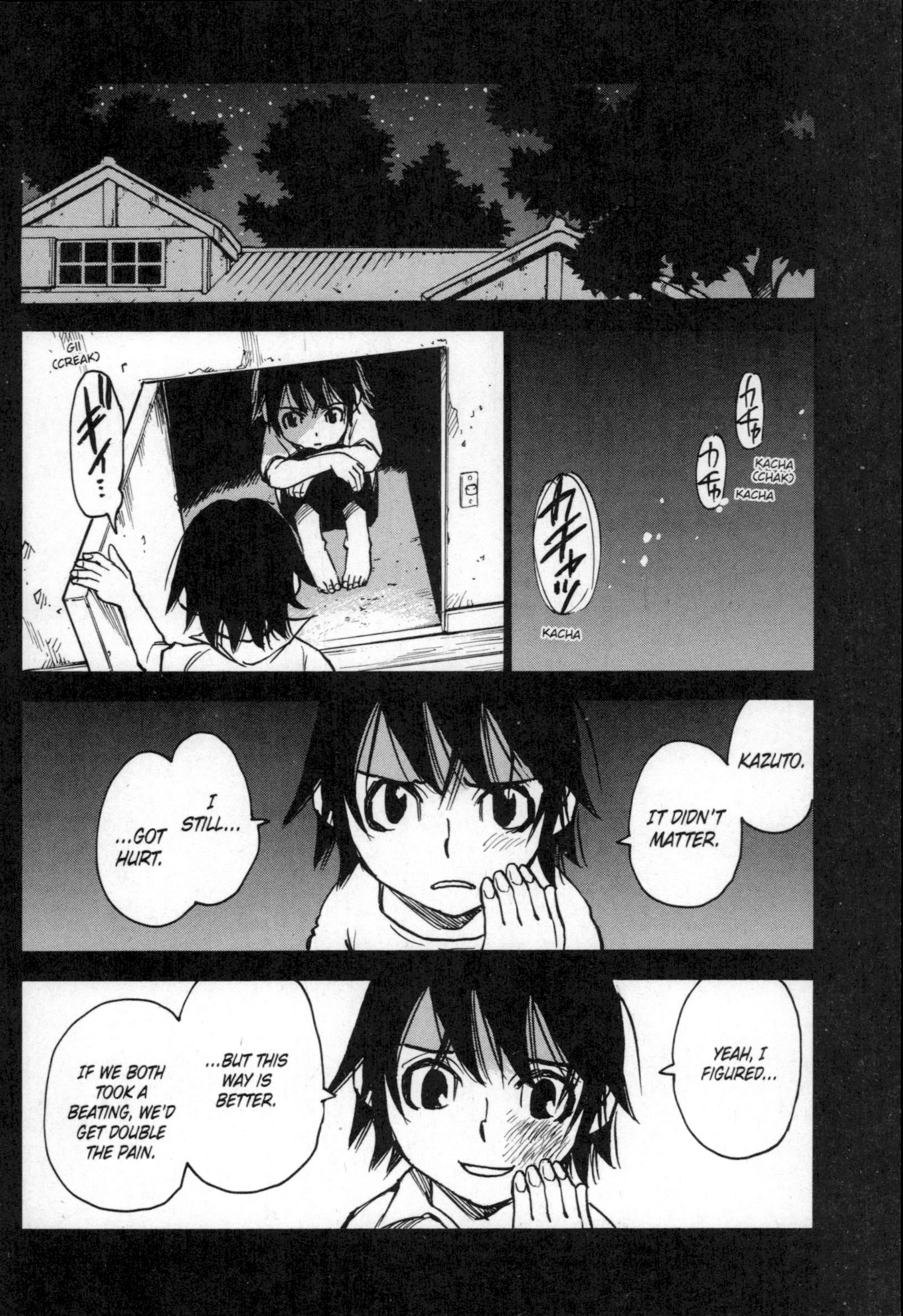
カチャ
KACHA (CHAK)
カチャ
KACHA
カチャッ
KACHA
ギイ…
GII (CREAK)
KAZUTO.
IT DIDN'T MATTER.
I STILL...
...GOT HURT.
YEAH, I FIGURED...
...BUT THIS WAY IS BETTER.
IF WE BOTH TOOK A BEATING, WE'D GET DOUBLE THE PAIN.

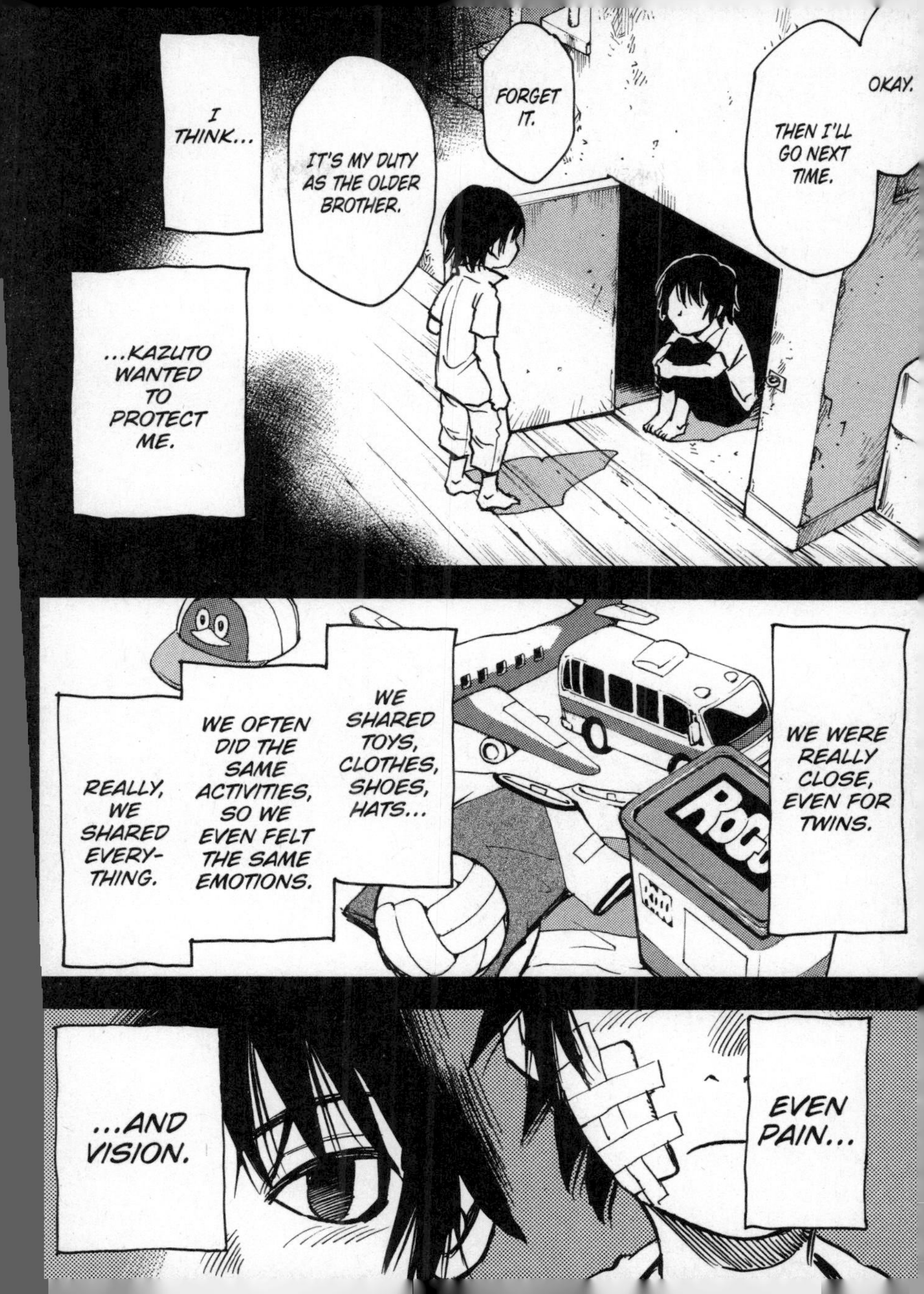
OKAY.
THEN I'LL GO NEXT TIME.
FORGET IT.
IT'S MY DUTY AS THE OLDER BROTHER.
I THINK...
...KAZUTO WANTED TO PROTECT ME.
WE WERE REALLY CLOSE, EVEN FOR TWINS.
WE SHARED TOYS, CLOTHES, SHOES, HATS...
WE OFTEN DID THE SAME ACTIVITIES, SO WE EVEN FELT THE SAME EMOTIONS.
REALLY, WE SHARED EVERY-THING.
EVEN PAIN...
...AND VISION.

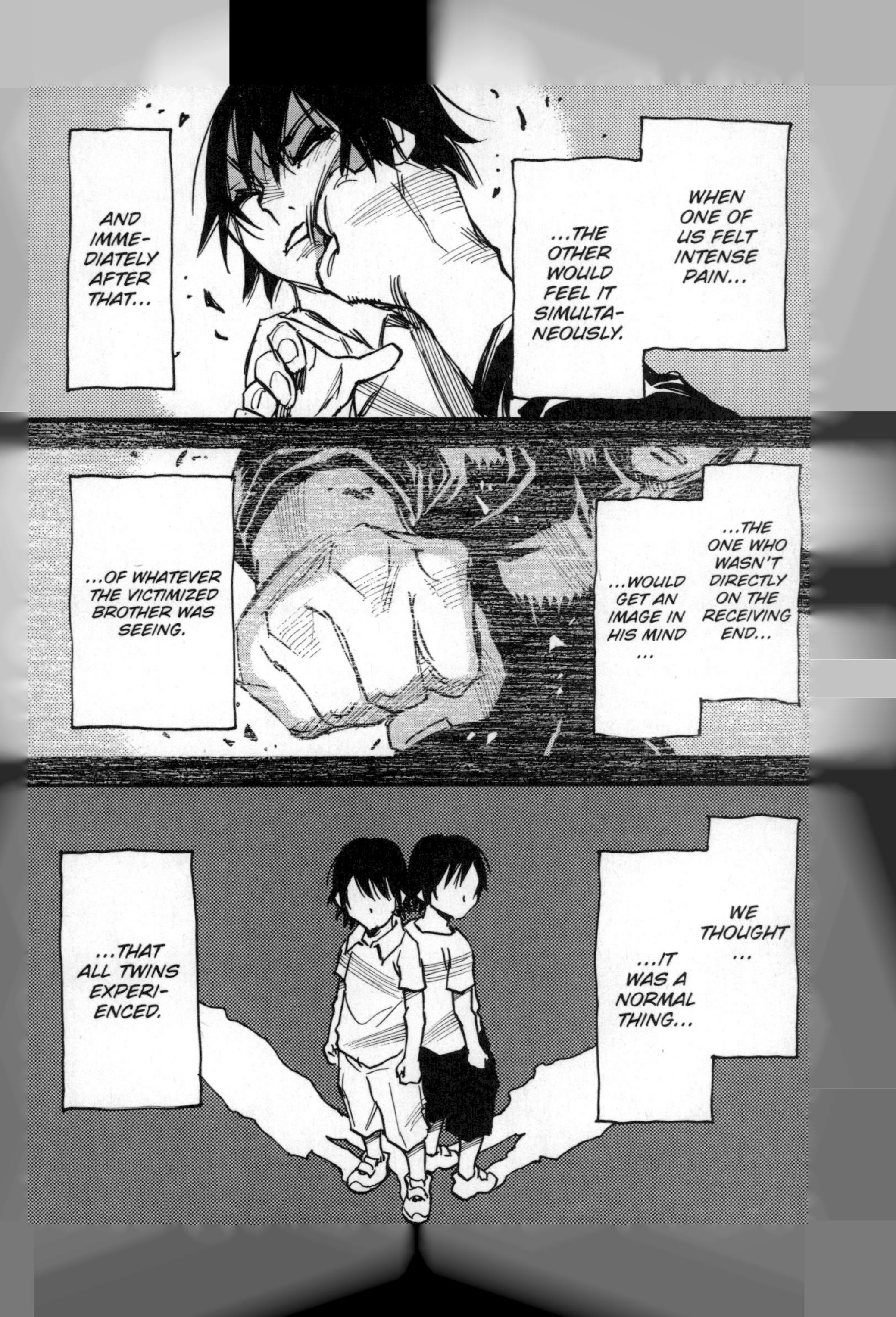
WHEN ONE OF US FELT INTENSE PAIN...
...THE OTHER WOULD FEEL IT SIMULTA-NEOUSLY.
AND IMME-DIATELY AFTER THAT...
...THE ONE WHO WASN'T DIRECTLY ON THE RECEIVING END...
...WOULD GET AN IMAGE IN HIS MIND ...
...OF WHATEVER THE VICTIMIZED BROTHER WAS SEEING.
WE THOUGHT ...
...IT WAS A NORMAL THING...
...THAT ALL TWINS EXPERI-ENCED.

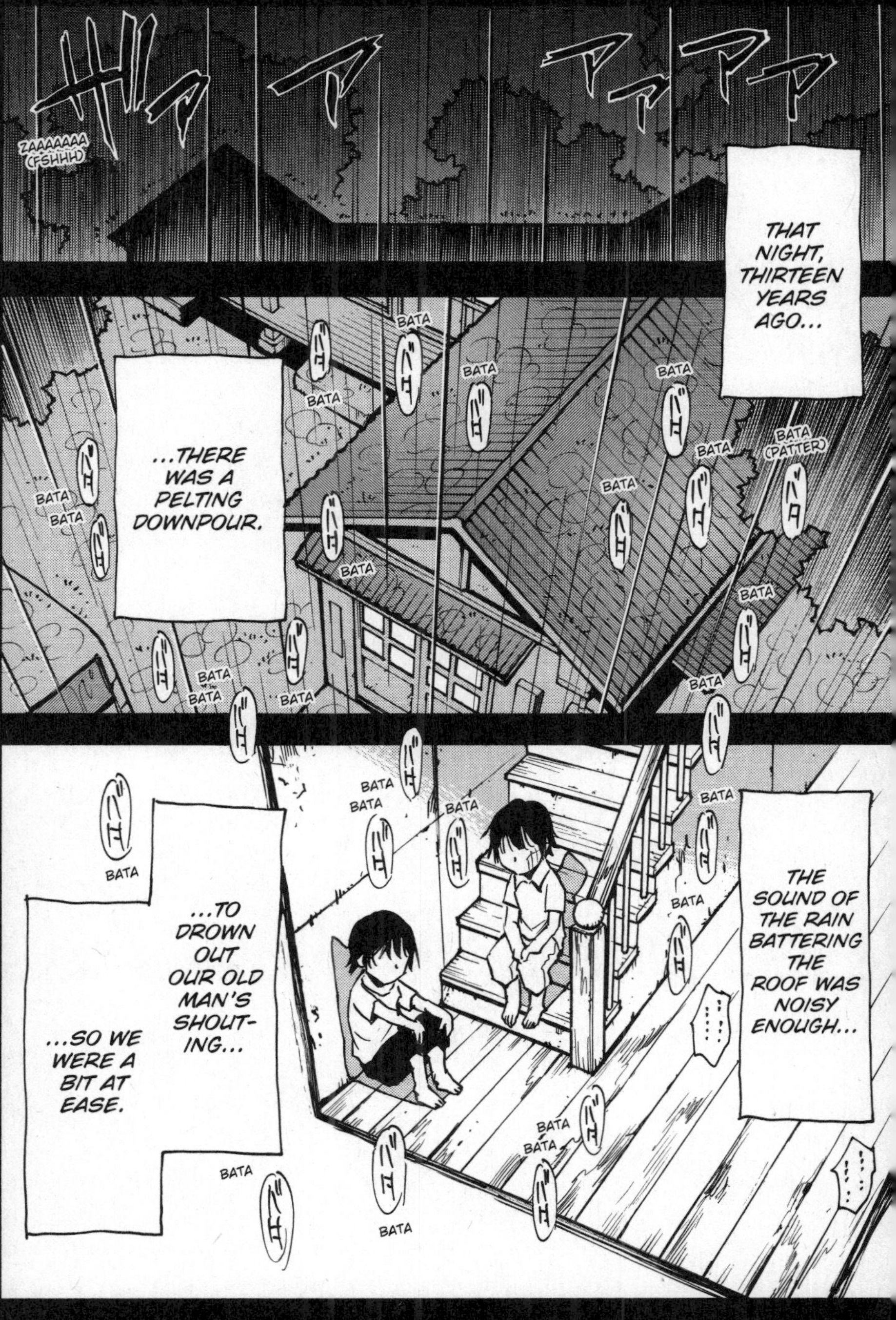
ZAAAAAAA (FSHHH)
THAT NIGHT, THIRTEEN YEARS AGO...
BATA (PATTER)
BATA
BATA
BATA
BATA
...THERE WAS A PELTING DOWNPOUR.
BATA BATA
THE SOUND OF THE RAIN BATTERING THE ROOF WAS NOISY ENOUGH...
......
......
BATA
BATA
BATA BATA
...TO DROWN OUT OUR OLD MAN'S SHOUTING...
...SO WE WERE A BIT AT EASE.
BATA
BATA BATA
BATA
BATA

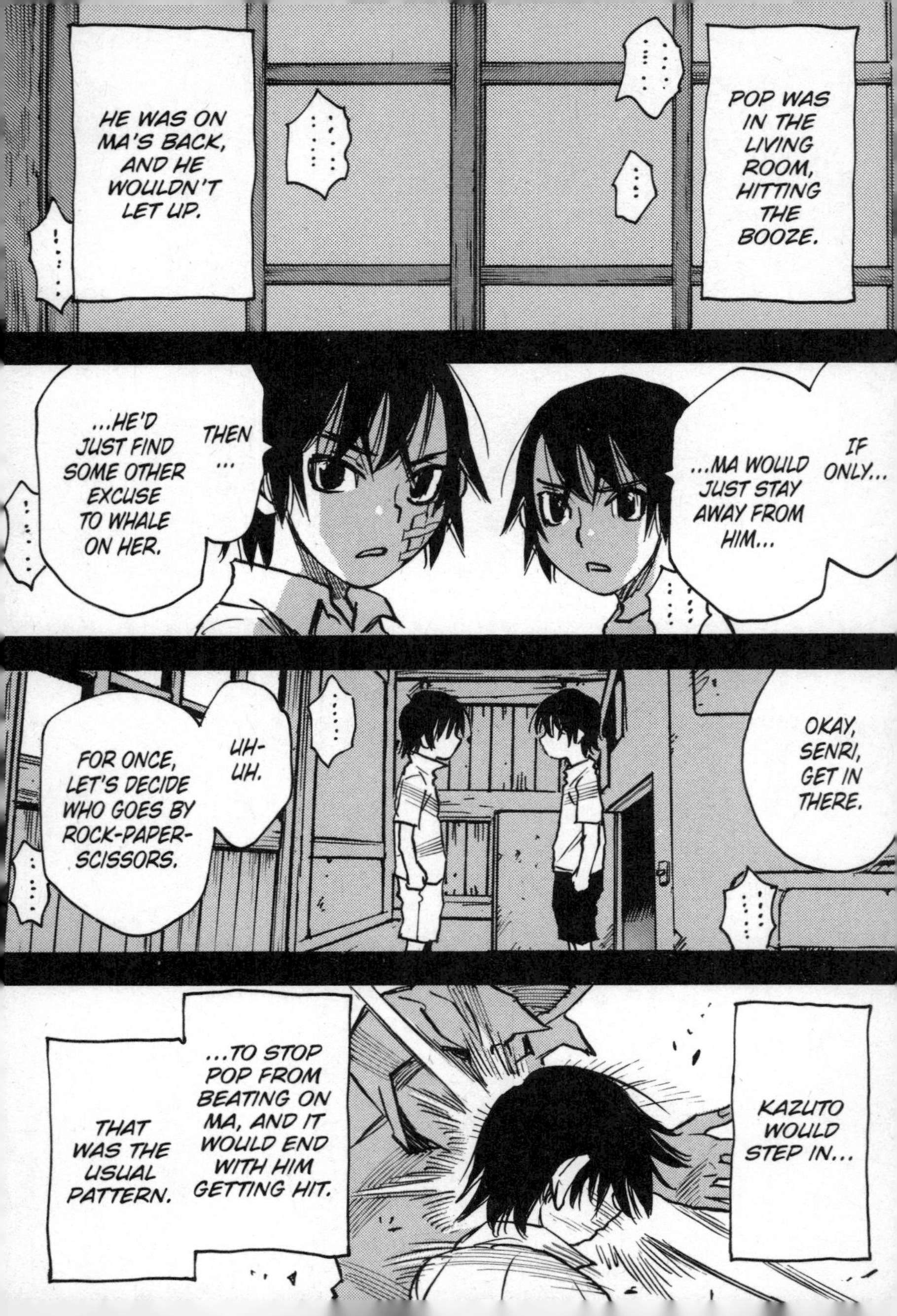
POP WAS IN THE LIVING ROOM, HITTING THE BOOZE.
......
...
......
HE WAS ON MA'S BACK, AND HE WOULDN'T LET UP.
IF ONLY...
...MA WOULD JUST STAY AWAY FROM HIM...
THEN ...
...HE'D JUST FIND SOME OTHER EXCUSE TO WHALE ON HER.
OKAY, SENRI, GET IN THERE.
UH-UH.
FOR ONCE, LET'S DECIDE WHO GOES BY ROCK-PAPER-SCISSORS.
KAZUTO WOULD STEP IN...
...TO STOP POP FROM BEATING ON MA, AND IT WOULD END WITH HIM GETTING HIT.
THAT WAS THE USUAL PATTERN.

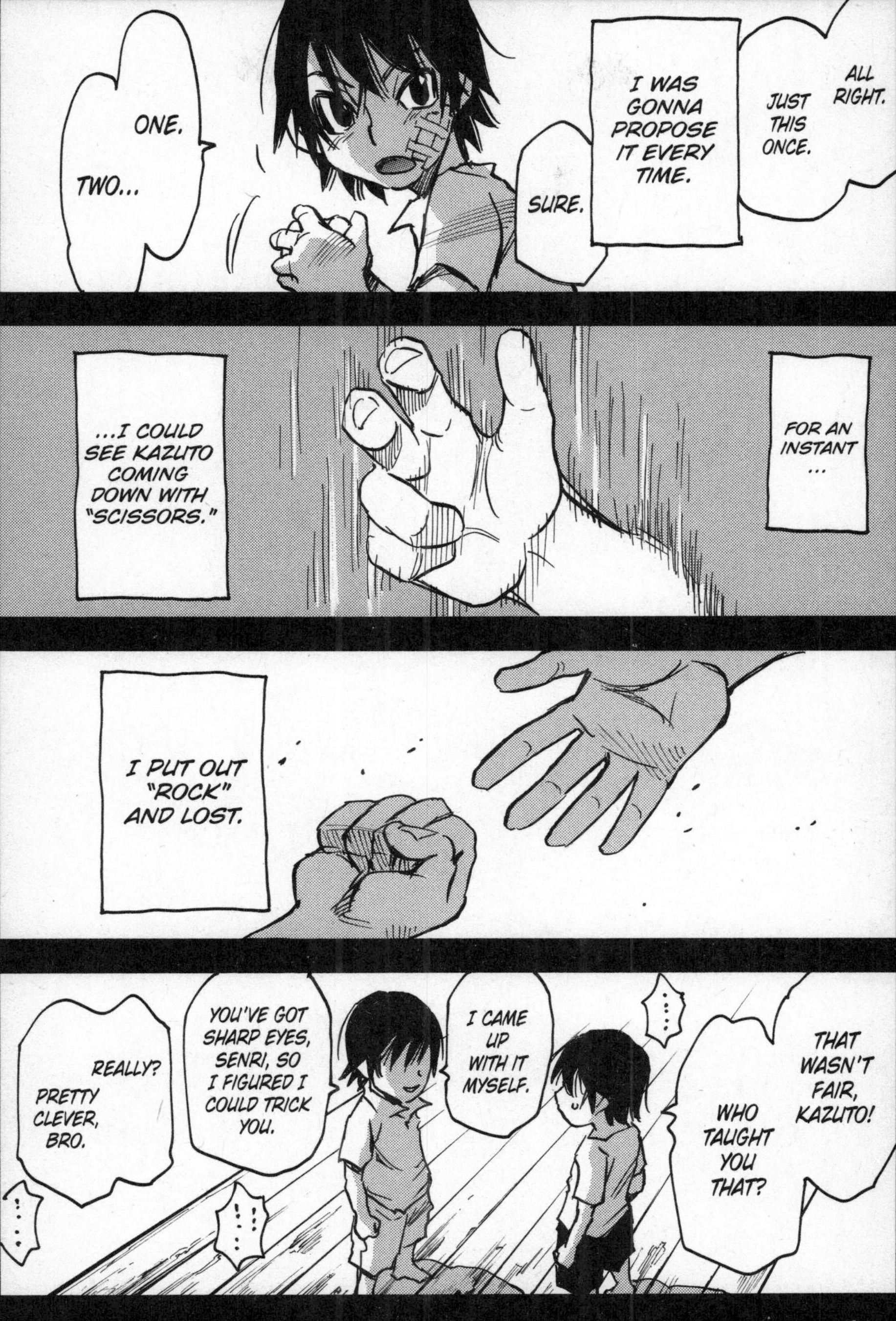
ALL RIGHT.
JUST THIS ONCE.
I WAS GONNA PROPOSE IT EVERY TIME.
SURE.
ONE.
TWO...
FOR AN INSTANT ...
...I COULD SEE KAZUTO COMING DOWN WITH "SCISSORS."
I PUT OUT "ROCK" AND LOST.
THAT WASN'T FAIR, KAZUTO!
WHO TAUGHT YOU THAT?
......
I CAME UP WITH IT MYSELF.
YOU'VE GOT SHARP EYES, SENRI, SO I FIGURED I COULD TRICK YOU.
!!...
REALLY?
PRETTY CLEVER, BRO.
.....

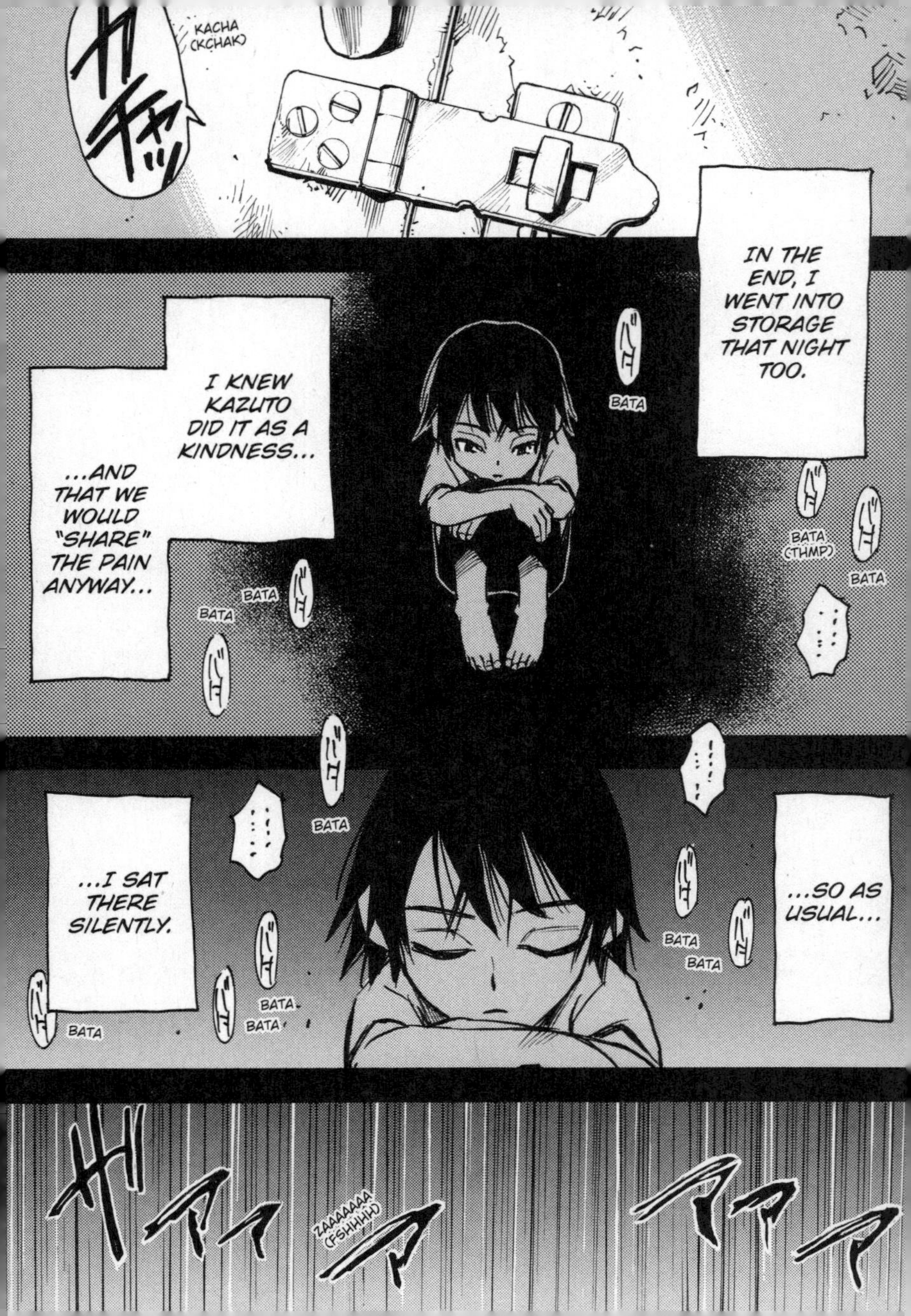
カチャッ
KACHA (KCHAK)
IN THE END, I WENT INTO STORAGE THAT NIGHT TOO.
BATA
BATA (THMP)
BATA
I KNEW KAZUTO DID IT AS A KINDNESS...
...AND THAT WE WOULD "SHARE" THE PAIN ANYWAY...
BATA
BATA
BATA
...SO AS USUAL...
BATA
BATA
...I SAT THERE SILENTLY.
BATA
BATA
BATA
ザァァァ アァァァ
ZAAAAAAA (FSHHHH)

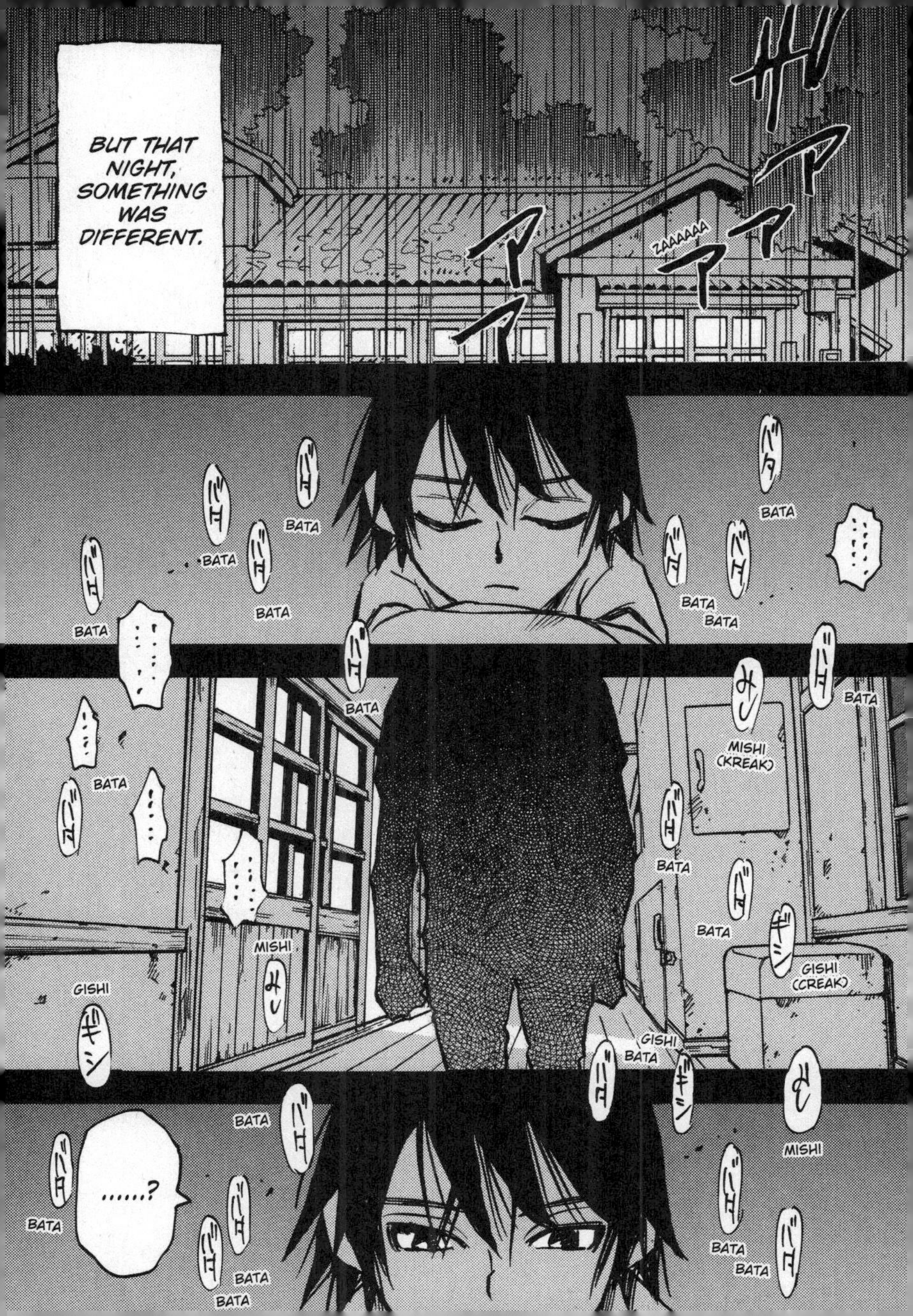
ZAAAAAA
BUT THAT NIGHT, SOMETHING WAS DIFFERENT.
BATA
......
BATA
BATA
BATA
BATA
BATA
BATA
......
BATA
BATA
MISHI (KREAK)
BATA
BATA
GISHI (CREAK)
GISHI
BATA
......
......
......
BATA
MISHI
GISHI
MISHI
BATA
BATA
BATA
BATA
......?
BATA
BATA
BATA

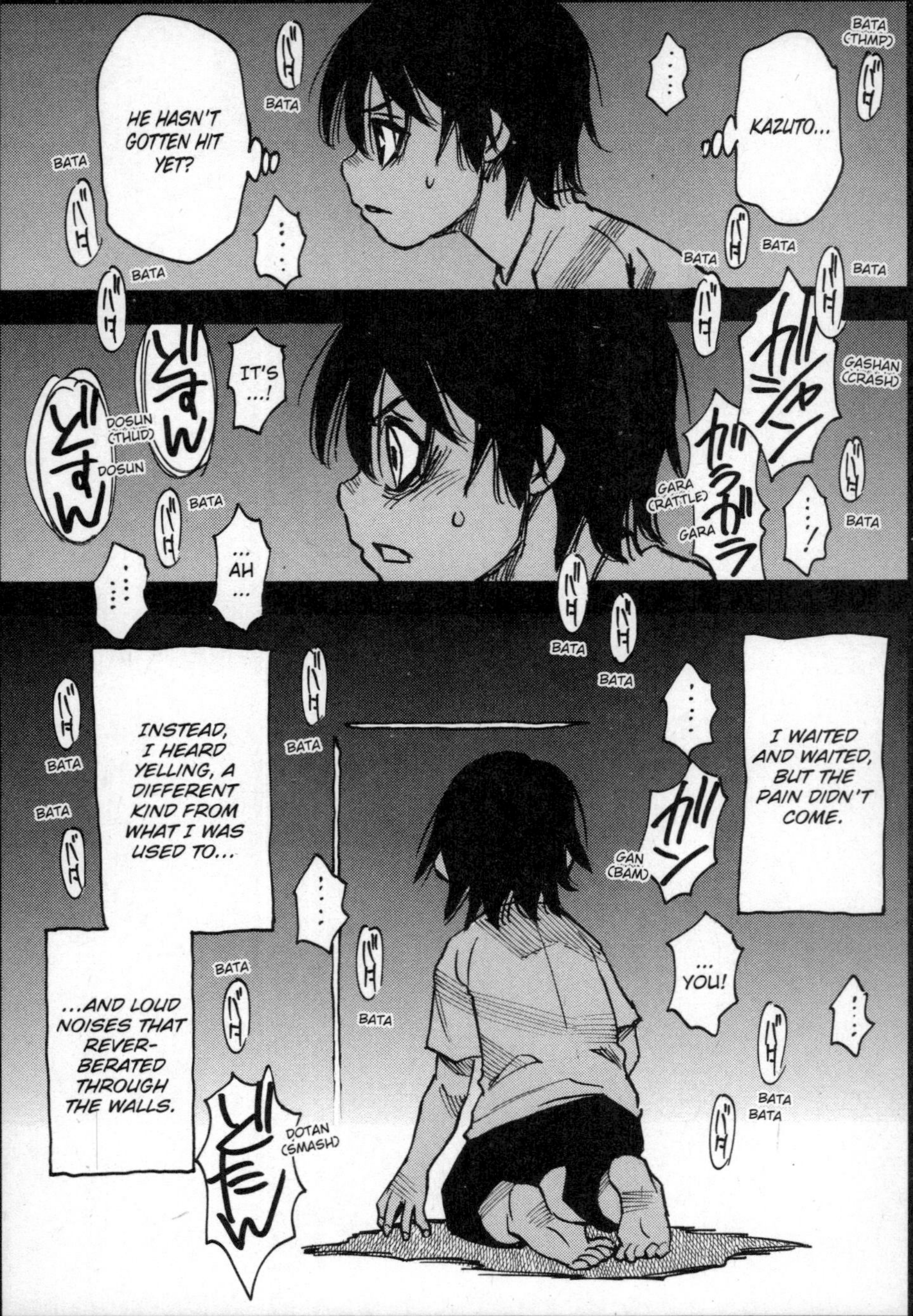
BATA (THMP)
KAZUTO...
......
HE HASN'T GOTTEN HIT YET?
BATA
BATA
BATA
....
BATA
BATA
GASHAN (CRASH)
BATA
...!
GARA (RATTLE)
GARA
IT'S ...!
... AH ...
DOSUN (THUD)
DOSUN
BATA
.....
BATA
BATA
I WAITED AND WAITED, BUT THE PAIN DIDN'T COME.
.....
GAN (BAM)
INSTEAD, I HEARD YELLING, A DIFFERENT KIND FROM WHAT I WAS USED TO...
BATA
BATA
BATA
.....
... YOU!
.....
BATA
BATA
BATA
BATA
...AND LOUD NOISES THAT REVER-BERATED THROUGH THE WALLS.
DOTAN (SMASH)

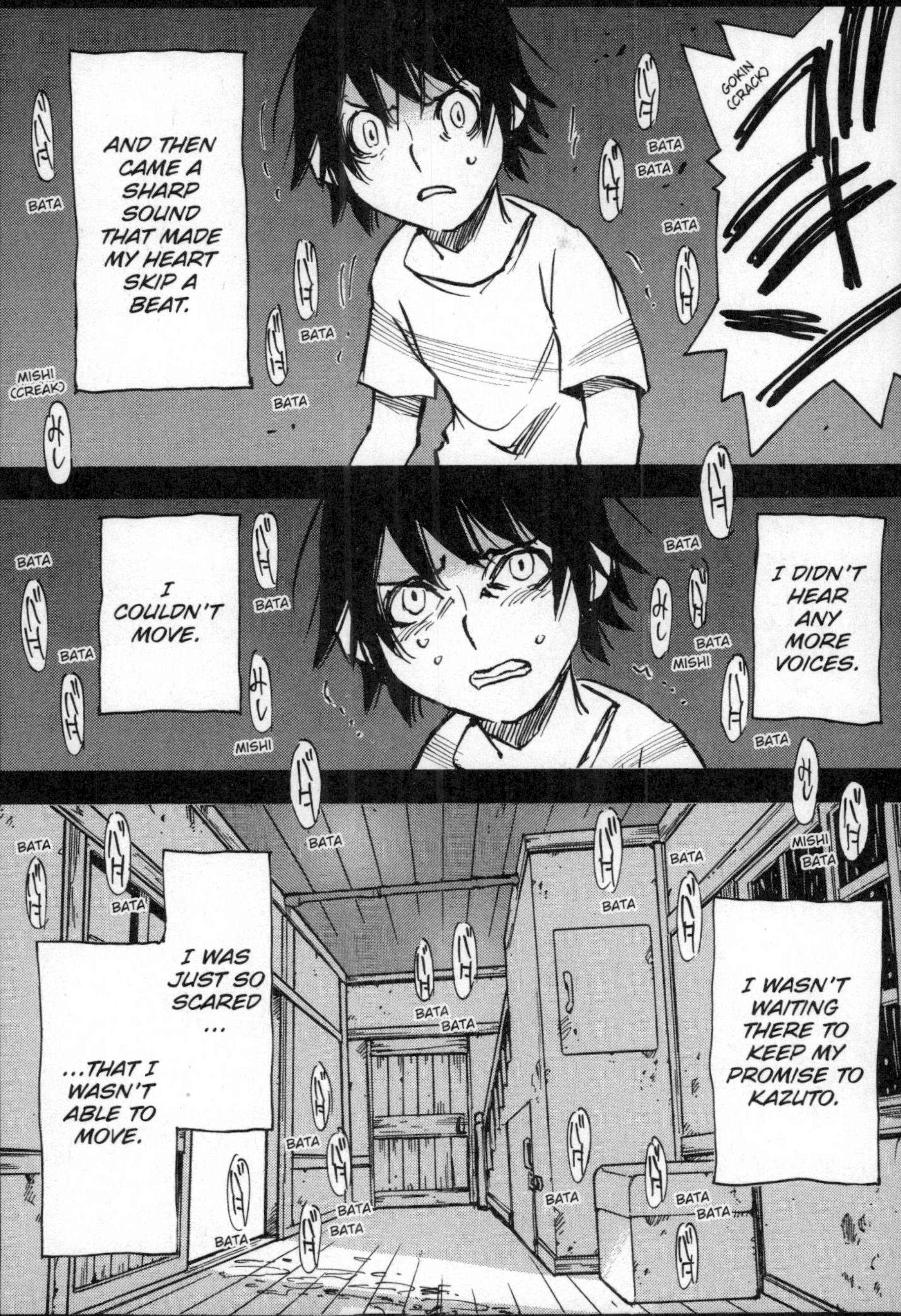
GOKIN (CRACK)
BATA
BATA
BATA
AND THEN CAME A SHARP SOUND THAT MADE MY HEART SKIP A BEAT.
BATA
BATA
BATA
MISHI (CREAK)
BATA
I DIDN'T HEAR ANY MORE VOICES.
BATA
MISHI
BATA
BATA
I COULDN'T MOVE.
MISHI
BATA
BATA
MISHI
BATA
I WASN'T WAITING THERE TO KEEP MY PROMISE TO KAZUTO.
BATA
BATA
BATA
BATA
BATA
BATA
BATA
I WAS JUST SO SCARED ...
...THAT I WASN'T ABLE TO MOVE.
BATA
BATA
BATA
BATA
BATA
BATA

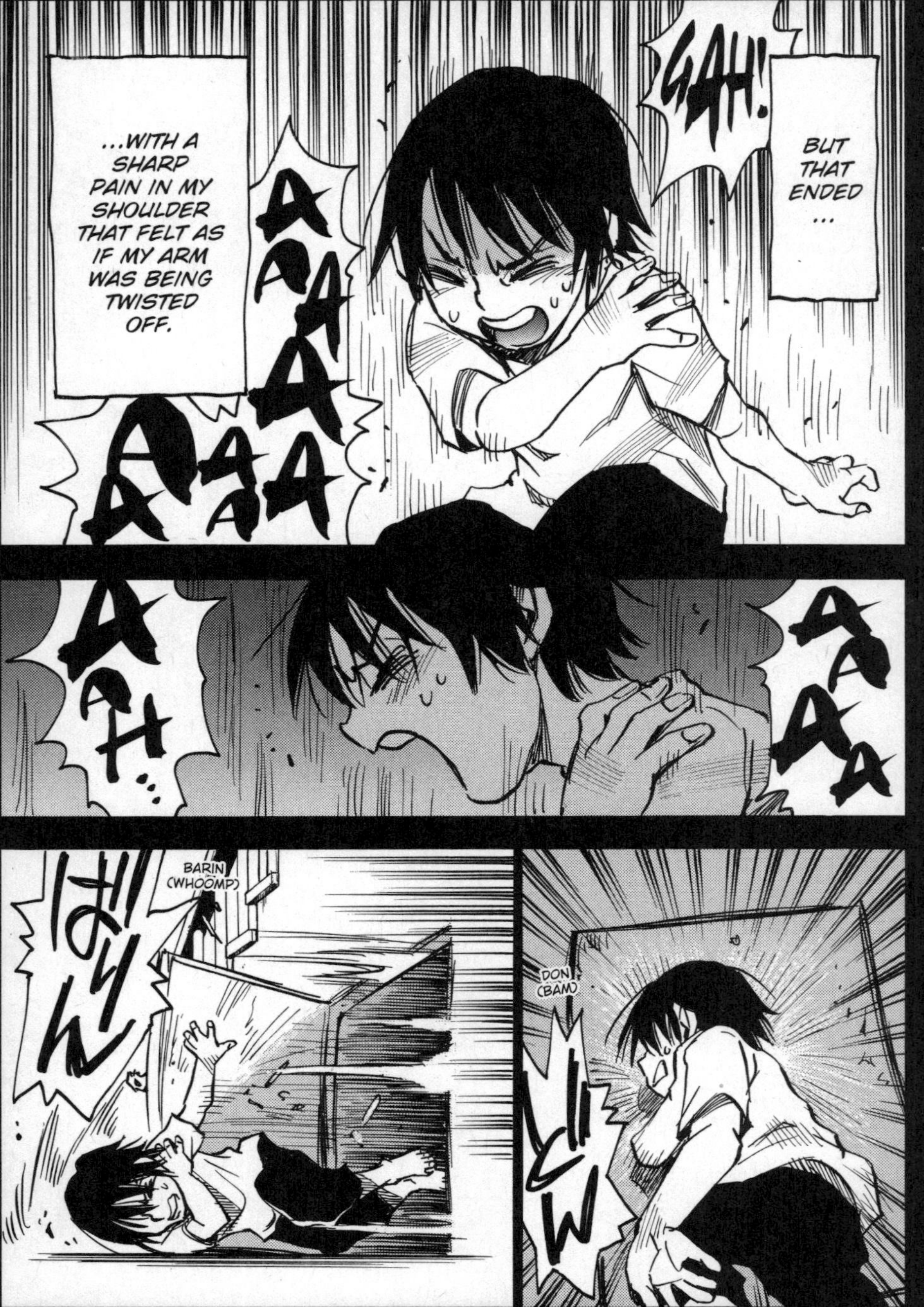
BUT THAT ENDED ...
GAH!
...WITH A SHARP PAIN IN MY SHOULDER THAT FELT AS IF MY ARM WAS BEING TWISTED OFF.
AAAAAAAAAAAA
AAAA
AAH...
DON (BAM)
BARIN (WHOOMP)
ばりん

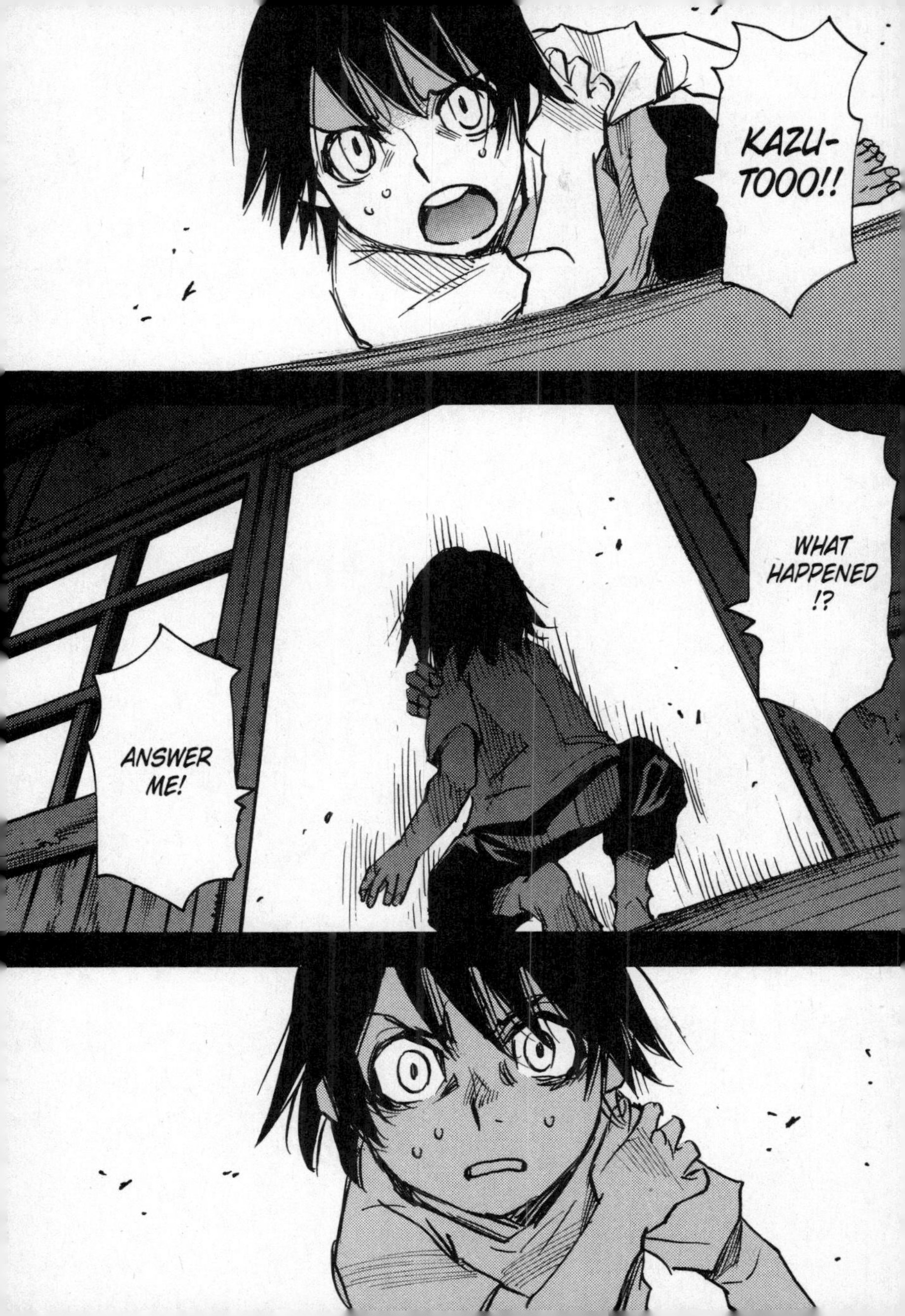
KAZU-TOOO!!
WHAT HAPPENED !?
ANSWER ME!

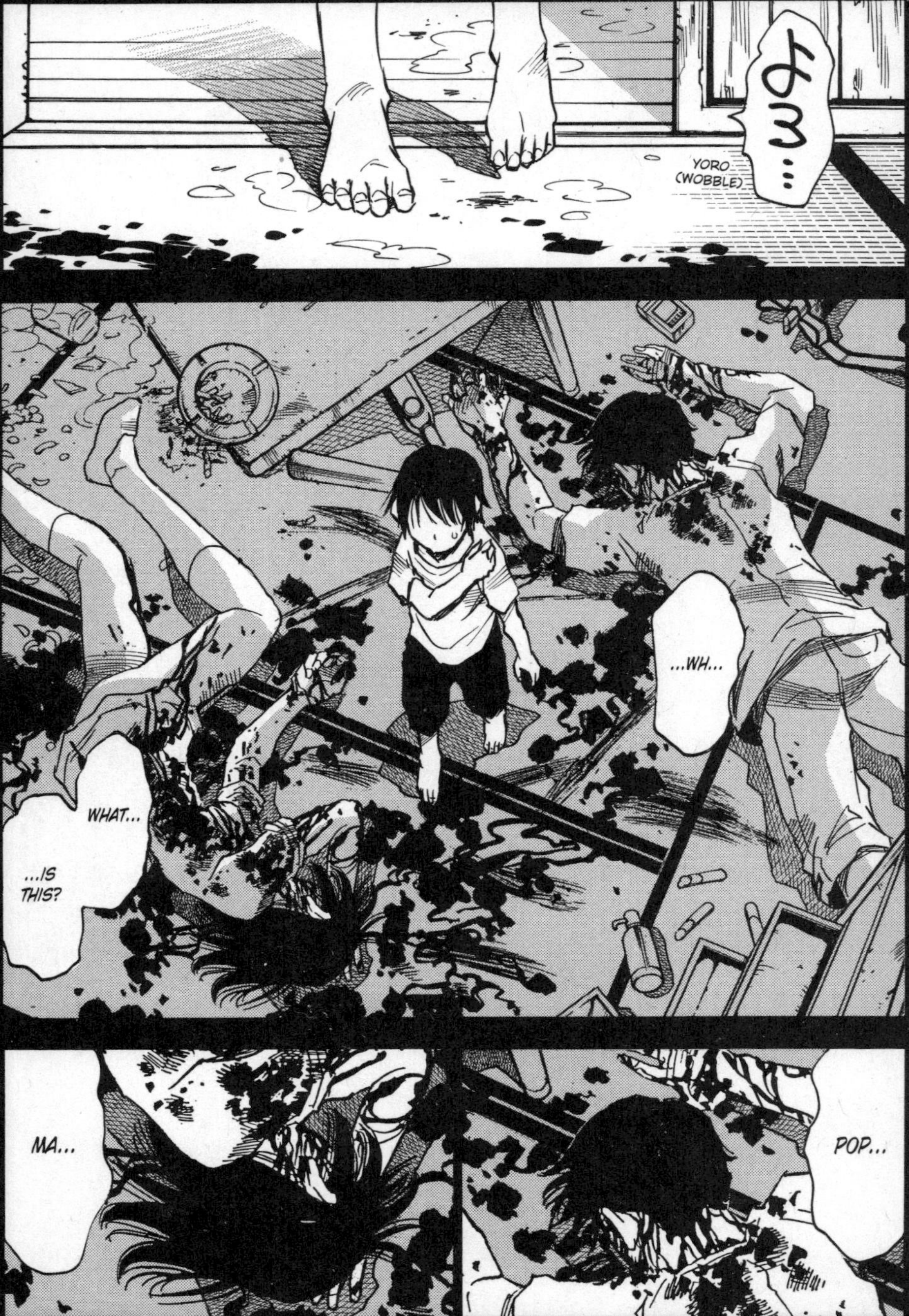
よろ…
YORO (WOBBLE)
...WH...
WHAT...
...IS THIS?
POP...
MA...

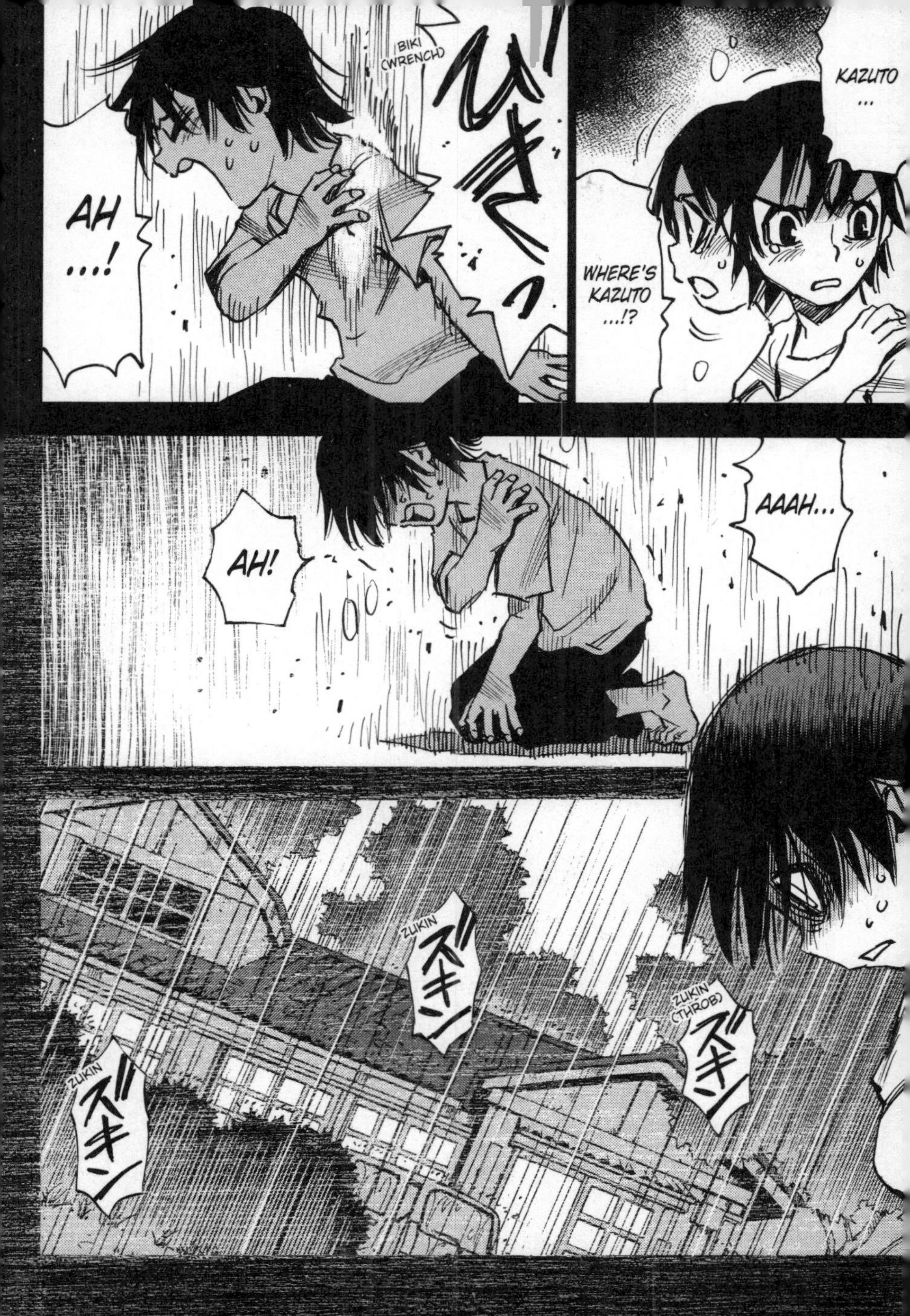
KAZUTO ...
WHERE'S KAZUTO ...!?
BIKI (WRENCH)
ひきっ
AH ...!
AAAH...
AH!
ZUKIN (THROB)
ズキン
ZUKIN
ズキン
ZUKIN
ズキン

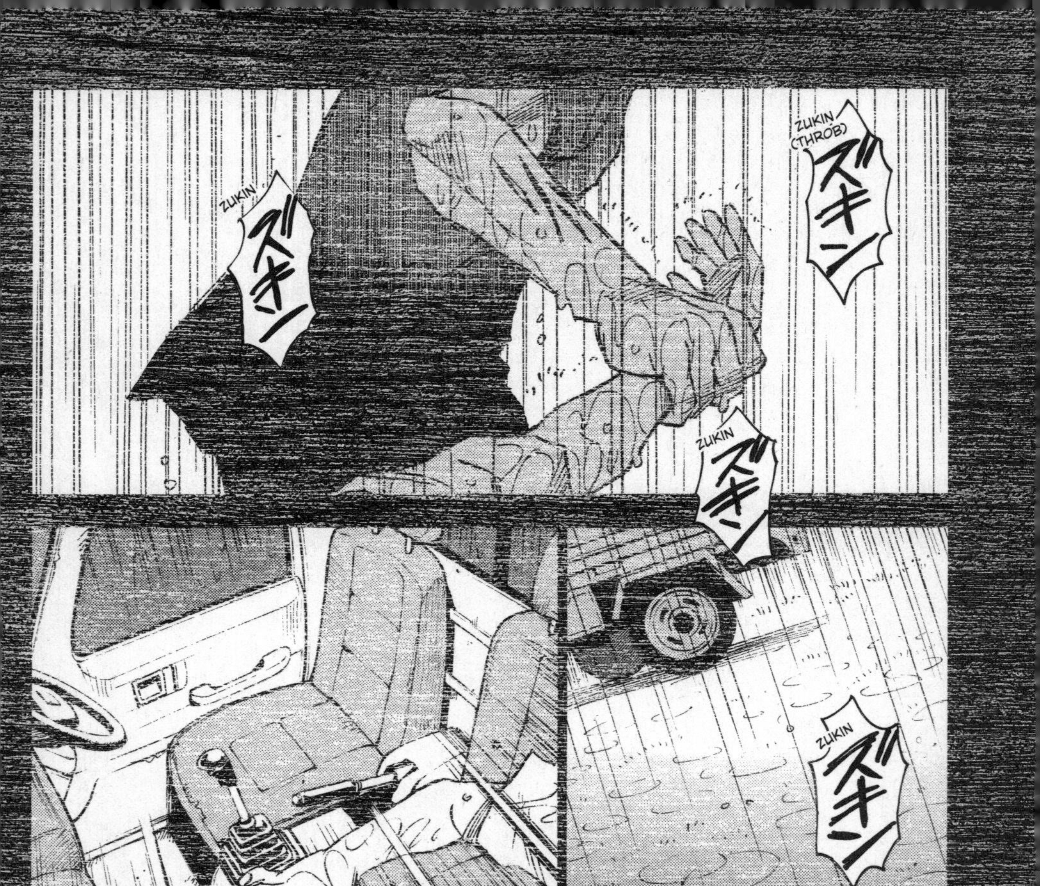
ZUKIN (THROB)
ズキン
ZUKIN
ズキン
ZUKIN
ズキン
ZUKIN
ズキン
...KA-ZUTO...
KAZUTO ...!

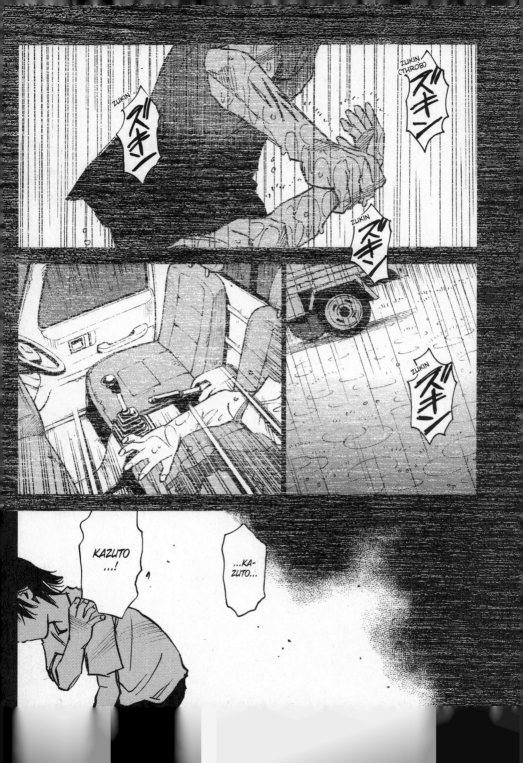

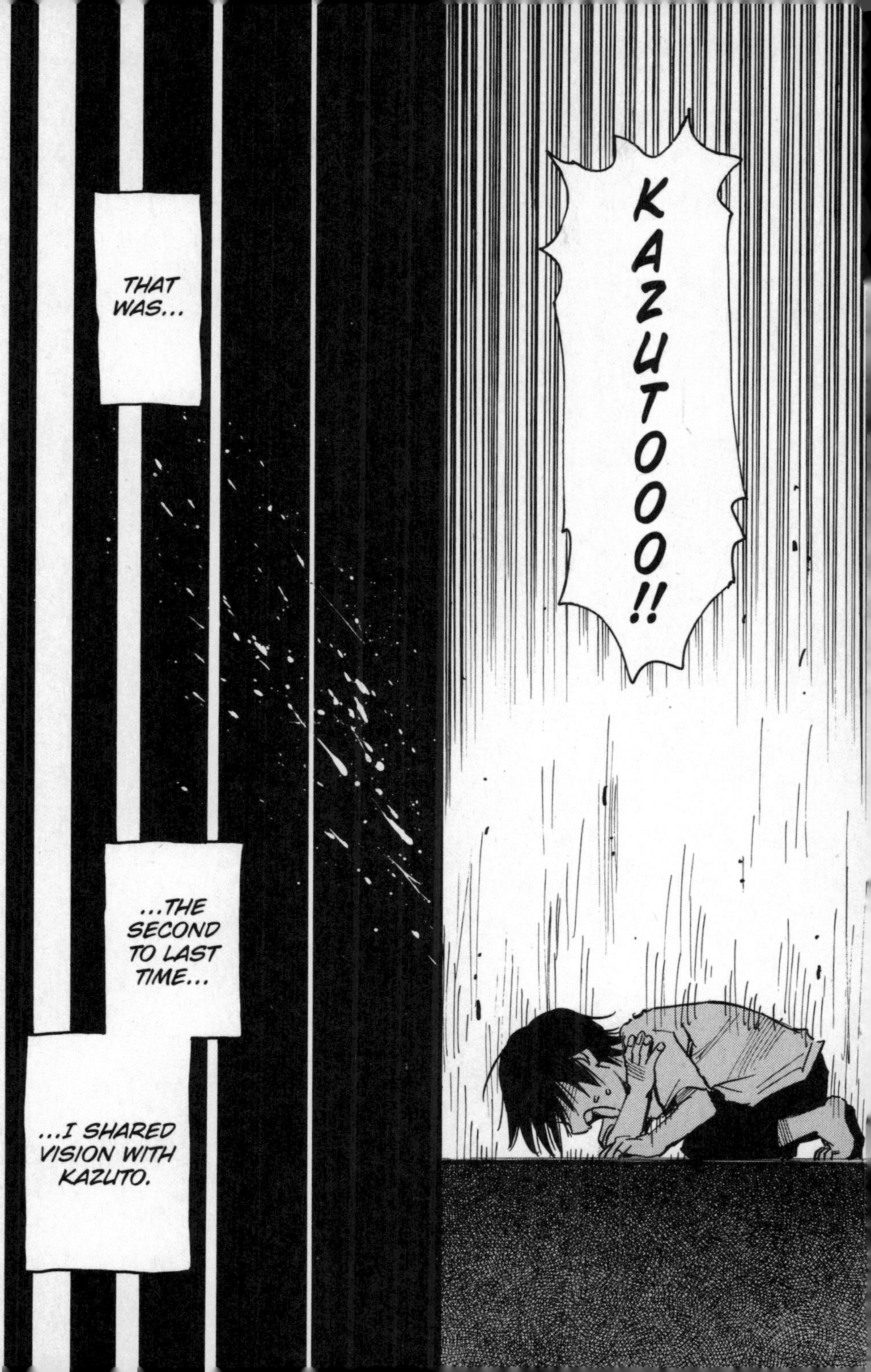
KAZUTOOOO!!
THAT WAS...
...THE SECOND TO LAST TIME...
...I SHARED VISION WITH KAZUTO.

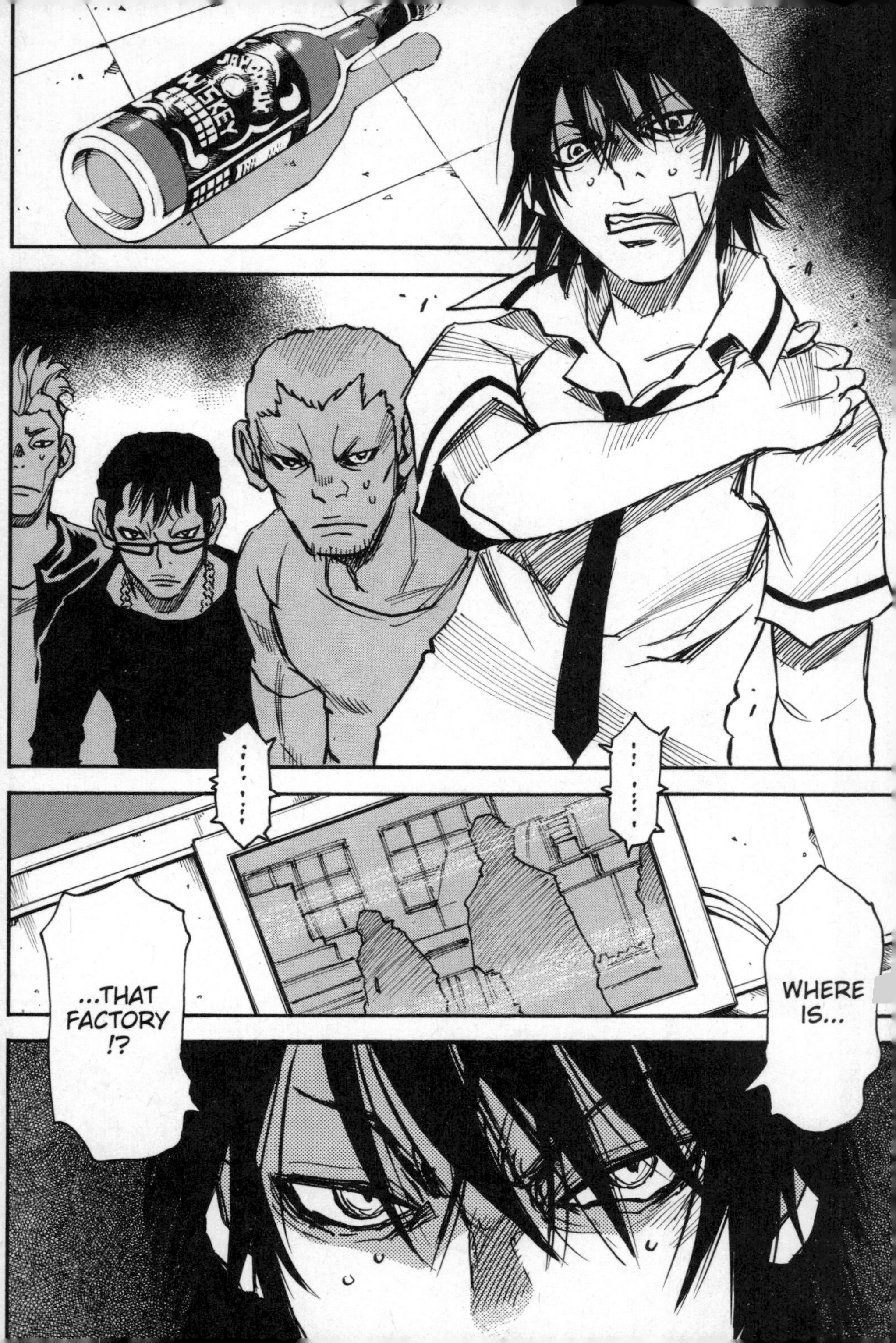
WISKEY
......!!
......!!
WHERE IS...
...THAT FACTORY !?

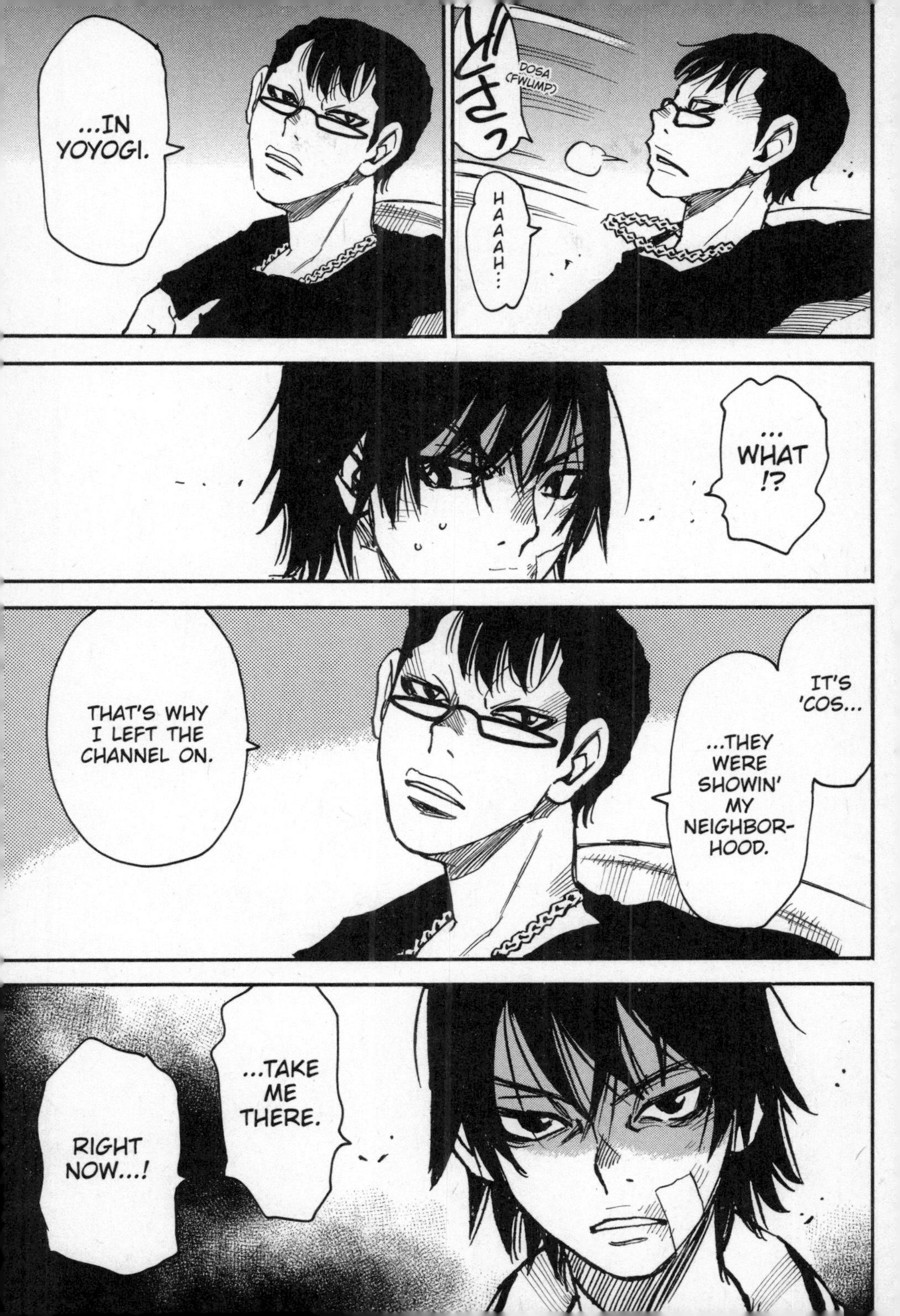
どさっ
DOSA (FWUMP)
HAAAH...
...IN YOYOGI.
... WHAT !?
IT'S 'COS...
...THEY WERE SHOWIN' MY NEIGHBORHOOD.
THAT'S WHY I LEFT THE CHANNEL ON.
...TAKE ME THERE.
RIGHT NOW...!

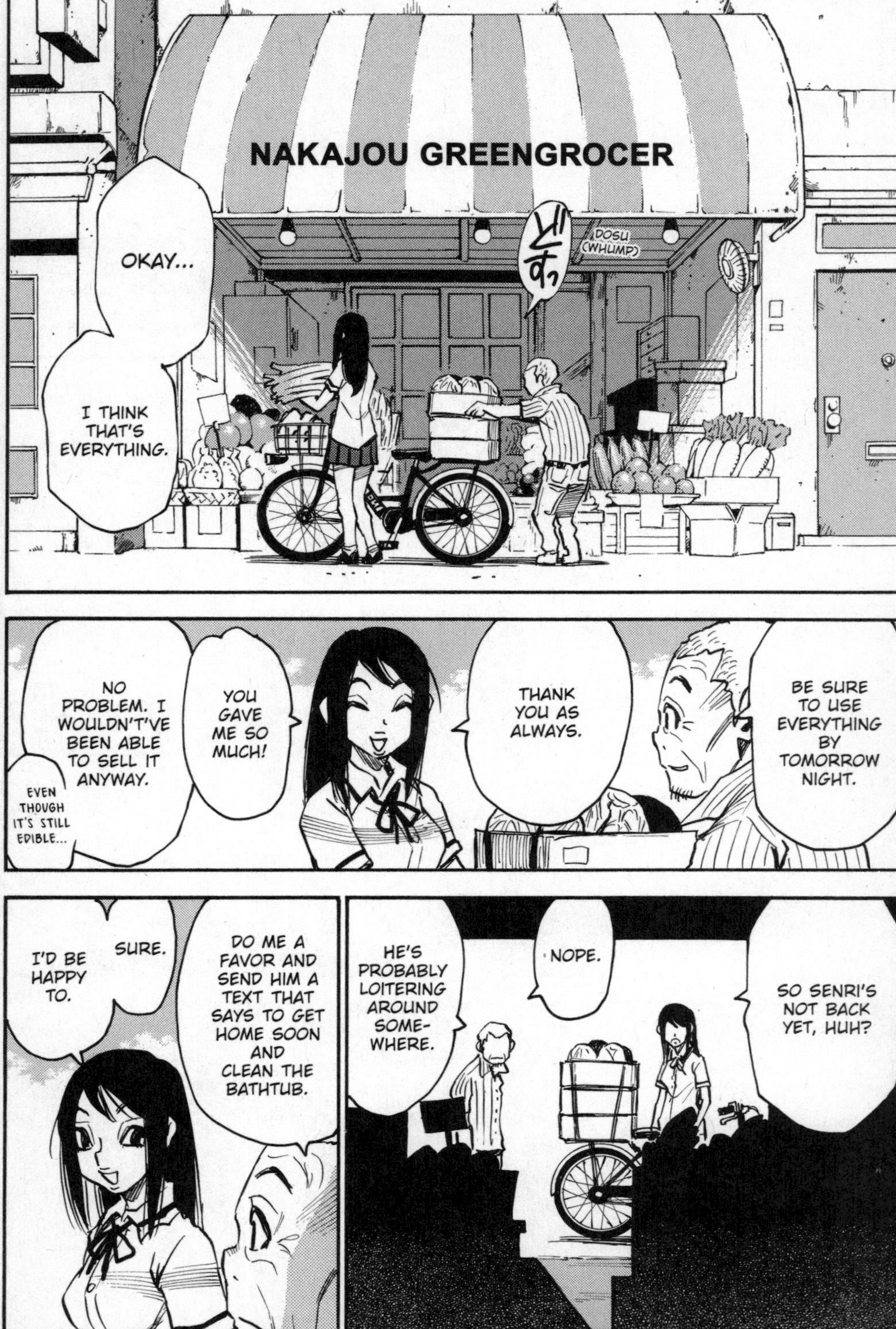
NAKAJOU GREENGROCER
どすっ
DOSU (WHUMP)
OKAY...
I THINK THAT'S EVERYTHING.
BE SURE TO USE EVERYTHING BY TOMORROW NIGHT.
THANK YOU AS ALWAYS.
YOU GAVE ME SO MUCH!
NO PROBLEM. I WOULDN'T'VE BEEN ABLE TO SELL IT ANYWAY.
EVEN THOUGH IT'S STILL EDIBLE...
SO SENRI'S NOT BACK YET, HUH?
NOPE.
HE'S PROBABLY LOITERING AROUND SOME-WHERE.
DO ME A FAVOR AND SEND HIM A TEXT THAT SAYS TO GET HOME SOON AND CLEAN THE BATHTUB.
SURE.
I'D BE HAPPY TO.

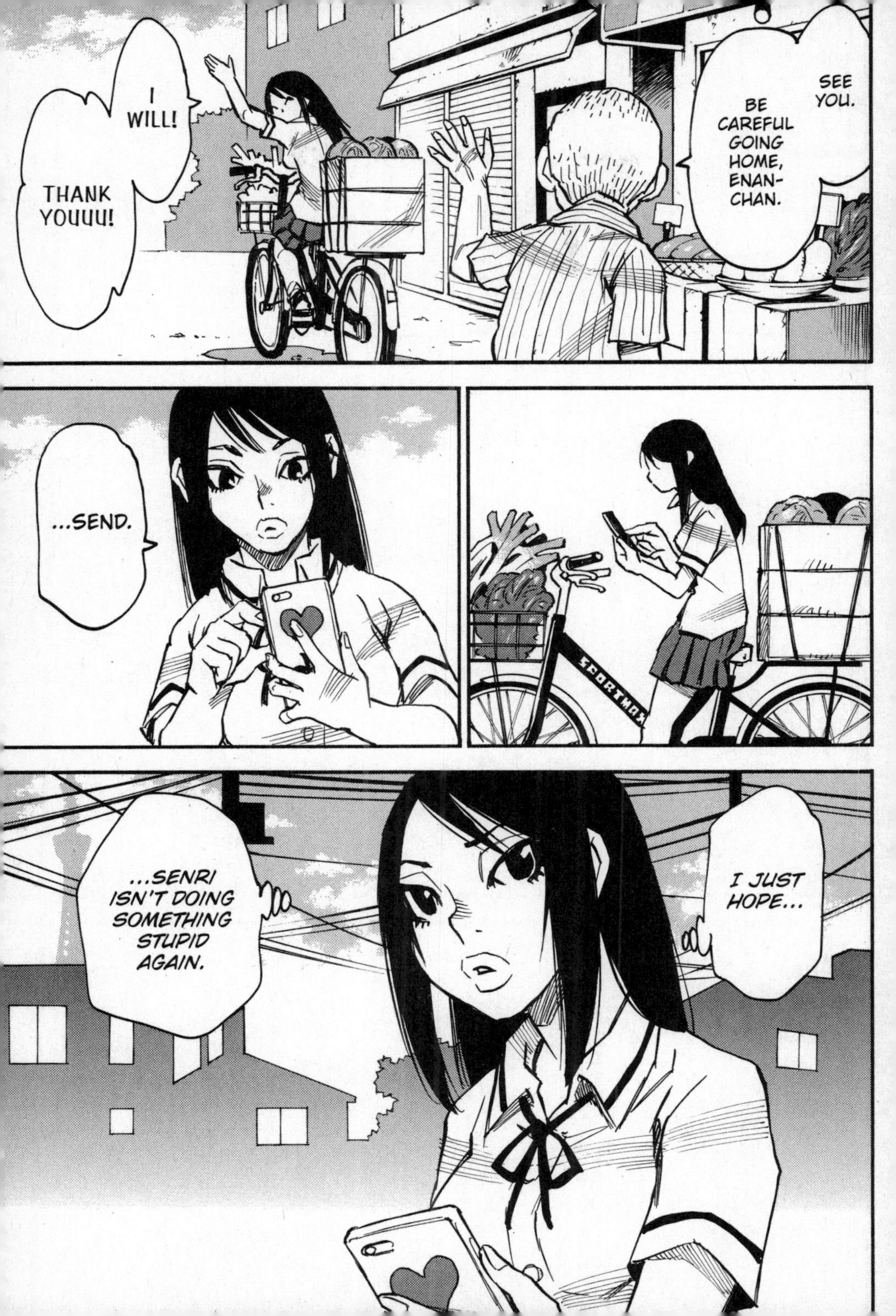
SEE YOU.
BE CAREFUL GOING HOME, ENAN-CHAN.
I WILL!
THANK YOUUU!
...SEND.
I JUST HOPE...
...SENRI ISN'T DOING SOMETHING STUPID AGAIN.

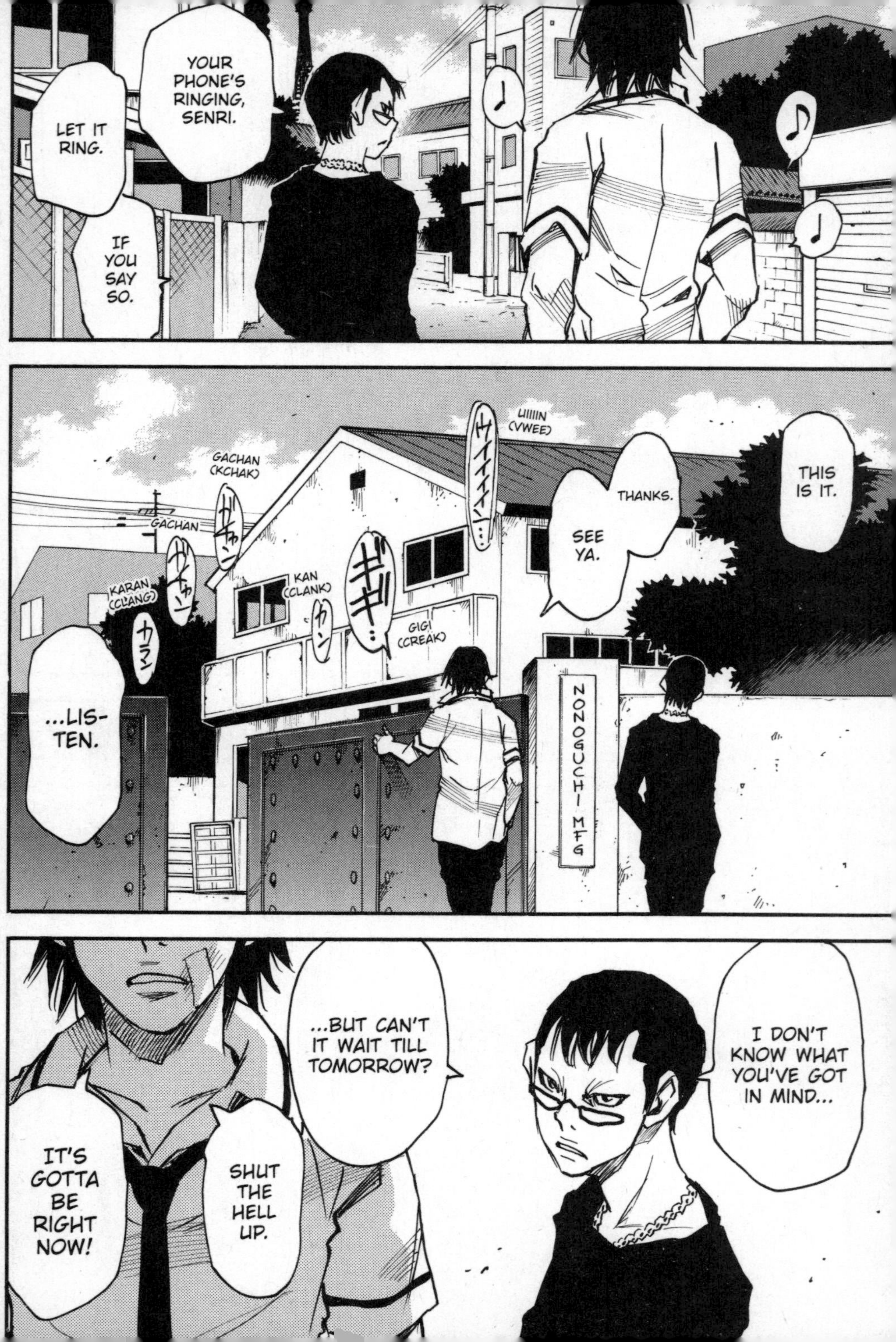
YOUR PHONE'S RINGING, SENRI.
LET IT RING.
IF YOU SAY SO.
THIS IS IT.
THANKS.
SEE YA.
UIIIIN (VWEE)
GIGI (CREAK)
KAN (CLANK)
GACHAN (KCHAK)
GACHAN
KARAN (CLANG)
...LIS-TEN.
NONOGUCHI MFG
I DON'T KNOW WHAT YOU'VE GOT IN MIND...
...BUT CAN'T IT WAIT TILL TOMORROW?
SHUT THE HELL UP.
IT'S GOTTA BE RIGHT NOW!

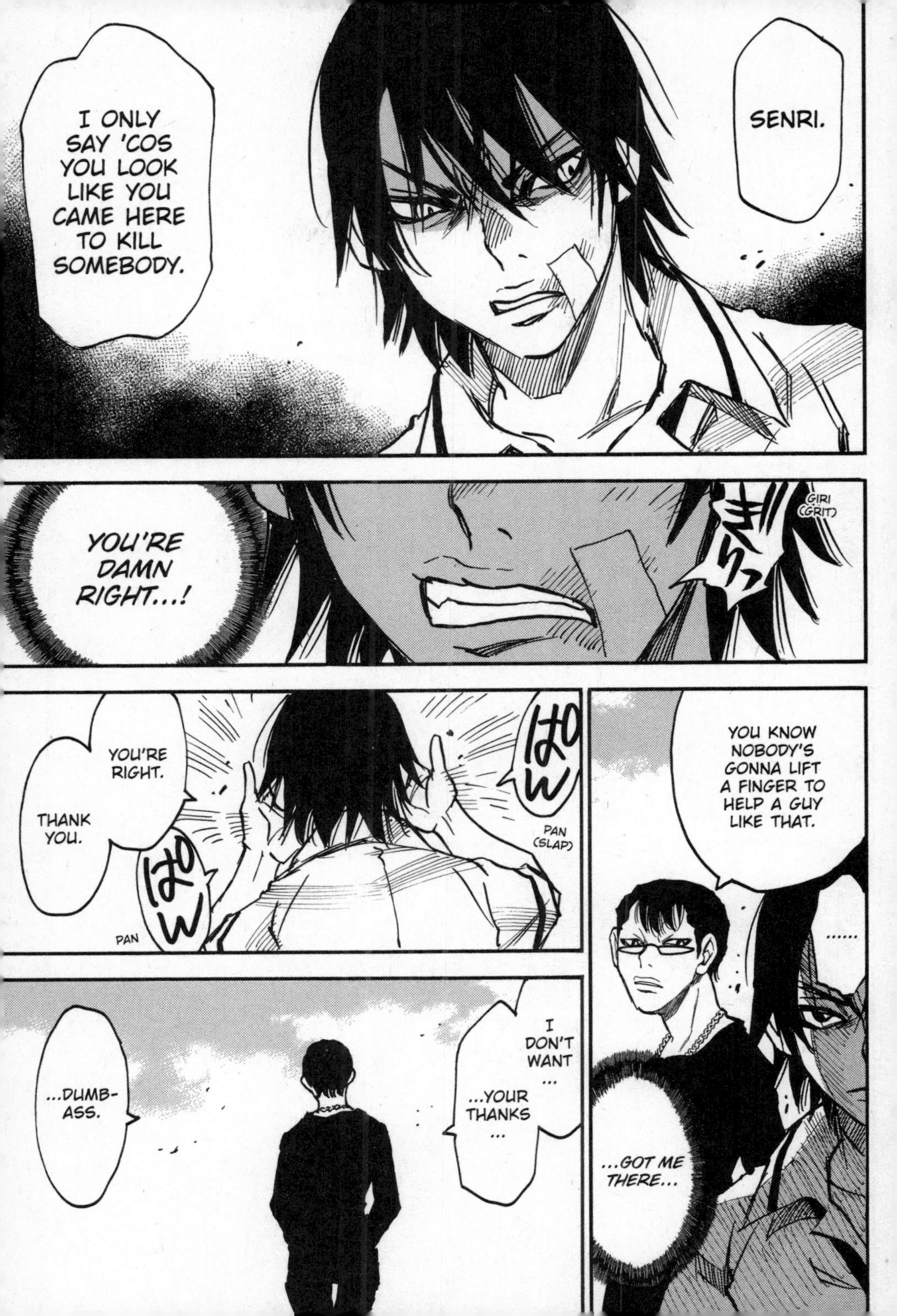
SENRI.
I ONLY SAY 'COS YOU LOOK LIKE YOU CAME HERE TO KILL SOMEBODY.
GIRI (GRIT)
YOU'RE DAMN RIGHT...!
YOU KNOW NOBODY'S GONNA LIFT A FINGER TO HELP A GUY LIKE THAT.
......
...GOT ME THERE...
PAN (SLAP)
YOU'RE RIGHT.
THANK YOU.
PAN
I DON'T WANT ...
...YOUR THANKS ...
...DUMB-ASS.

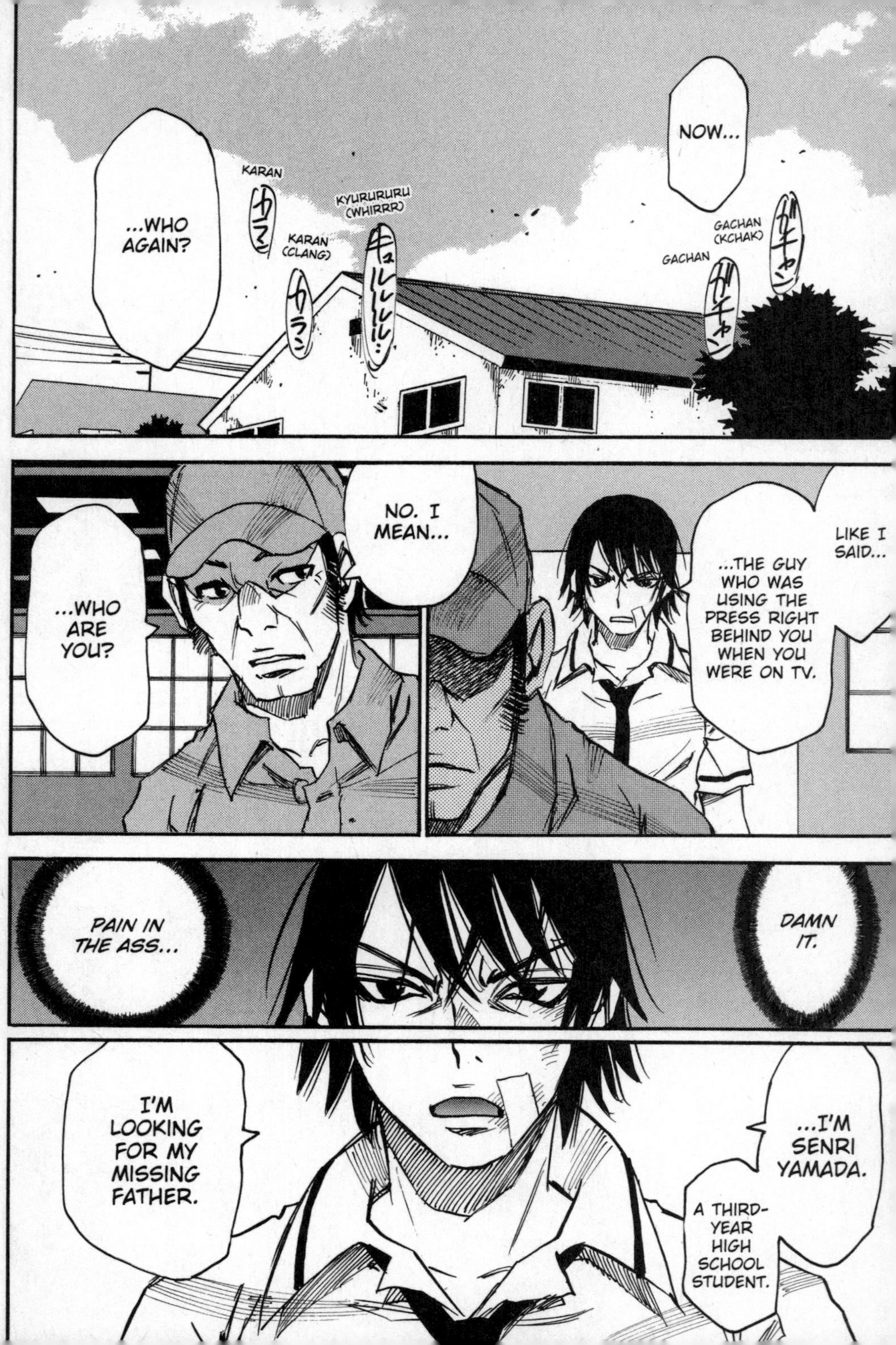
NOW...
GACHAN (KCHAK) ガチャン
GACHAN ガチャン
KYURURURU (WHIRRR) キュルルルル…
KARAN (CLANG) カラン
KARAN
...WHO AGAIN?
LIKE I SAID...
...THE GUY WHO WAS USING THE PRESS RIGHT BEHIND YOU WHEN YOU WERE ON TV.
NO. I MEAN...
...WHO ARE YOU?
DAMN IT.
PAIN IN THE ASS...
...I'M SENRI YAMADA.
A THIRD-YEAR HIGH SCHOOL STUDENT.
I'M LOOKING FOR MY MISSING FATHER.

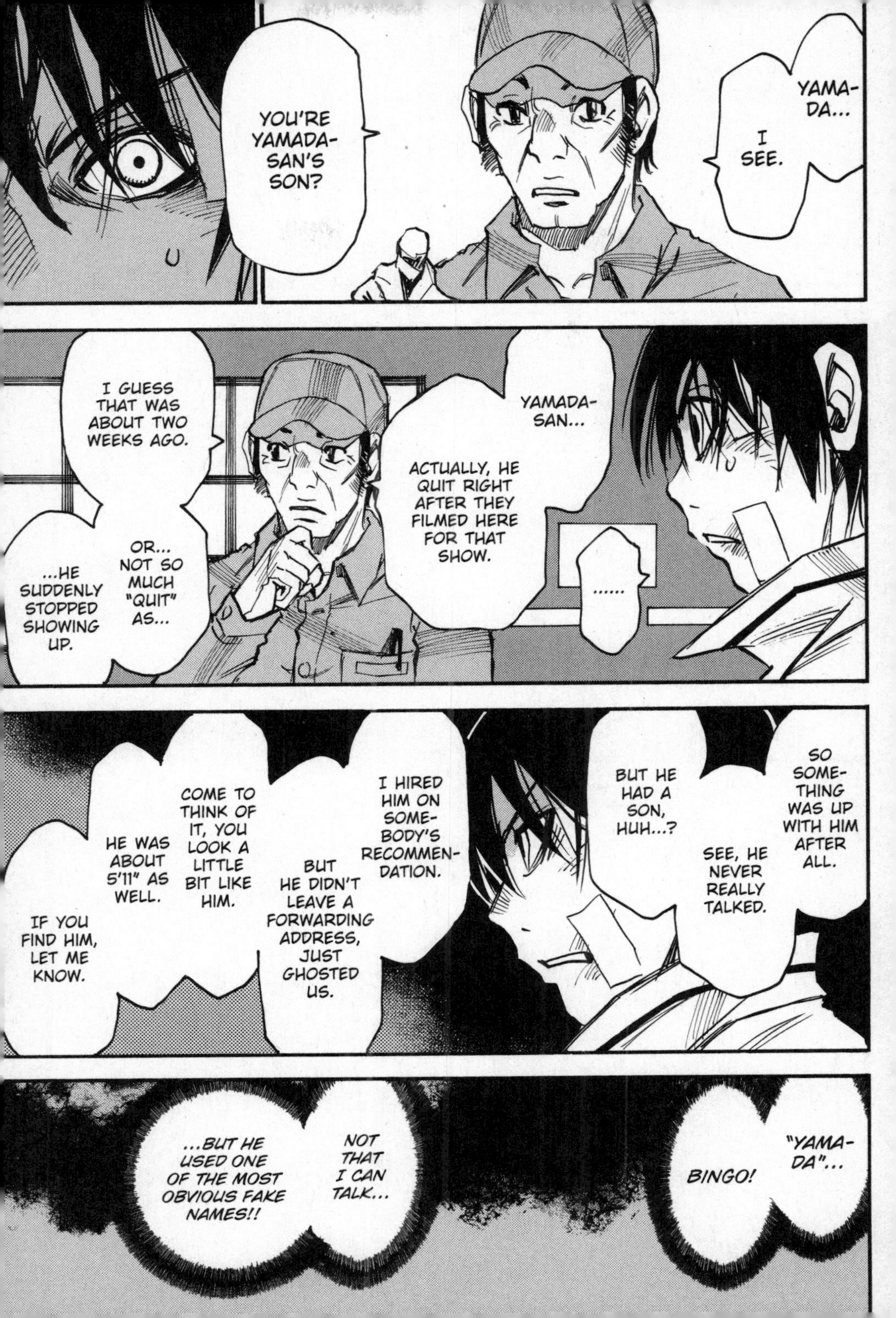
YAMADA...
I SEE.
YOU'RE YAMADA-SAN'S SON?
YAMADA-SAN...
ACTUALLY, HE QUIT RIGHT AFTER THEY FILMED HERE FOR THAT SHOW.
......
I GUESS THAT WAS ABOUT TWO WEEKS AGO.
OR... NOT SO MUCH "QUIT" AS...
...HE SUDDENLY STOPPED SHOWING UP.
SO SOMETHING WAS UP WITH HIM AFTER ALL.
SEE, HE NEVER REALLY TALKED.
BUT HE HAD A SON, HUH...?
I HIRED HIM ON SOMEBODY'S RECOMMENDATION.
BUT HE DIDN'T LEAVE A FORWARDING ADDRESS, JUST GHOSTED US.
COME TO THINK OF IT, YOU LOOK A LITTLE BIT LIKE HIM.
HE WAS ABOUT 5'11" AS WELL.
IF YOU FIND HIM, LET ME KNOW.
"YAMADA"...
BINGO!
NOT THAT I CAN TALK...
...BUT HE USED ONE OF THE MOST OBVIOUS FAKE NAMES!!

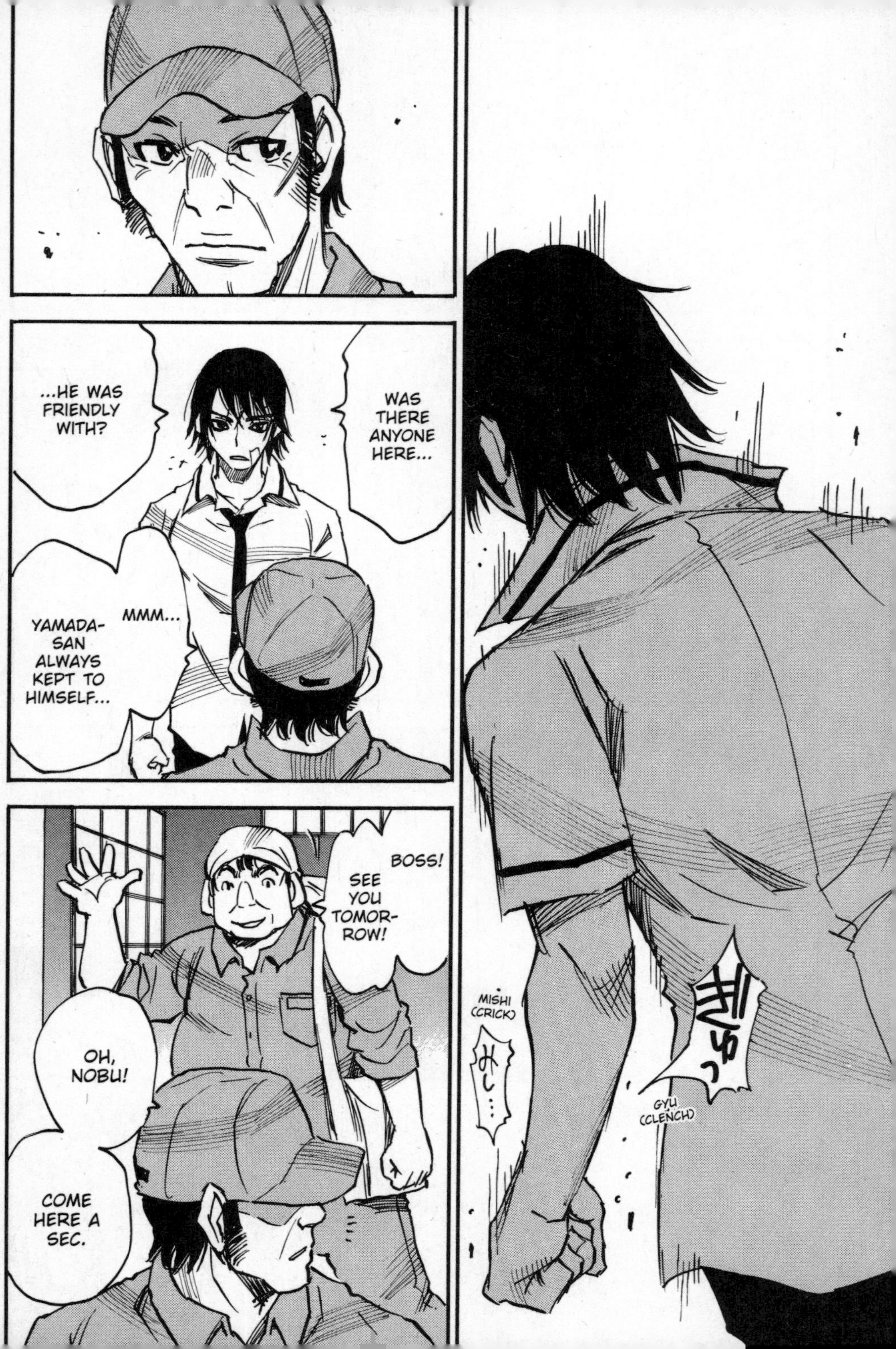
ぎゅっ
GYU (CLENCH)
みし…
MISHI (CRICK)
WAS THERE ANYONE HERE...
...HE WAS FRIENDLY WITH?
MMM...
YAMADA-SAN ALWAYS KEPT TO HIMSELF...
BOSS! SEE YOU TOMOR-ROW!
OH, NOBU!
COME HERE A SEC.

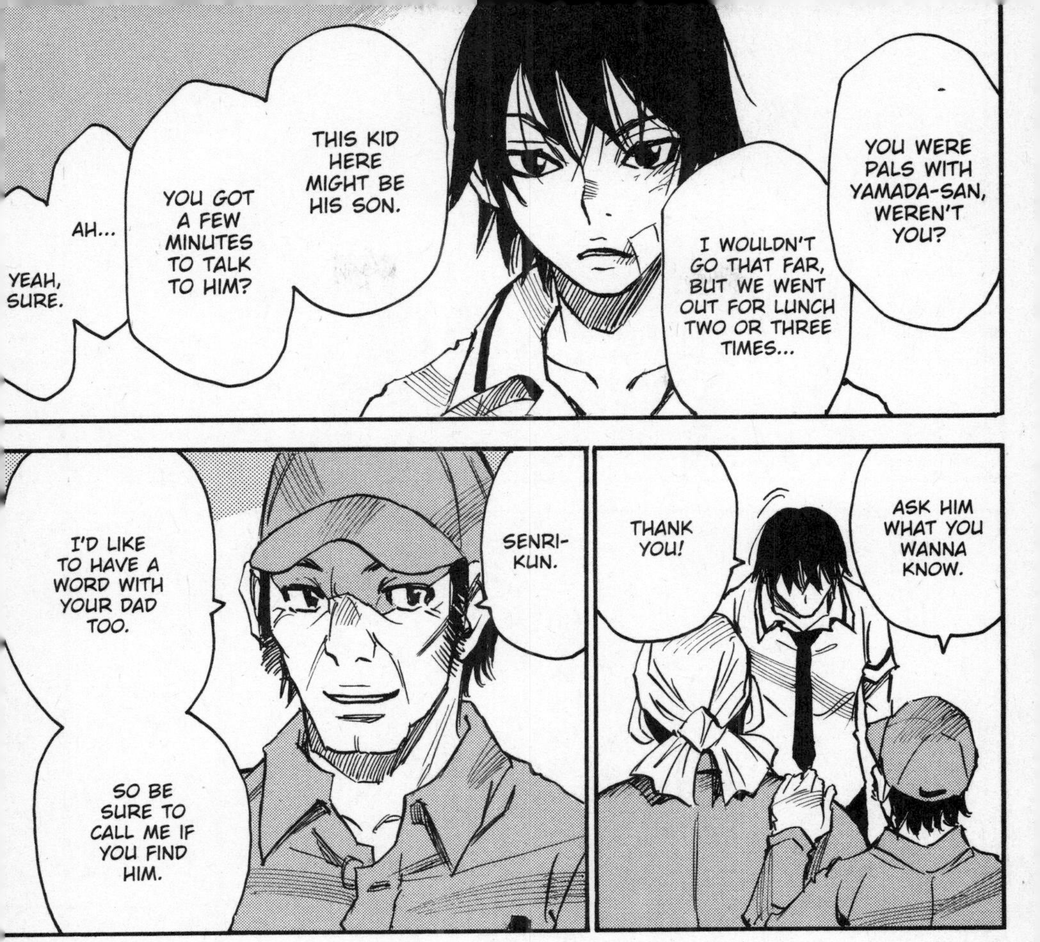
YOU WERE PALS WITH YAMADA-SAN, WEREN'T YOU?
I WOULDN'T GO THAT FAR, BUT WE WENT OUT FOR LUNCH TWO OR THREE TIMES...
THIS KID HERE MIGHT BE HIS SON.
YOU GOT A FEW MINUTES TO TALK TO HIM?
AH...
YEAH, SURE.
ASK HIM WHAT YOU WANNA KNOW.
THANK YOU!
SENRI-KUN.
I'D LIKE TO HAVE A WORD WITH YOUR DAD TOO.
SO BE SURE TO CALL ME IF YOU FIND HIM.

CURTAIN: FLAME-BROILED FOOD, DEEP-FRIED FOOD, MINAKATSU RESTAURANT
SIGNS (L-R): ENTRANCE / OPEN / RECOMMENDED: DEEP-FRIED HORSE MACKEREL

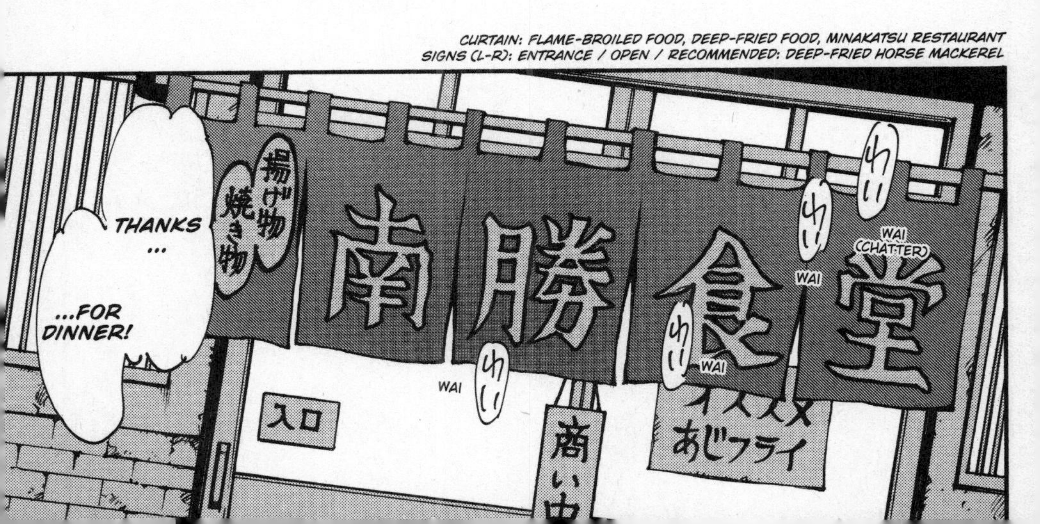
わい
わい
WAI (CHATTER)
WAI
わい
WAI
わい
WAI
南勝食堂
揚げ物
焼き物
オススメ
あじフライ
商い中
入口
THANKS...
...FOR DINNER!

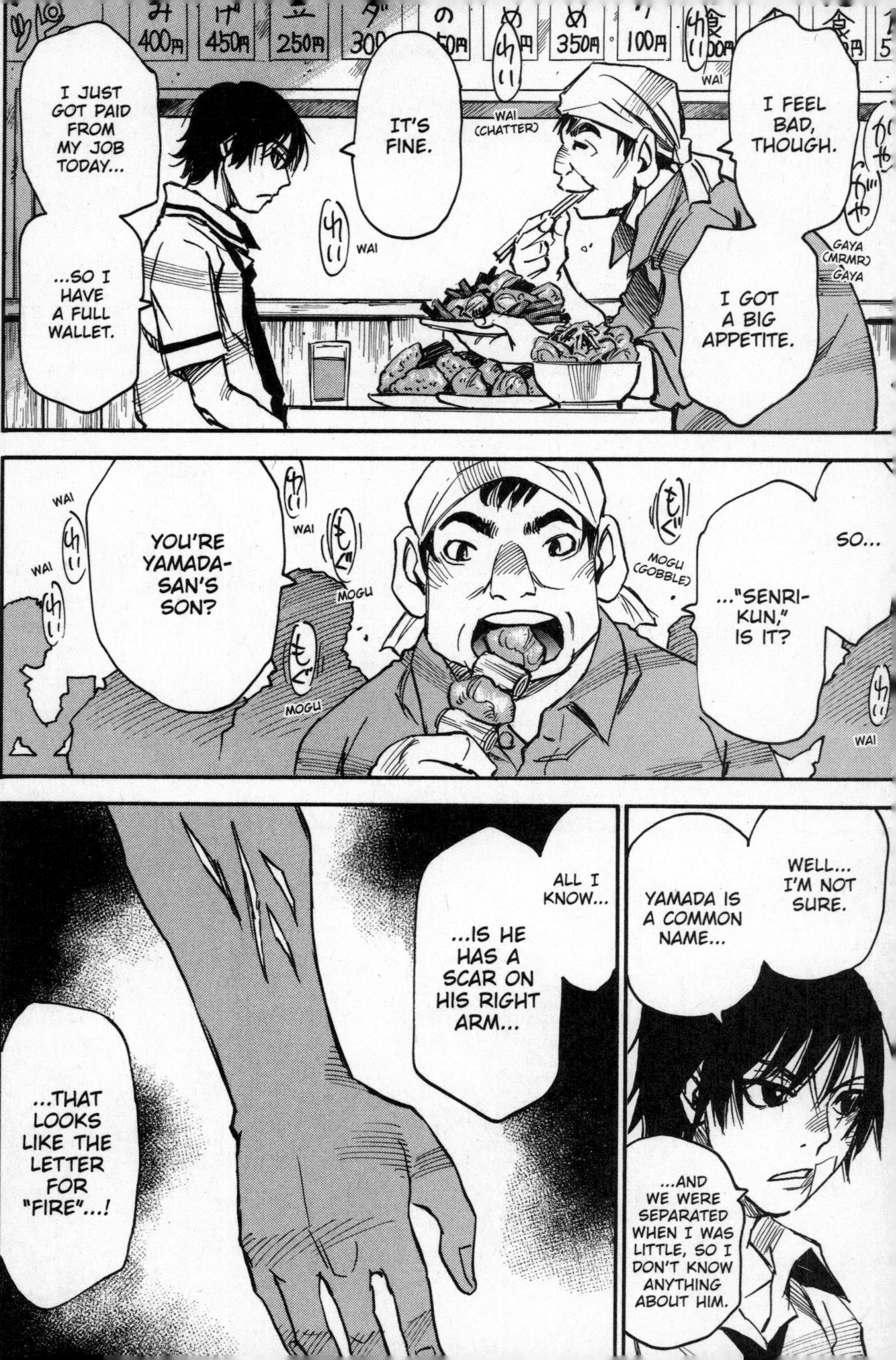
I FEEL BAD, THOUGH.
WAI
GAYA (MRMR) GAYA
I GOT A BIG APPETITE.
WAI (CHATTER)
IT'S FINE.
I JUST GOT PAID FROM MY JOB TODAY...
...SO I HAVE A FULL WALLET.
WAI
SO...
..."SENRI-KUN," IS IT?
WAI
MOGU (GOBBLE)
MOGU
MOGU
WAI
YOU'RE YAMADA-SAN'S SON?
WAI
WAI
WELL... I'M NOT SURE.
YAMADA IS A COMMON NAME...
...AND WE WERE SEPARATED WHEN I WAS LITTLE, SO I DON'T KNOW ANYTHING ABOUT HIM.
ALL I KNOW...
...IS HE HAS A SCAR ON HIS RIGHT ARM...
...THAT LOOKS LIKE THE LETTER FOR "FIRE"...!

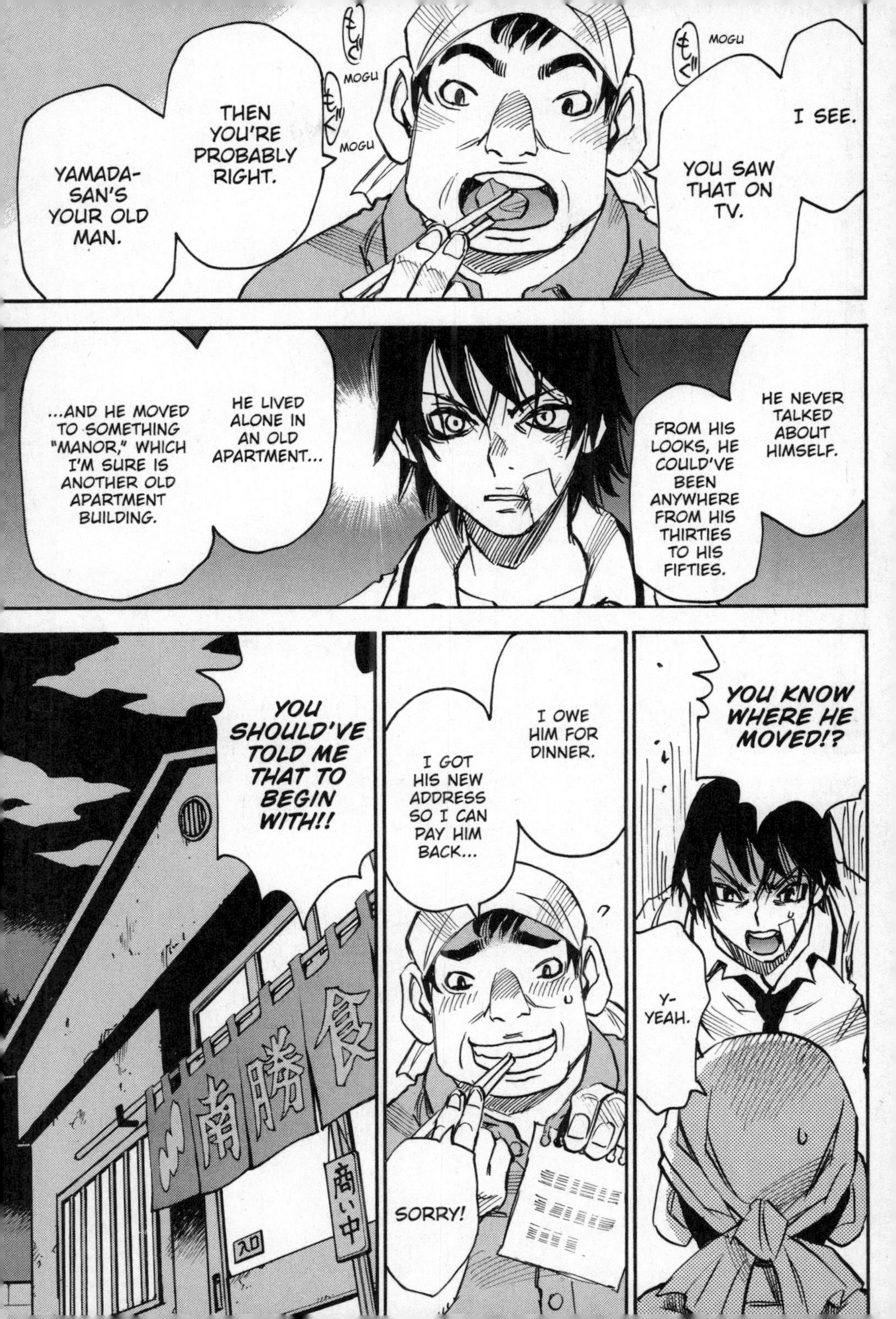
もぐ
MOGU
I SEE.
YOU SAW THAT ON TV.
もぐ
MOGU
もぐ
MOGU
THEN YOU'RE PROBABLY RIGHT.
YAMADA-SAN'S YOUR OLD MAN.
HE NEVER TALKED ABOUT HIMSELF.
FROM HIS LOOKS, HE COULD'VE BEEN ANYWHERE FROM HIS THIRTIES TO HIS FIFTIES.
HE LIVED ALONE IN AN OLD APARTMENT...
...AND HE MOVED TO SOMETHING "MANOR," WHICH I'M SURE IS ANOTHER OLD APARTMENT BUILDING.
YOU KNOW WHERE HE MOVED!?
Y-YEAH.
I OWE HIM FOR DINNER.
I GOT HIS NEW ADDRESS SO I CAN PAY HIM BACK...
SORRY!
YOU SHOULD'VE TOLD ME THAT TO BEGIN WITH!!
食
南勝
商い中
入口

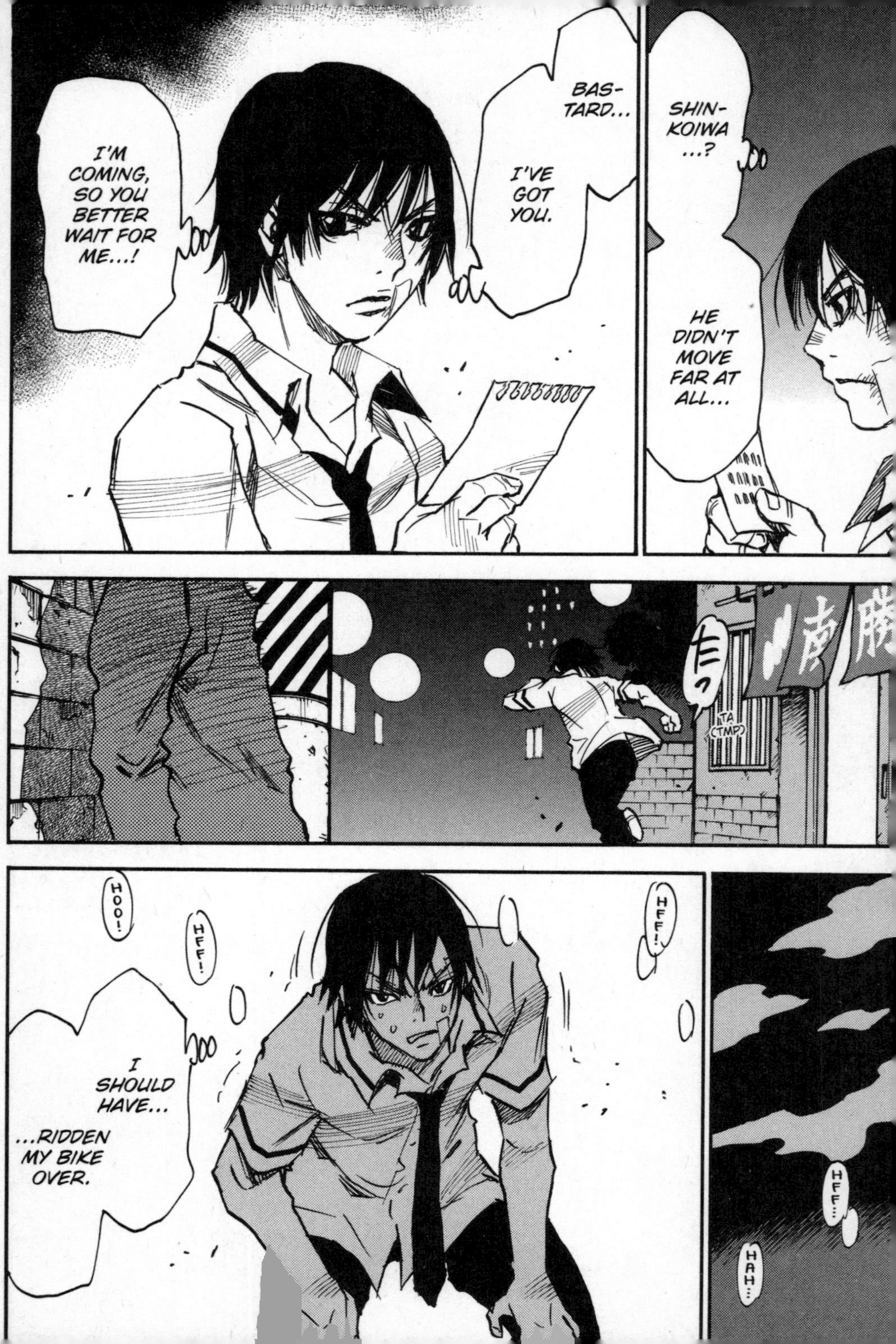
SHIN-KOIWA ...?
HE DIDN'T MOVE FAR AT ALL...
BASTARD...
I'VE GOT YOU.
I'M COMING, SO YOU BETTER WAIT FOR ME...!
たっ
TA (TMP)
HFF...
HAH...
HFF!
HFF!
HOO!
I SHOULD HAVE...
...RIDDEN MY BIKE OVER.

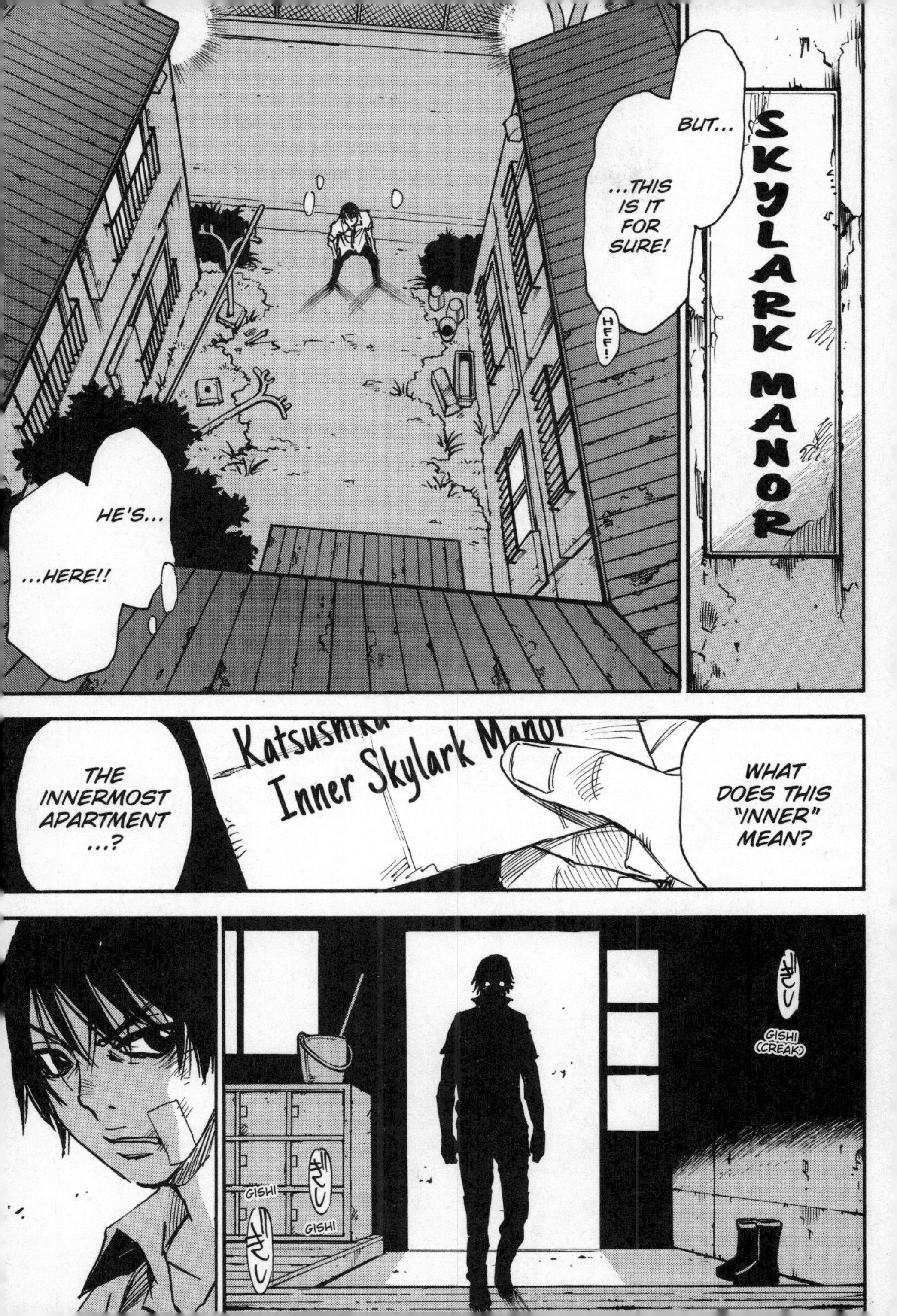
SKYLARK MANOR
BUT...
...THIS IS IT FOR SURE!
HFF!
HE'S...
...HERE!!
WHAT DOES THIS "INNER" MEAN?
Katsushika
Inner Skylark Manor
THE INNERMOST APARTMENT ...?
ぎし
GISHI (CREAK)
ぎし
GISHI
ぎし
GISHI

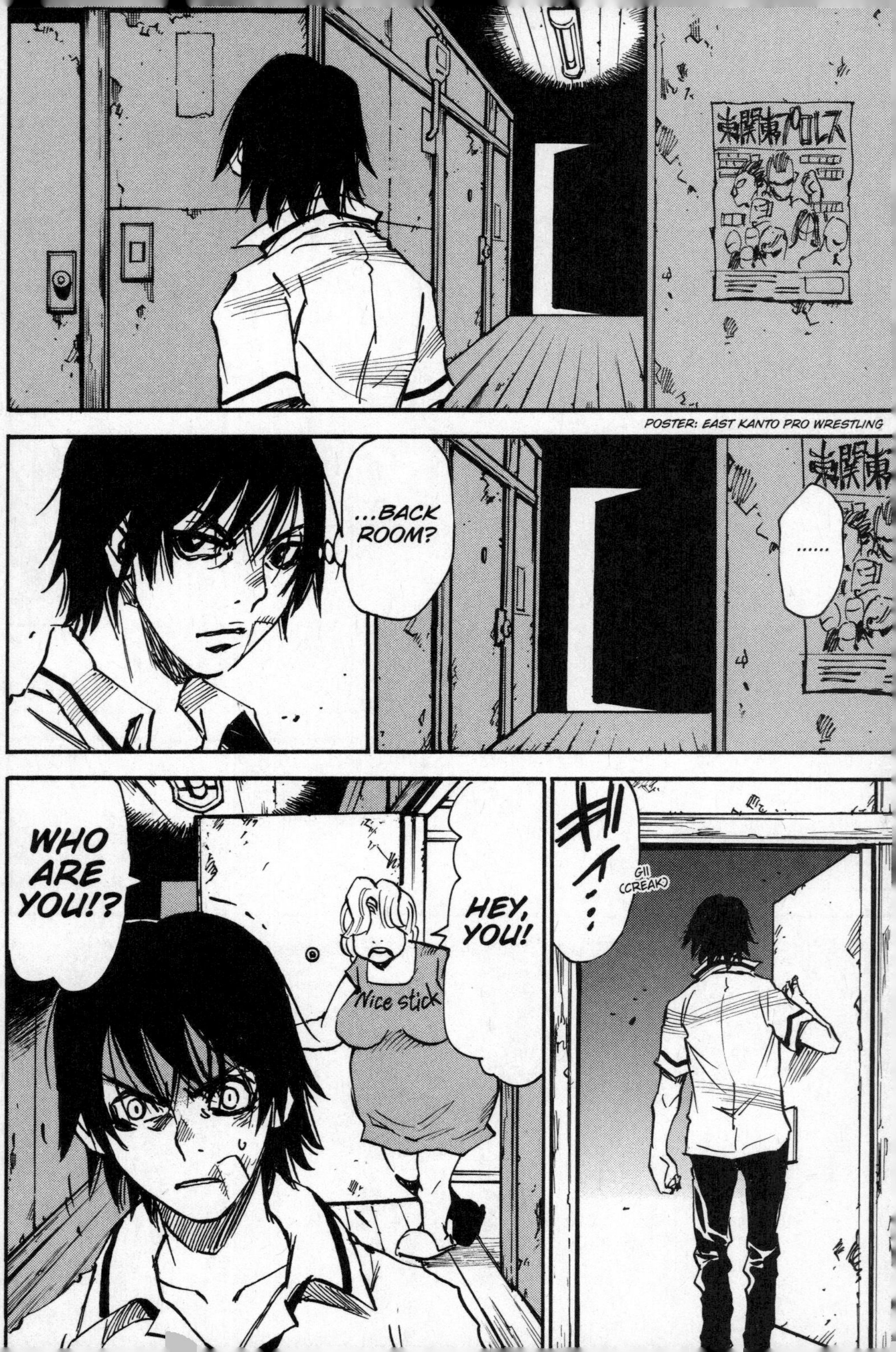
東関東プロレス
POSTER: EAST KANTO PRO WRESTLING
......
...BACK ROOM?
ギィ…
GII (CREAK)
HEY, YOU!
Nice stick
WHO ARE YOU!?

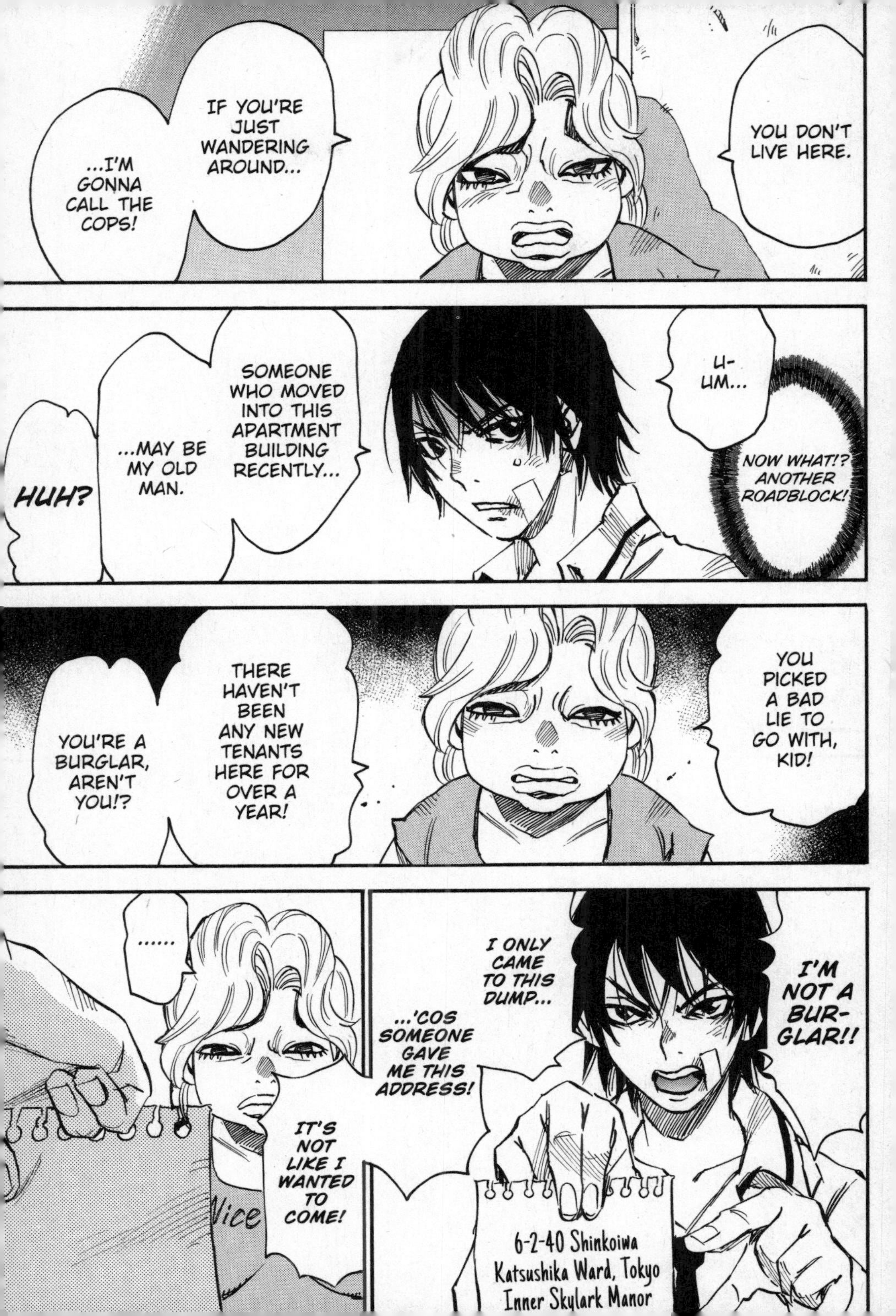
YOU DON'T LIVE HERE.
IF YOU'RE JUST WANDERING AROUND...
...I'M GONNA CALL THE COPS!
U-UM...
NOW WHAT!? ANOTHER ROADBLOCK!
SOMEONE WHO MOVED INTO THIS APARTMENT BUILDING RECENTLY...
...MAY BE MY OLD MAN.
HUH?
YOU PICKED A BAD LIE TO GO WITH, KID!
THERE HAVEN'T BEEN ANY NEW TENANTS HERE FOR OVER A YEAR!
YOU'RE A BURGLAR, AREN'T YOU!?
I'M NOT A BUR-GLAR!!
I ONLY CAME TO THIS DUMP...
...'COS SOMEONE GAVE ME THIS ADDRESS!
IT'S NOT LIKE I WANTED TO COME!
6-2-40 Shinkoiwa
Katsushika Ward, Tokyo
Inner Skylark Manor
......
Vice

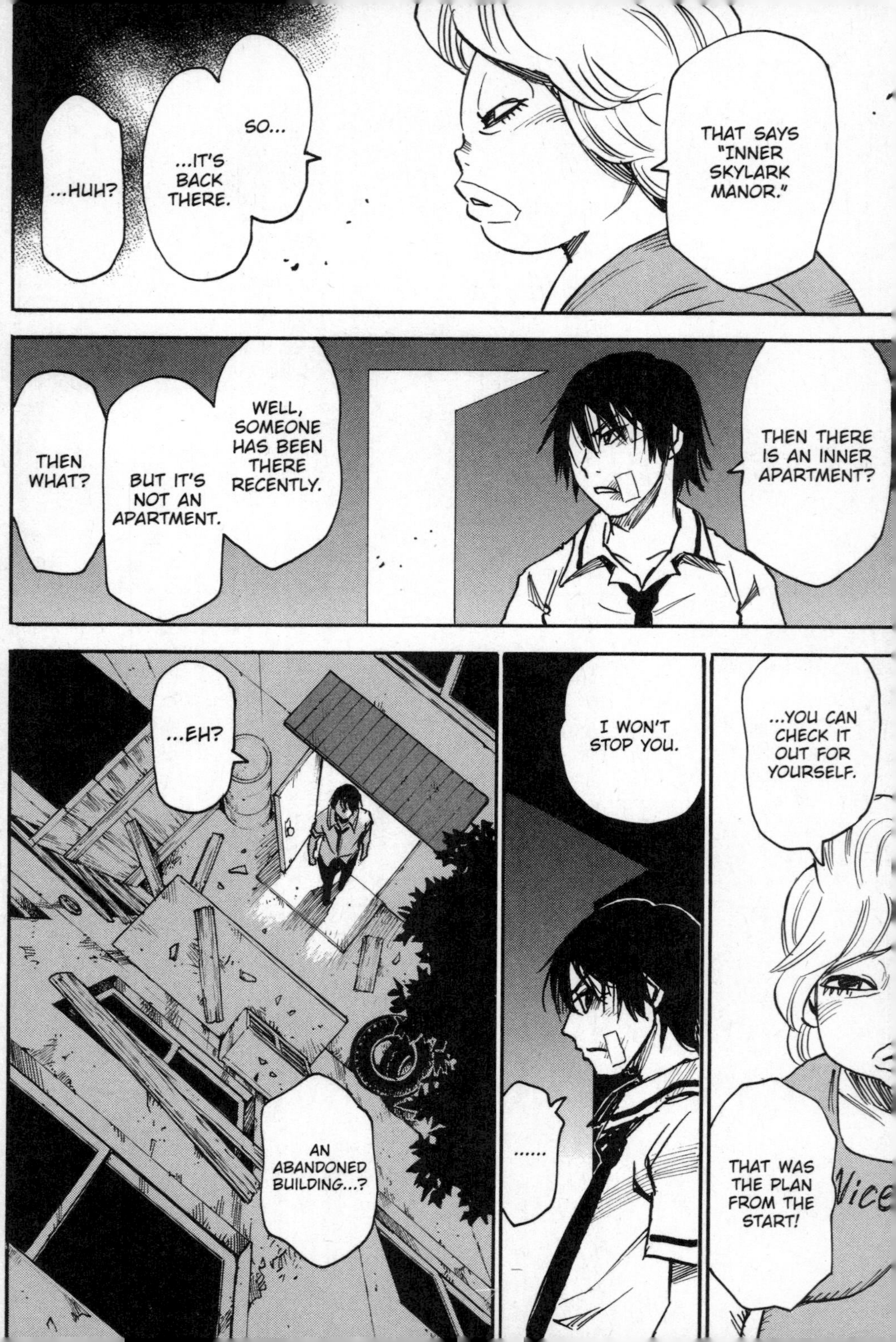
THAT SAYS "INNER SKYLARK MANOR."
SO... ...IT'S BACK THERE.
...HUH?
THEN THERE IS AN INNER APARTMENT?
WELL, SOMEONE HAS BEEN THERE RECENTLY.
BUT IT'S NOT AN APARTMENT.
THEN WHAT?
...YOU CAN CHECK IT OUT FOR YOURSELF.
THAT WAS THE PLAN FROM THE START!
I WON'T STOP YOU.
......
...EH?
AN ABANDONED BUILDING...?

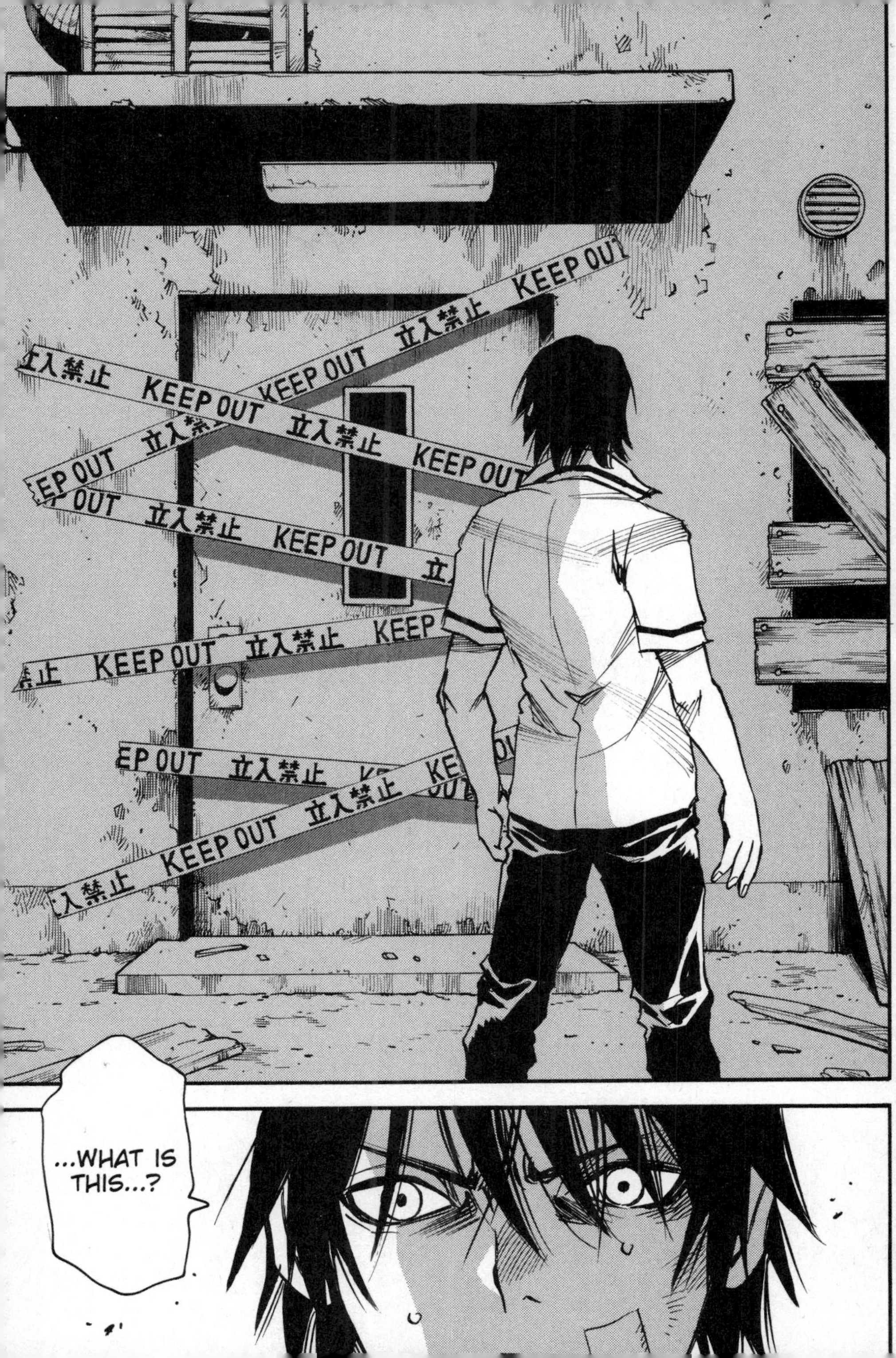
立入禁止 KEEP OUT 立入禁止 KEEP OUT
KEEP OUT 立入禁止 KEEP OUT
KEEP OUT 立入禁止 KEEP OUT 立入禁止
KEEP OUT 立入禁止 KEEP
EP OUT 立入禁止
入禁止 KEEP OUT 立入禁止
...WHAT IS THIS...?

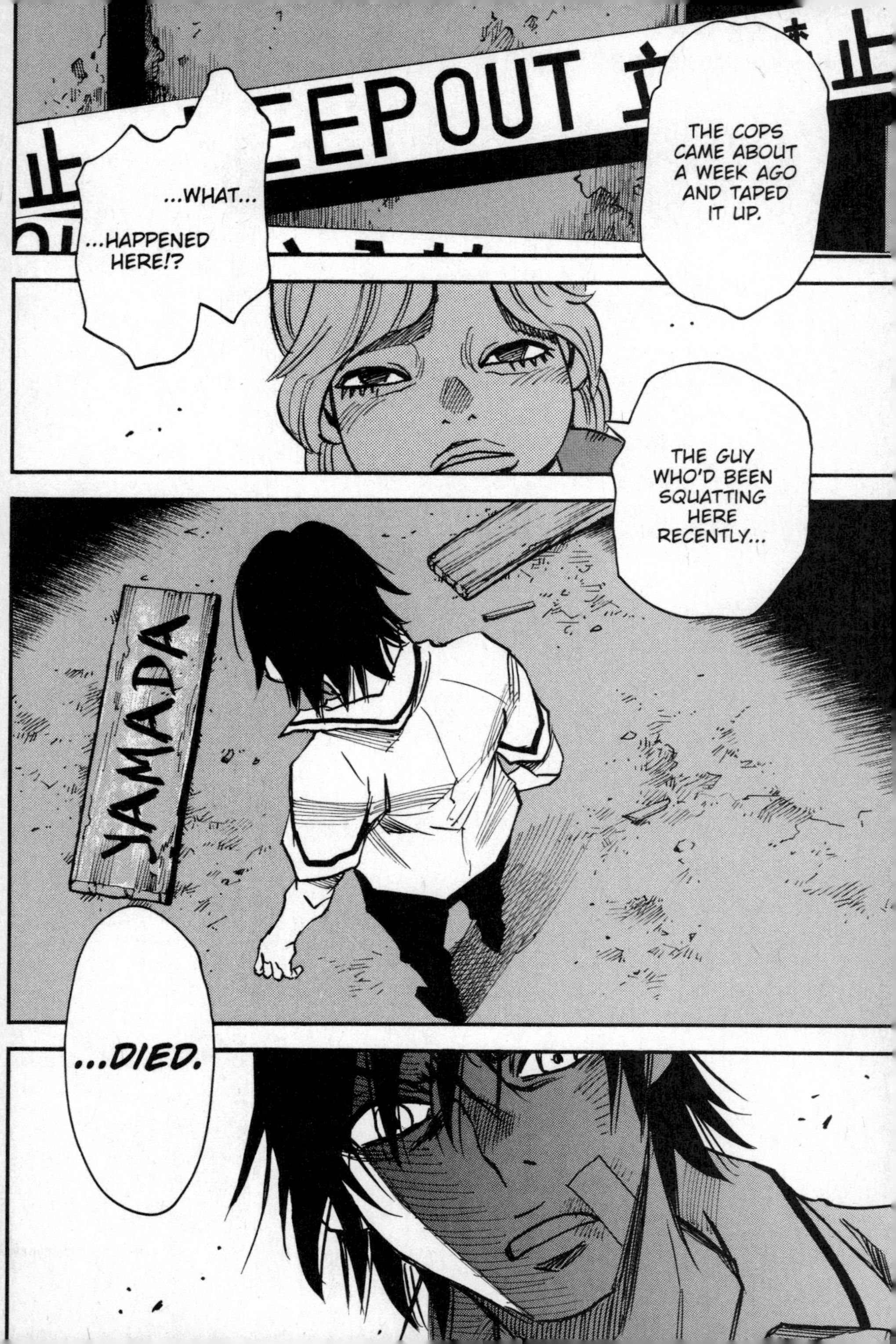
EEP OUT
THE COPS CAME ABOUT A WEEK AGO AND TAPED IT UP.
...WHAT...
...HAPPENED HERE!?
THE GUY WHO'D BEEN SQUATTING HERE RECENTLY...
YAMADA
...DIED.
#2 END

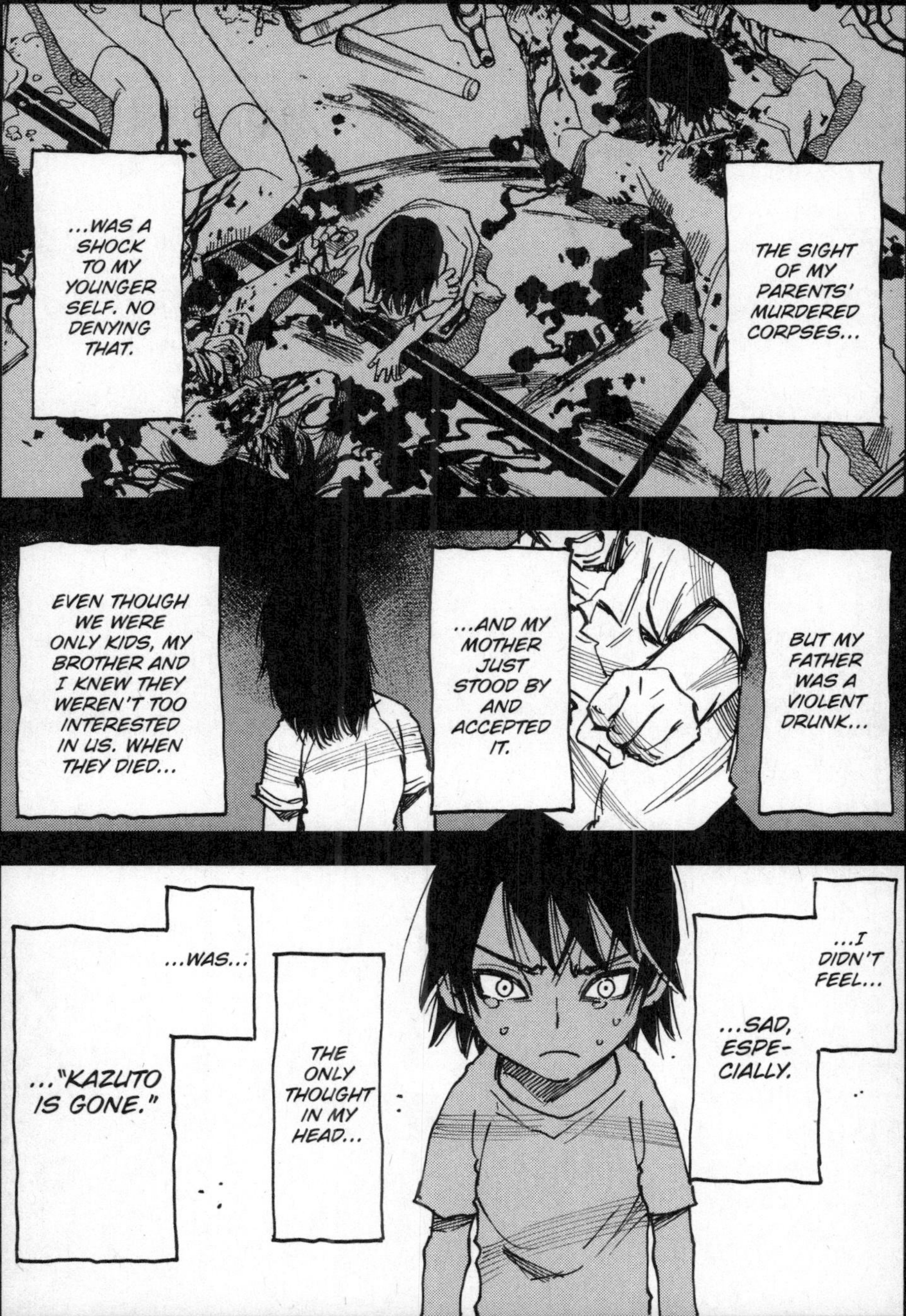
THE SIGHT OF MY PARENTS' MURDERED CORPSES...
...WAS A SHOCK TO MY YOUNGER SELF. NO DENYING THAT.
BUT MY FATHER WAS A VIOLENT DRUNK...
...AND MY MOTHER JUST STOOD BY AND ACCEPTED IT.
EVEN THOUGH WE WERE ONLY KIDS, MY BROTHER AND I KNEW THEY WEREN'T TOO INTERESTED IN US. WHEN THEY DIED...
...I DIDN'T FEEL...
...SAD, ESPE-CIALLY.
THE ONLY THOUGHT IN MY HEAD...
...WAS...
..."KAZUTO IS GONE."

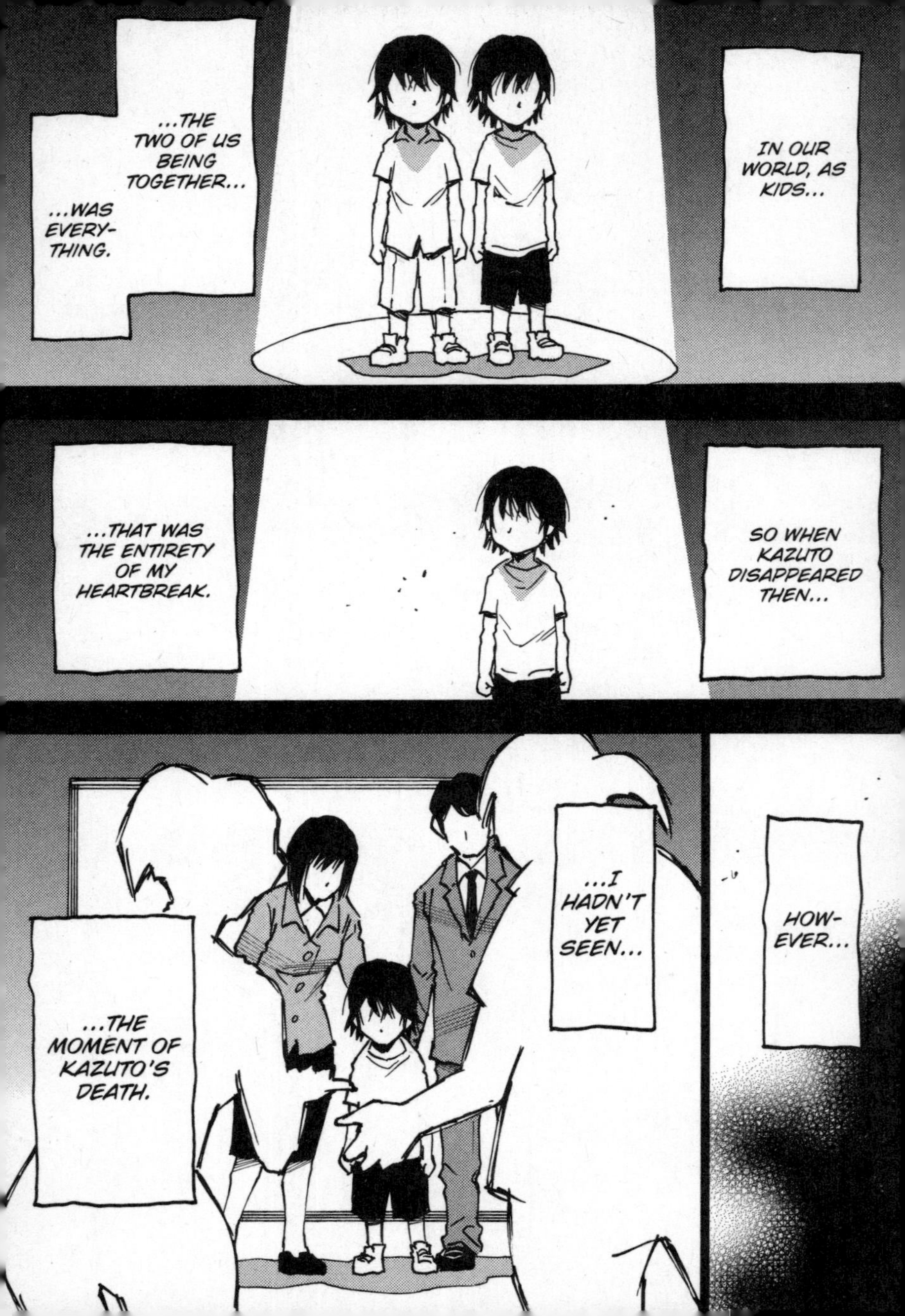
IN OUR WORLD, AS KIDS...
...THE TWO OF US BEING TOGETHER...
...WAS EVERYTHING.
SO WHEN KAZUTO DISAPPEARED THEN...
...THAT WAS THE ENTIRETY OF MY HEARTBREAK.
HOWEVER...
...I HADN'T YET SEEN...
...THE MOMENT OF KAZUTO'S DEATH.

#3 Decided to Kill Him

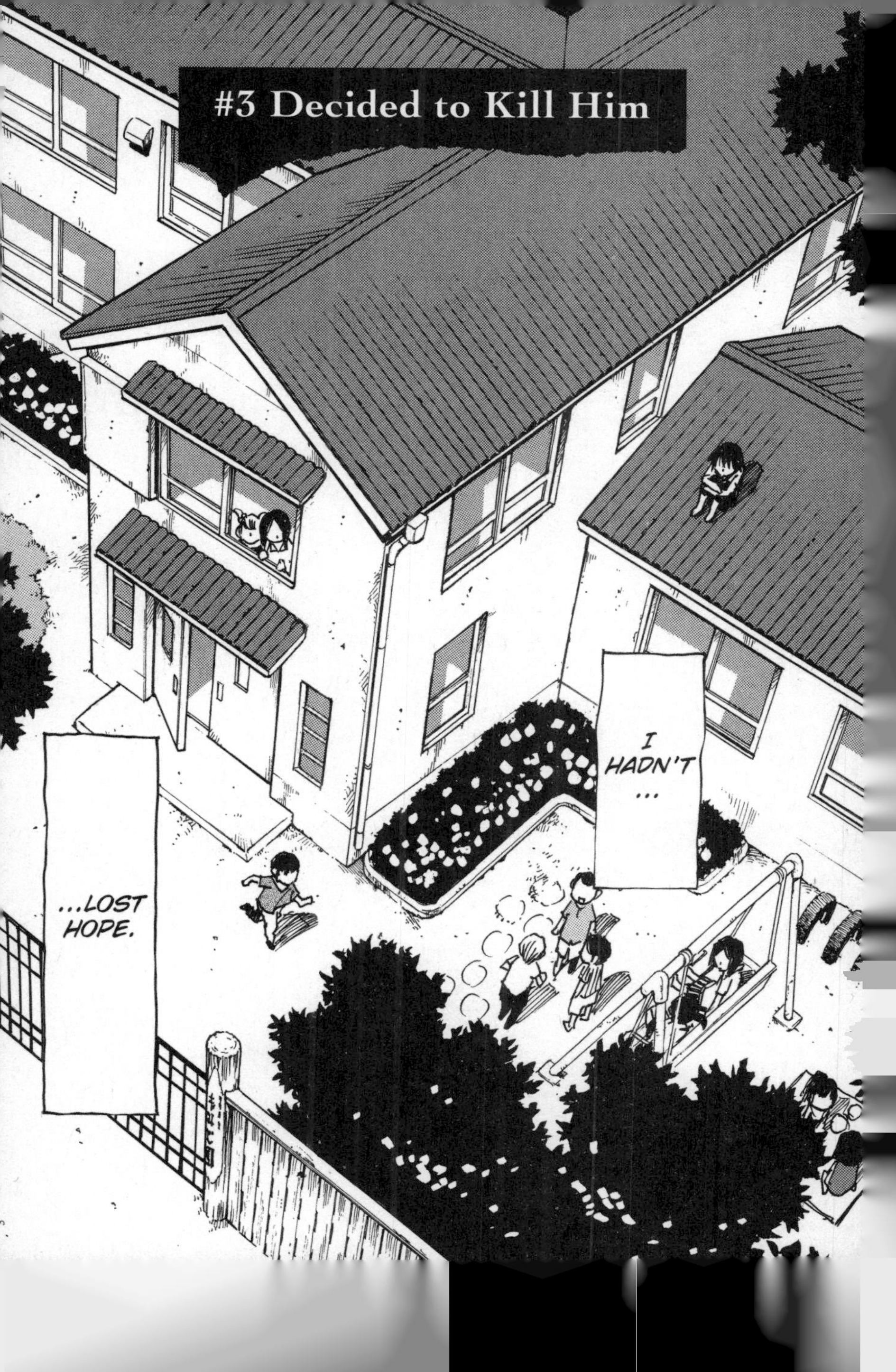
I HADN'T ...
...LOST HOPE.

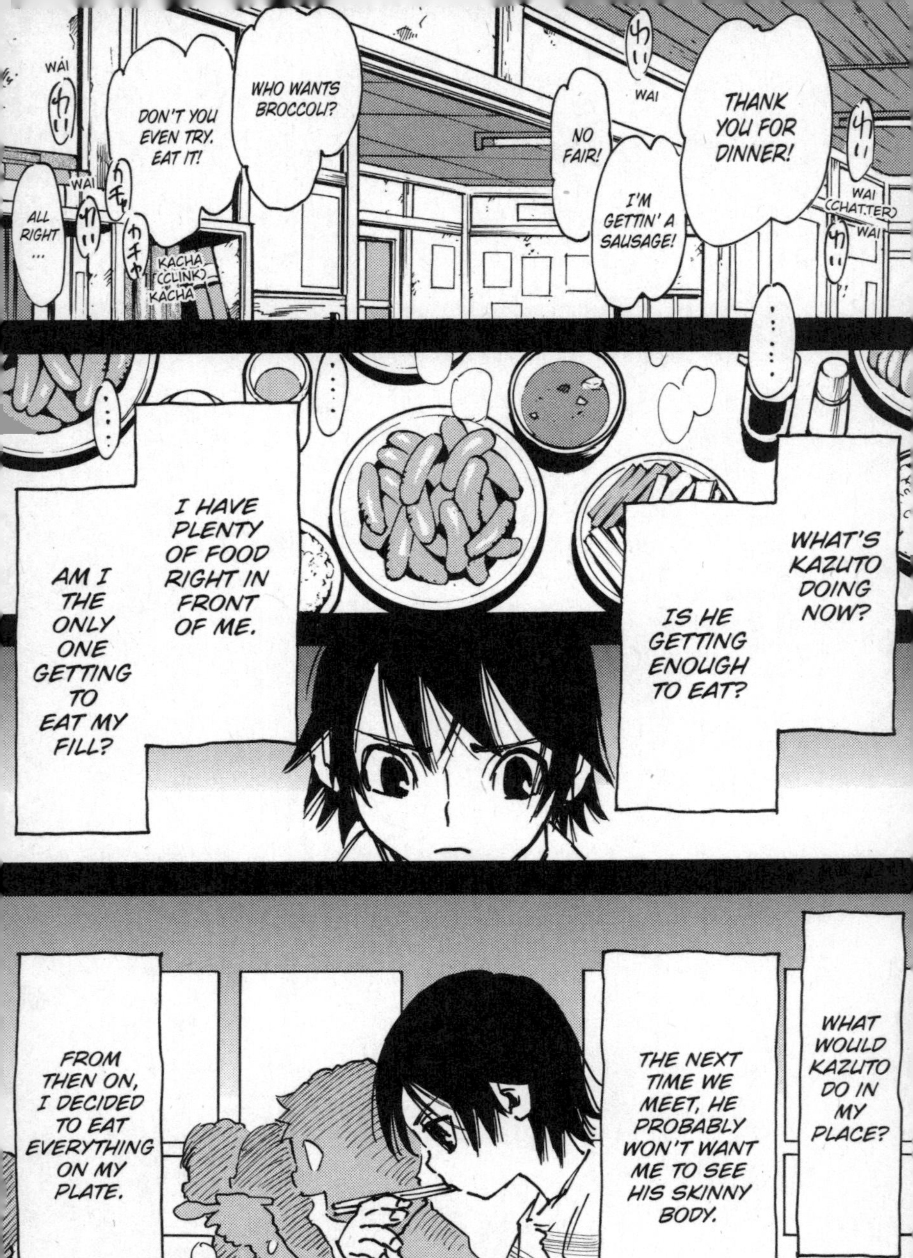
WAI (CHAT.TER) WAI
THANK YOU FOR DINNER!
WAI
NO FAIR!
I'M GETTIN' A SAUSAGE!
WHO WANTS BROCCOLI?
DON'T YOU EVEN TRY. EAT IT!
KACHA (CLINK) KACHA
WAI
WAI
ALL RIGHT ...
......
......
......
WHAT'S KAZUTO DOING NOW?
IS HE GETTING ENOUGH TO EAT?
I HAVE PLENTY OF FOOD RIGHT IN FRONT OF ME.
AM I THE ONLY ONE GETTING TO EAT MY FILL?
WHAT WOULD KAZUTO DO IN MY PLACE?
THE NEXT TIME WE MEET, HE PROBABLY WON'T WANT ME TO SEE HIS SKINNY BODY.
FROM THEN ON, I DECIDED TO EAT EVERYTHING ON MY PLATE.

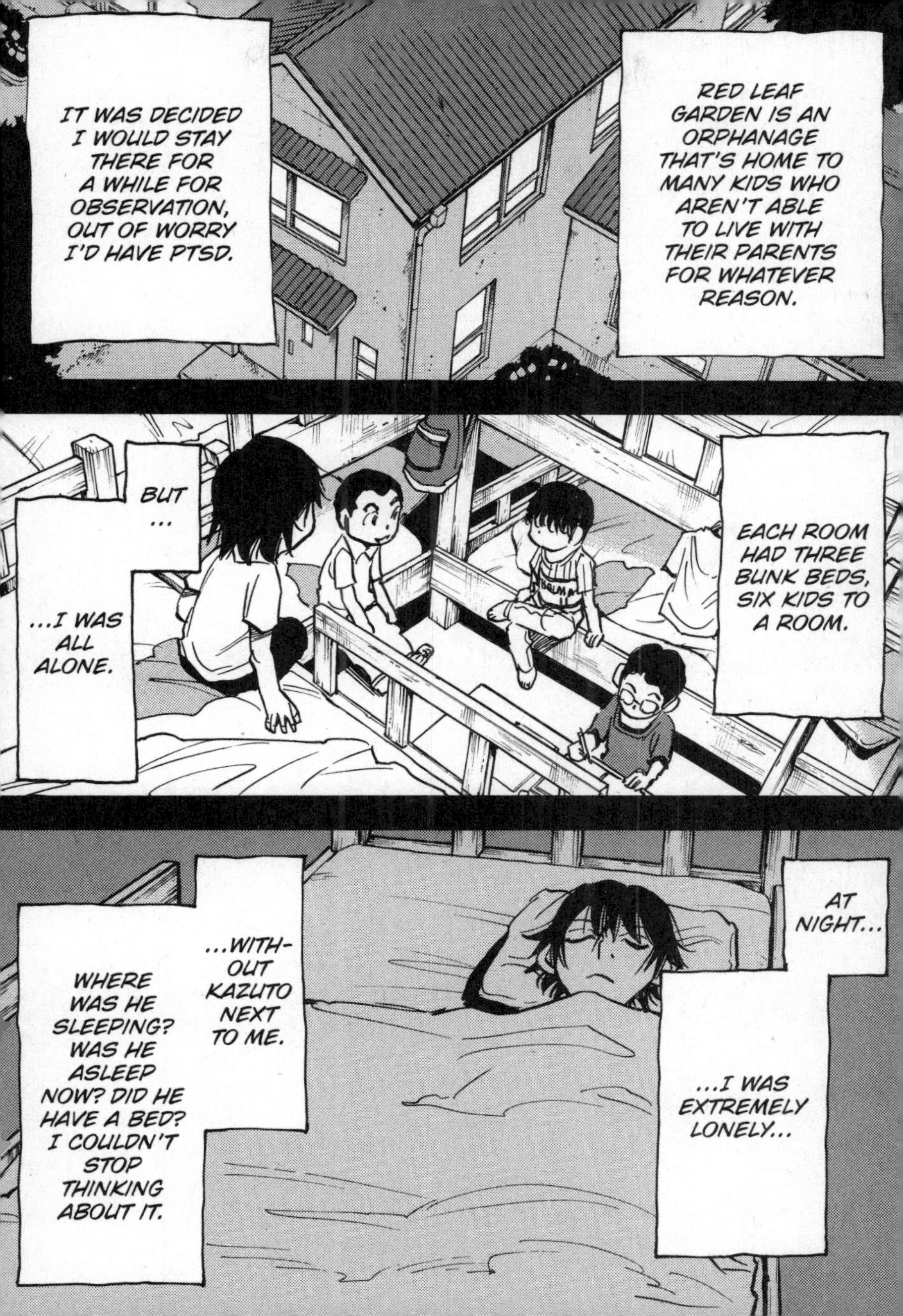
RED LEAF GARDEN IS AN ORPHANAGE THAT'S HOME TO MANY KIDS WHO AREN'T ABLE TO LIVE WITH THEIR PARENTS FOR WHATEVER REASON.
IT WAS DECIDED I WOULD STAY THERE FOR A WHILE FOR OBSERVATION, OUT OF WORRY I'D HAVE PTSD.
EACH ROOM HAD THREE BUNK BEDS, SIX KIDS TO A ROOM.
BUT...
...I WAS ALL ALONE.
AT NIGHT...
...I WAS EXTREMELY LONELY...
...WITH-OUT KAZUTO NEXT TO ME.
WHERE WAS HE SLEEPING? WAS HE ASLEEP NOW? DID HE HAVE A BED? I COULDN'T STOP THINKING ABOUT IT.

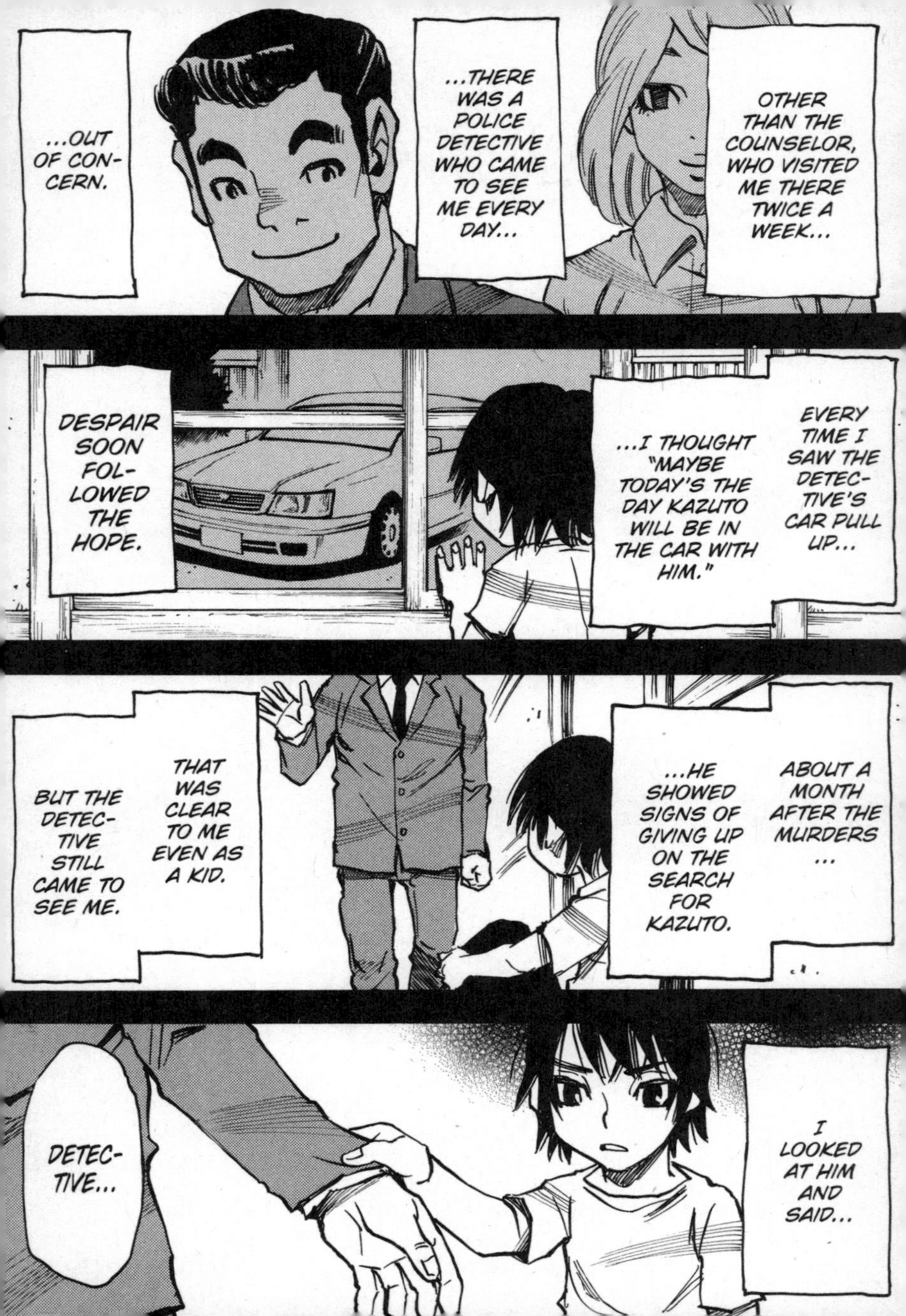
OTHER THAN THE COUNSELOR, WHO VISITED ME THERE TWICE A WEEK...
...THERE WAS A POLICE DETECTIVE WHO CAME TO SEE ME EVERY DAY...
...OUT OF CONCERN.
EVERY TIME I SAW THE DETECTIVE'S CAR PULL UP...
...I THOUGHT "MAYBE TODAY'S THE DAY KAZUTO WILL BE IN THE CAR WITH HIM."
DESPAIR SOON FOLLOWED THE HOPE.
ABOUT A MONTH AFTER THE MURDERS...
...HE SHOWED SIGNS OF GIVING UP ON THE SEARCH FOR KAZUTO.
THAT WAS CLEAR TO ME EVEN AS A KID.
BUT THE DETECTIVE STILL CAME TO SEE ME.
I LOOKED AT HIM AND SAID...
DETECTIVE...

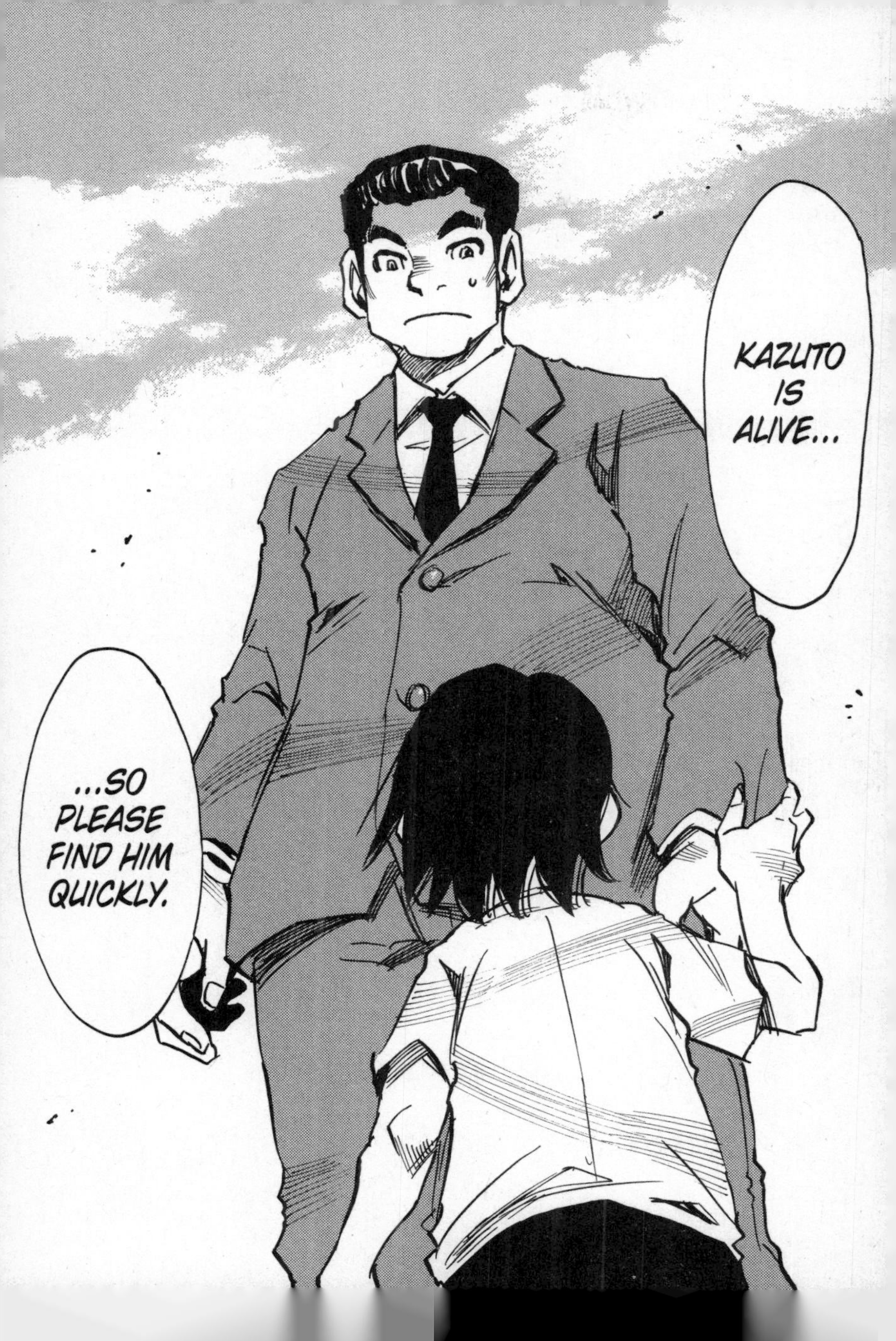
KAZUTO IS ALIVE...
...SO PLEASE FIND HIM QUICKLY.

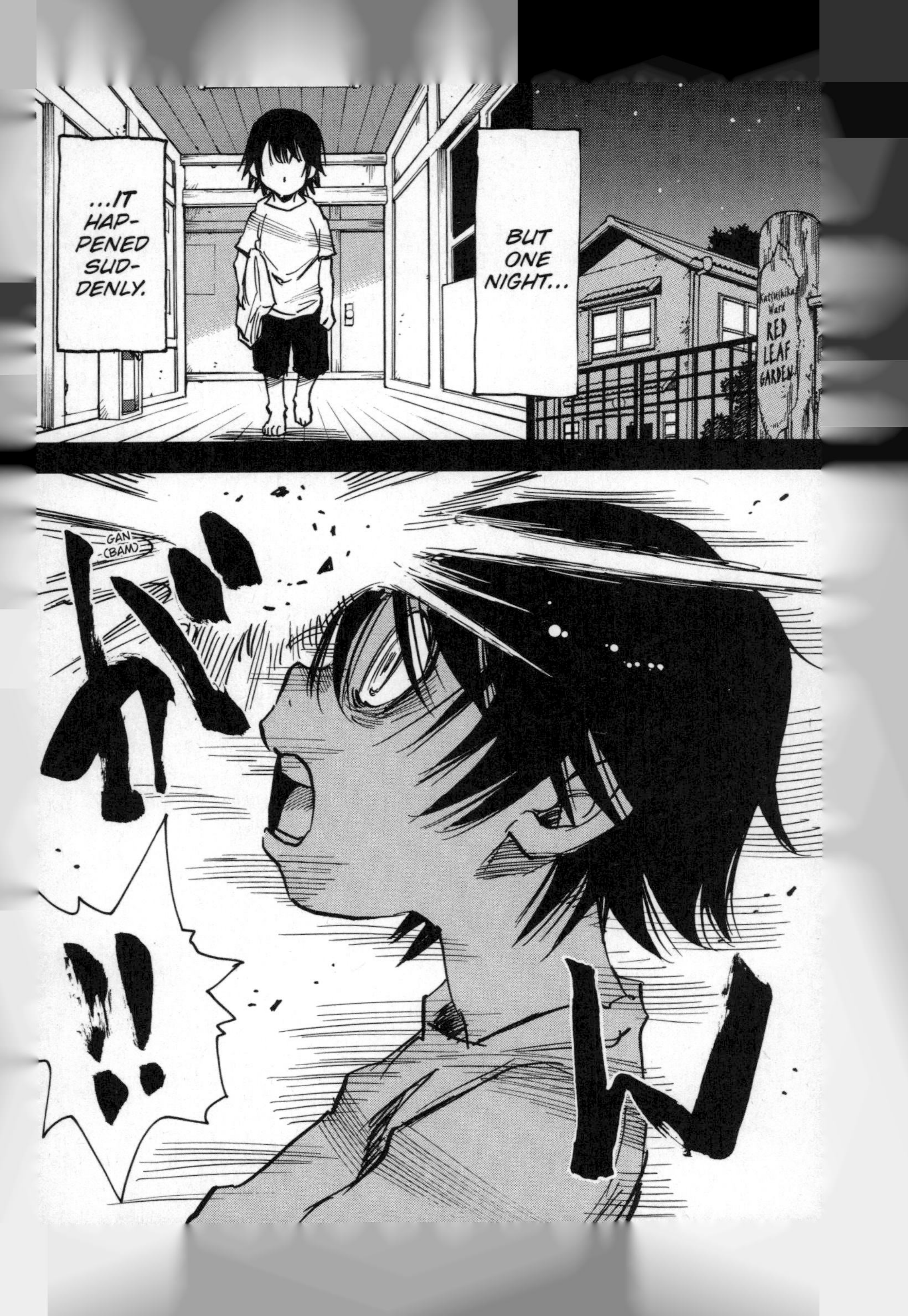
BUT ONE NIGHT...
Katsushika Ward
RED LEAF GARDEN
...IT HAPPENED SUDDENLY.
GAN (BAM)
!!

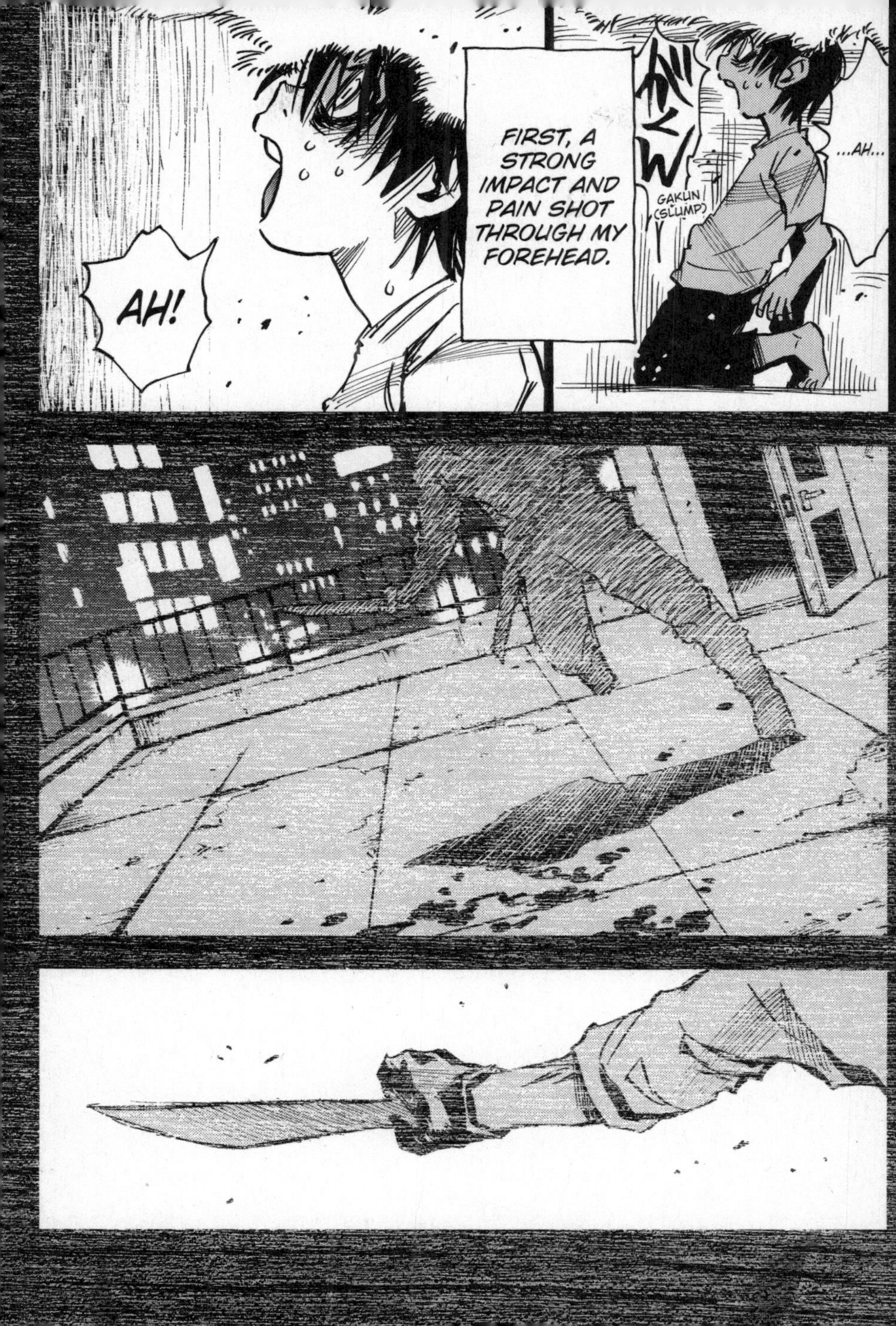
GAKUN (SLUMP)
...AH...
FIRST, A STRONG IMPACT AND PAIN SHOT THROUGH MY FOREHEAD.
AH!

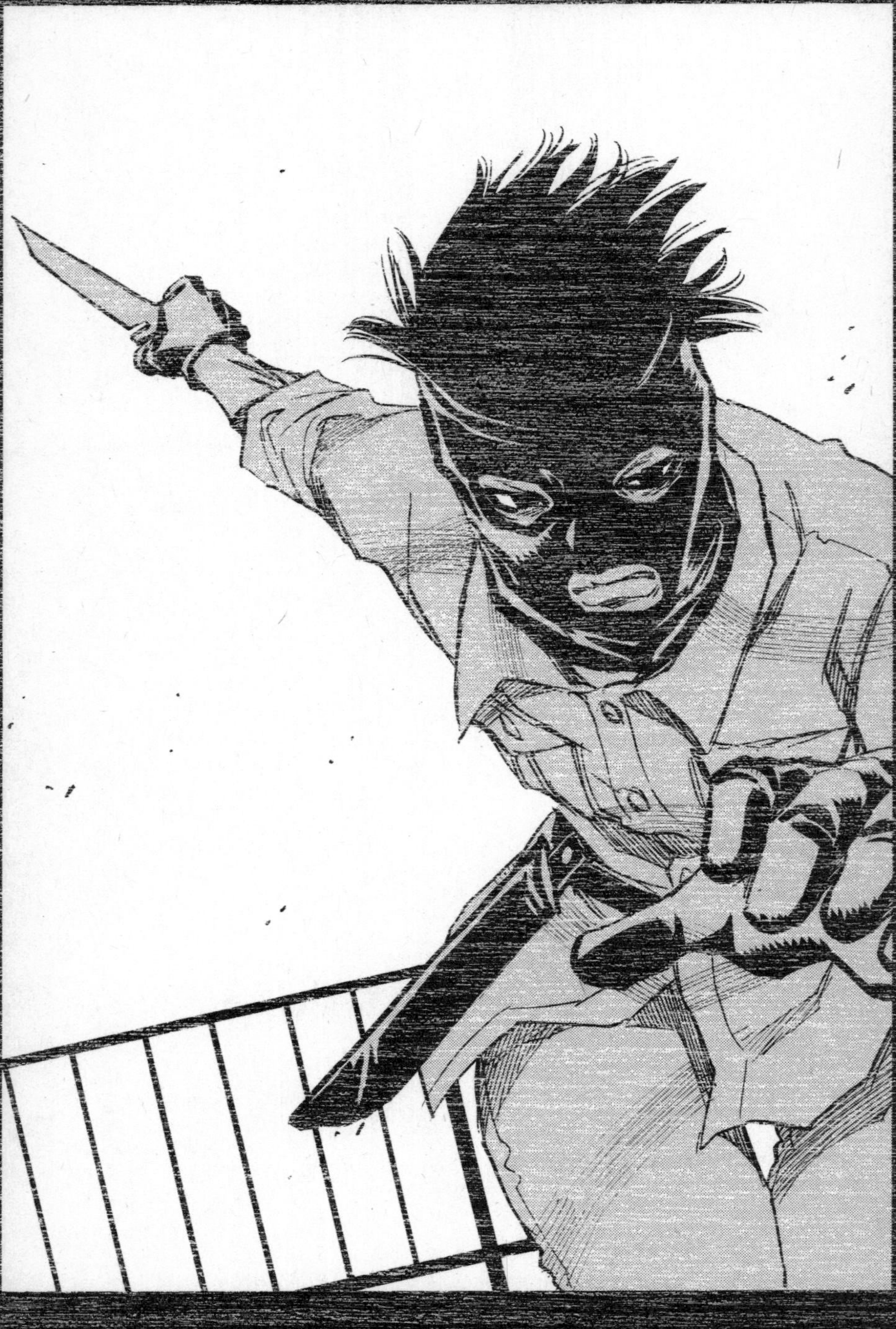

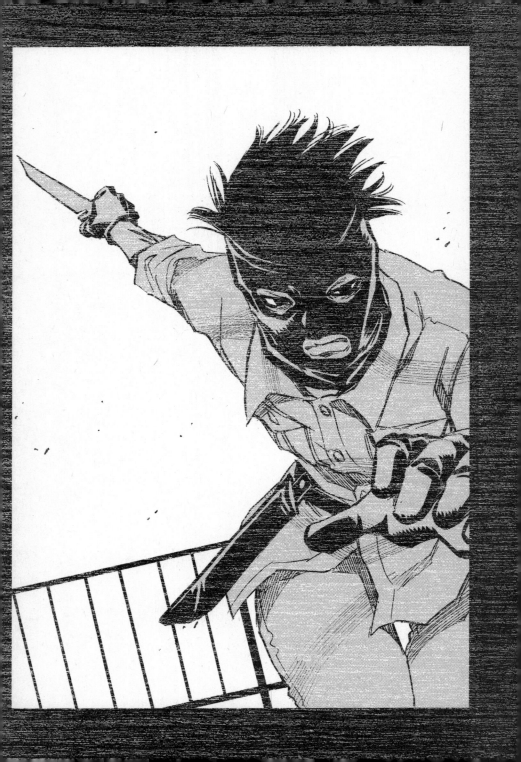

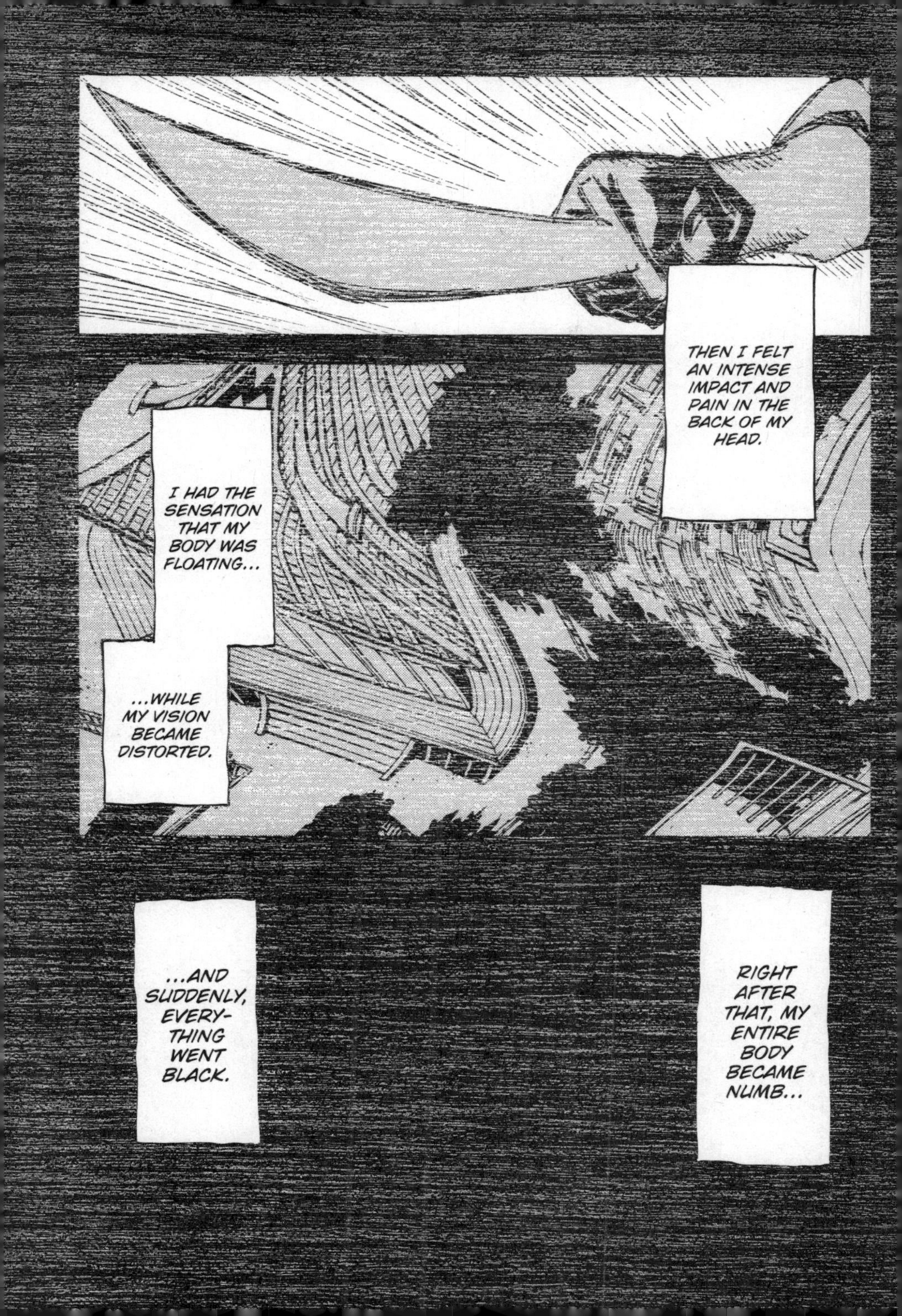
THEN I FELT AN INTENSE IMPACT AND PAIN IN THE BACK OF MY HEAD.
I HAD THE SENSATION THAT MY BODY WAS FLOATING...
...WHILE MY VISION BECAME DISTORTED.
RIGHT AFTER THAT, MY ENTIRE BODY BECAME NUMB...
...AND SUDDENLY, EVERY-THING WENT BLACK.

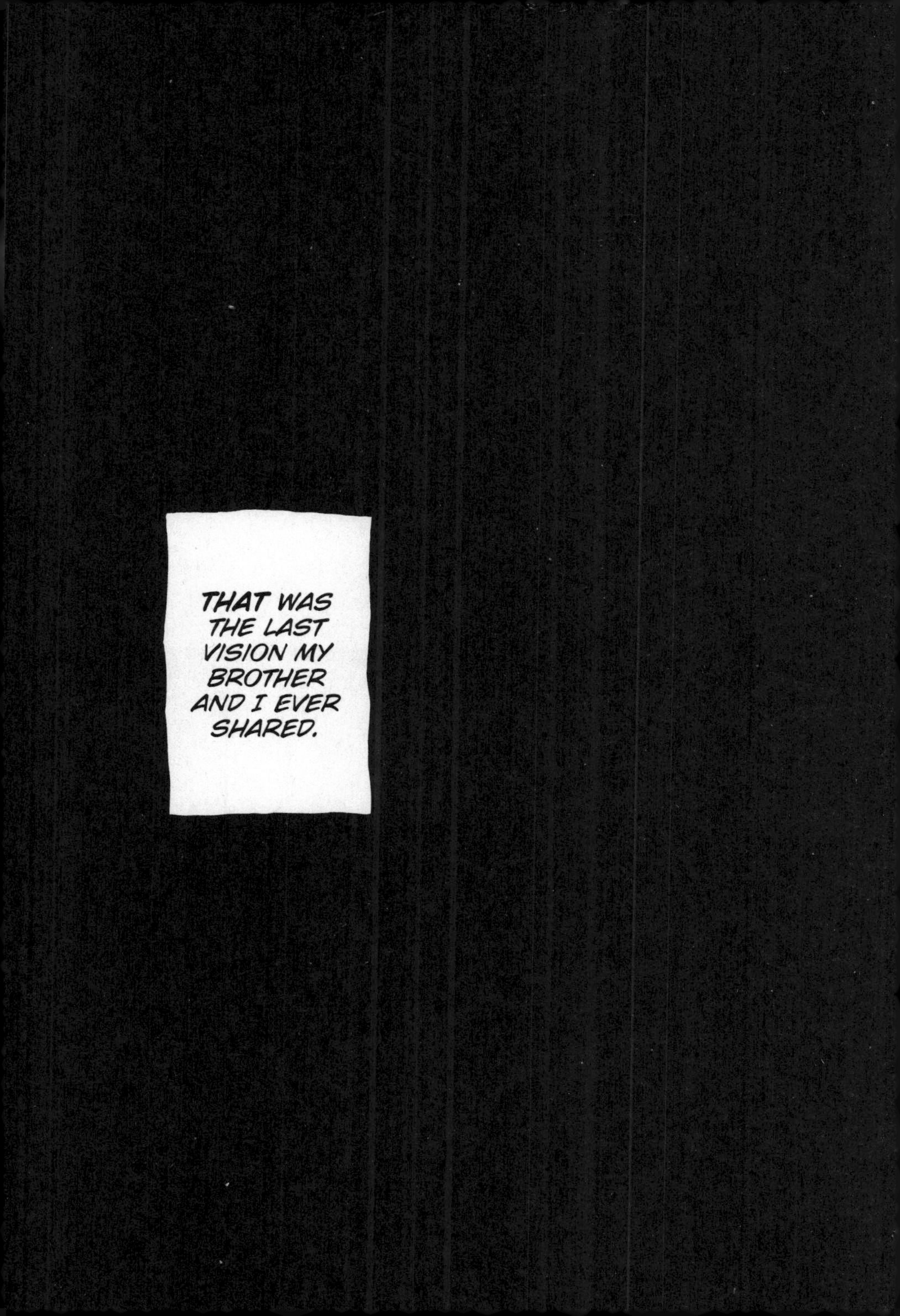
THAT WAS THE LAST VISION MY BROTHER AND I EVER SHARED.

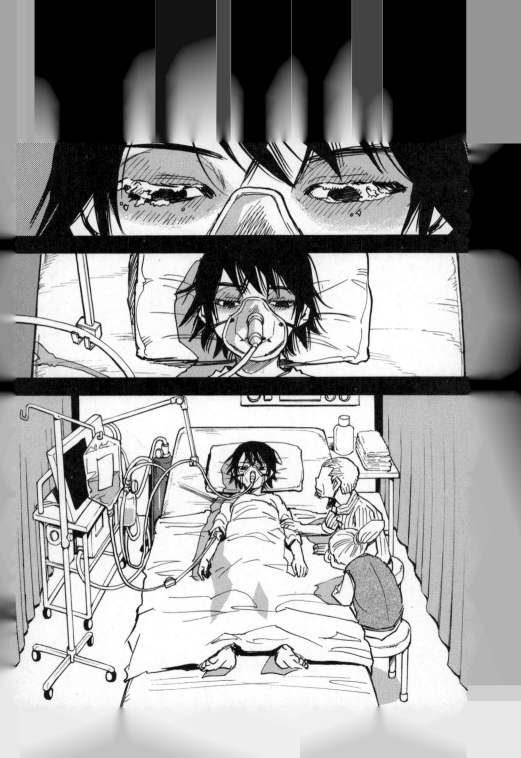

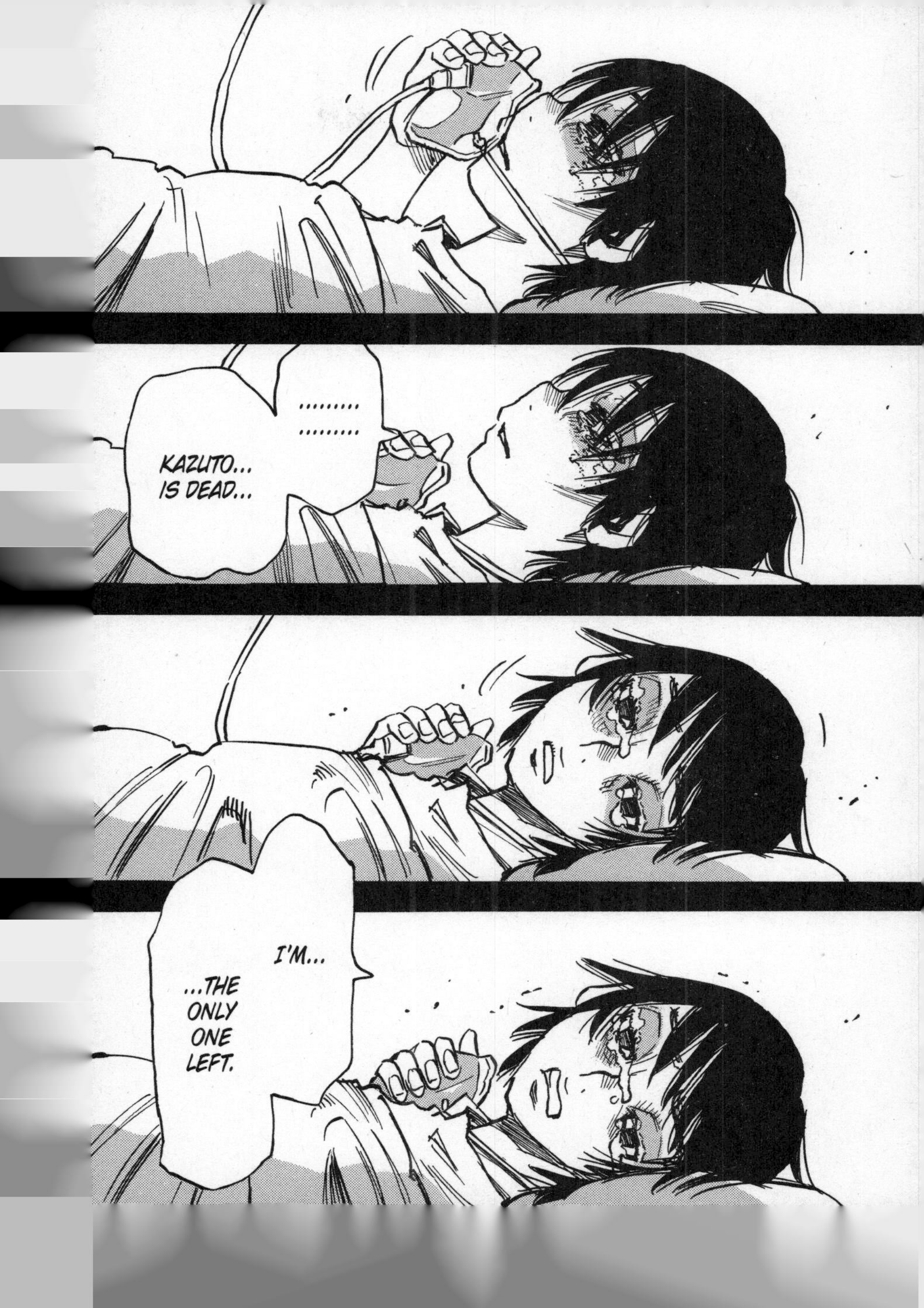
....
....
KAZUTO... IS DEAD...
I'M...
...THE ONLY ONE LEFT.

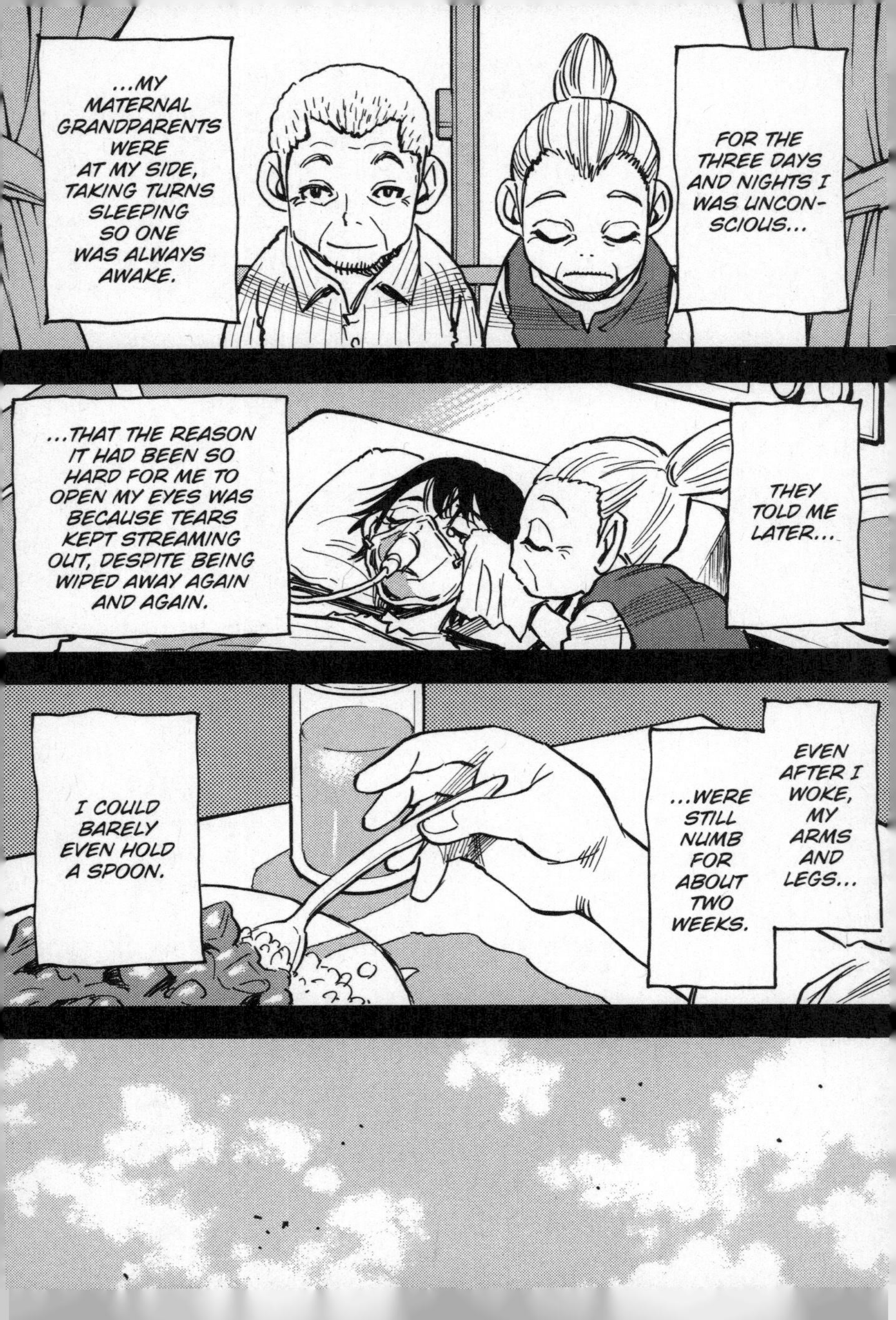
FOR THE THREE DAYS AND NIGHTS I WAS UNCONSCIOUS...
...MY MATERNAL GRANDPARENTS WERE AT MY SIDE, TAKING TURNS SLEEPING SO ONE WAS ALWAYS AWAKE.
THEY TOLD ME LATER...
...THAT THE REASON IT HAD BEEN SO HARD FOR ME TO OPEN MY EYES WAS BECAUSE TEARS KEPT STREAMING OUT, DESPITE BEING WIPED AWAY AGAIN AND AGAIN.
EVEN AFTER I WOKE, MY ARMS AND LEGS...
...WERE STILL NUMB FOR ABOUT TWO WEEKS.
I COULD BARELY EVEN HOLD A SPOON.

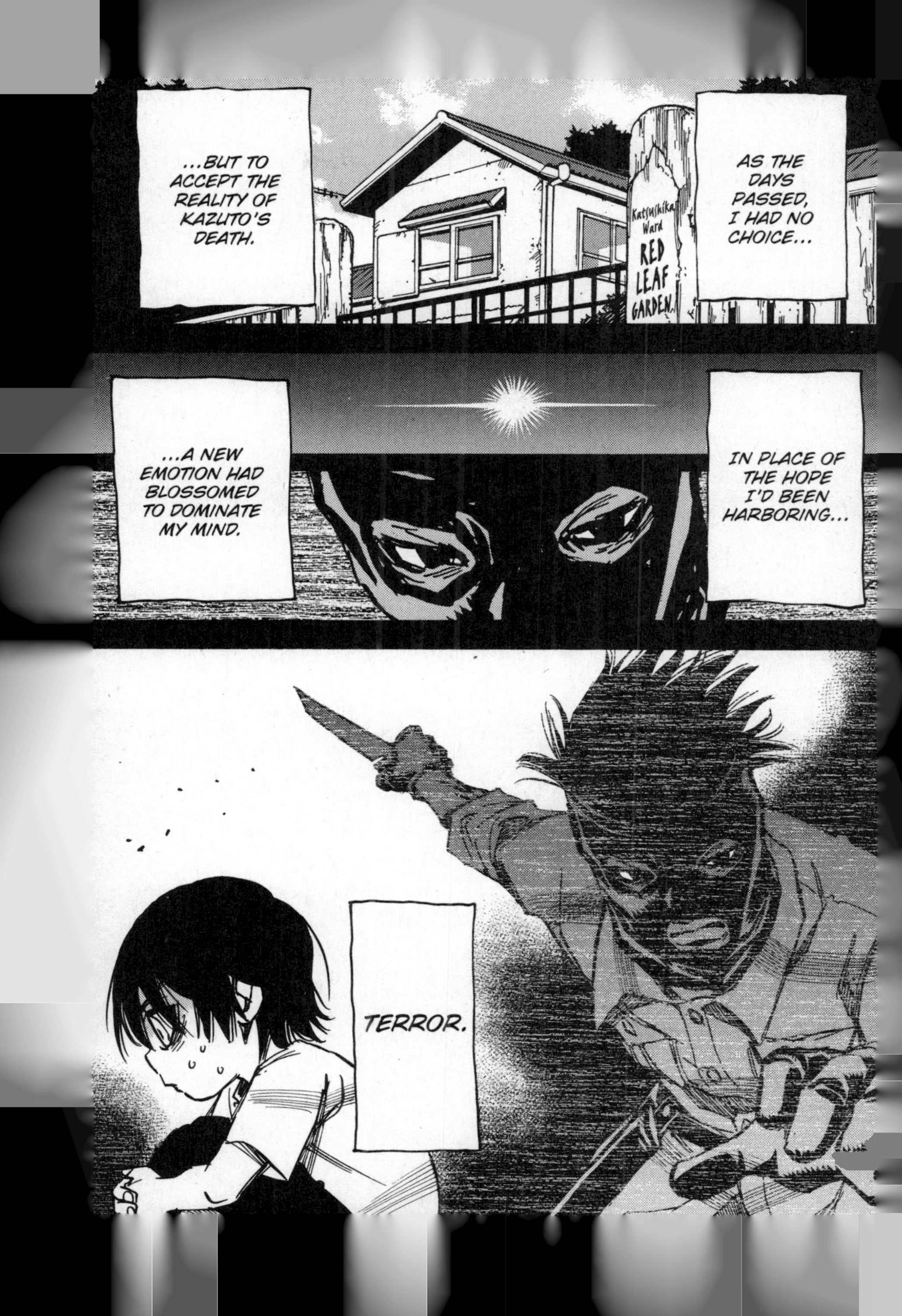
AS THE DAYS PASSED, I HAD NO CHOICE...
Katsushika Ward RED LEAF GARDEN
...BUT TO ACCEPT THE REALITY OF KAZUTO'S DEATH.
IN PLACE OF THE HOPE I'D BEEN HARBORING...
...A NEW EMOTION HAD BLOSSOMED TO DOMINATE MY MIND.
TERROR.

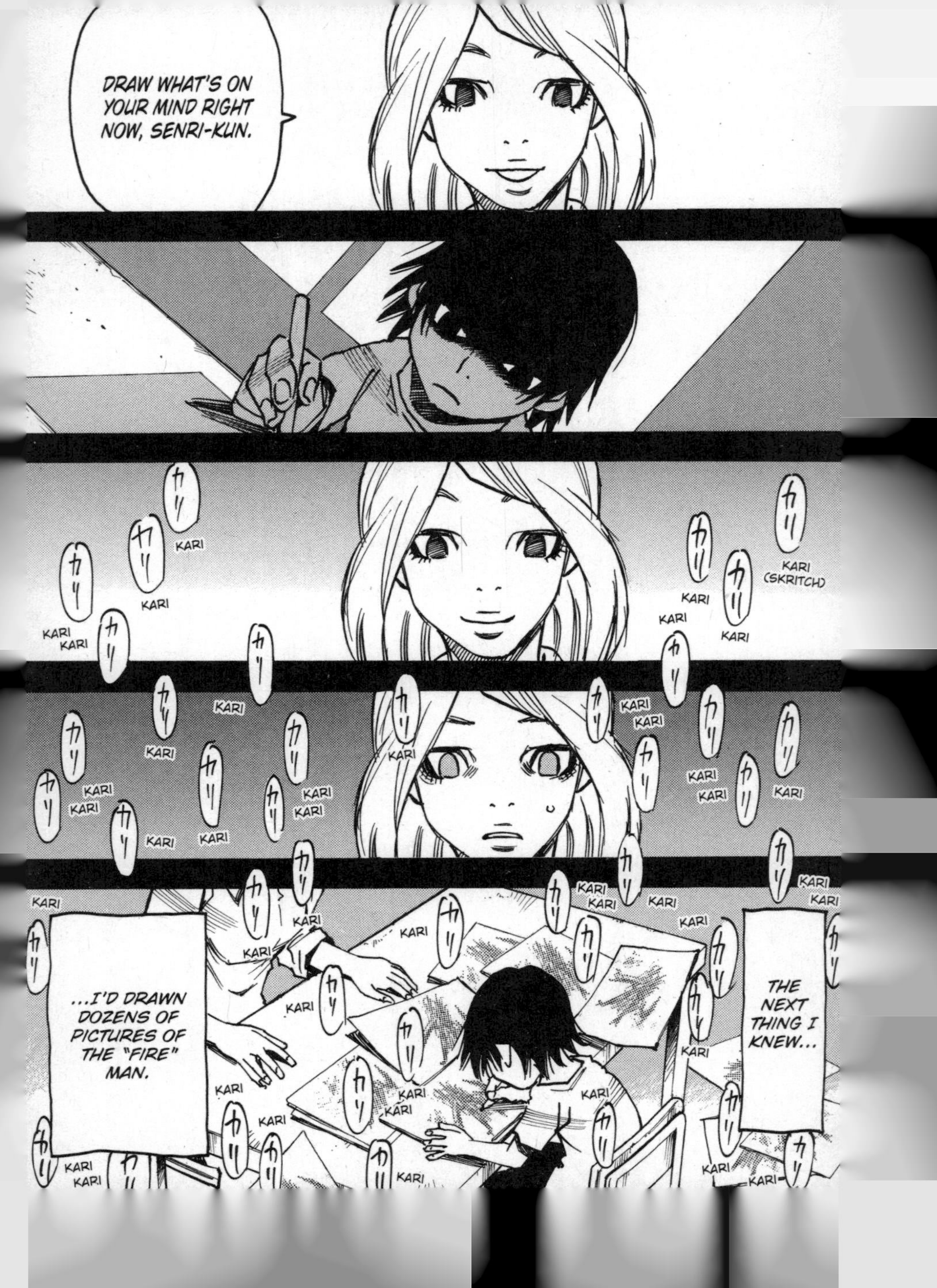
DRAW WHAT'S ON YOUR MIND RIGHT NOW, SENRI-KUN.
カリ
KARI (SKRITCH)
カリ
KARI
カリ
KARI
カリ
KARI
カリ
KARI
カリ
KARI KARI
カリ
KARI KARI
カリ
KARI KARI
カリ
KARI
カリ
KARI KARI
カリ
KARI KARI
カリ
KARI
カリ
KARI
カリ
KARI KARI
カリ
KARI
THE NEXT THING I KNEW...
...I'D DRAWN DOZENS OF PICTURES OF THE "FIRE" MAN.
カリ
KARI KARI
カリ
KARI
カリ
KARI
カリ
KARI
カリ
KARI KARI

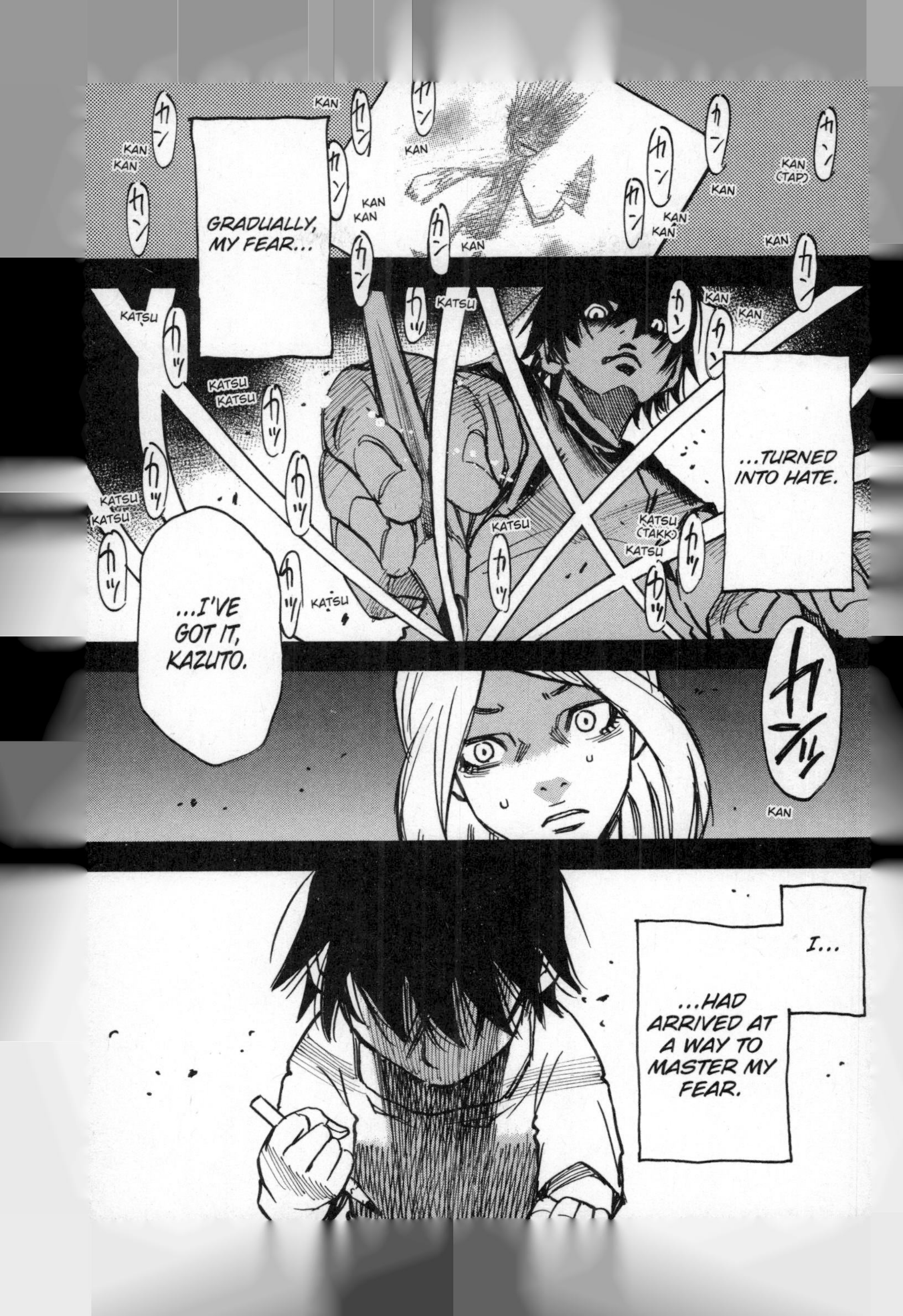
KAN (TAP)
KAN
KAN KAN
KAN
KAN KAN
KAN
KAN
KAN KAN
GRADUALLY, MY FEAR...
KAN KAN
...TURNED INTO HATE.
KATSU (TAKK) KATSU
KATSU
KATSU
KATSU
KATSU KATSU
KATSU KATSU
KATSU
...I'VE GOT IT, KAZUTO.
KAN
I...
...HAD ARRIVED AT A WAY TO MASTER MY FEAR.

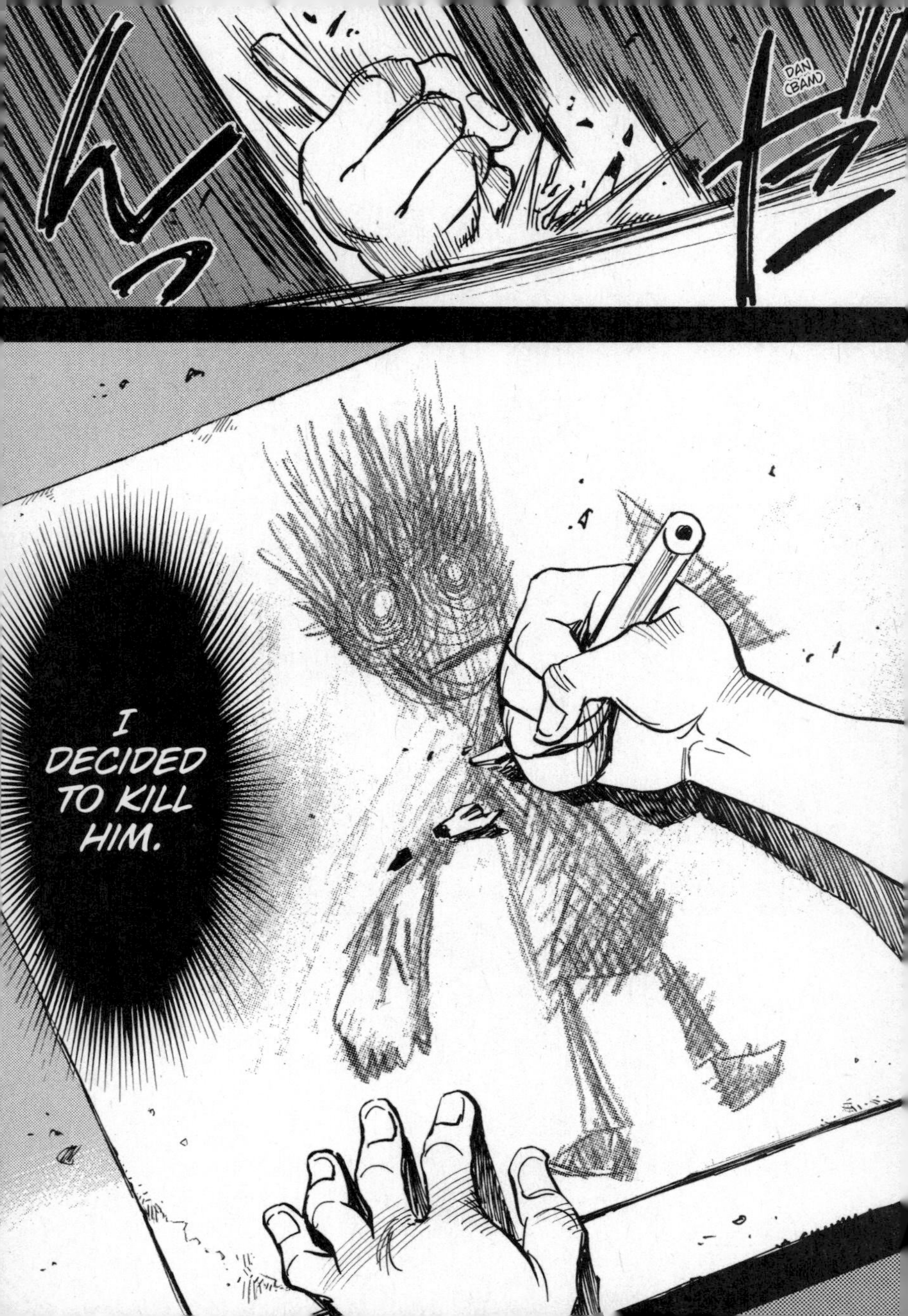
DAN (BAM)
I DECIDED TO KILL HIM.

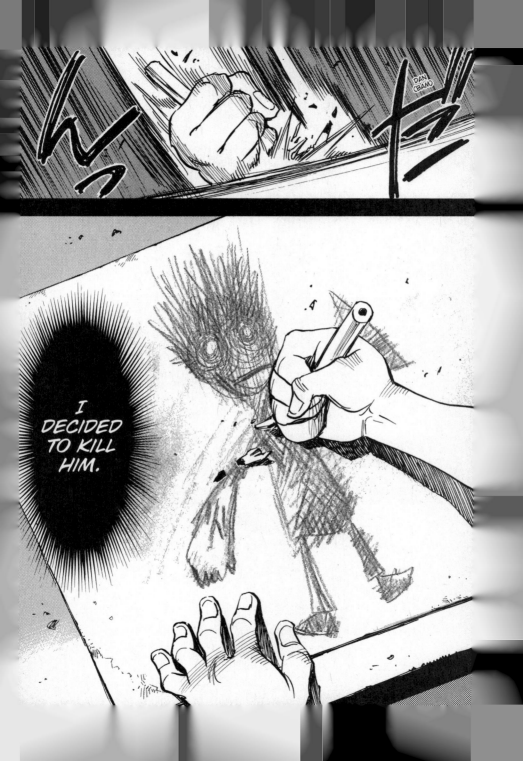

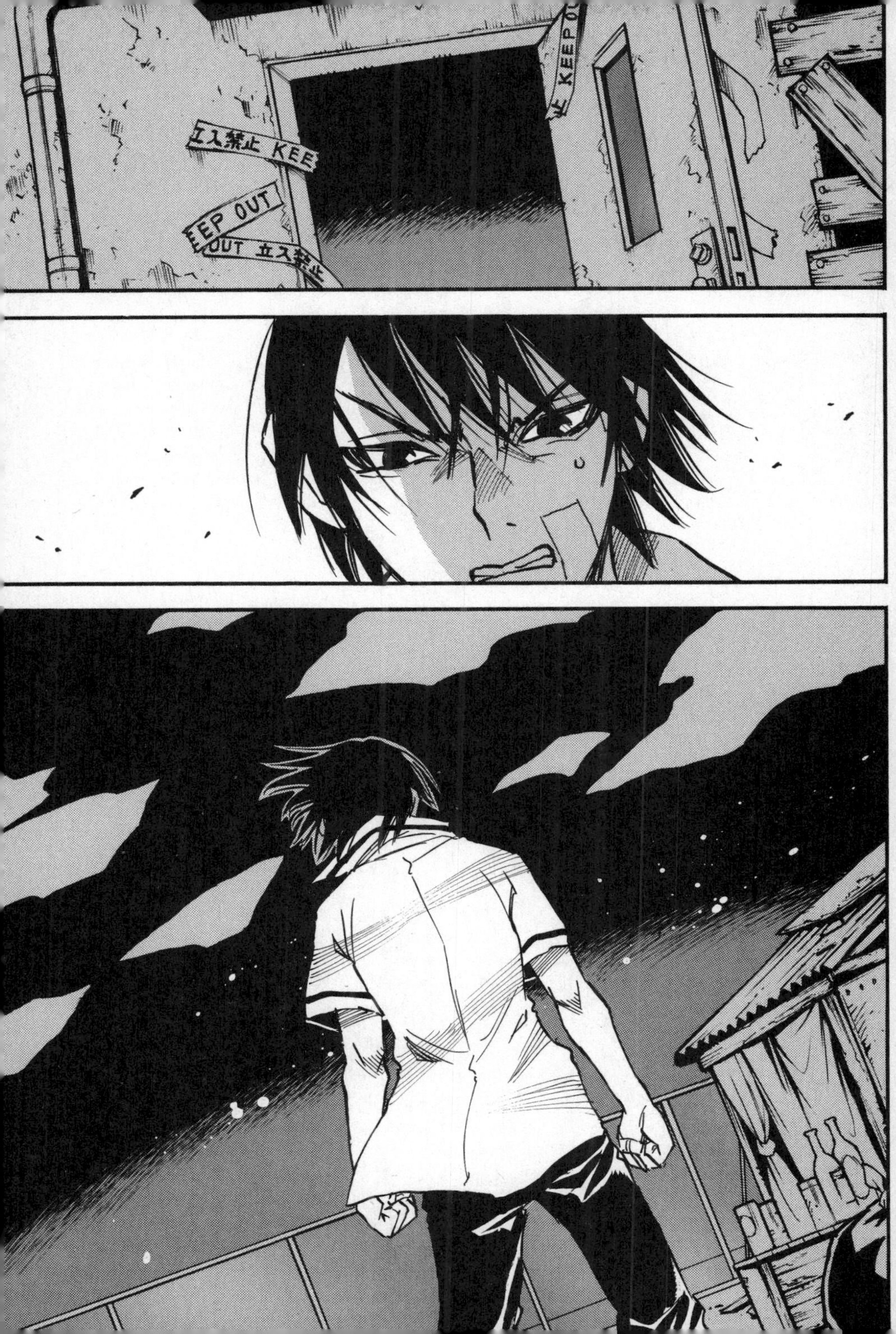KEEP OU
入禁止 KEE
EEP OUT
OUT 立入禁止

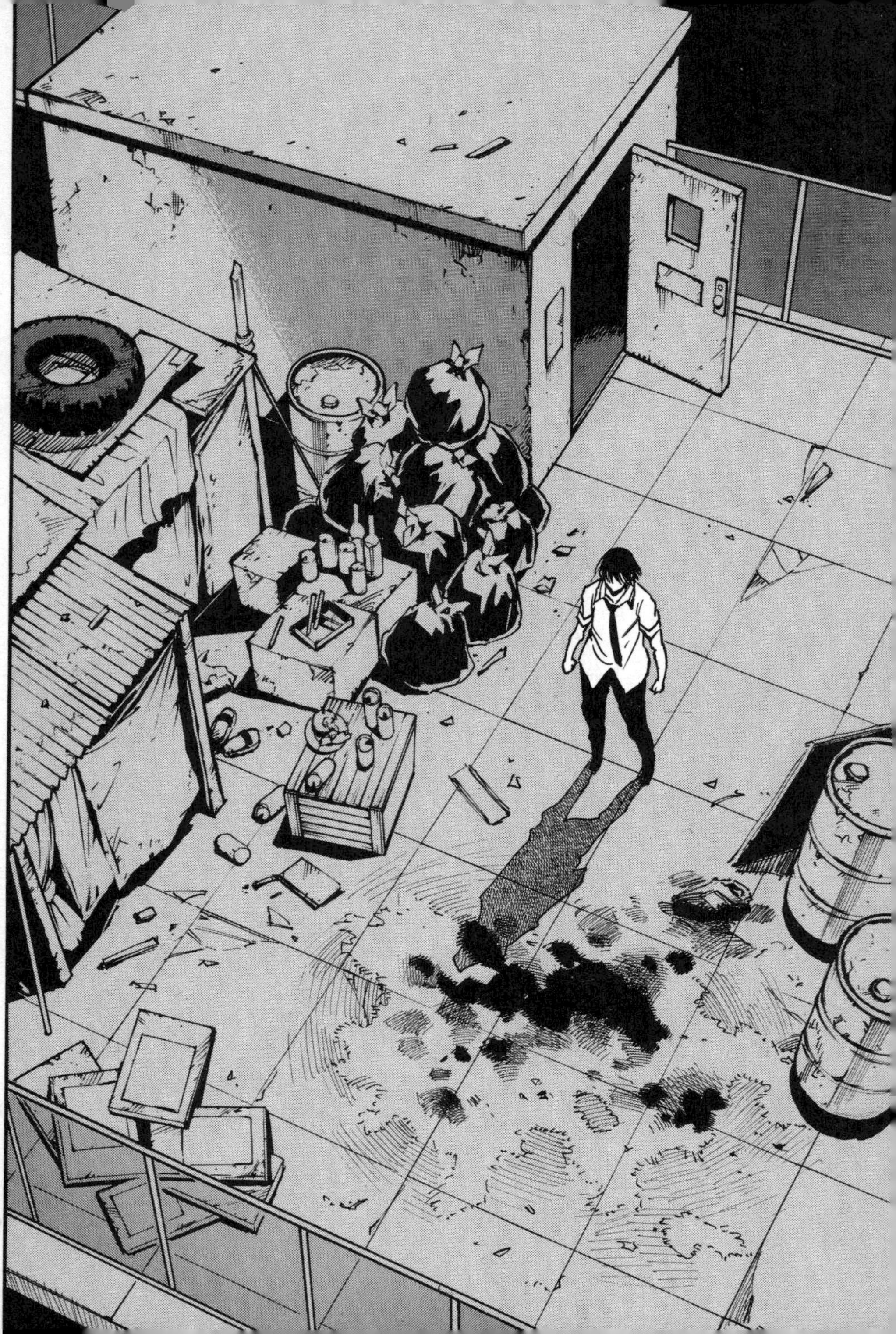

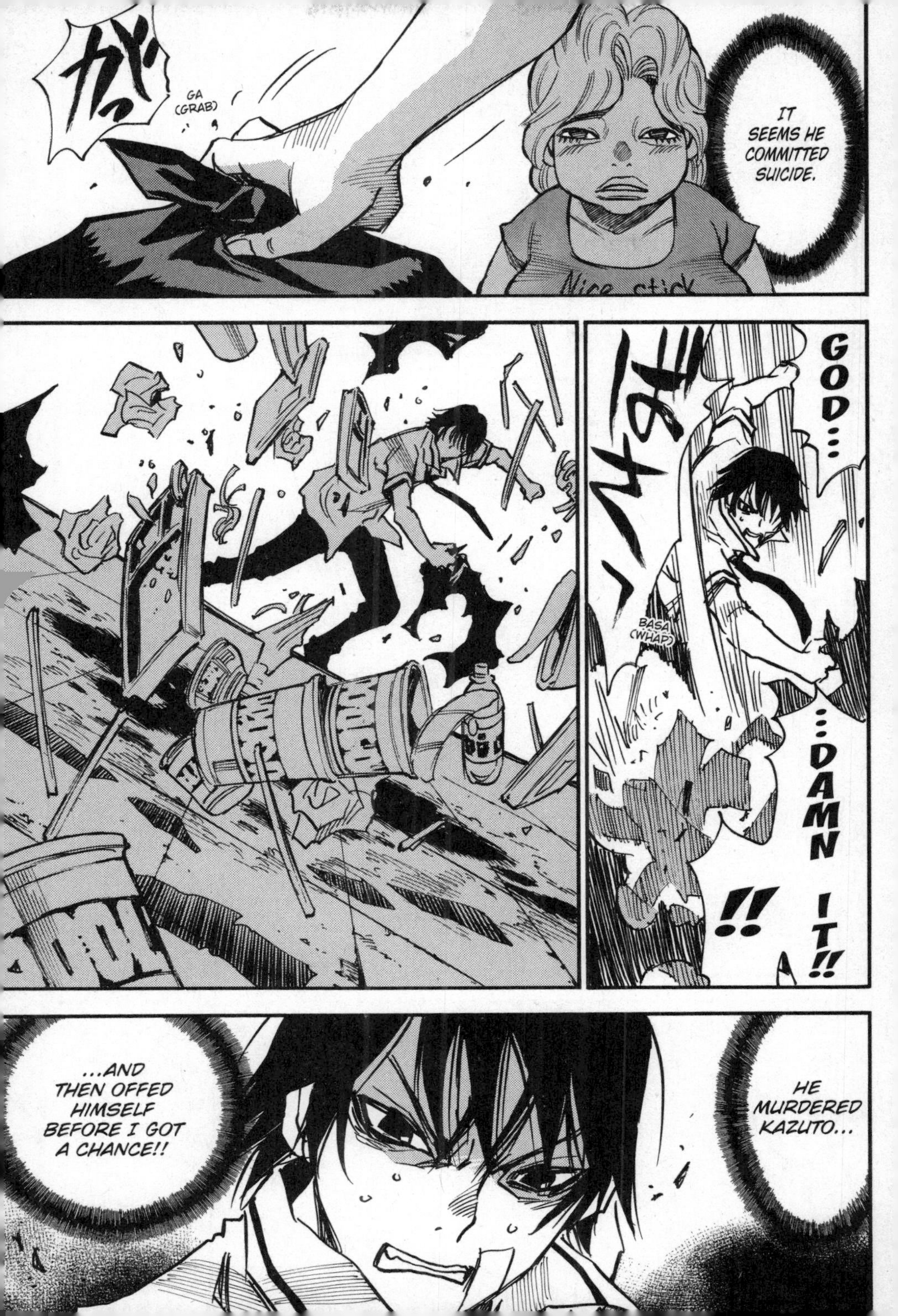

IT SEEMS HE COMMITTED SUICIDE.
Nice stick
がっ
GA (GRAB)
GOD...
...DAMN IT!!
!!
BASA (WHAP)
HE MURDERED KAZUTO...
...AND THEN OFFED HIMSELF BEFORE I GOT A CHANCE!!

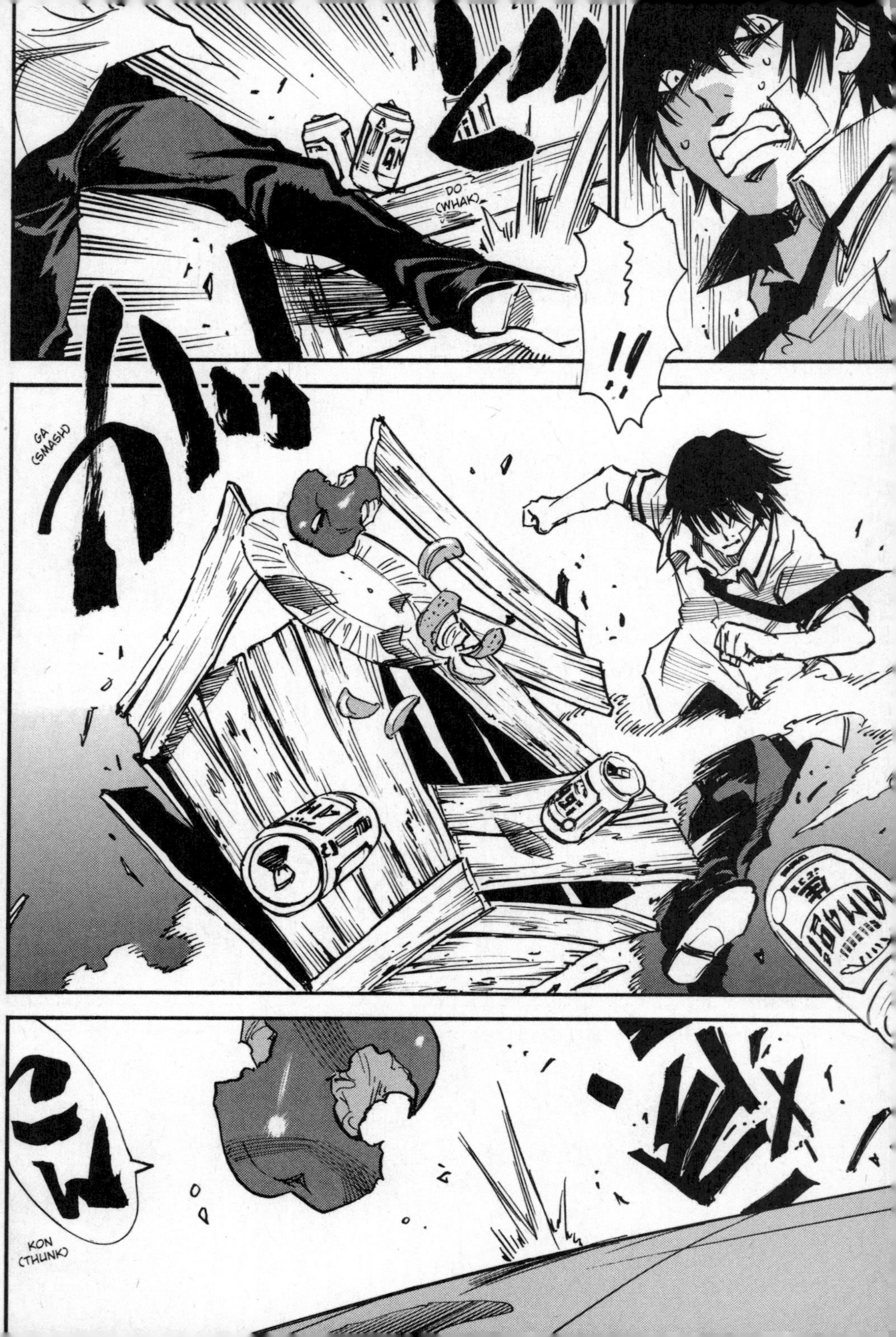
DO (WHAK)
GA (SMASH)
KON (THUNK)

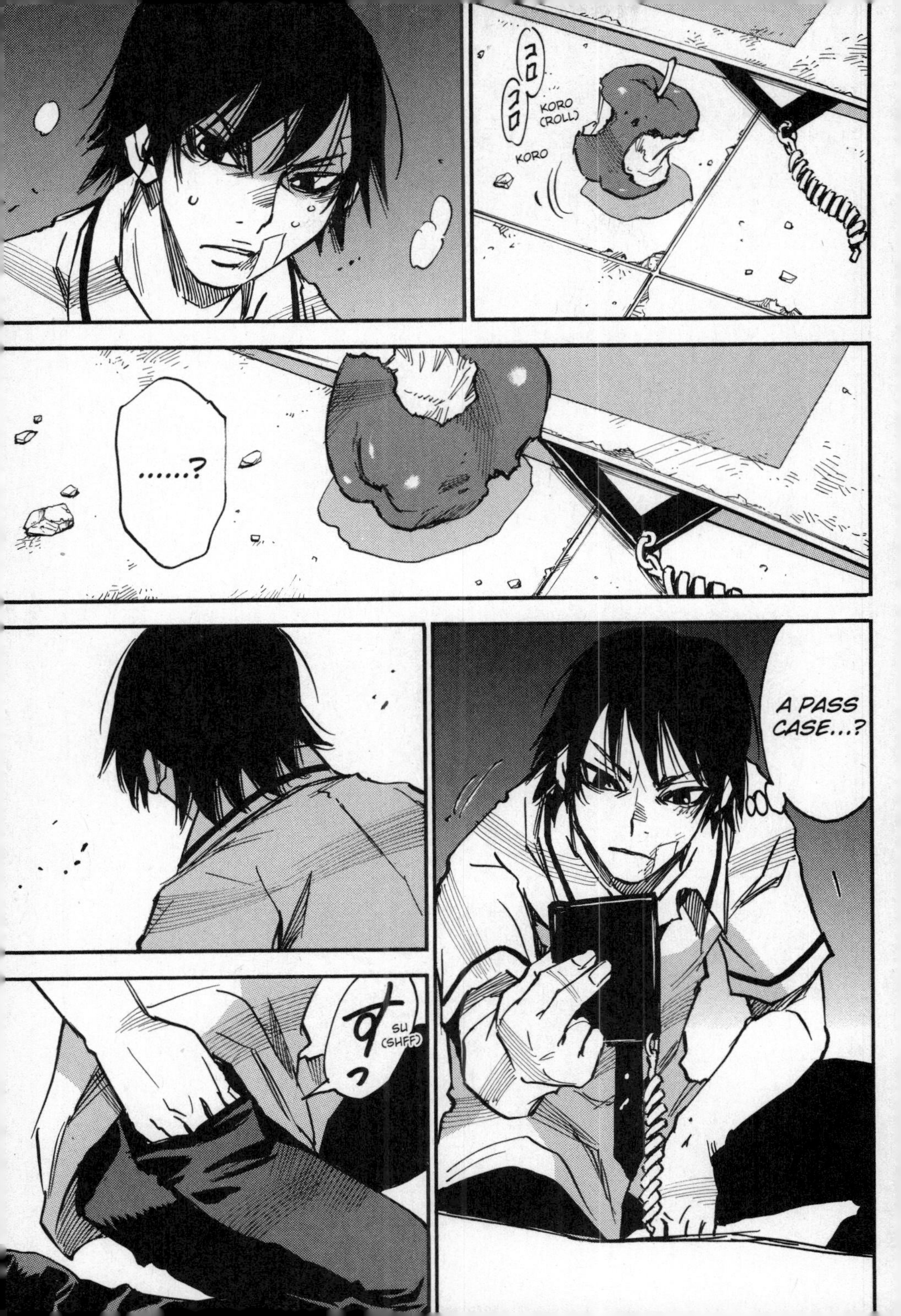
コロ
コロ
KORO (ROLL)
KORO
......?
A PASS CASE...?
すっ
SU (SHFF)

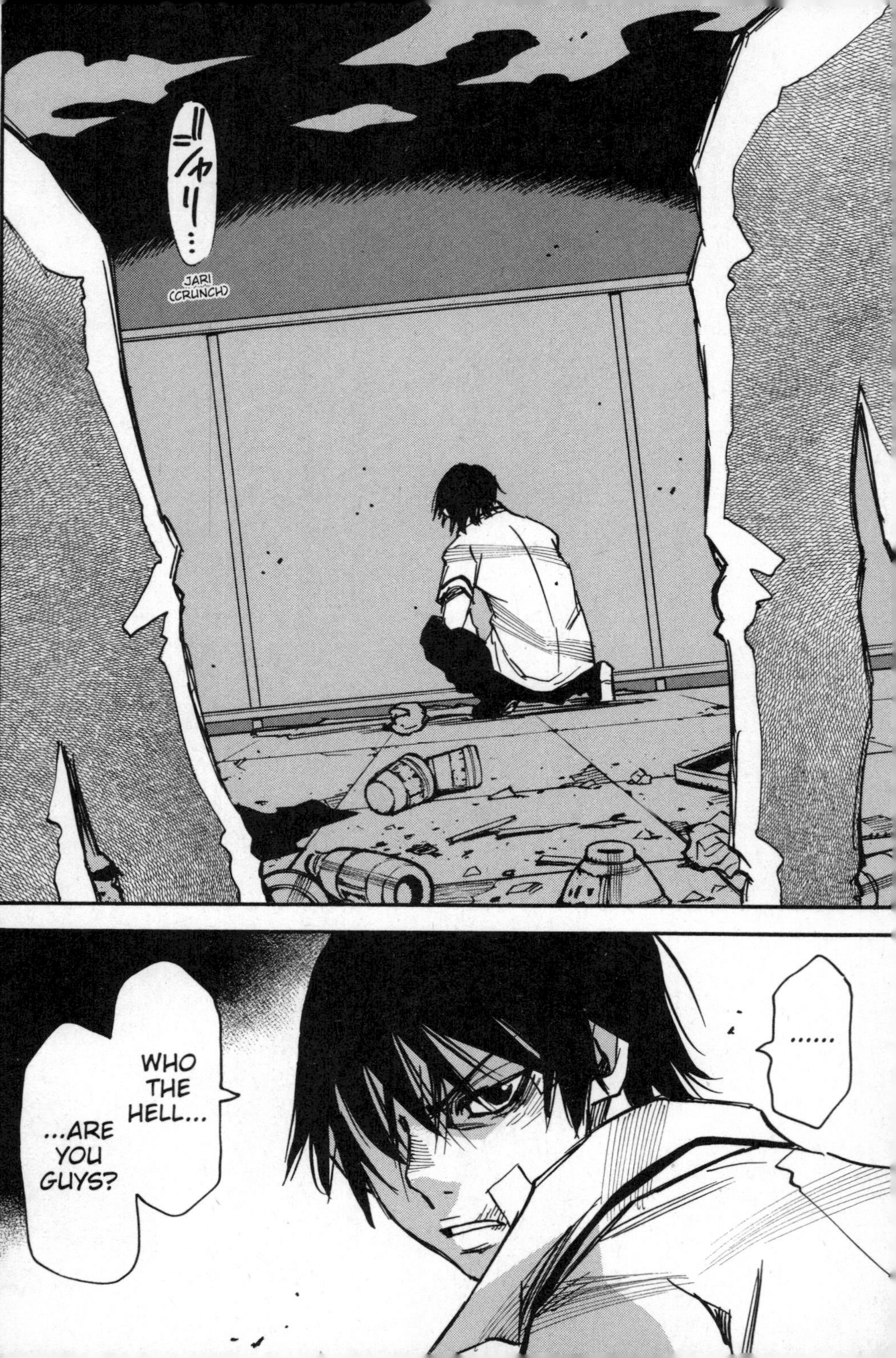
ジャリ…
JARI (CRUNCH)
......
WHO THE HELL...
...ARE YOU GUYS?

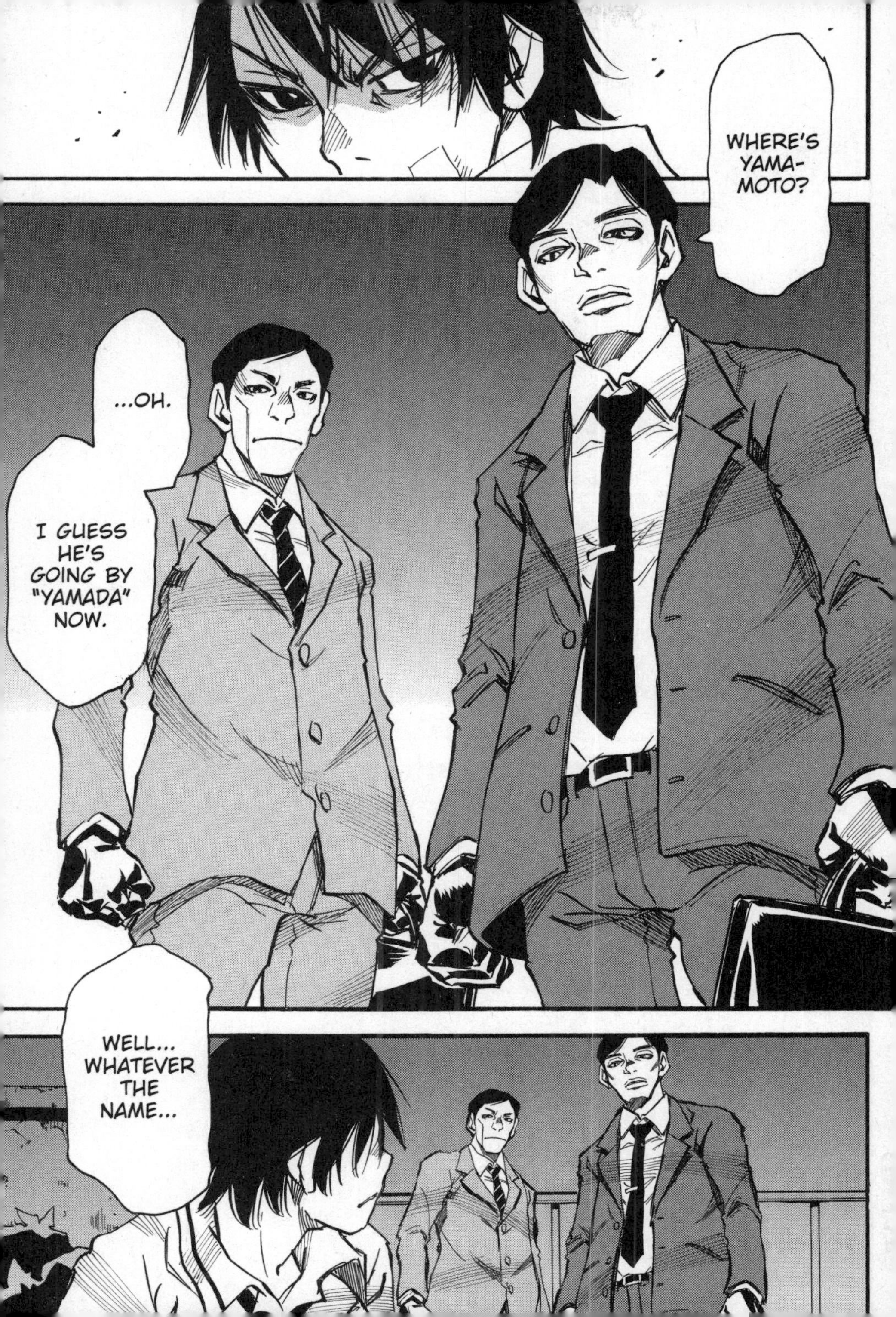
WHERE'S YAMA-MOTO?
...OH.
I GUESS HE'S GOING BY "YAMADA" NOW.
WELL... WHATEVER THE NAME...

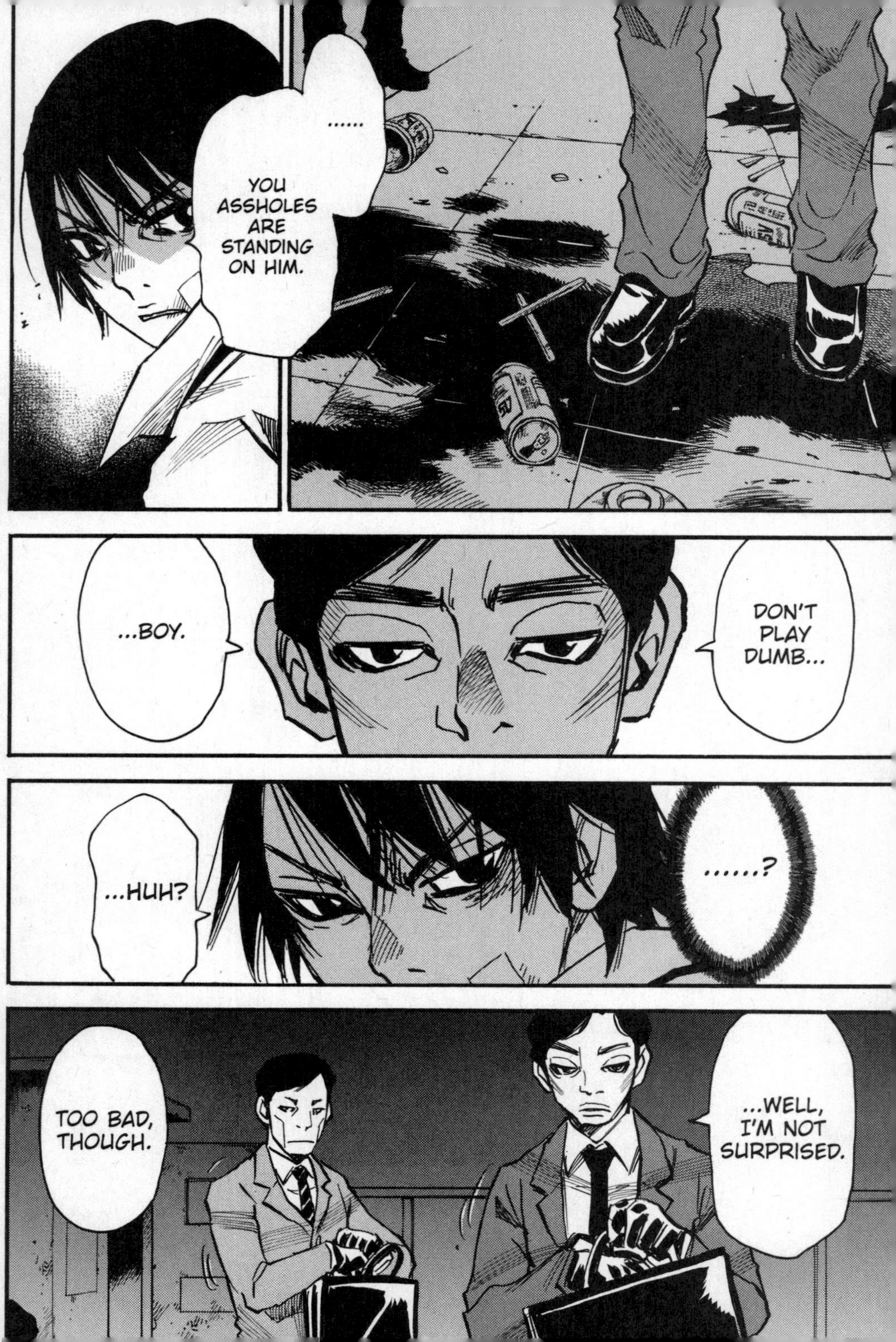
......
YOU ASSHOLES ARE STANDING ON HIM.
DON'T PLAY DUMB...
...BOY.
......?
...HUH?
...WELL, I'M NOT SURPRISED.
TOO BAD, THOUGH.

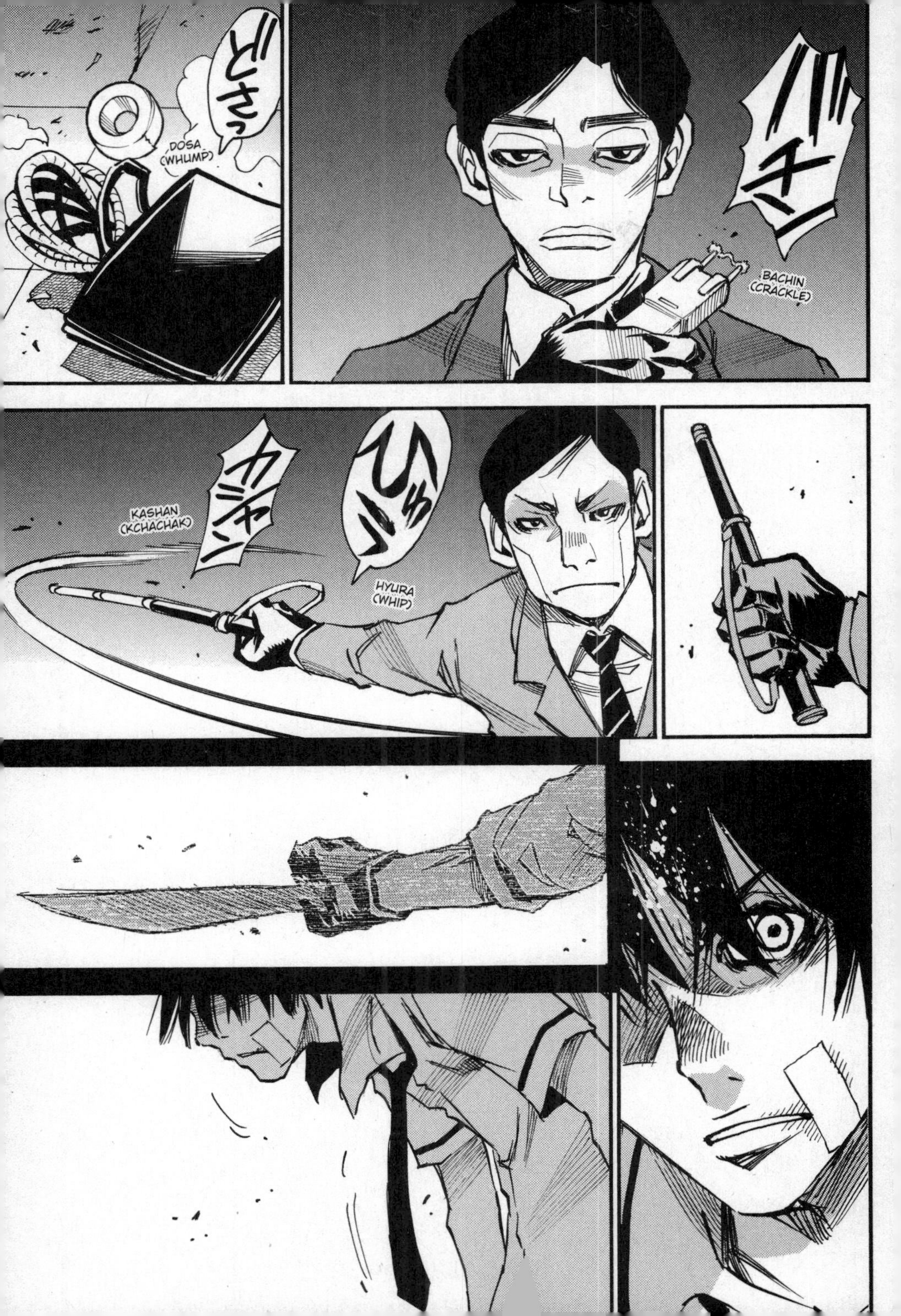
バチン
BACHIN (CRACKLE)
どさっ
DOSA (WHUMP)
ひゅらっ
HYURA (WHIP)
カシャン
KASHAN (KCHACHAK)

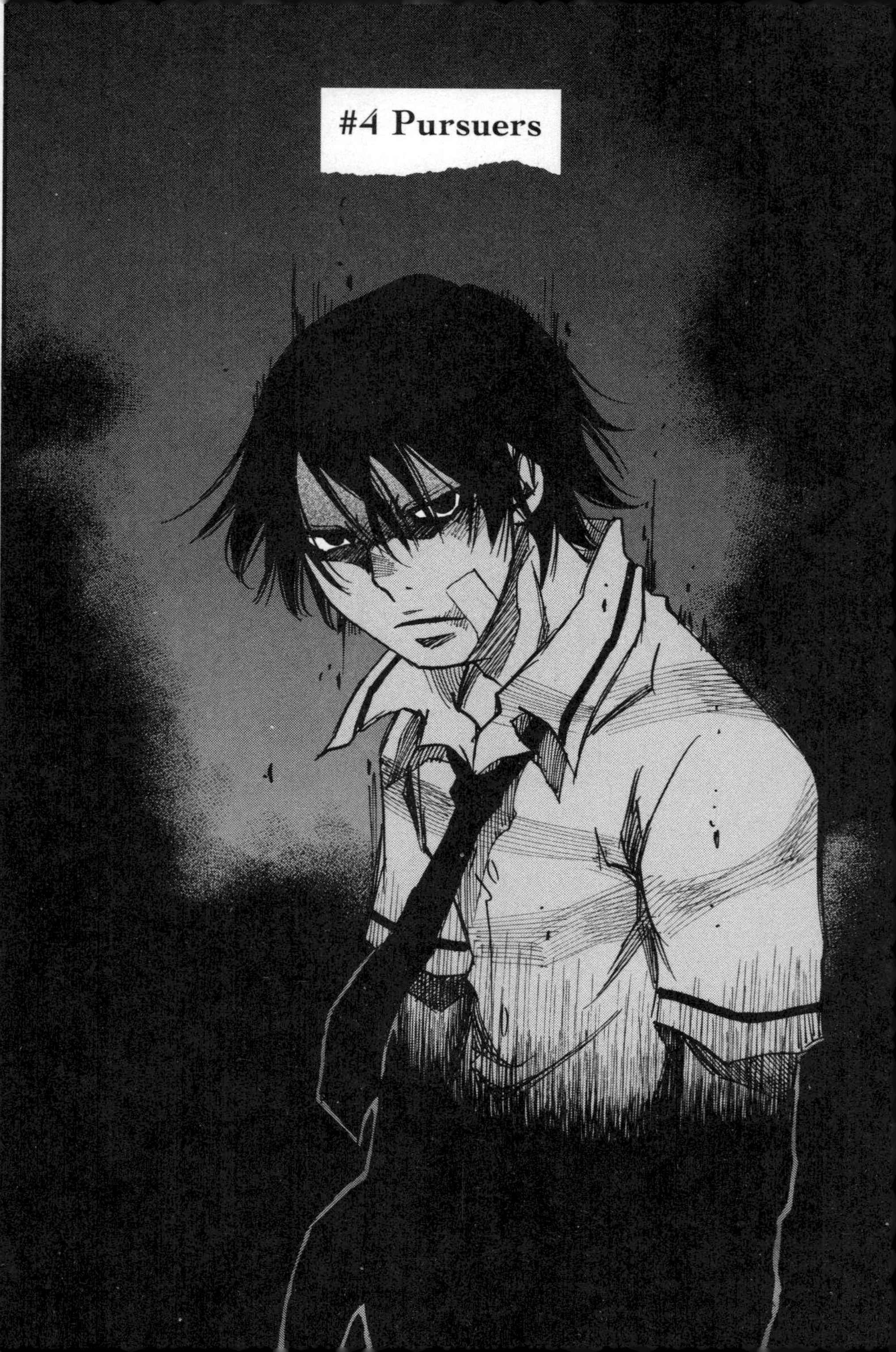
#4 Pursuers

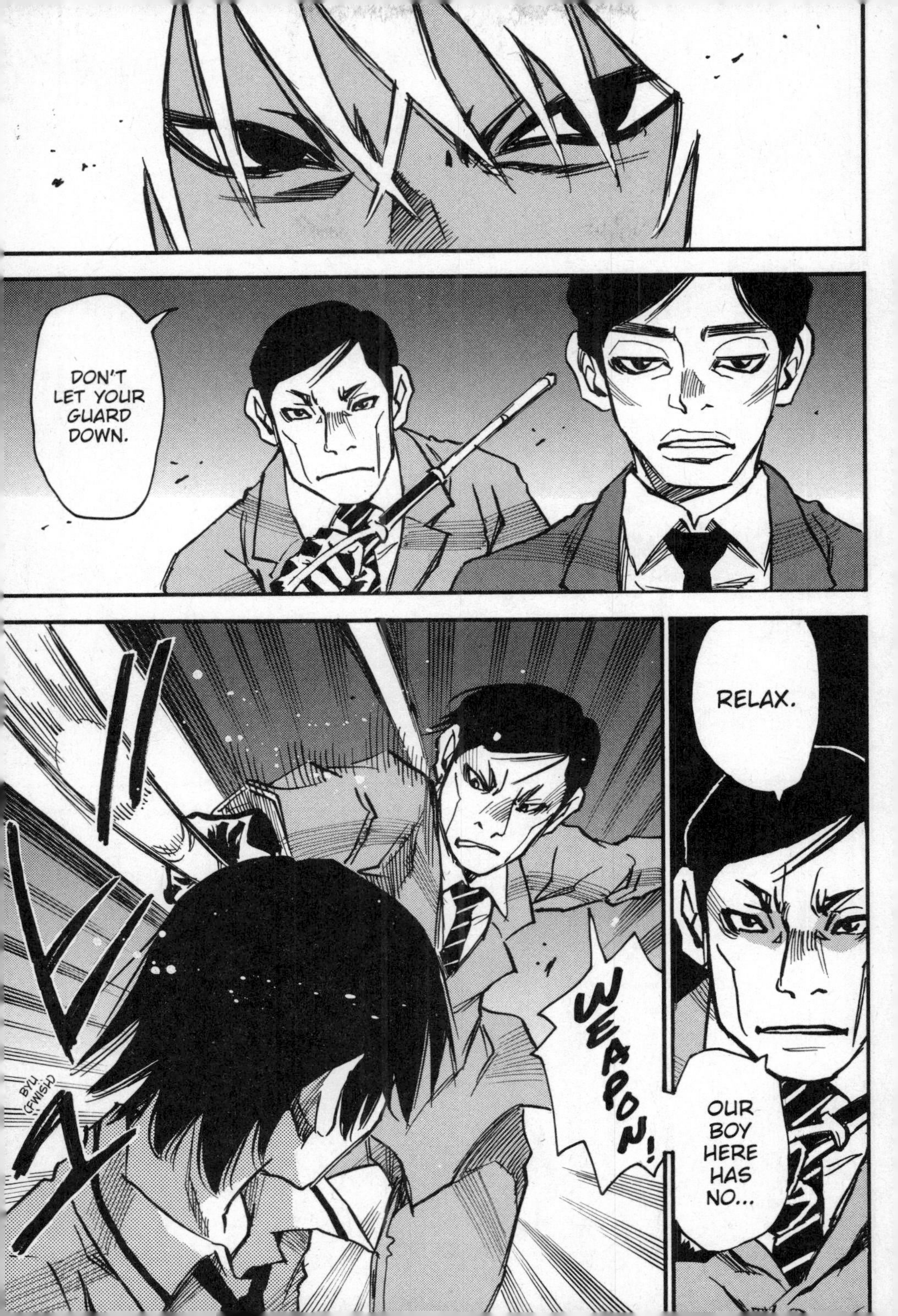
DON'T LET YOUR GUARD DOWN.
RELAX.
OUR BOY HERE HAS NO...
WEAPON!
BYU (FWISH)

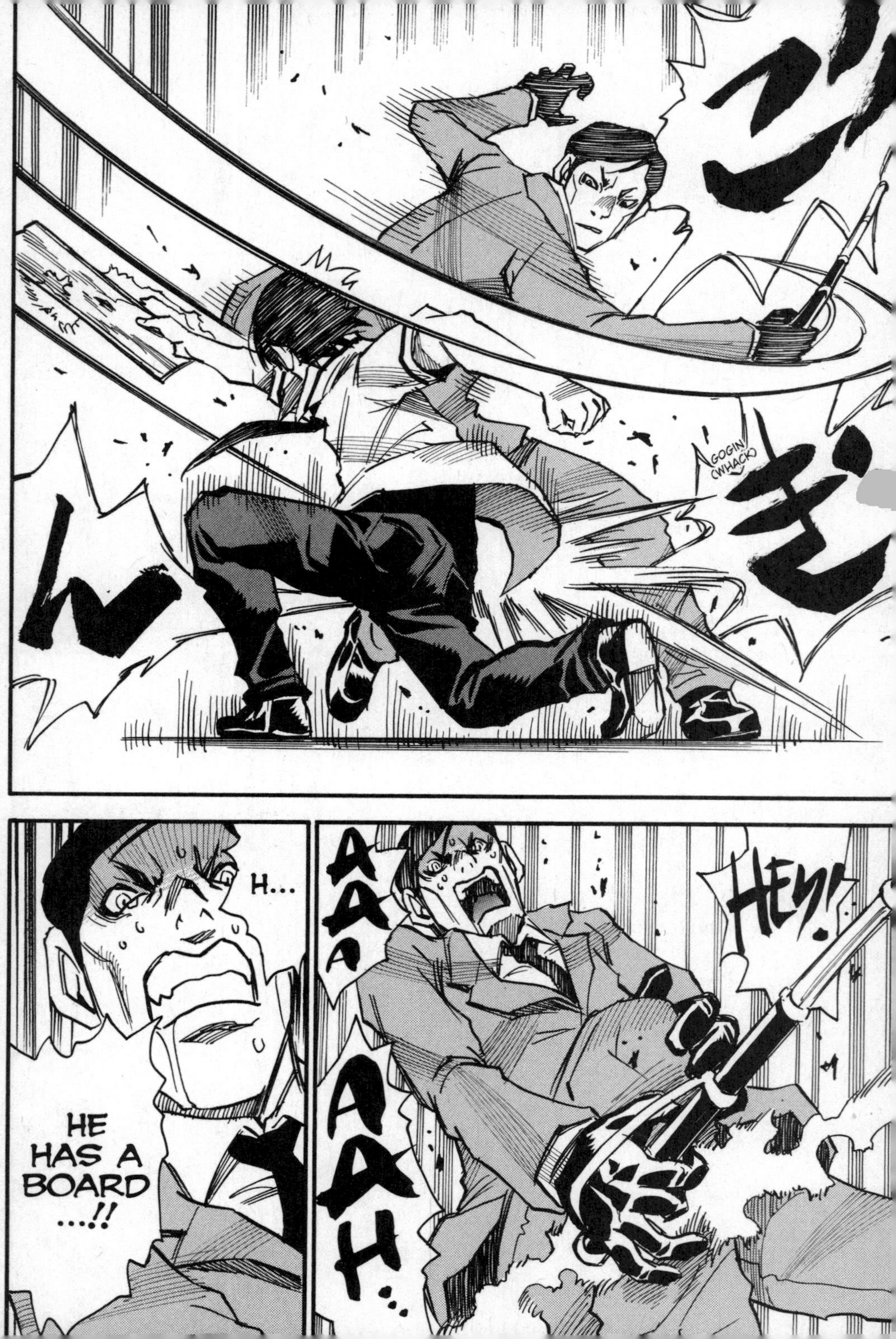
GOGIN (WHACK)
HEY!
AAAAAH...
H...
HE HAS A BOARD ...!!

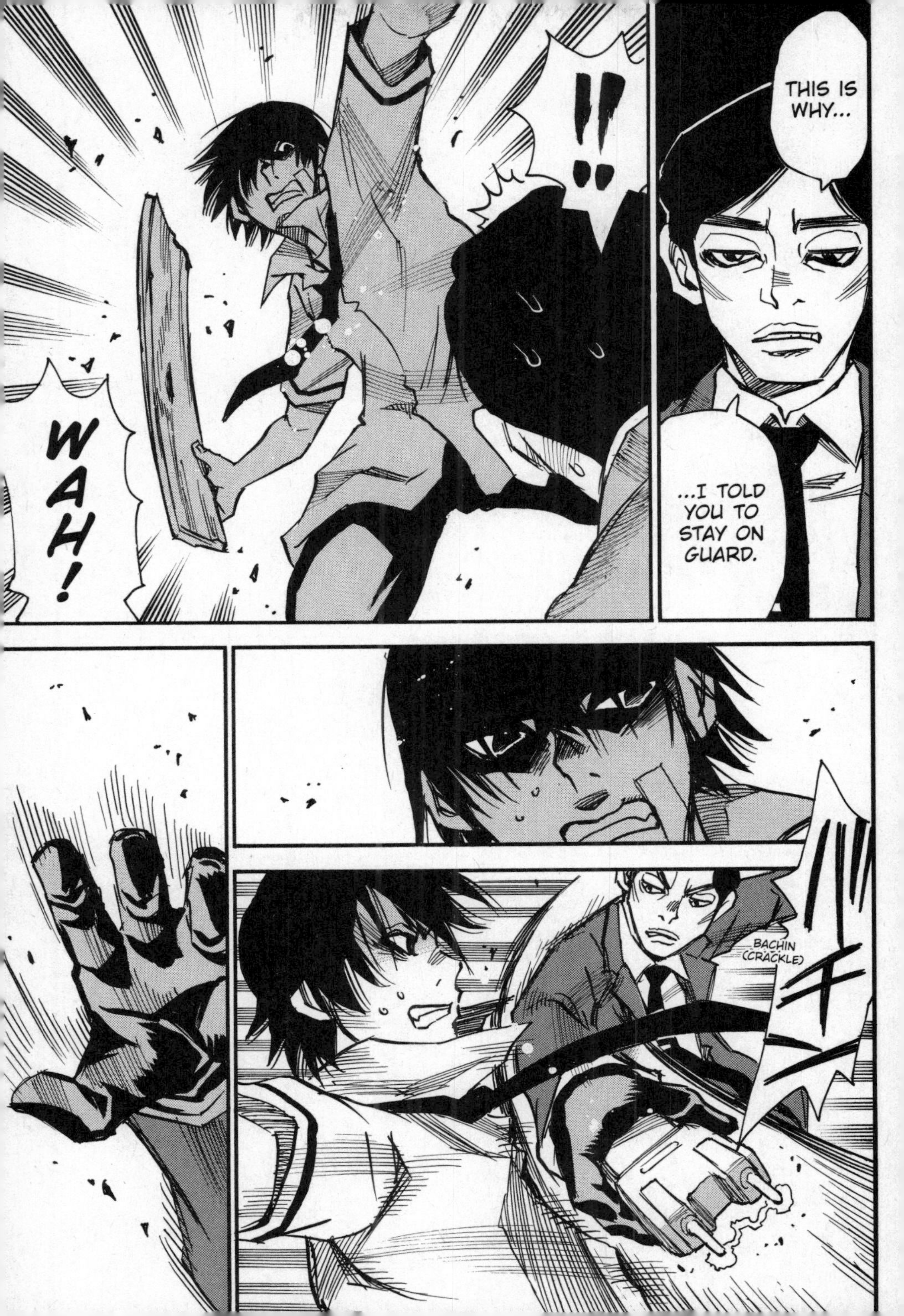
THIS IS WHY...
...I TOLD YOU TO STAY ON GUARD.
!!
WAH!
BACHIN (CRACKLE)

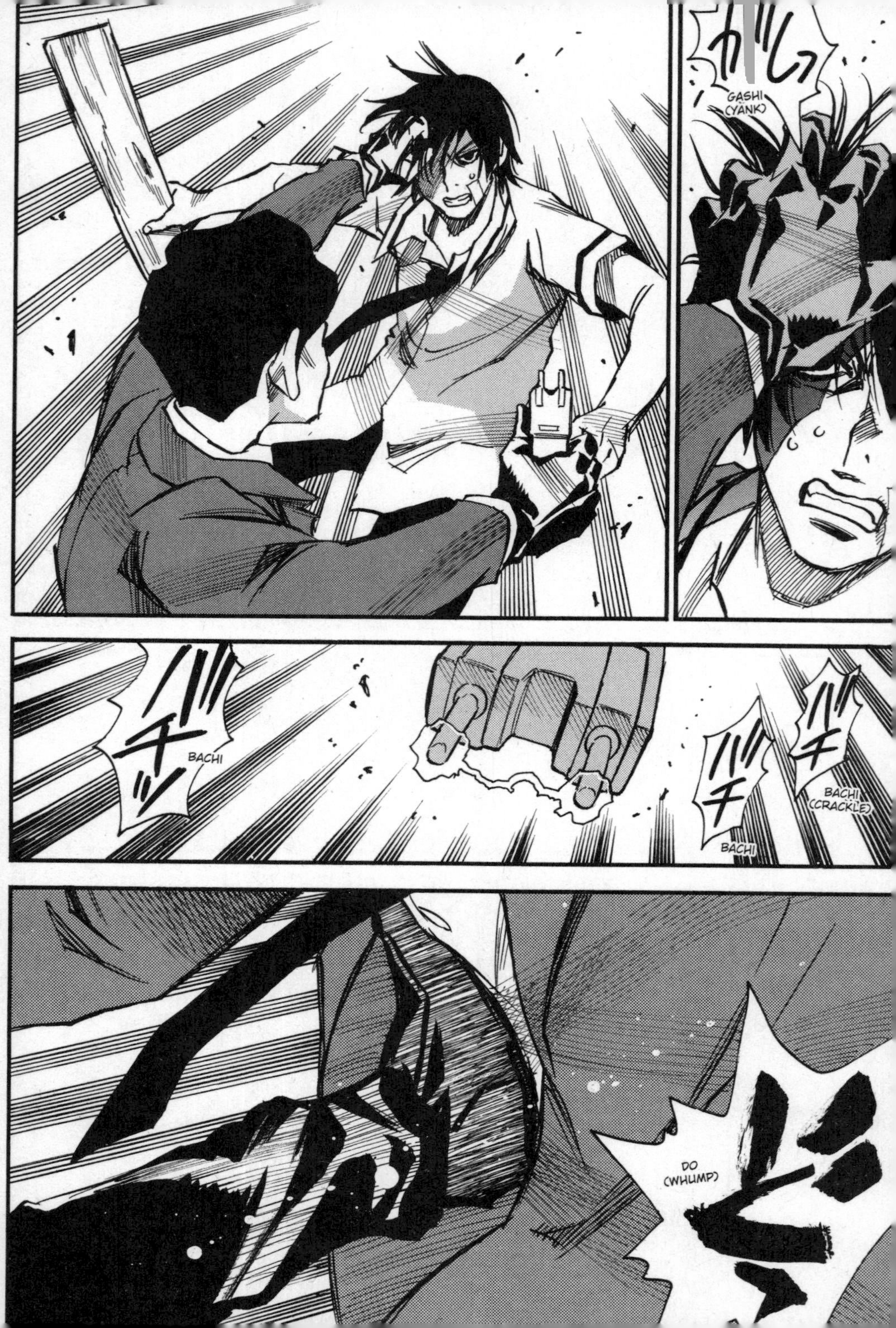

ガシッ
GASHI (YANK)
バチ
BACHI (CRACKLE)
バチ
BACHI
バチッ
BACHI
DO (WHUMP)

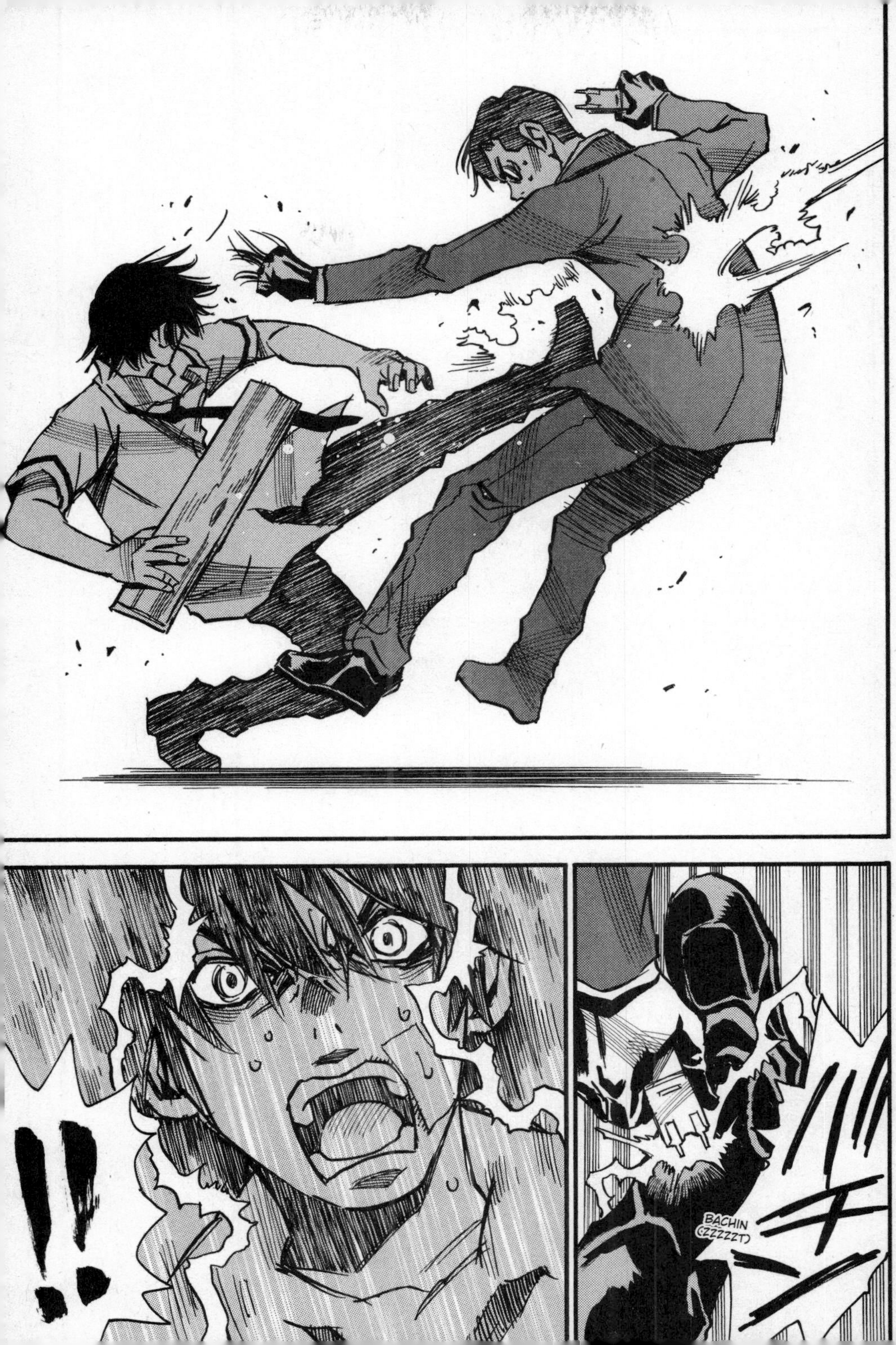
BACHIN
(ZZZZZT)
!!

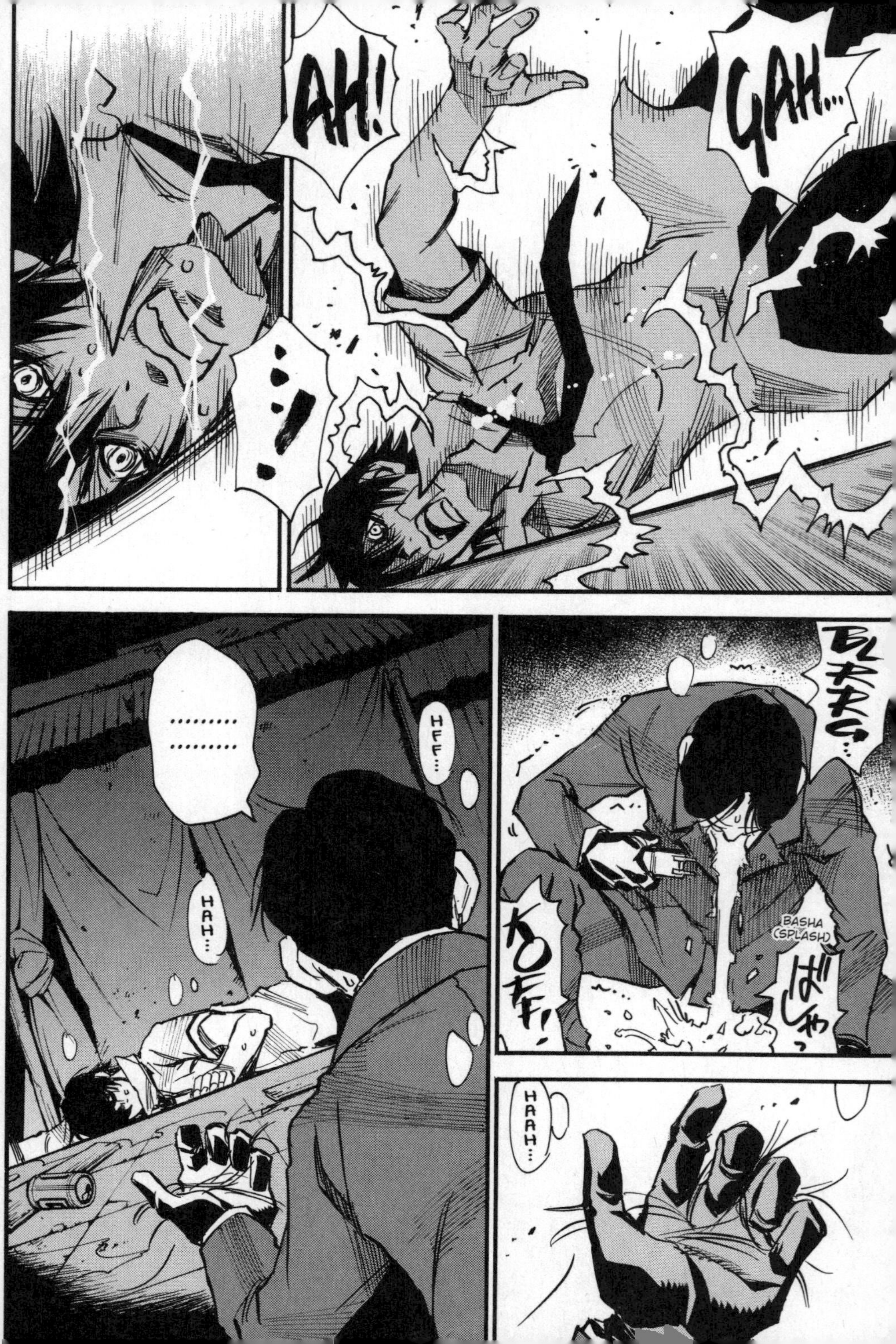
AH!
GAH...
!!
BLRRRG...
KOFF!
BASHA (SPLASH)
ばしゃっ
HAAH...
....
....
HFF...
HAH...

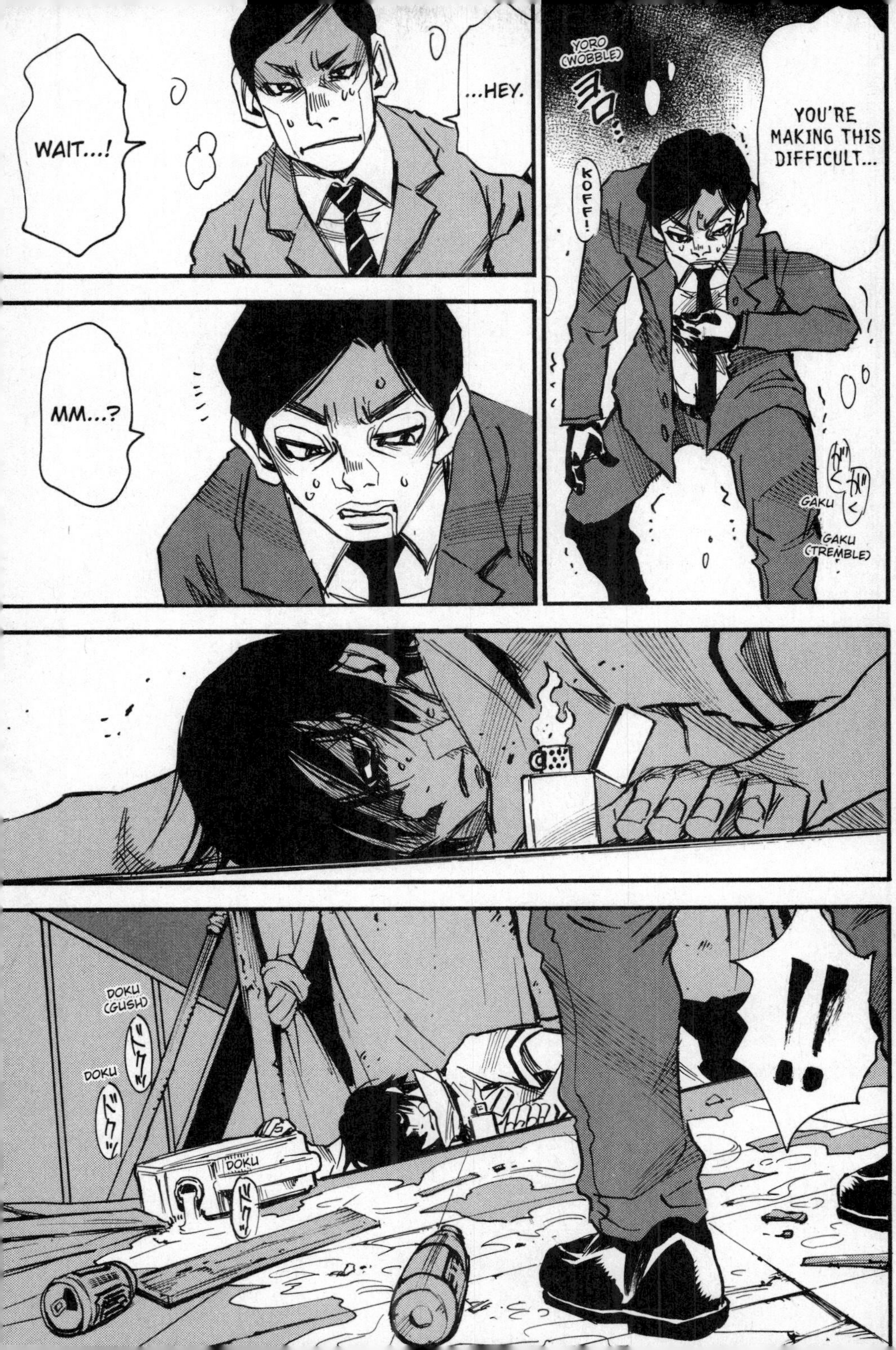
YOU'RE MAKING THIS DIFFICULT...
YORO (WOBBLE)
ヨロ
KOFF!
GAKU
GAKU (TREMBLE)
...HEY.
WAIT...!
MM...?
!!
DOKU (GUSH)
DOKU
DOKU

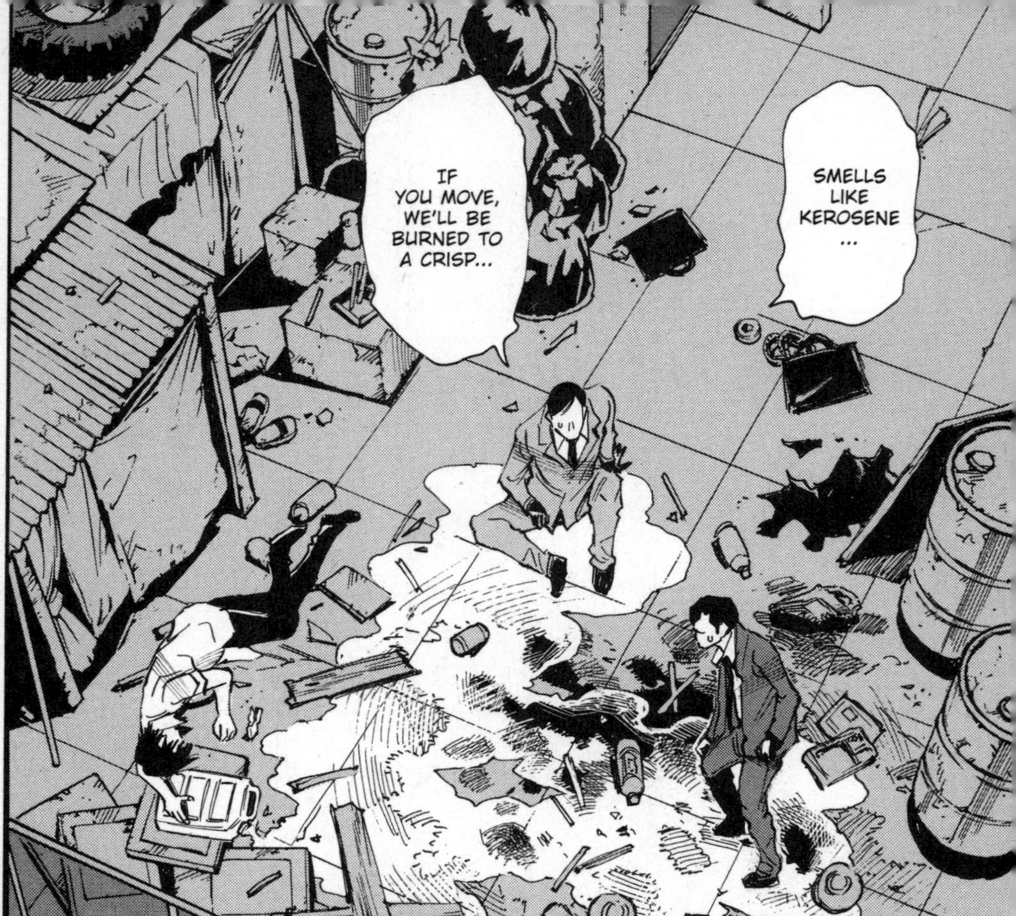
SMELLS LIKE KEROSENE ...
IF YOU MOVE, WE'LL BE BURNED TO A CRISP...
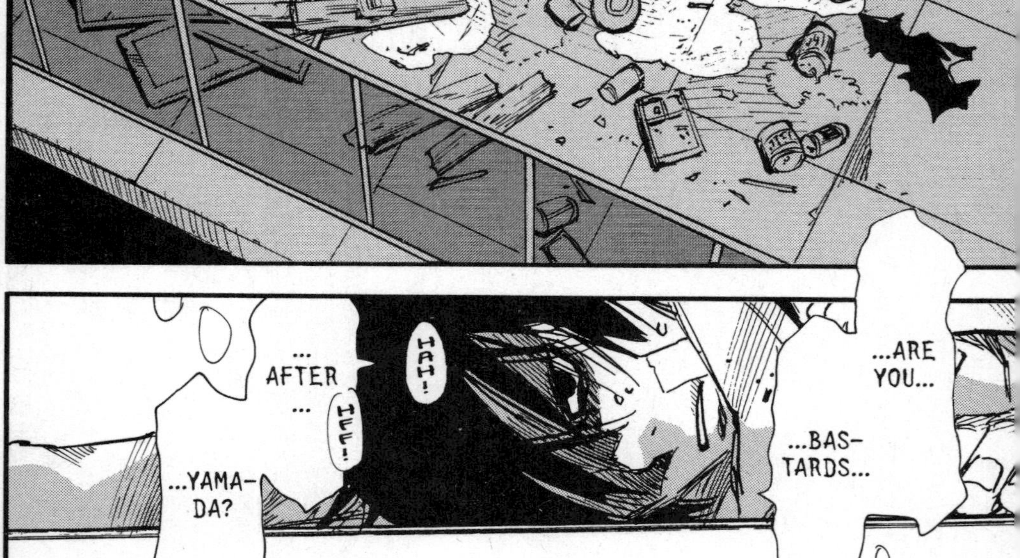
...ARE YOU...
...BAS-TARDS...
HAH!
HFF!
... AFTER ...
...YAMA-DA?

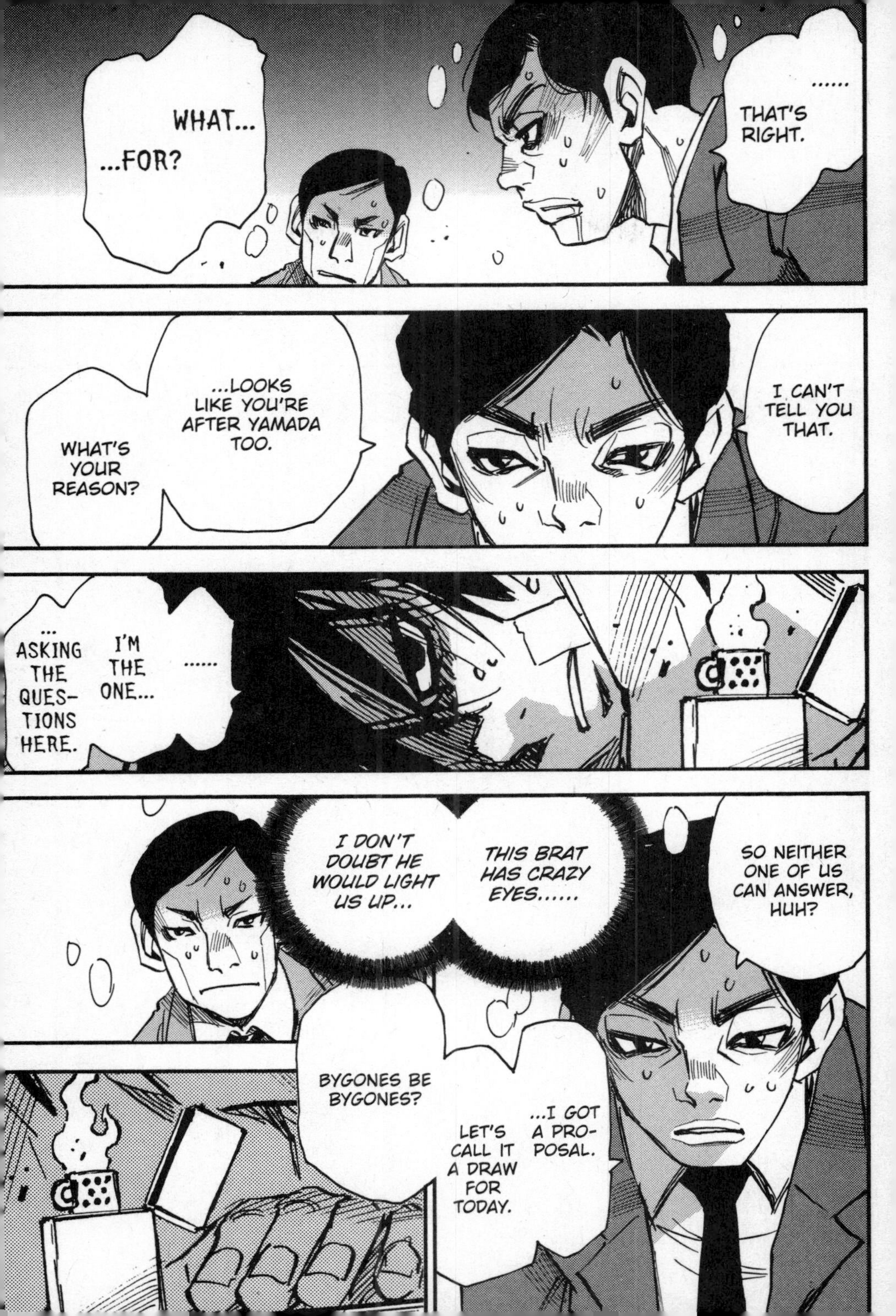
......
THAT'S RIGHT.
WHAT... ...FOR?
I CAN'T TELL YOU THAT.
...LOOKS LIKE YOU'RE AFTER YAMADA TOO.
WHAT'S YOUR REASON?
......
I'M THE ONE...
...ASKING THE QUES-TIONS HERE.
SO NEITHER ONE OF US CAN ANSWER, HUH?
THIS BRAT HAS CRAZY EYES......
I DON'T DOUBT HE WOULD LIGHT US UP...
...I GOT A PRO-POSAL.
LET'S CALL IT A DRAW FOR TODAY.
BYGONES BE BYGONES?

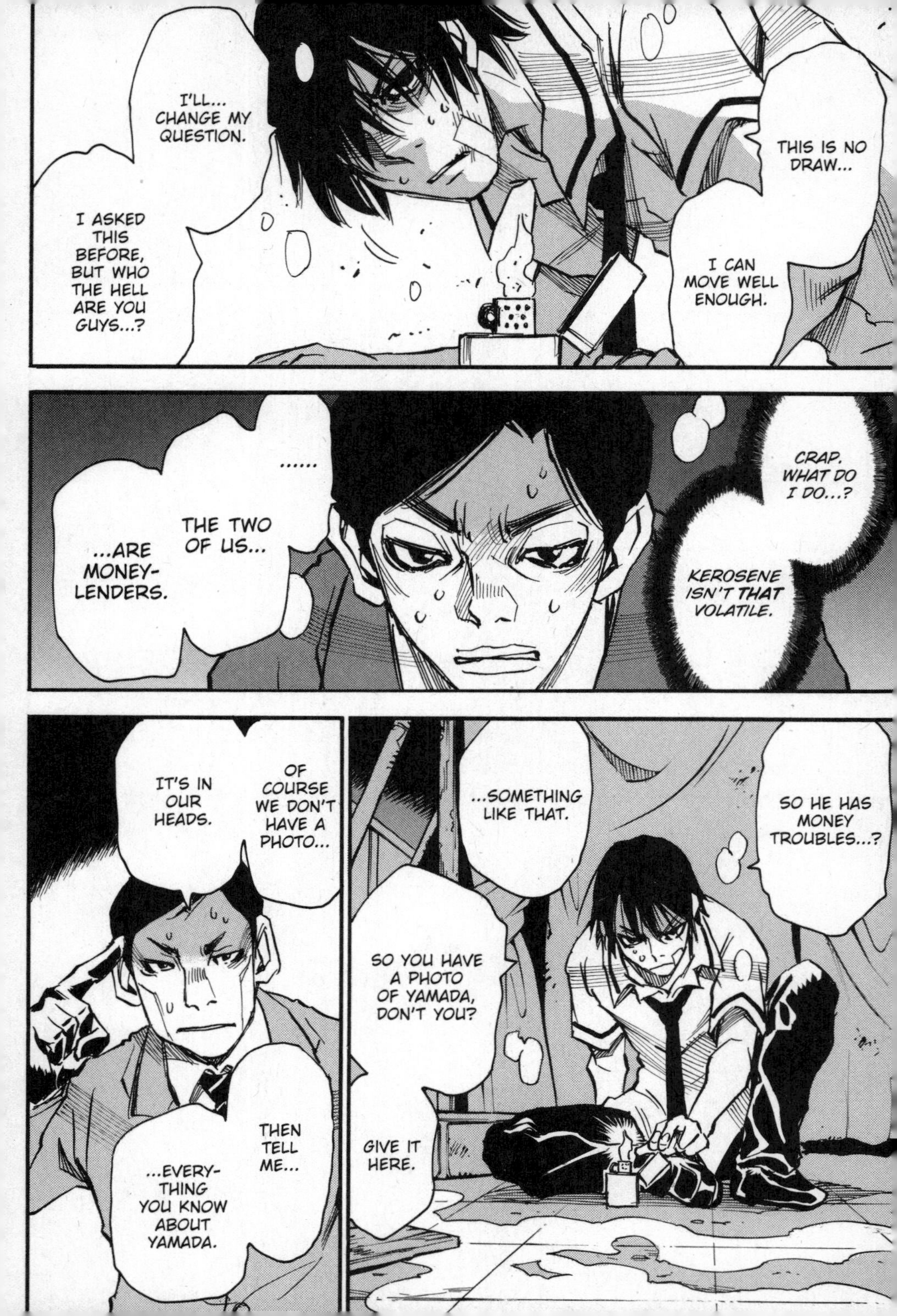
THIS IS NO DRAW...
I CAN MOVE WELL ENOUGH.
I'LL... CHANGE MY QUESTION.
I ASKED THIS BEFORE, BUT WHO THE HELL ARE YOU GUYS...?
CRAP. WHAT DO I DO...?
KEROSENE ISN'T THAT VOLATILE.
......
THE TWO OF US...
...ARE MONEY-LENDERS.
SO HE HAS MONEY TROUBLES...?
...SOMETHING LIKE THAT.
SO YOU HAVE A PHOTO OF YAMADA, DON'T YOU?
GIVE IT HERE.
OF COURSE WE DON'T HAVE A PHOTO...
IT'S IN OUR HEADS.
THEN TELL ME...
...EVERY-THING YOU KNOW ABOUT YAMADA.

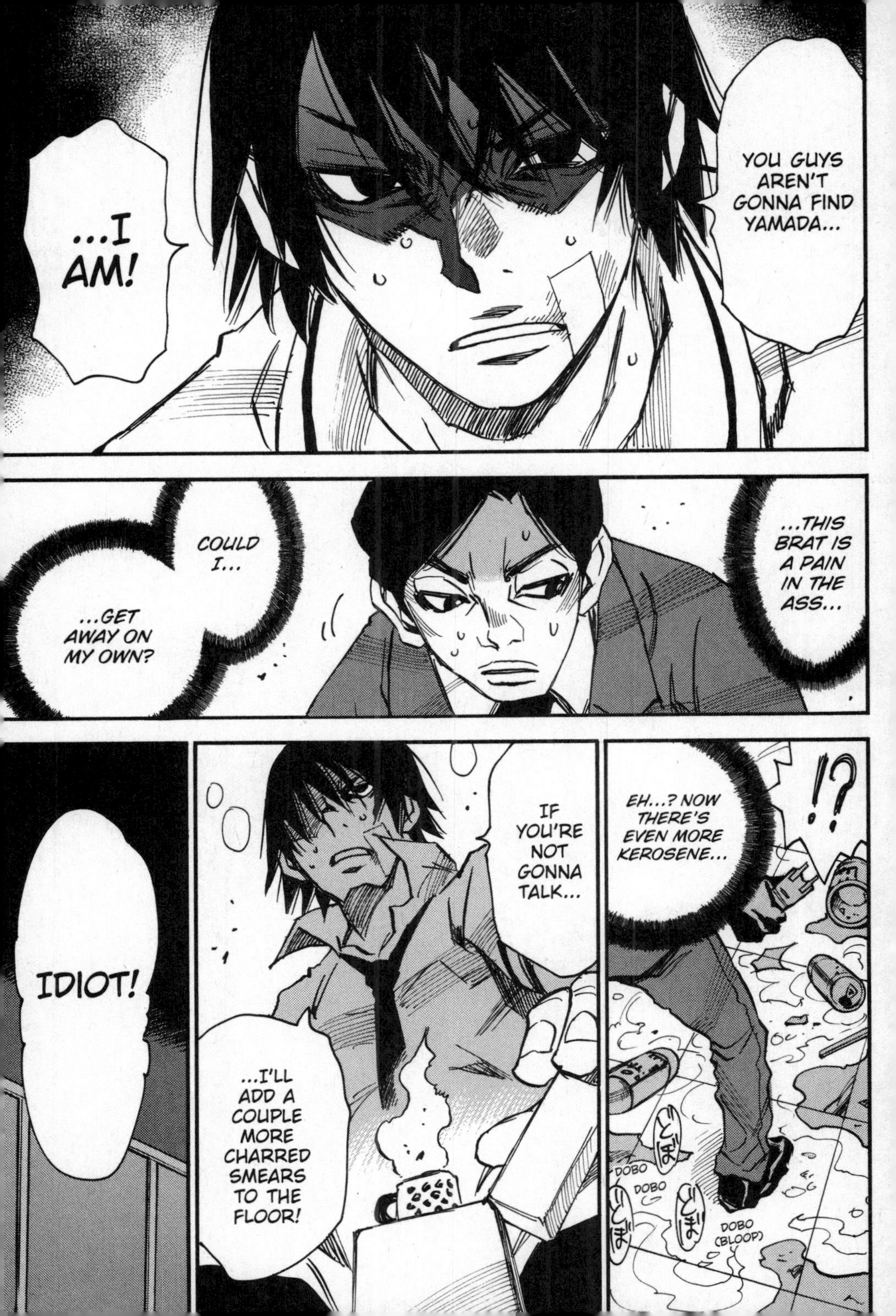
YOU GUYS AREN'T GONNA FIND YAMADA...
...I AM!
...THIS BRAT IS A PAIN IN THE ASS...
COULD I...
...GET AWAY ON MY OWN?
!?
EH...? NOW THERE'S EVEN MORE KEROSENE...
DOBO
DOBO
DOBO (BLOOP)
IF YOU'RE NOT GONNA TALK...
...I'LL ADD A COUPLE MORE CHARRED SMEARS TO THE FLOOR!
IDIOT!

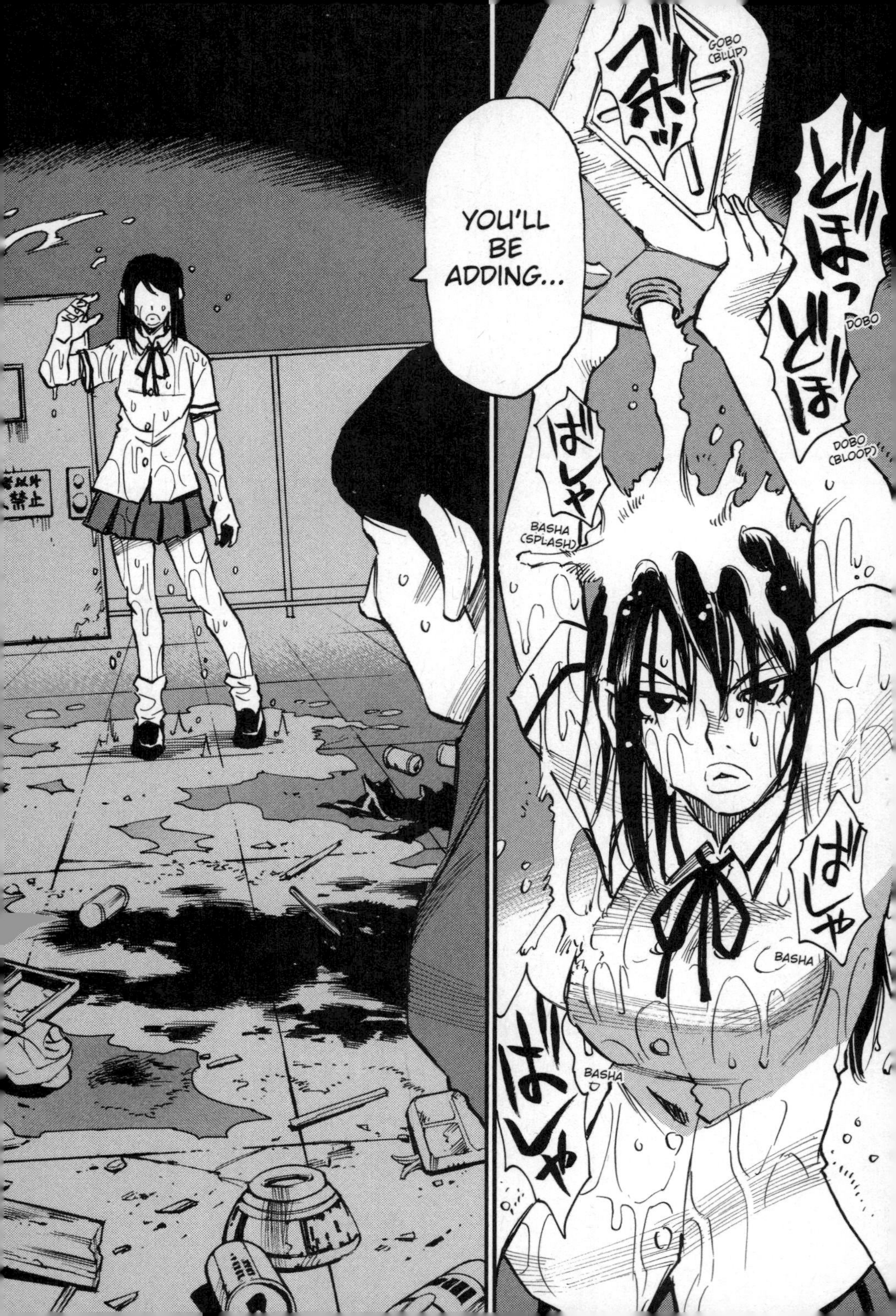
ゴボッ
GOBO (BLUP)
どぼっ
DOBO
どぼ
DOBO (BLOOP)
ばしゃ
BASHA (SPLASH)
ばしゃ
BASHA
ばしゃ
BASHA
YOU'LL BE ADDING...

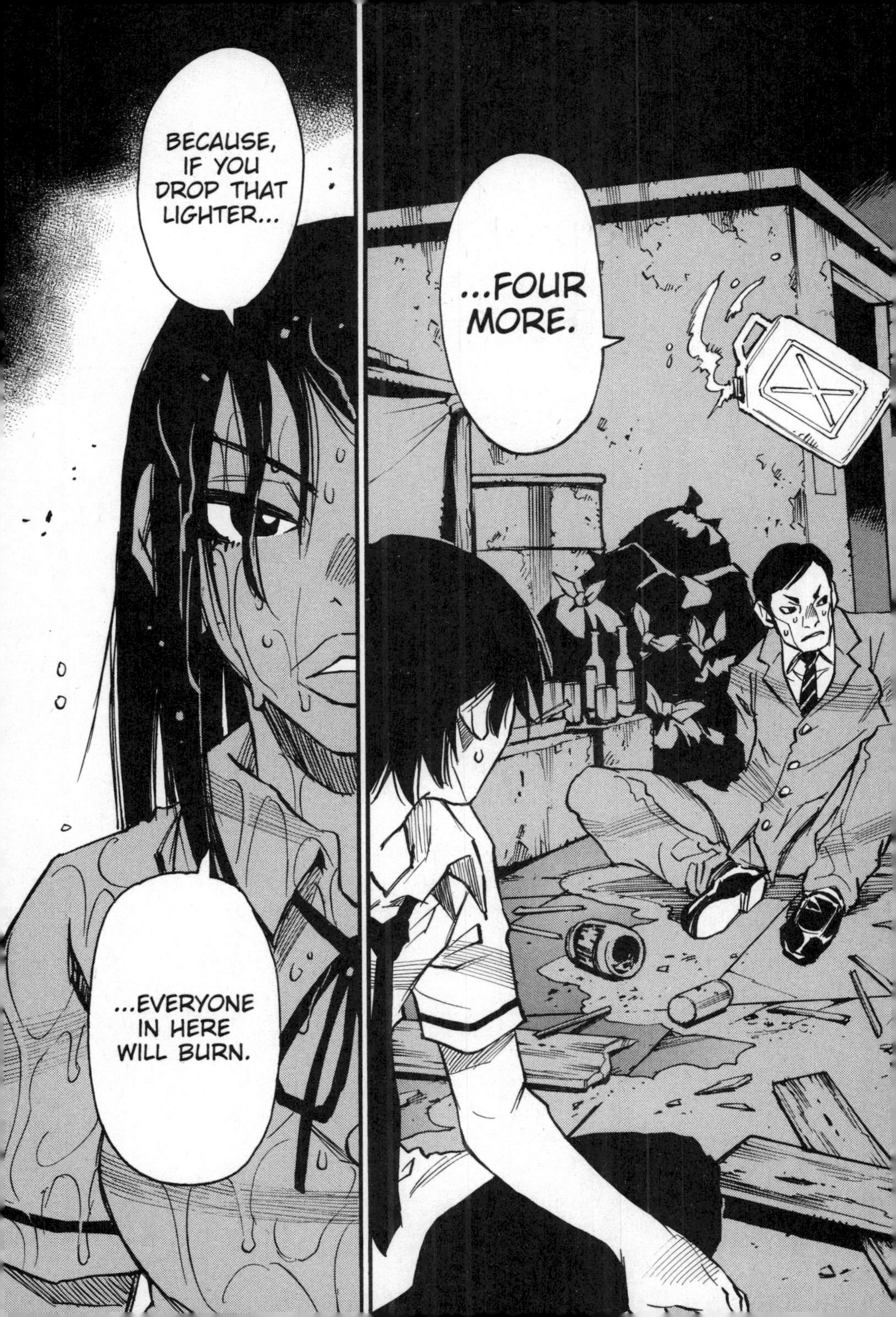
...FOUR MORE.
BECAUSE, IF YOU DROP THAT LIGHTER...
...EVERYONE IN HERE WILL BURN.

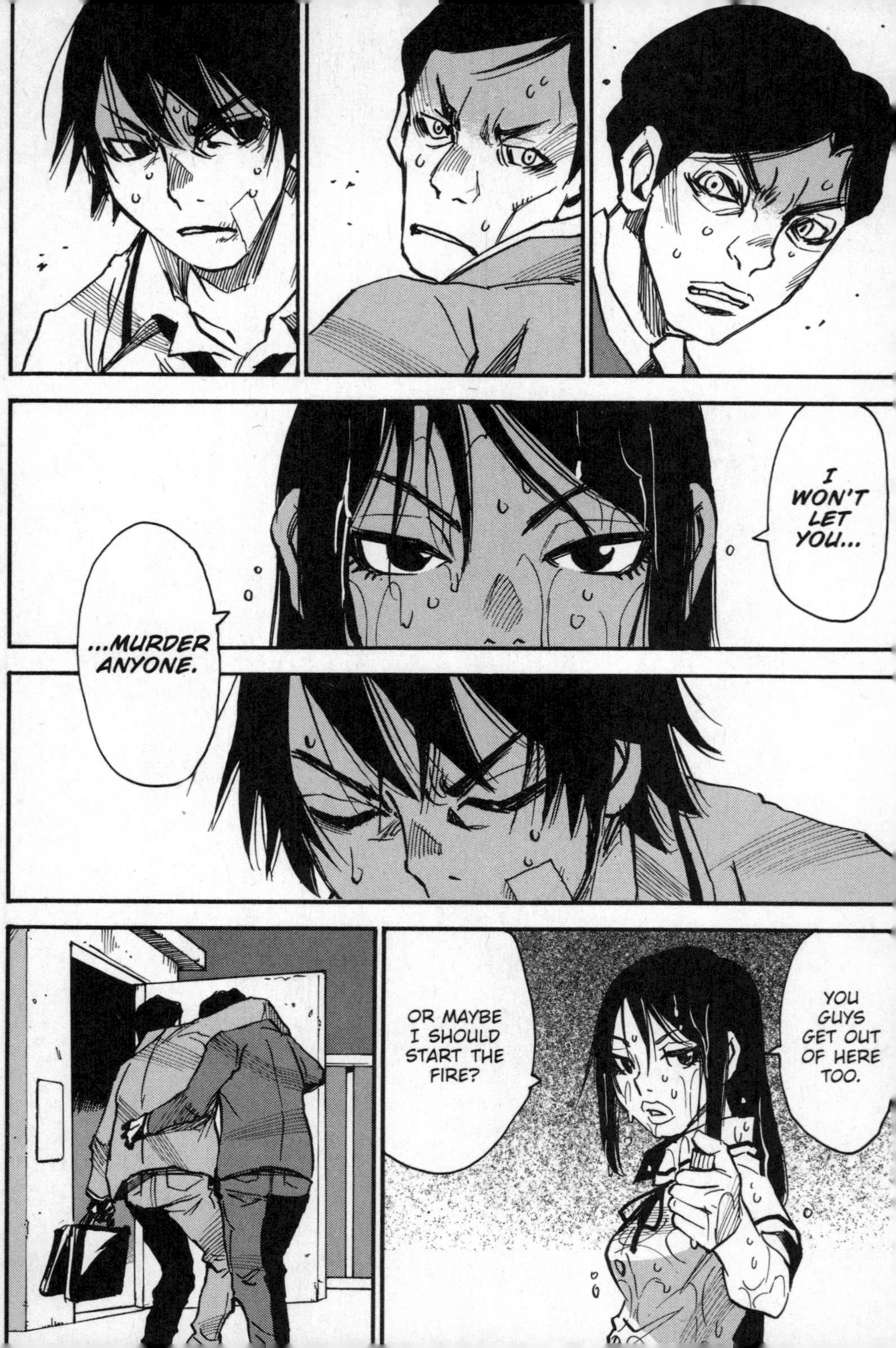
I WON'T LET YOU...
...MURDER ANYONE.
YOU GUYS GET OUT OF HERE TOO.
OR MAYBE I SHOULD START THE FIRE?

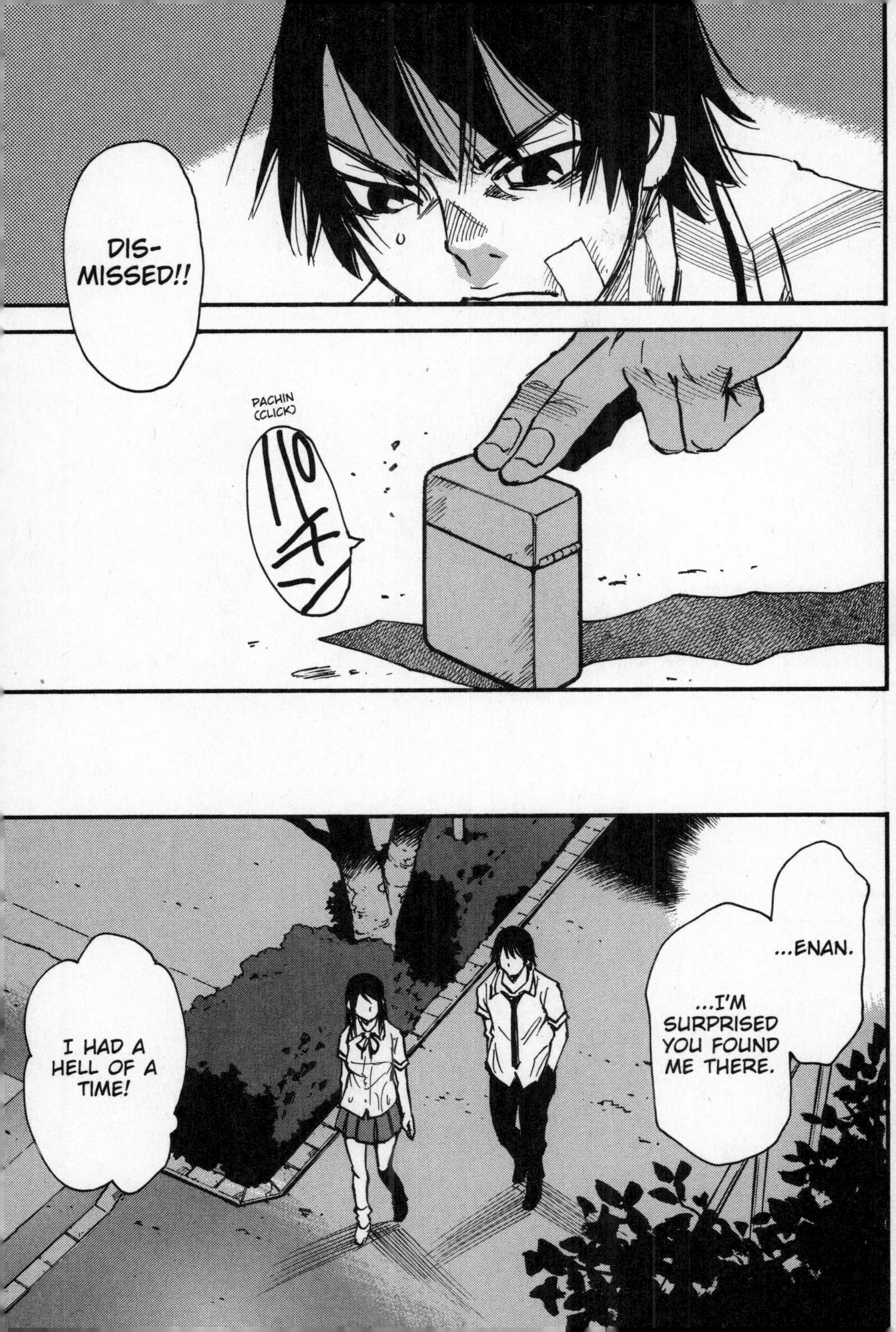
DIS-MISSED!!
PACHIN (CLICK)
...ENAN.
...I'M SURPRISED YOU FOUND ME THERE.
I HAD A HELL OF A TIME!

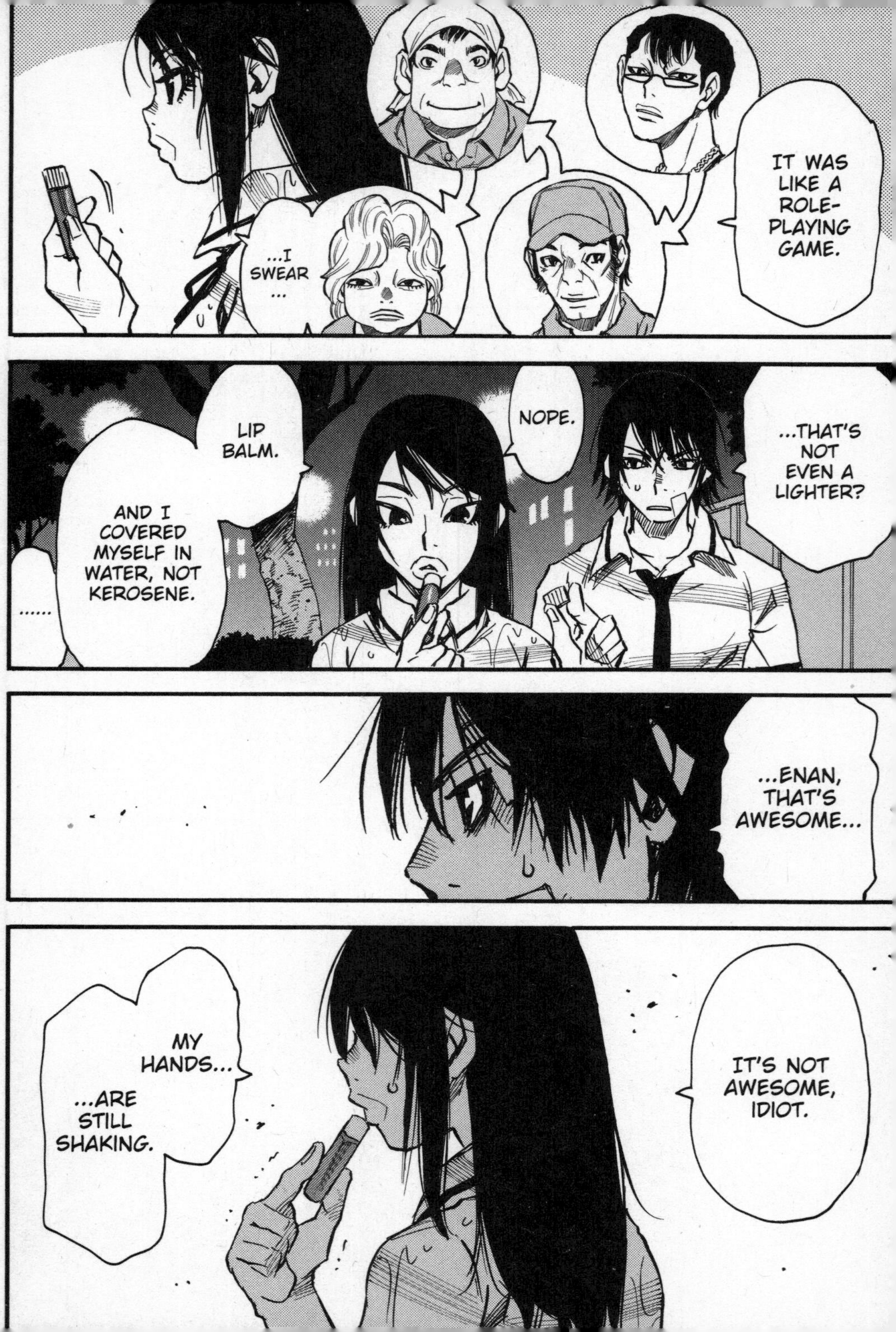
IT WAS LIKE A ROLE-PLAYING GAME.
...I SWEAR ...
...THAT'S NOT EVEN A LIGHTER?
NOPE.
LIP BALM.
AND I COVERED MYSELF IN WATER, NOT KEROSENE.
......
...ENAN, THAT'S AWESOME...
IT'S NOT AWESOME, IDIOT.
MY HANDS...
...ARE STILL SHAKING.

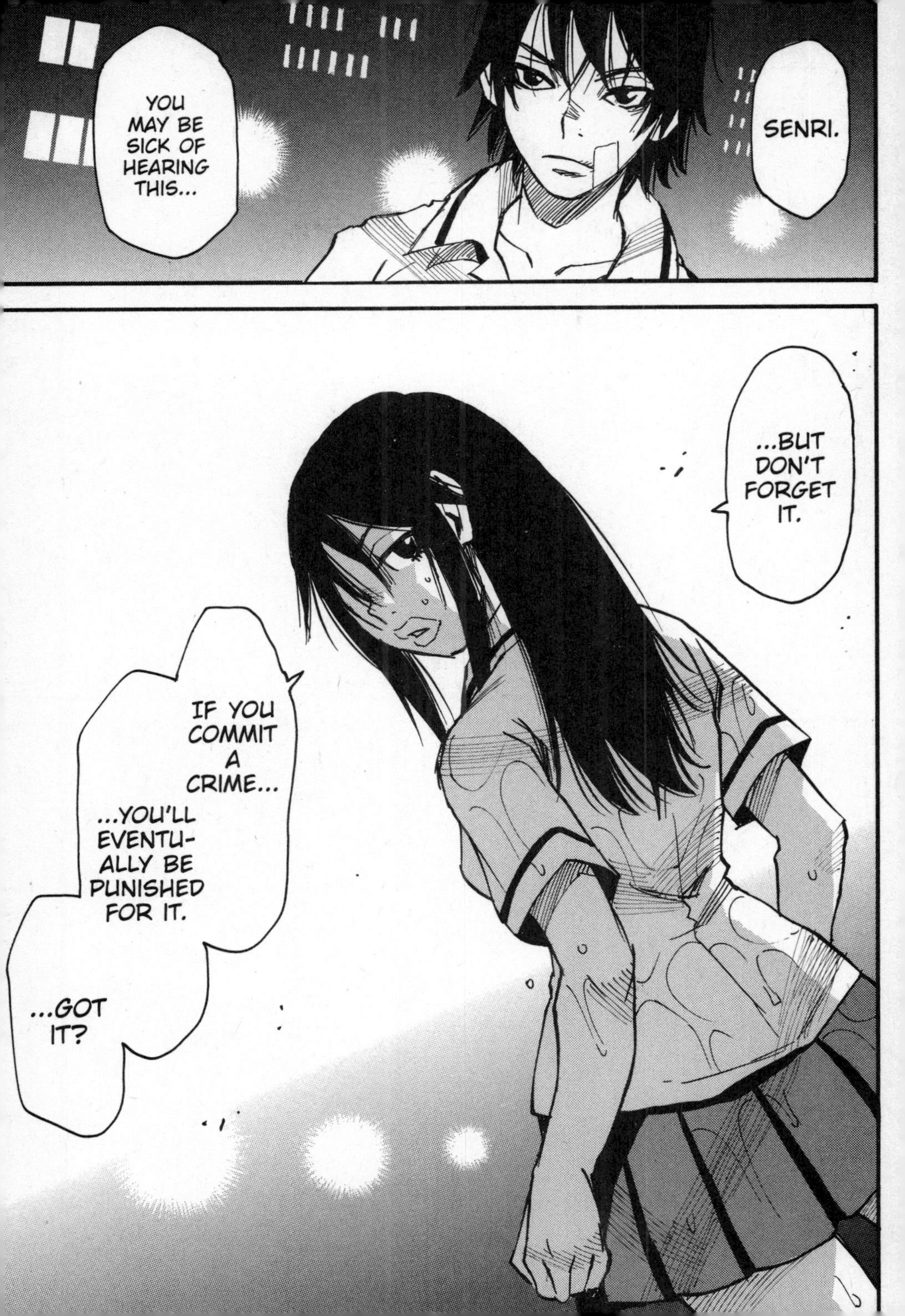
SENRI.
YOU MAY BE SICK OF HEARING THIS...
...BUT DON'T FORGET IT.
IF YOU COMMIT A CRIME...
...YOU'LL EVENTU-ALLY BE PUNISHED FOR IT.
...GOT IT?

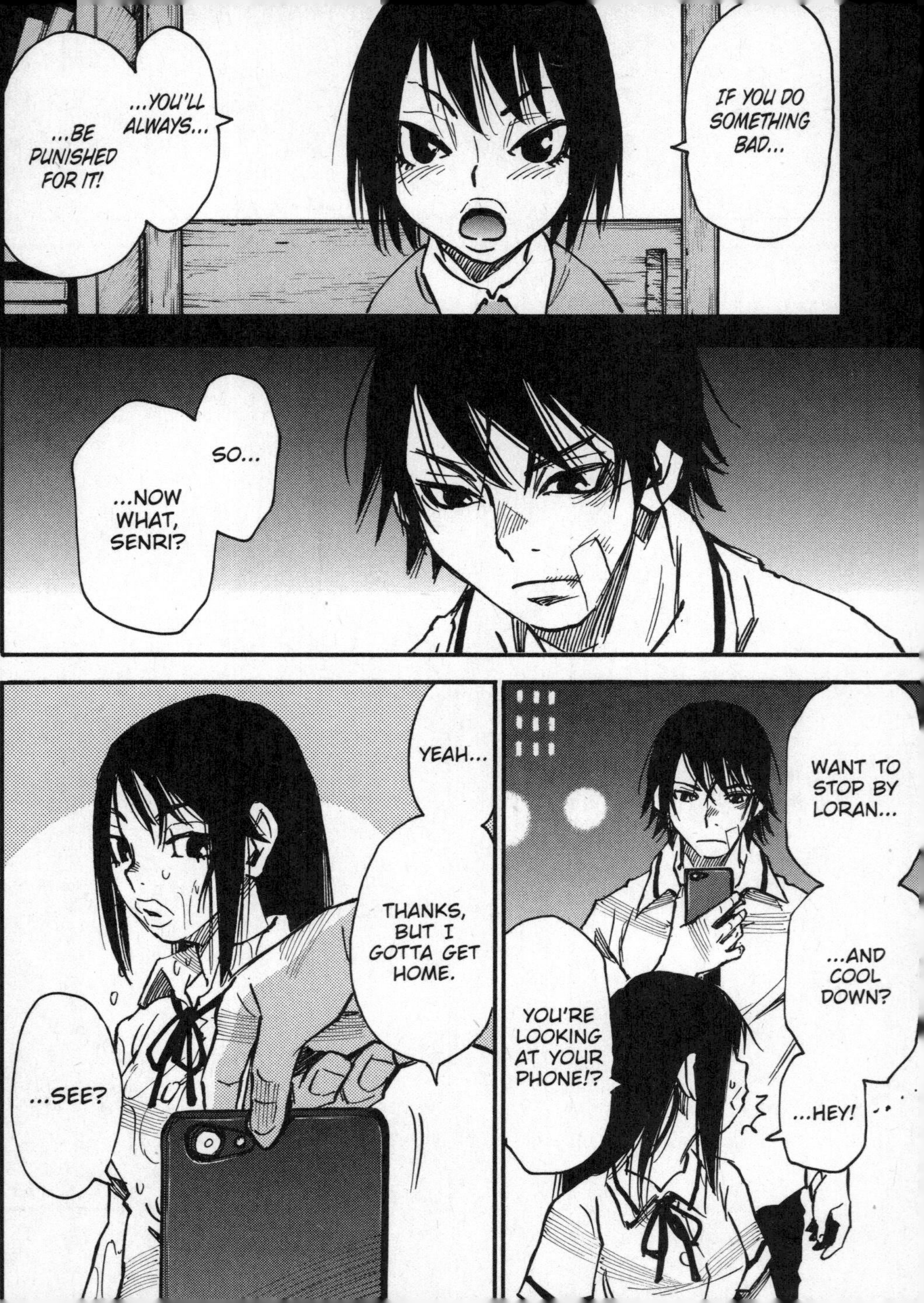
IF YOU DO SOMETHING BAD...
...YOU'LL ALWAYS...
...BE PUNISHED FOR IT!
SO...
...NOW WHAT, SENRI?
WANT TO STOP BY LORAN...
...AND COOL DOWN?
...HEY!
YOU'RE LOOKING AT YOUR PHONE!?
YEAH...
THANKS, BUT I GOTTA GET HOME.
...SEE?

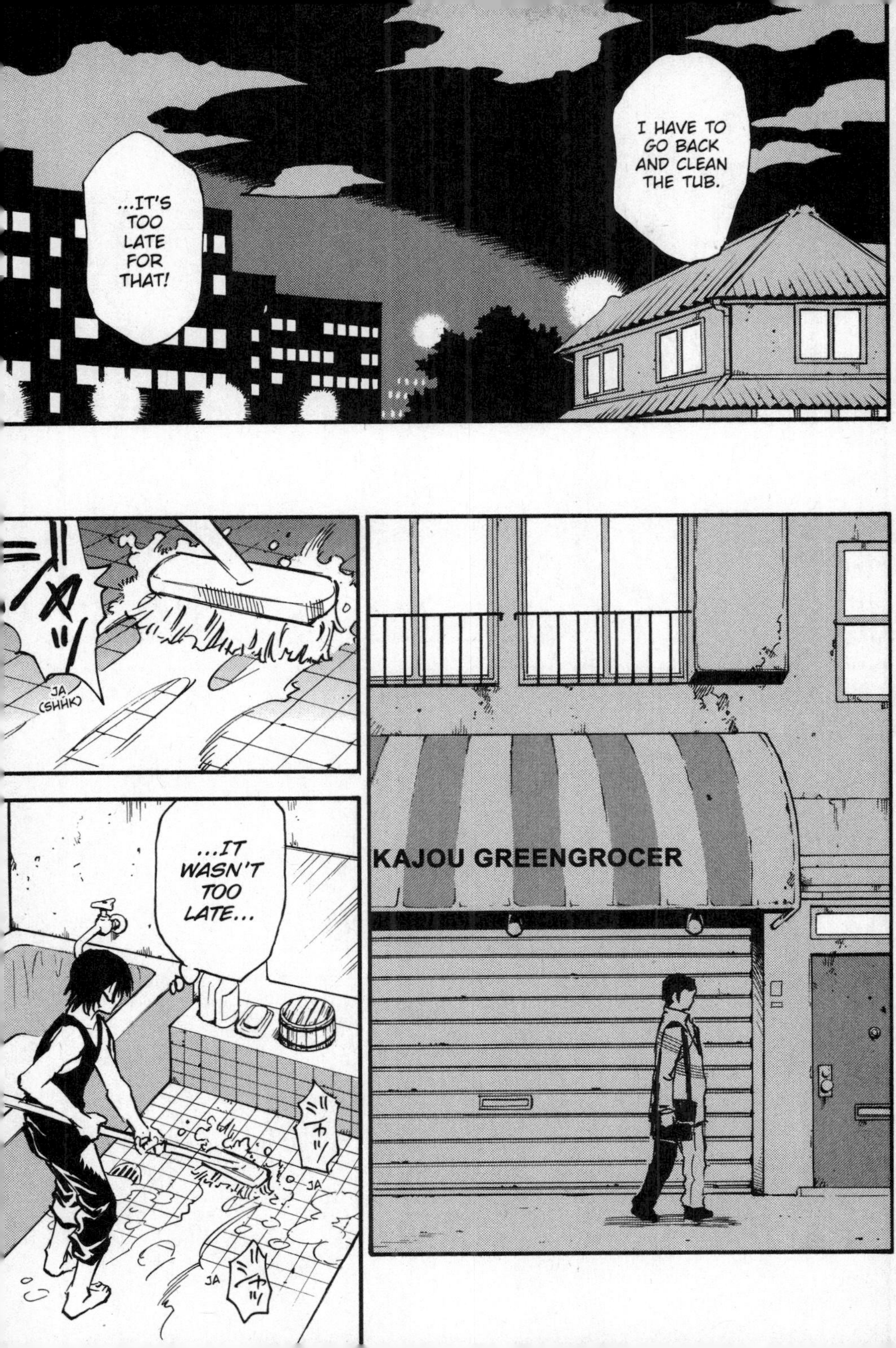

I HAVE TO GO BACK AND CLEAN THE TUB.
...IT'S TOO LATE FOR THAT!
KAJOU GREENGROCER
JA (SHHK)
...IT WASN'T TOO LATE...
JA
JA

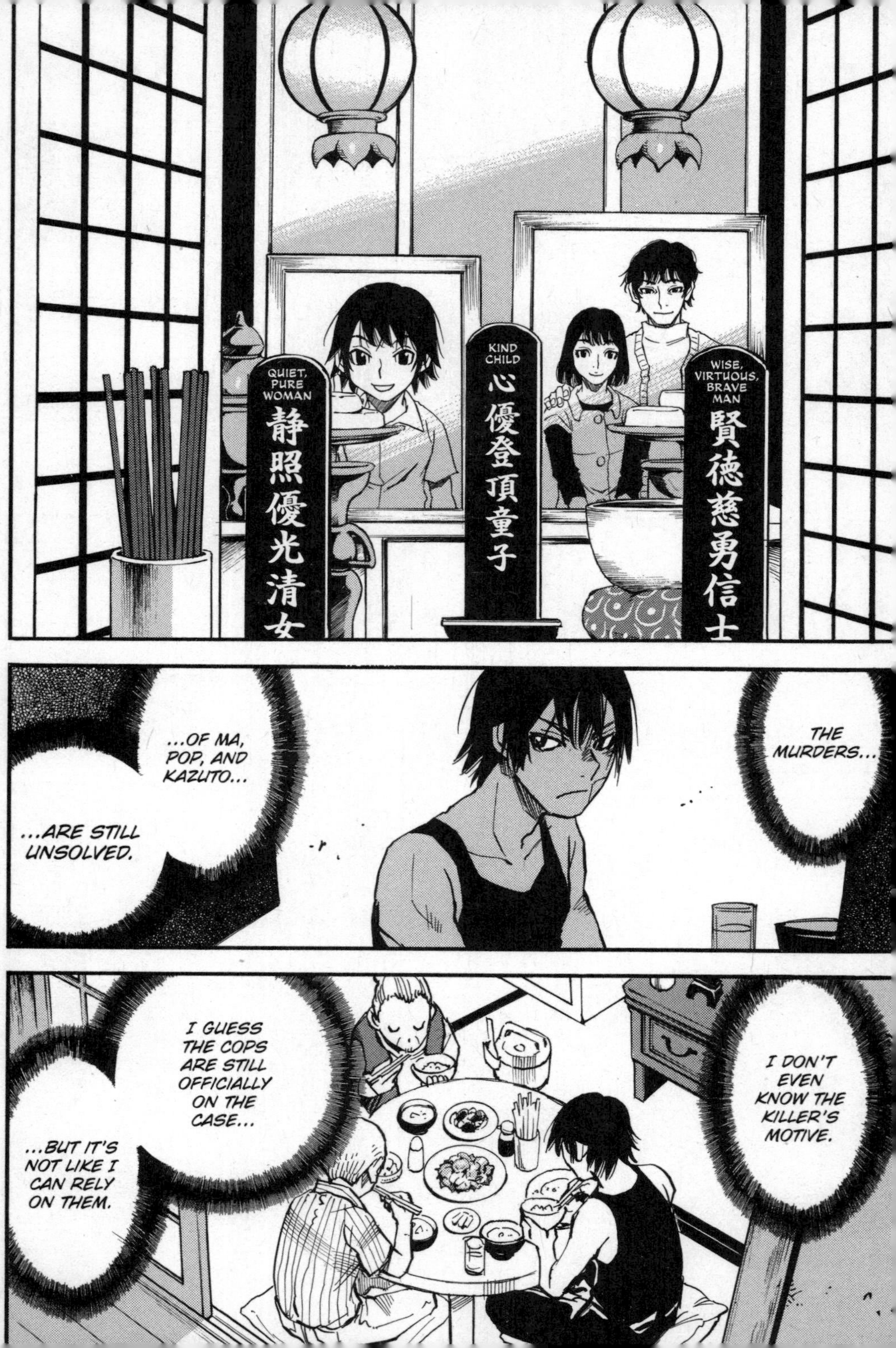
WISE, VIRTUOUS, BRAVE MAN
賢徳慈勇信士
KIND CHILD
心優登頂童子
QUIET, PURE WOMAN
静照優光清女
THE MURDERS...
...OF MA, POP, AND KAZUTO...
...ARE STILL UNSOLVED.
I DON'T EVEN KNOW THE KILLER'S MOTIVE.
I GUESS THE COPS ARE STILL OFFICIALLY ON THE CASE...
...BUT IT'S NOT LIKE I CAN RELY ON THEM.

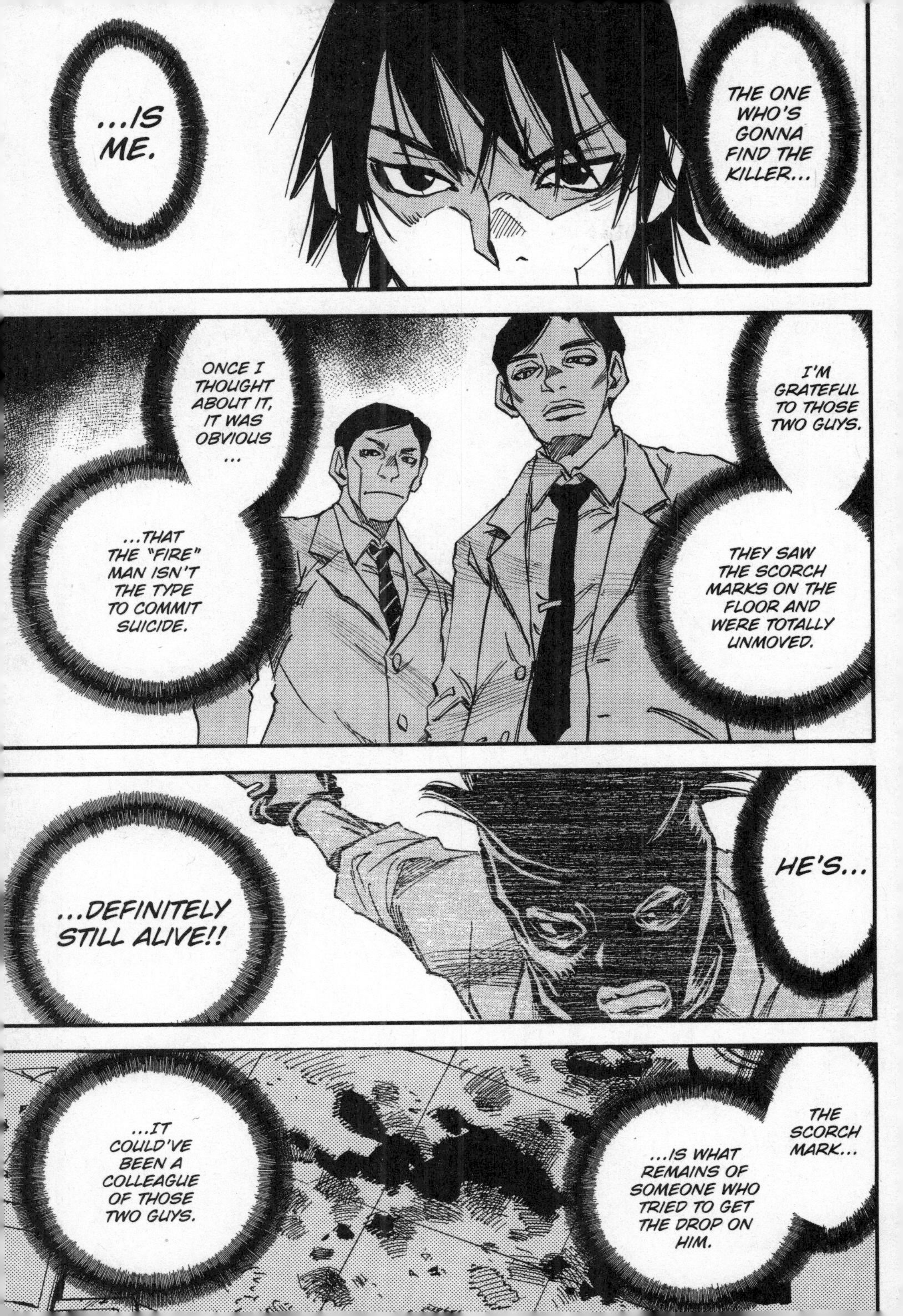
THE ONE WHO'S GONNA FIND THE KILLER...
...IS ME.
I'M GRATEFUL TO THOSE TWO GUYS.
THEY SAW THE SCORCH MARKS ON THE FLOOR AND WERE TOTALLY UNMOVED.
ONCE I THOUGHT ABOUT IT, IT WAS OBVIOUS...
...THAT THE "FIRE" MAN ISN'T THE TYPE TO COMMIT SUICIDE.
HE'S...
...DEFINITELY STILL ALIVE!!
THE SCORCH MARK...
...IS WHAT REMAINS OF SOMEONE WHO TRIED TO GET THE DROP ON HIM.
...IT COULD'VE BEEN A COLLEAGUE OF THOSE TWO GUYS.

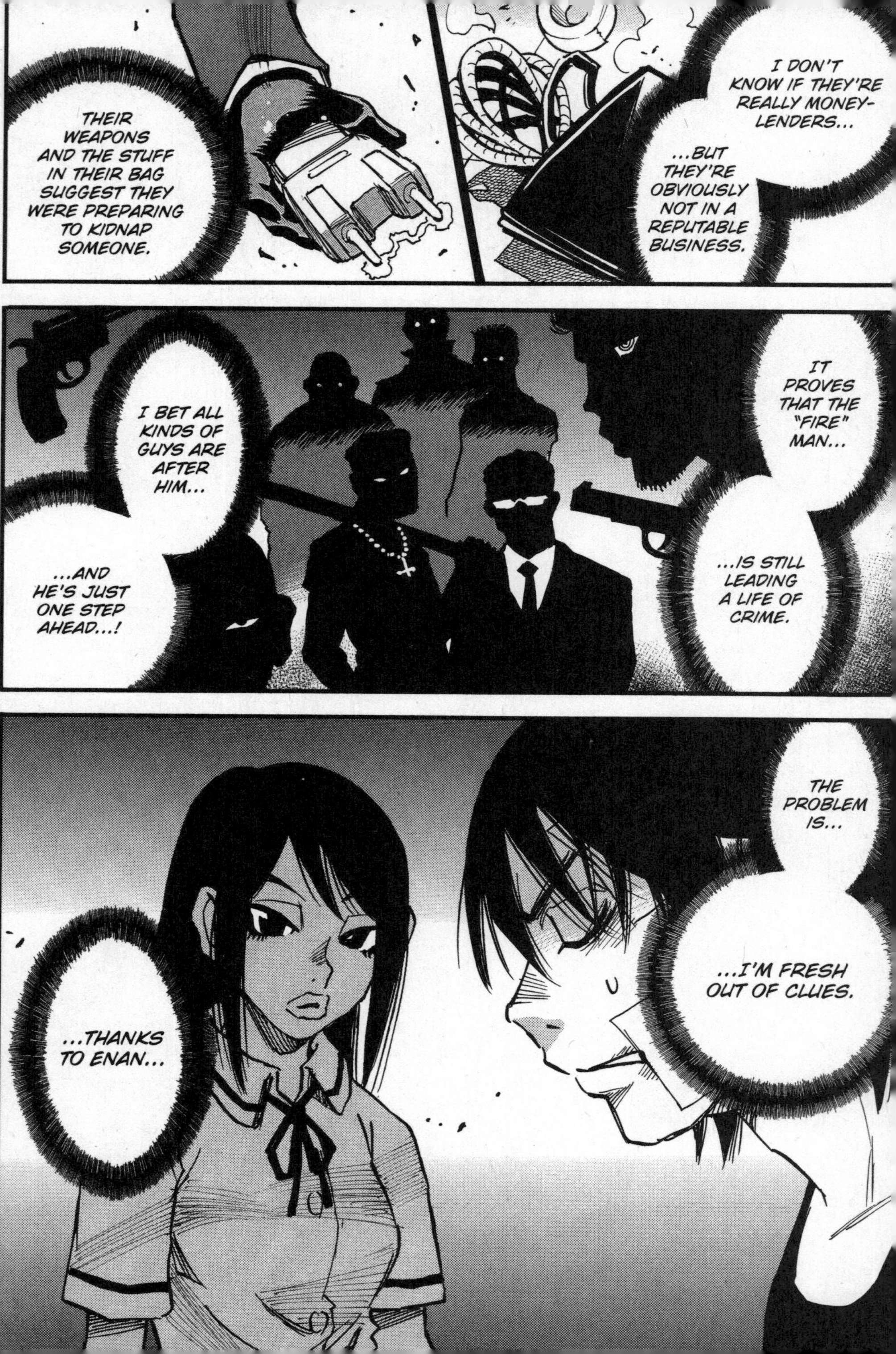
I DON'T KNOW IF THEY'RE REALLY MONEY-LENDERS...
...BUT THEY'RE OBVIOUSLY NOT IN A REPUTABLE BUSINESS.
THEIR WEAPONS AND THE STUFF IN THEIR BAG SUGGEST THEY WERE PREPARING TO KIDNAP SOMEONE.
IT PROVES THAT THE "FIRE" MAN...
...IS STILL LEADING A LIFE OF CRIME.
I BET ALL KINDS OF GUYS ARE AFTER HIM...
...AND HE'S JUST ONE STEP AHEAD...!
THE PROBLEM IS...
...I'M FRESH OUT OF CLUES.
...THANKS TO ENAN...

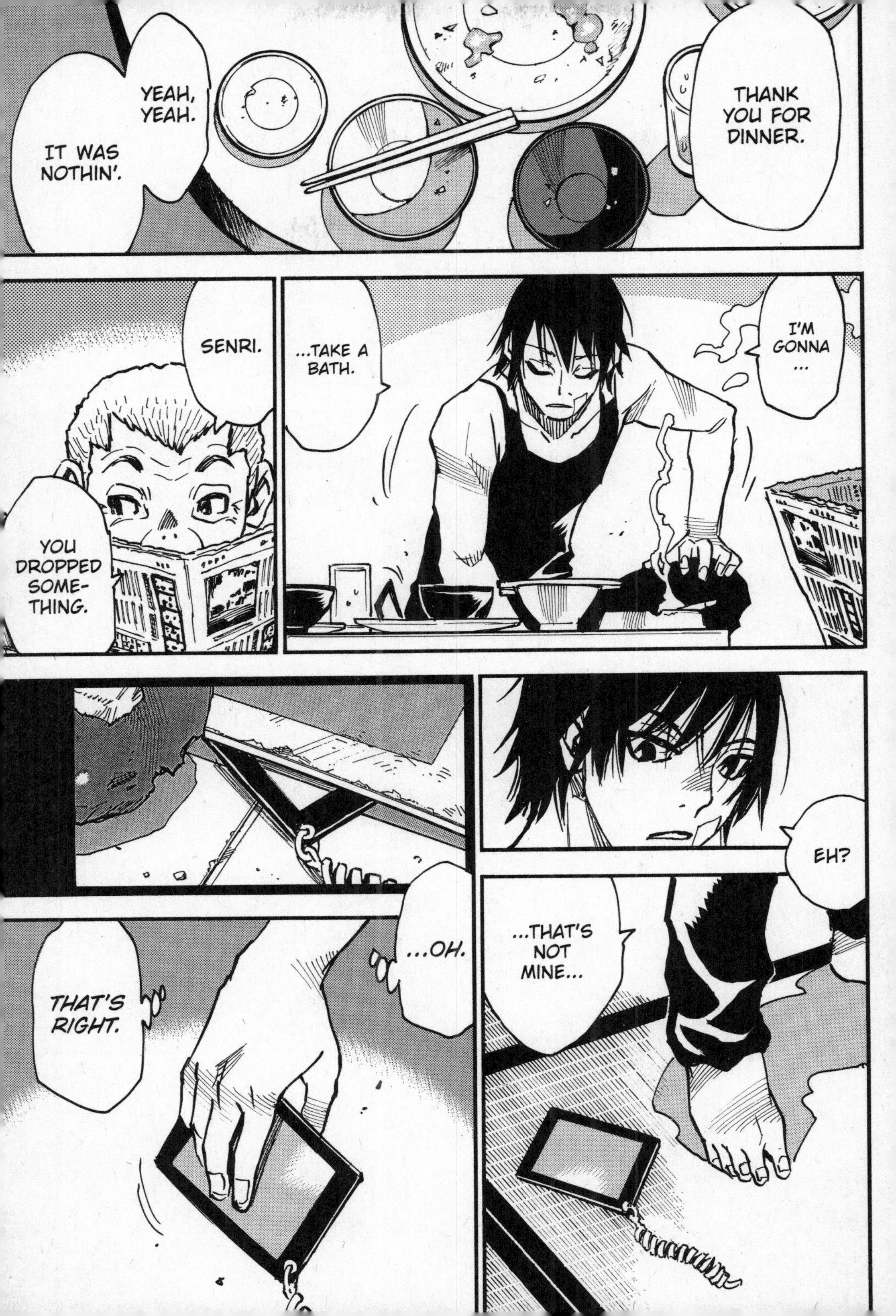
THANK YOU FOR DINNER.
YEAH, YEAH.
IT WAS NOTHIN'.
I'M GONNA ...
...TAKE A BATH.
SENRI.
YOU DROPPED SOME-THING.
EH?
...THAT'S NOT MINE...
...OH.
THAT'S RIGHT.

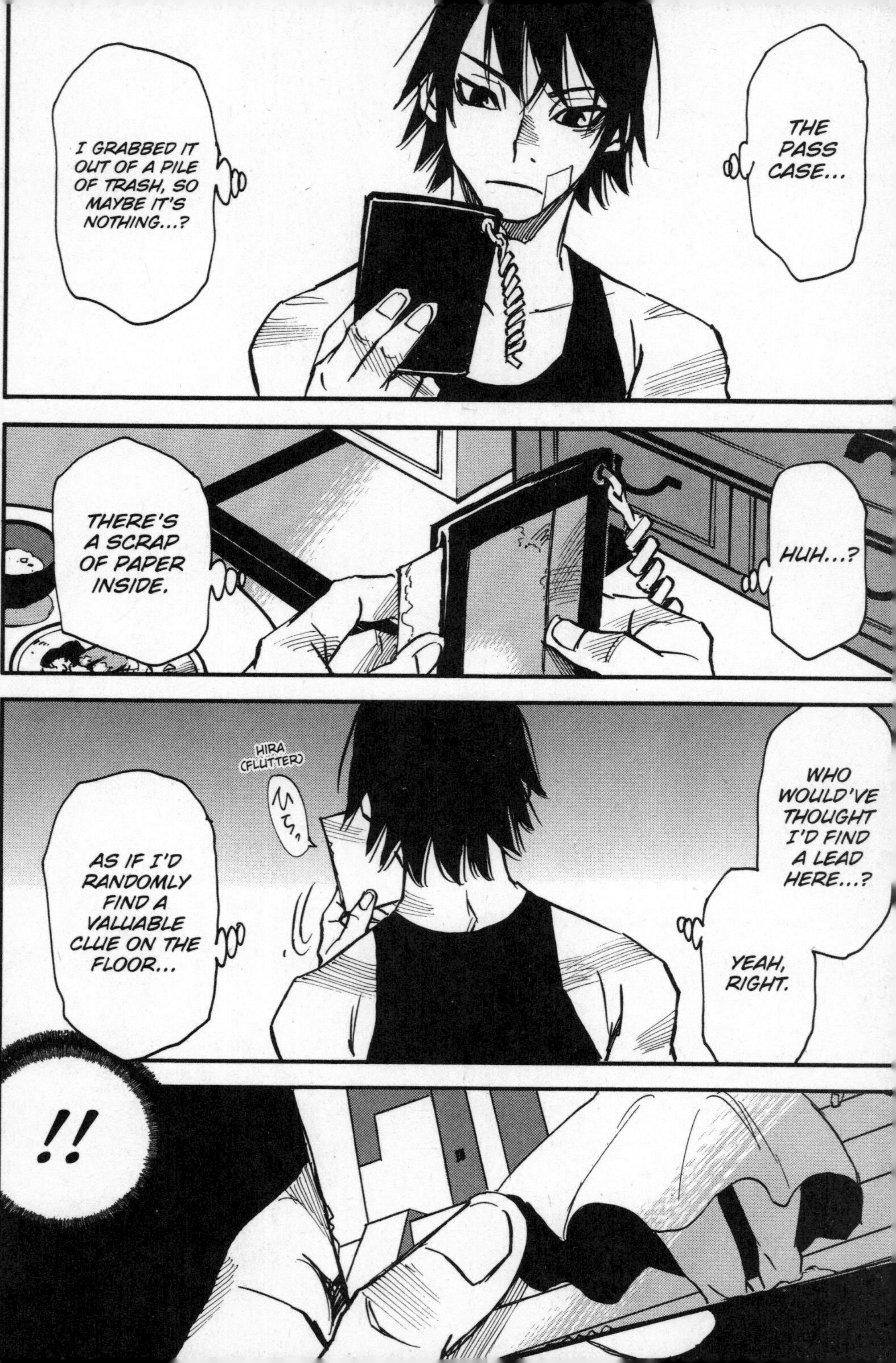
THE PASS CASE...
I GRABBED IT OUT OF A PILE OF TRASH, SO MAYBE IT'S NOTHING...?
HUH...?
THERE'S A SCRAP OF PAPER INSIDE.
WHO WOULD'VE THOUGHT I'D FIND A LEAD HERE...?
YEAH, RIGHT.
HIRA (FLUTTER)
AS IF I'D RANDOMLY FIND A VALUABLE CLUE ON THE FLOOR...
!!

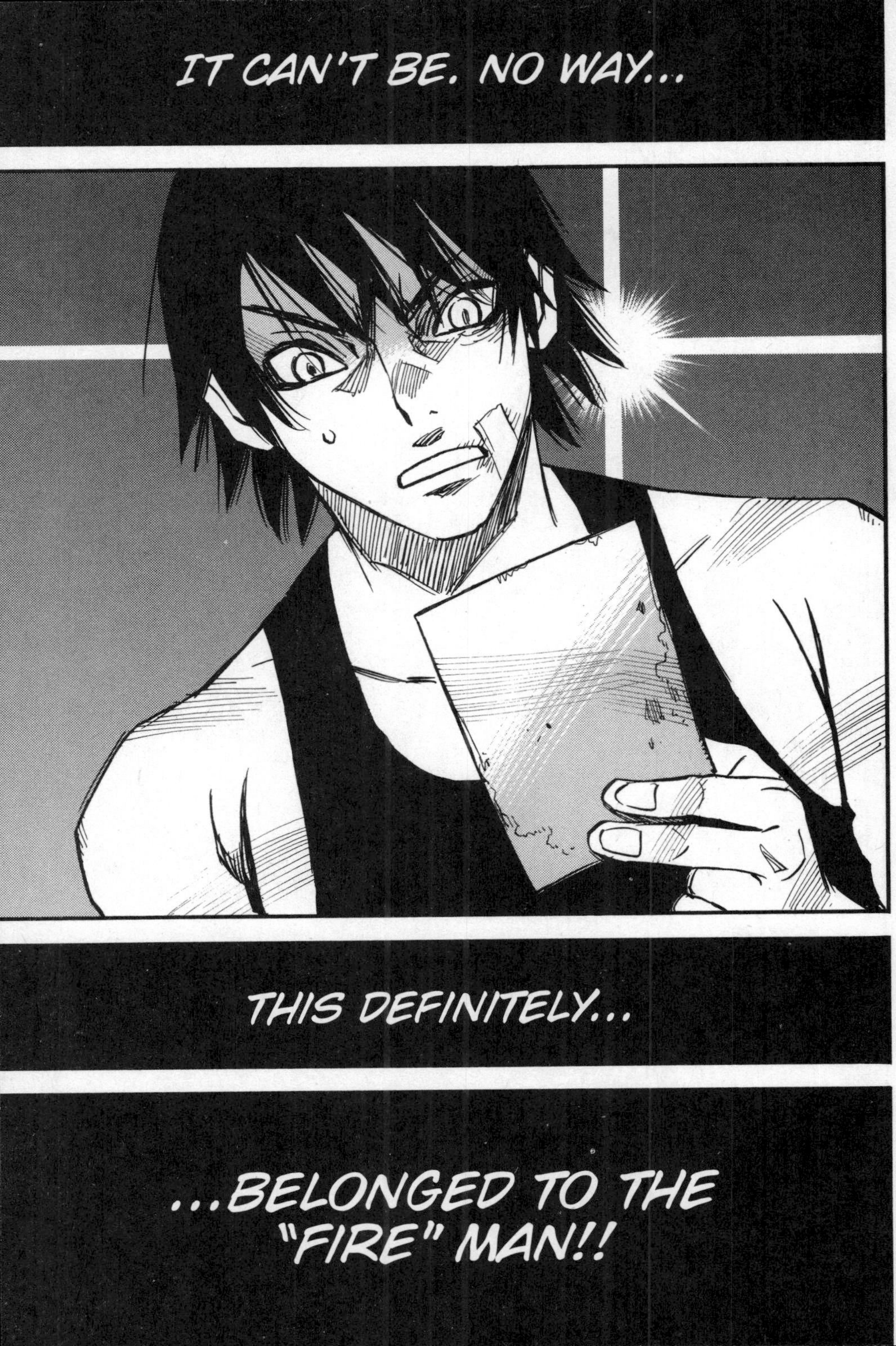
IT CAN'T BE. NO WAY...
THIS DEFINITELY...
...BELONGED TO THE "FIRE" MAN!!

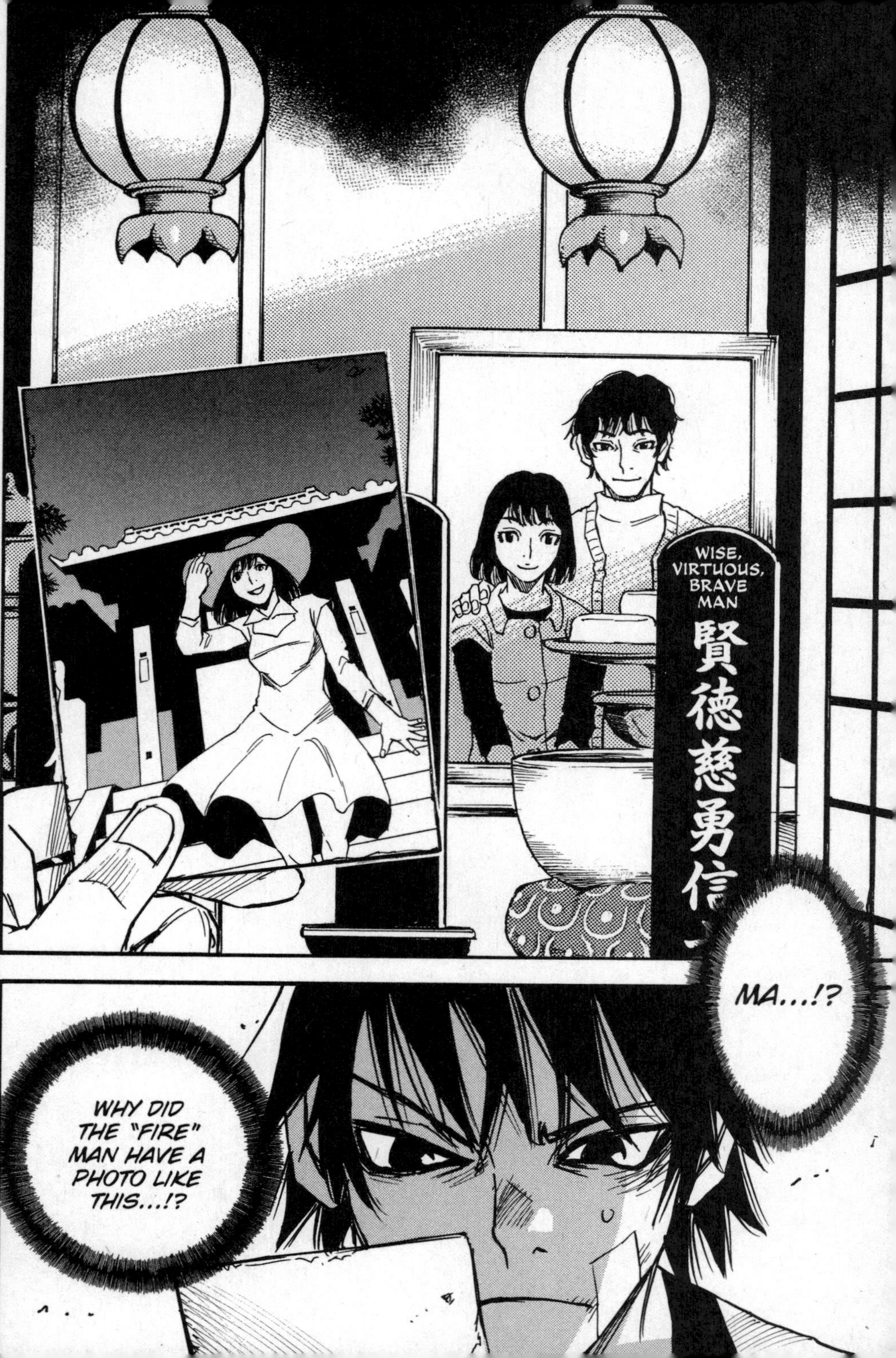
WISE, VIRTUOUS, BRAVE MAN
賢徳慈勇信
MA...!?
WHY DID THE "FIRE" MAN HAVE A PHOTO LIKE THIS...!?

#4 END

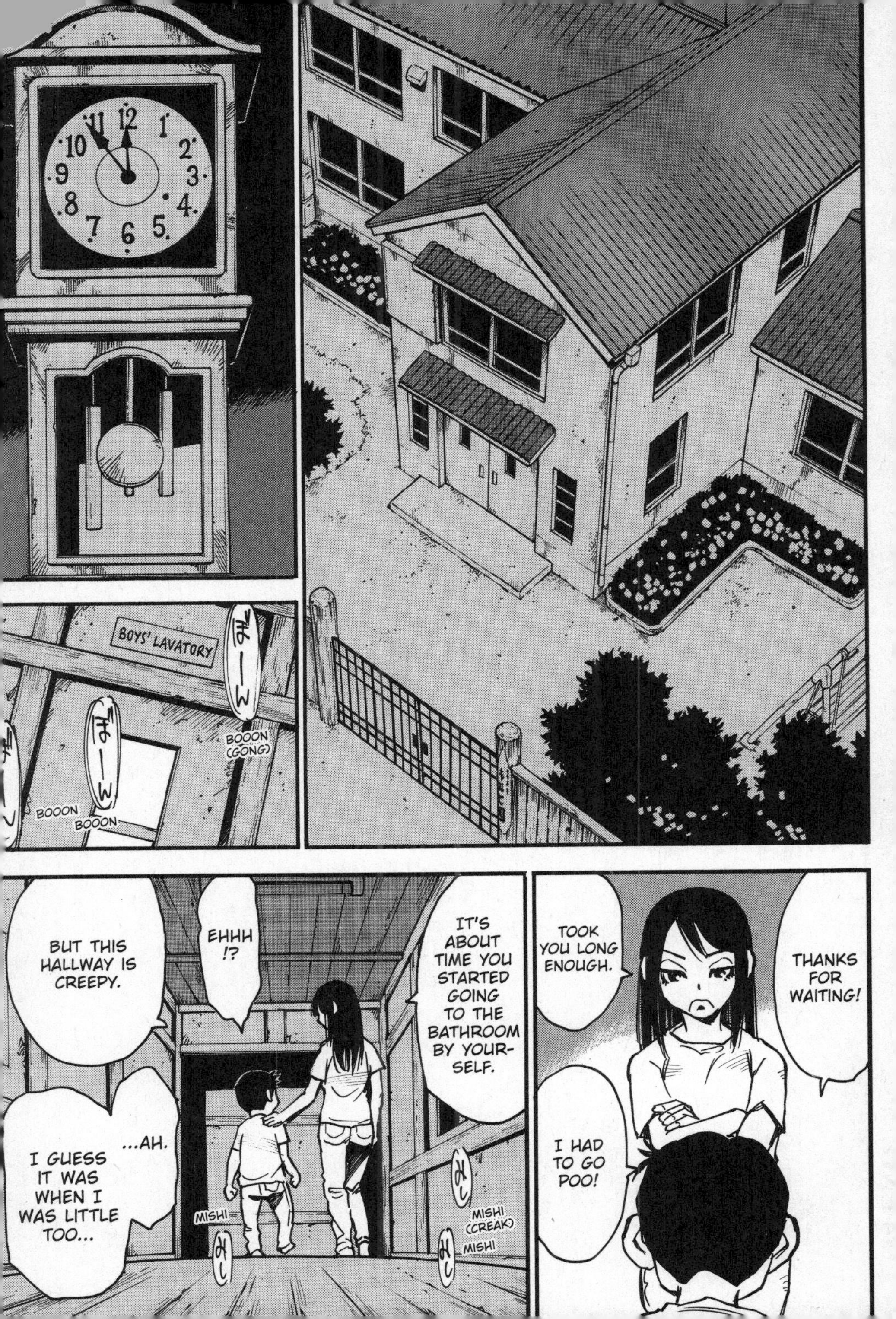
BOYS' LAVATORY
ぼーーん
BOOON (GONG)
ぼーーん
BOOON
BOOON
THANKS FOR WAITING!
TOOK YOU LONG ENOUGH.
I HAD TO GO POO!
IT'S ABOUT TIME YOU STARTED GOING TO THE BATHROOM BY YOURSELF.
EHHH !?
BUT THIS HALLWAY IS CREEPY.
...AH.
I GUESS IT WAS WHEN I WAS LITTLE TOO...
みし
MISHI (CREAK)
みし
MISHI
MISHI
みし

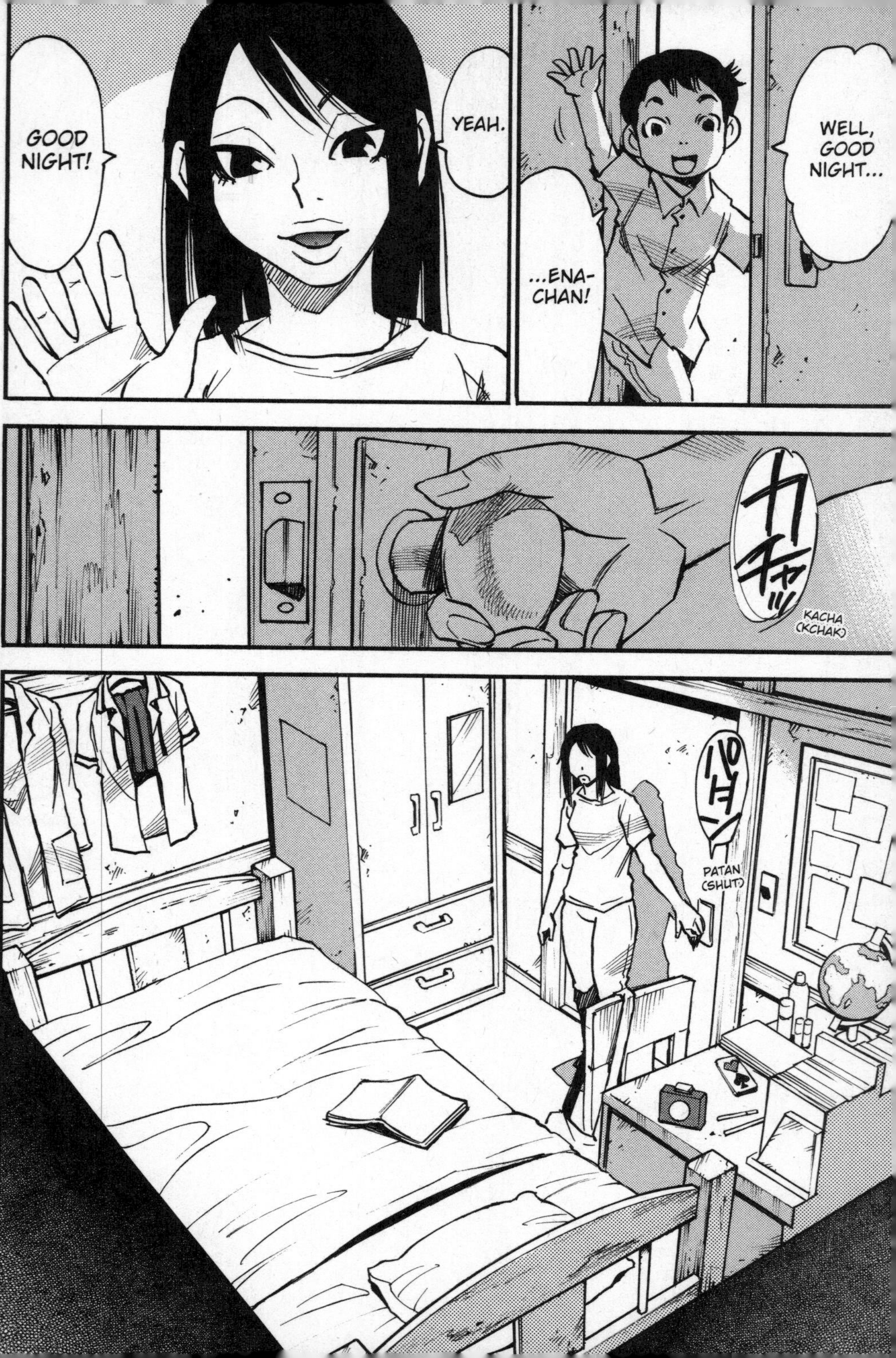
WELL, GOOD NIGHT...
...ENA-CHAN!
YEAH.
GOOD NIGHT!
カチャッ
KACHA (KCHAK)
パタン
PATAN (SHUT)

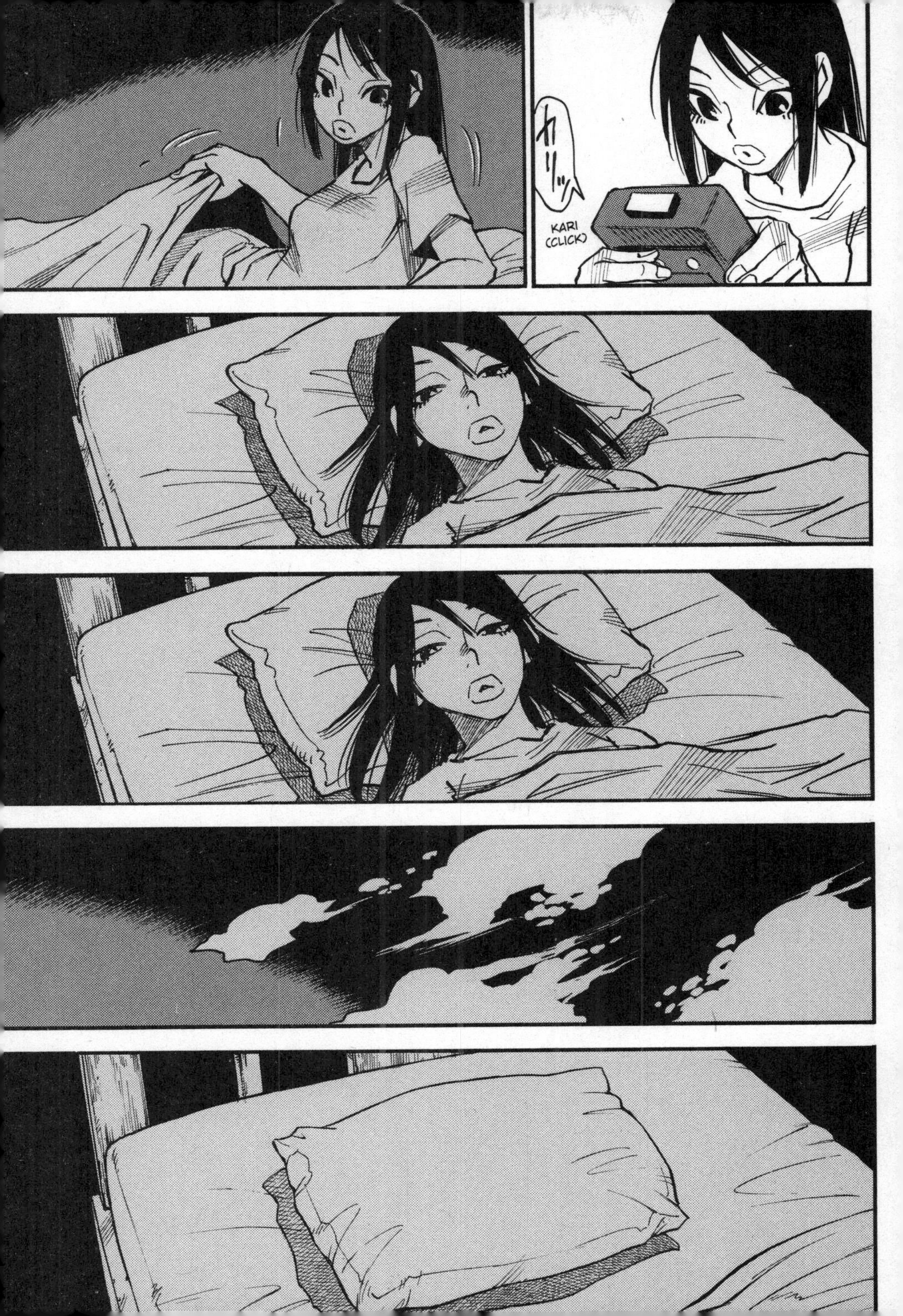
カリッ
KARI
(CLICK)

#5 Retribution

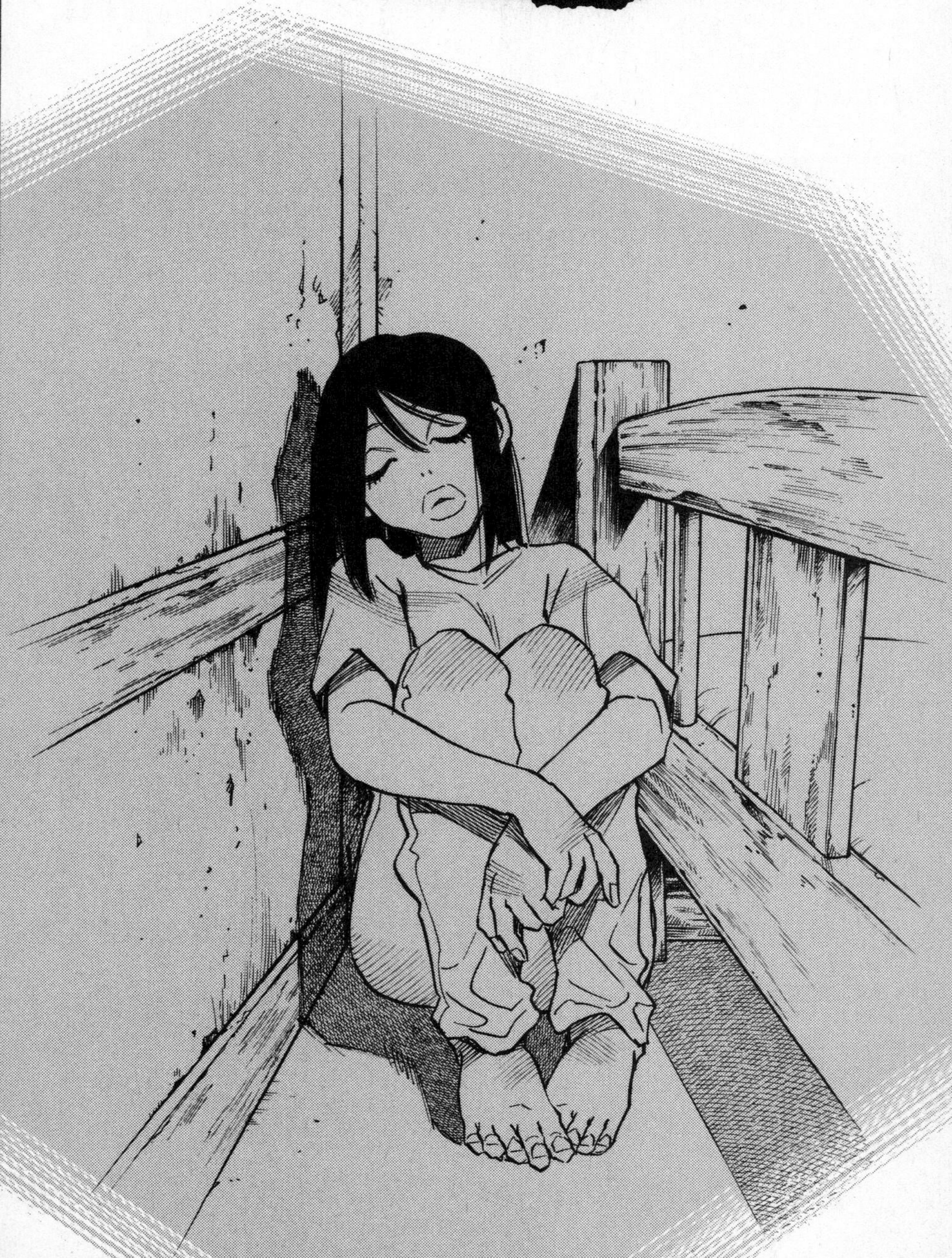

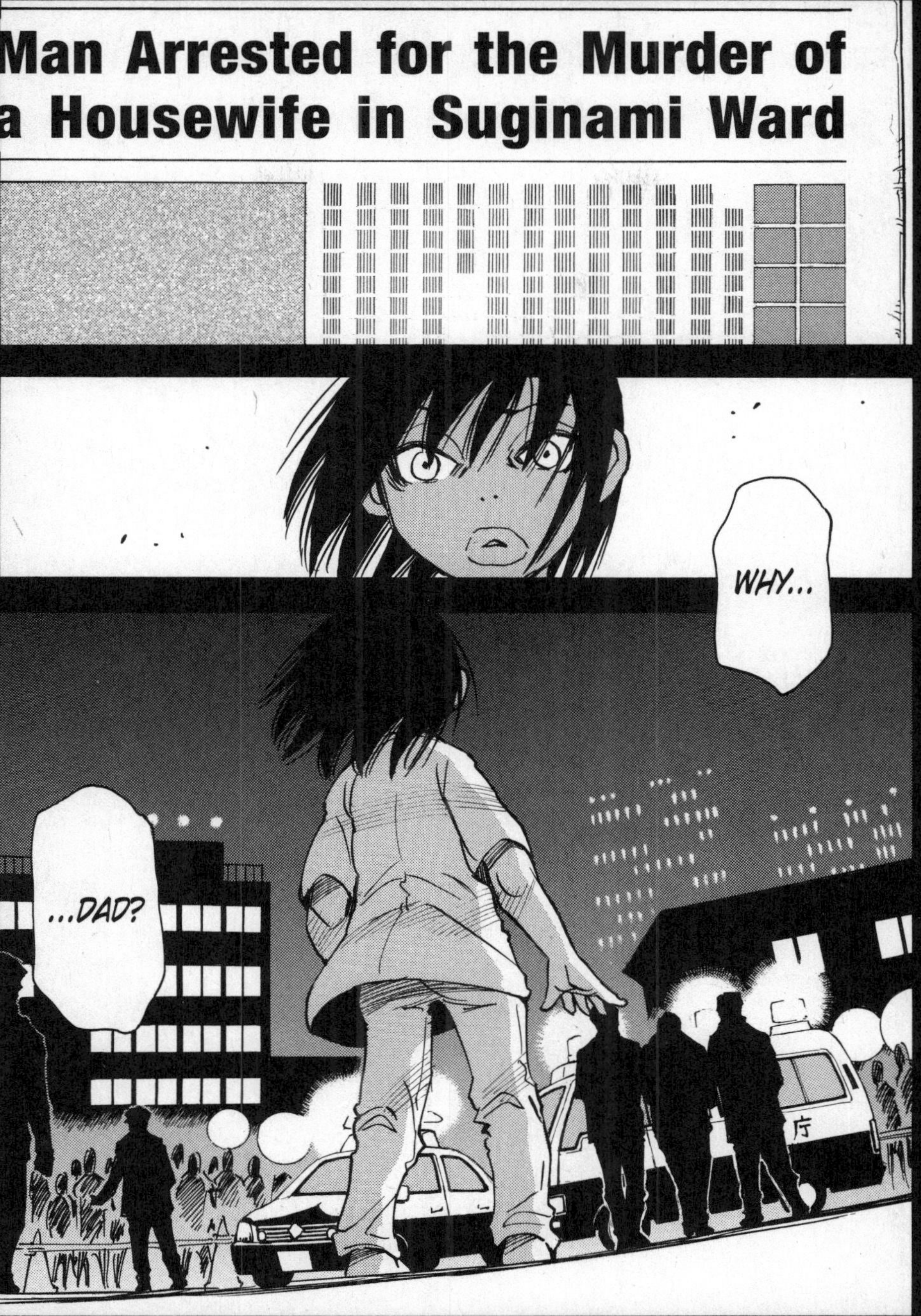
Man Arrested for the Murder of a Housewife in Suginami Ward
WHY...
...DAD?

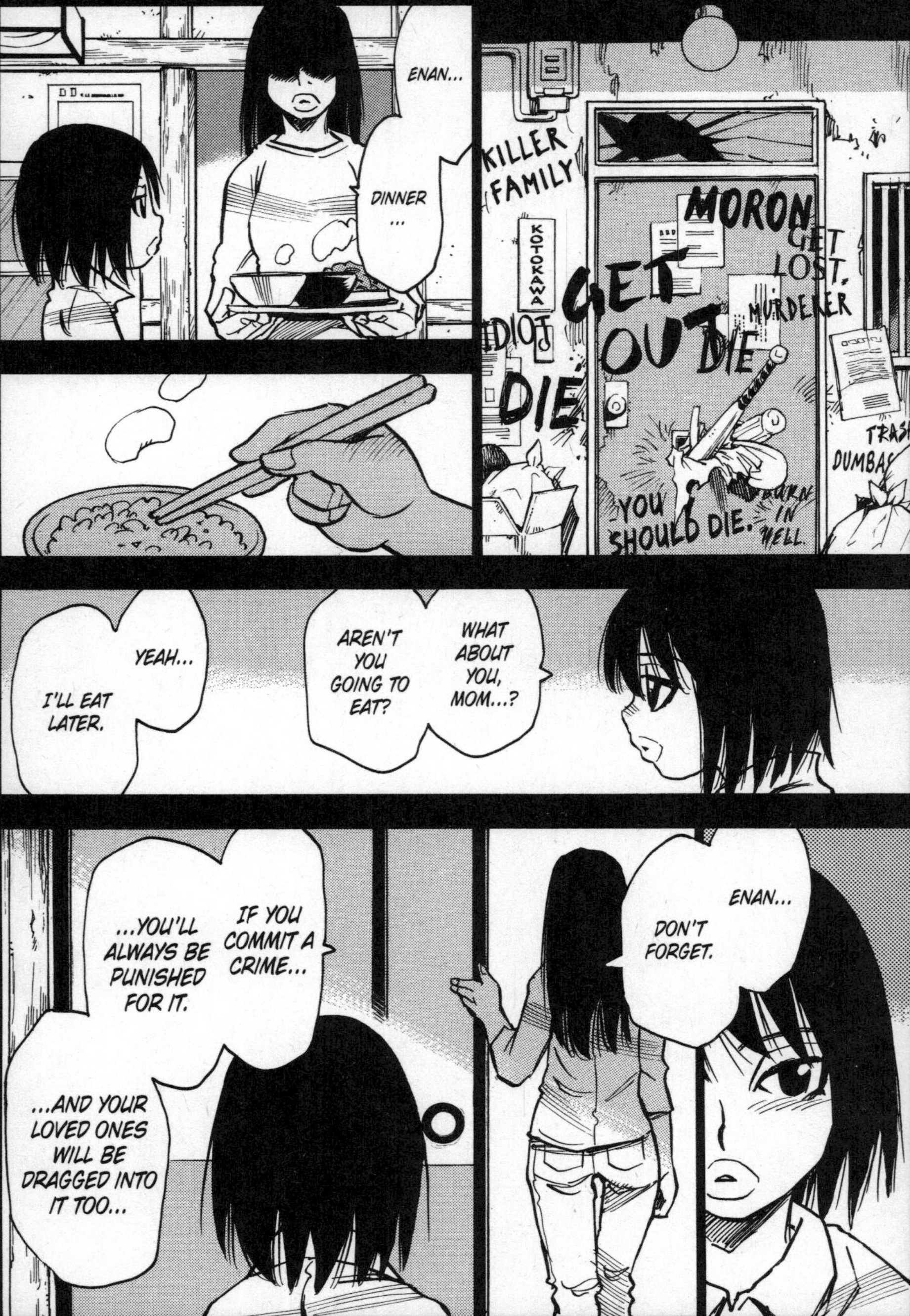
MORON
GET LOST.
MURDERER
KOTOKAWA
KILLER FAMILY
GET OUT
DIE
IDIOT
DIE
BURN IN HELL.
YOU SHOULD DIE.
ENAN...
DINNER ...
WHAT ABOUT YOU, MOM...?
AREN'T YOU GOING TO EAT?
YEAH...
I'LL EAT LATER.
ENAN...
DON'T FORGET.
IF YOU COMMIT A CRIME...
...YOU'LL ALWAYS BE PUNISHED FOR IT.
...AND YOUR LOVED ONES WILL BE DRAGGED INTO IT TOO...

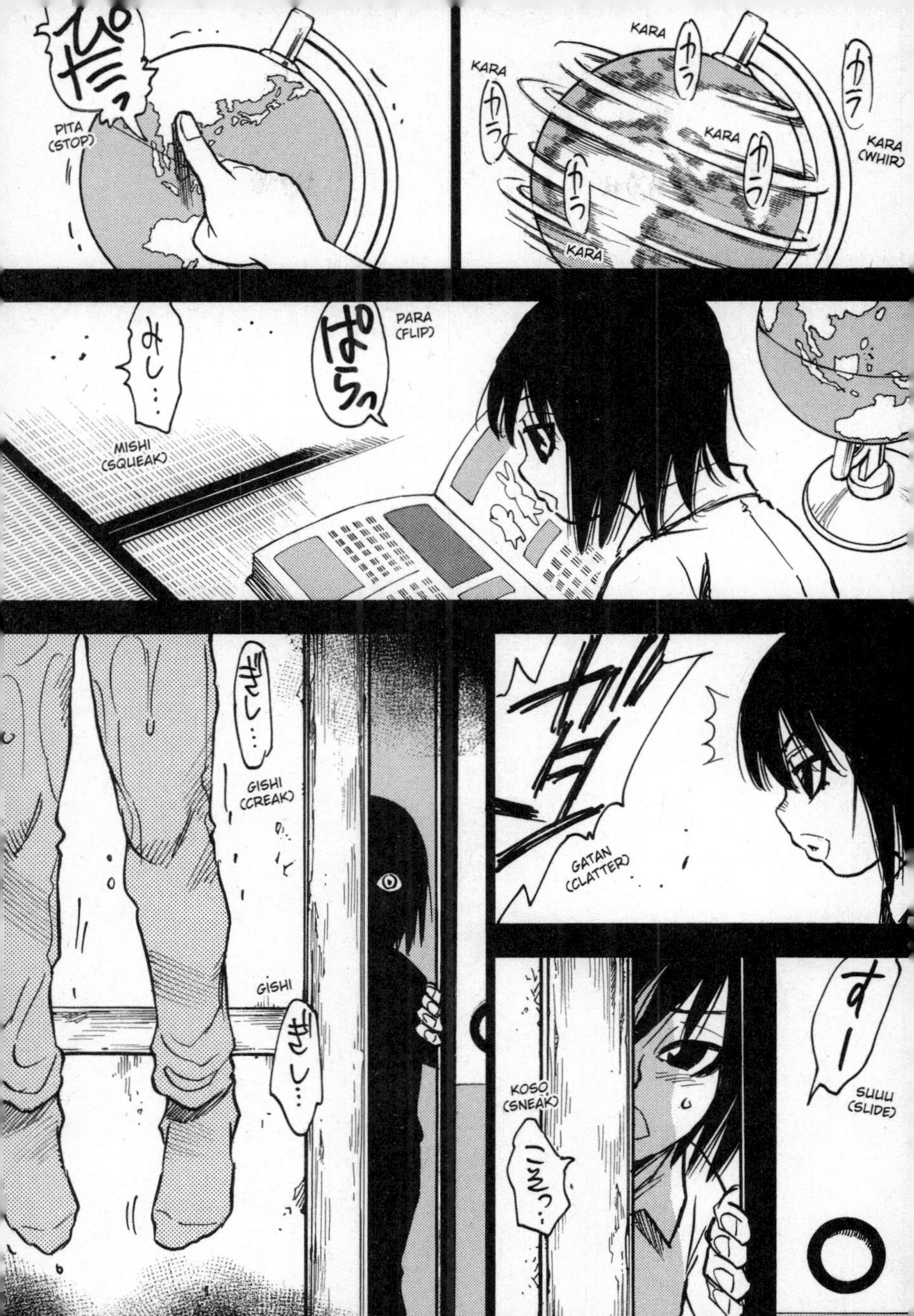

カラ
KARA (WHIR)
KARA
カラ
KARA
カラ
KARA
カラ
KARA
カラ
KARA
ぴたっ
PITA (STOP)
ぱらっ
PARA (FLIP)
みし…
MISHI (SQUEAK)
GATAN (CLATTER)
すー
SUUU (SLIDE)
こそっ…
KOSO (SNEAK)
ぎし…
GISHI (CREAK)
ぎし…
GISHI

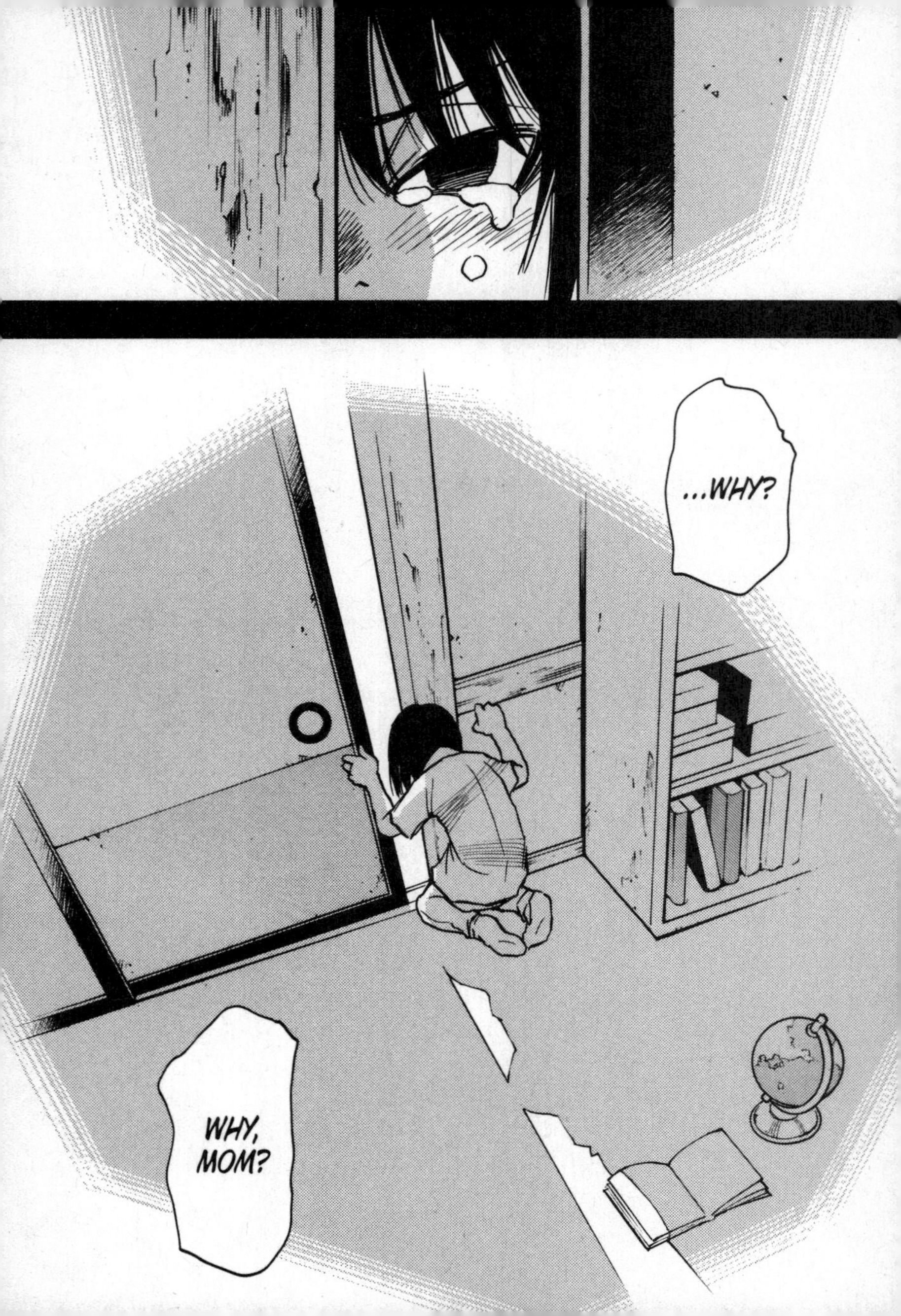
...WHY?
WHY, MOM?

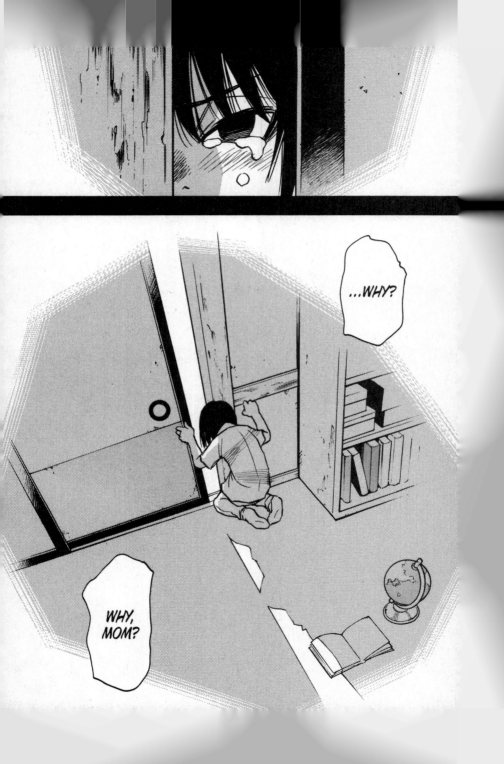

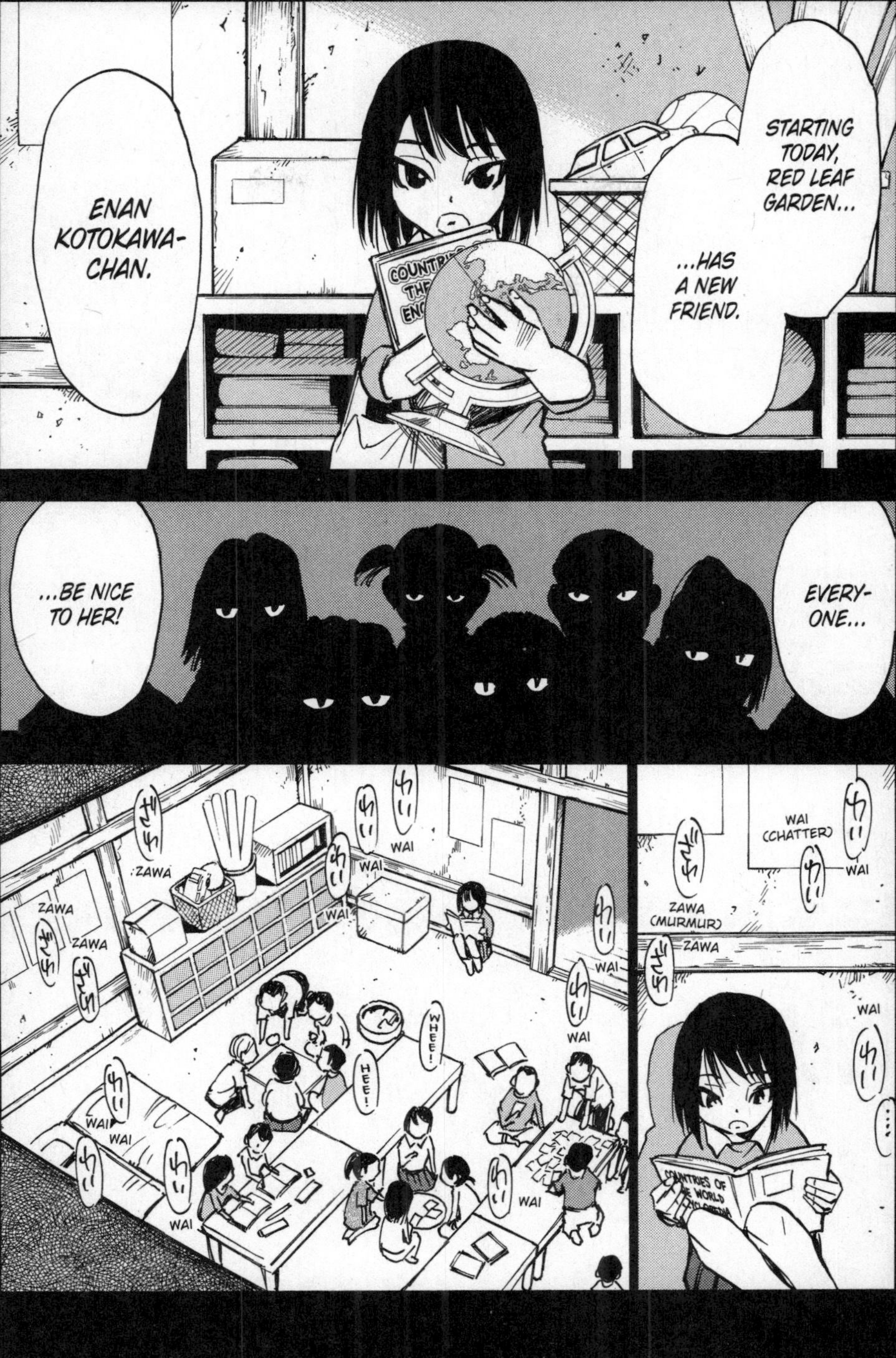
STARTING TODAY, RED LEAF GARDEN...
...HAS A NEW FRIEND.
ENAN KOTOKAWA-CHAN.
EVERY-ONE...
...BE NICE TO HER!
WAI (CHATTER)
WAI
ZAWA (MURMUR)
ZAWA
WAI
...
WAI
WAI
ZAWA
ZAWA
ZAWA
WAI
WAI
WAI
WHEE!
HEE!
WAI
WAI
WAI
WAI
WAI

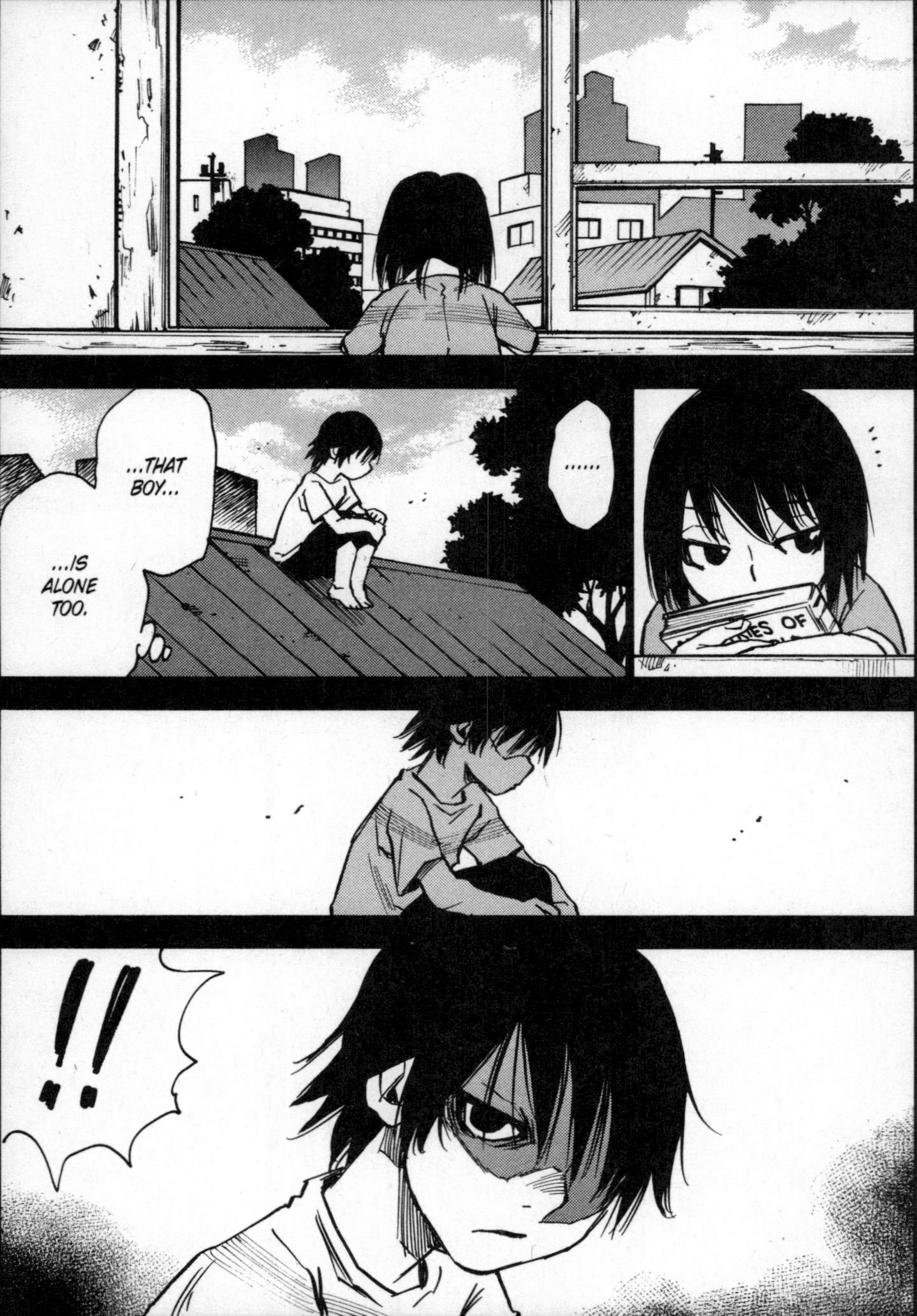
......
...THAT BOY...
...IS ALONE TOO.
!!

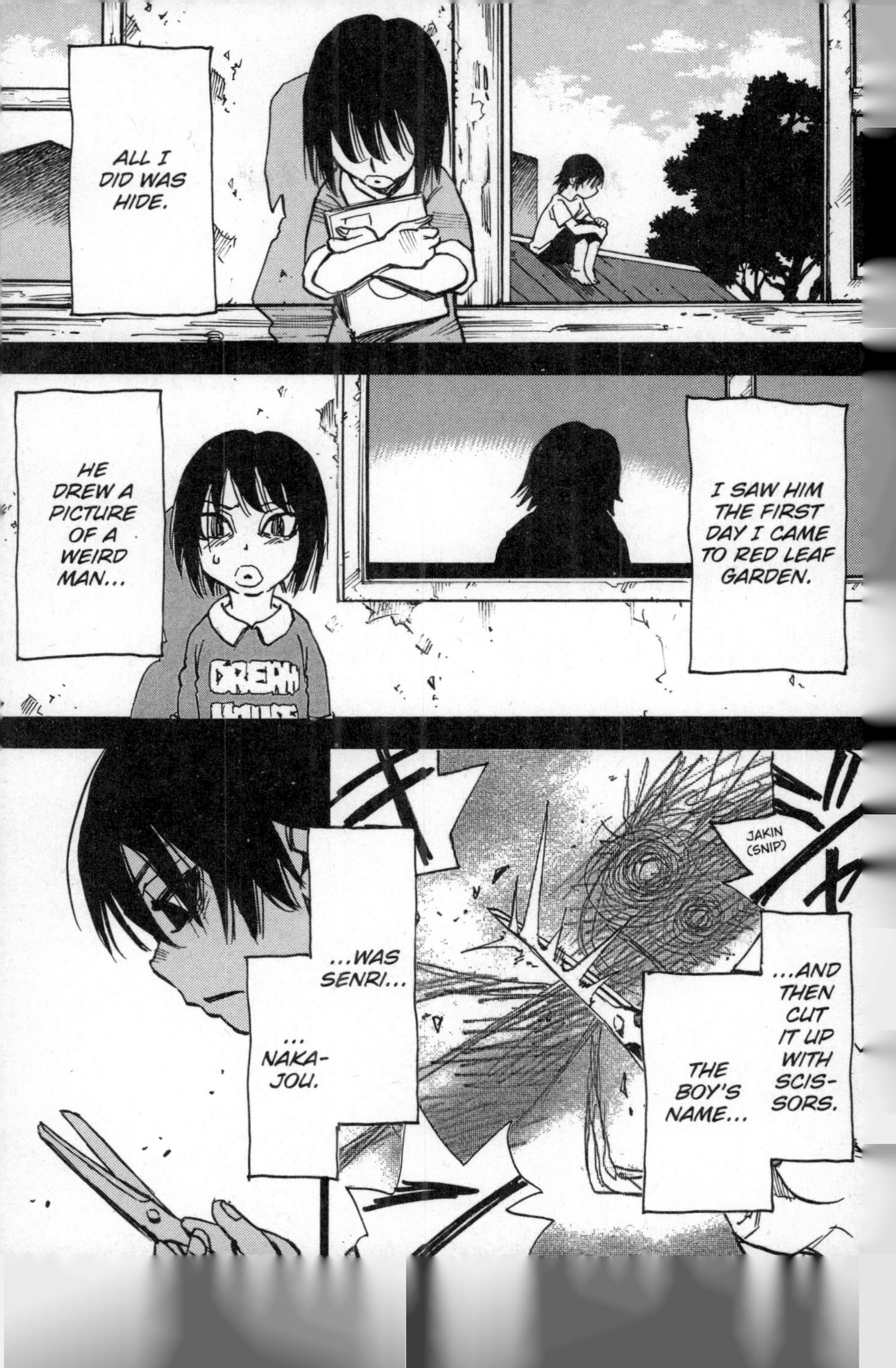
ALL I DID WAS HIDE.
I SAW HIM THE FIRST DAY I CAME TO RED LEAF GARDEN.
HE DREW A PICTURE OF A WEIRD MAN...
JAKIN (SNIP)
...AND THEN CUT IT UP WITH SCISSORS.
THE BOY'S NAME...
...WAS SENRI...
...NAKAJOU.

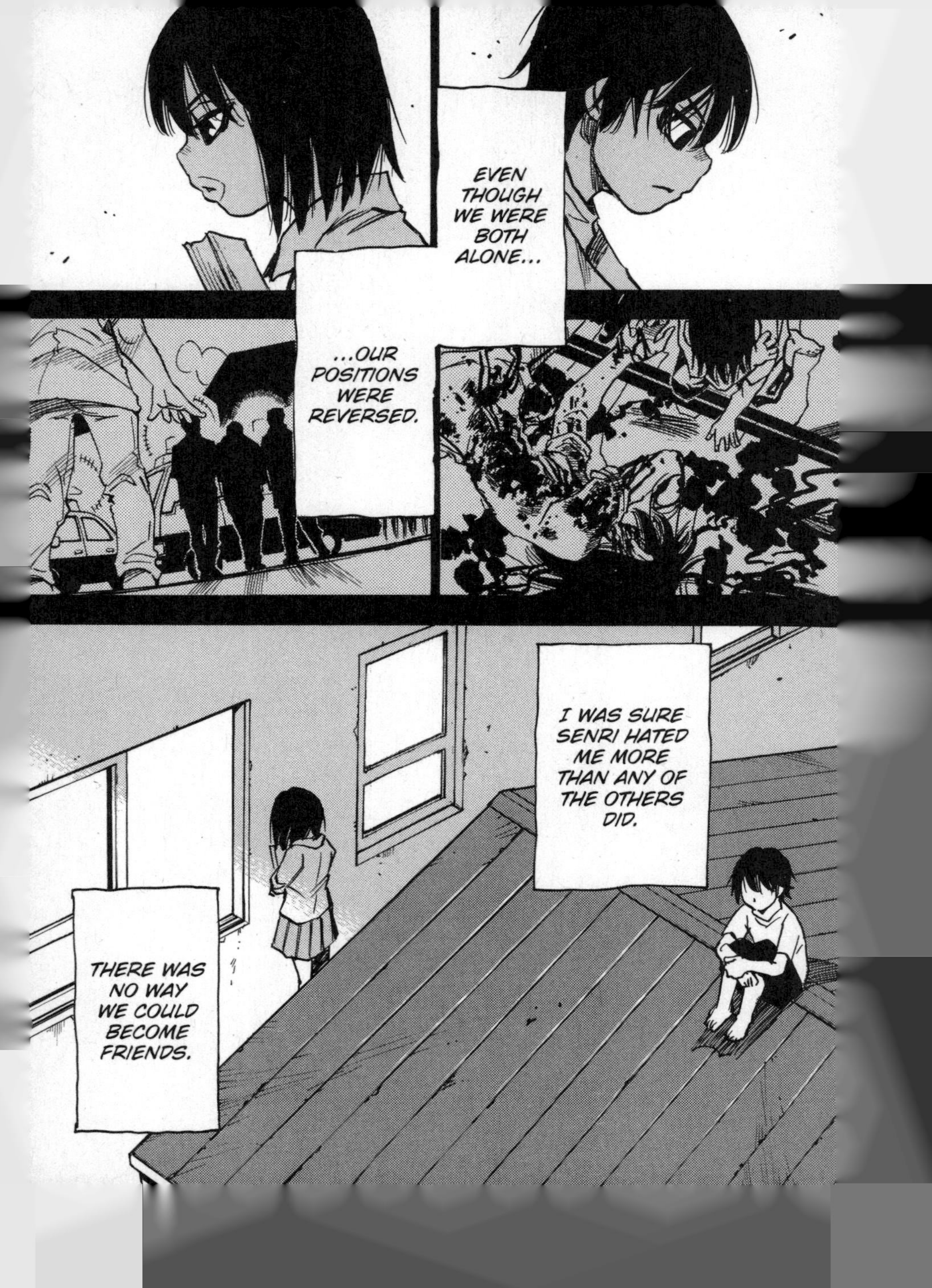
EVEN THOUGH WE WERE BOTH ALONE...
...OUR POSITIONS WERE REVERSED.
I WAS SURE SENRI HATED ME MORE THAN ANY OF THE OTHERS DID.
THERE WAS NO WAY WE COULD BECOME FRIENDS.

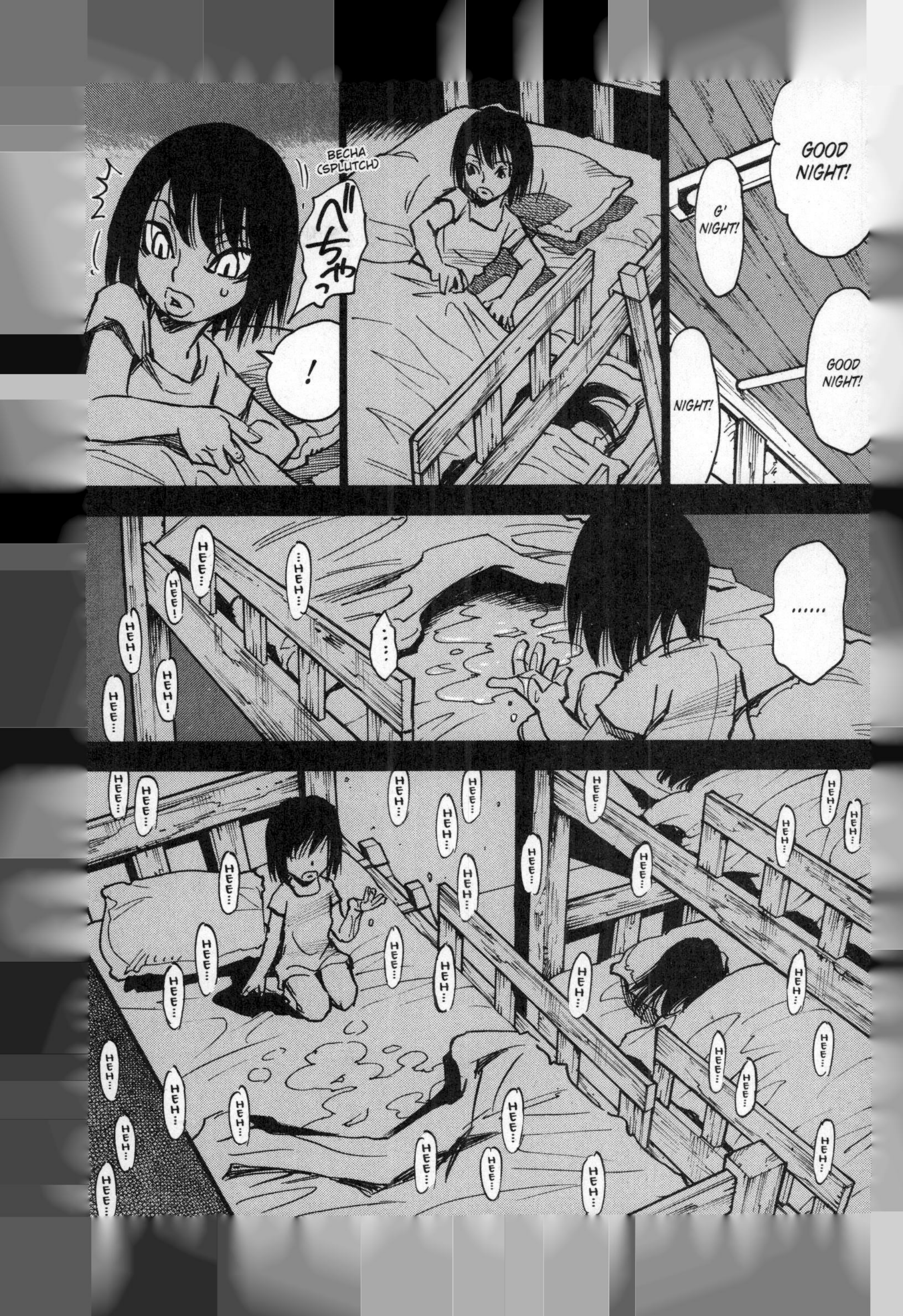
GOOD NIGHT!
G' NIGHT!
GOOD NIGHT!
NIGHT!
BECHA (SPLUTCH)
べちゃっ
!
......
...
...HEH...
HEE!
HEE!
HEH!
HEH!
HEE...
HEH...
HEH...
HEH...
HEE...
HEE...
HEE...
HEE...
HEH...
HEH...
HEH...
HEE...
HEH...
HEE...
HEH...
HEE...
HEE...
HEH...
HEE...
HEH...
HEE...
HEE...
HEE...
HEE...
HEE...
HEE...
HEE...
HEE...
HEE...
HEE...
HEH...
HEH...
HEH...
HEH...
HEH...
HEE...

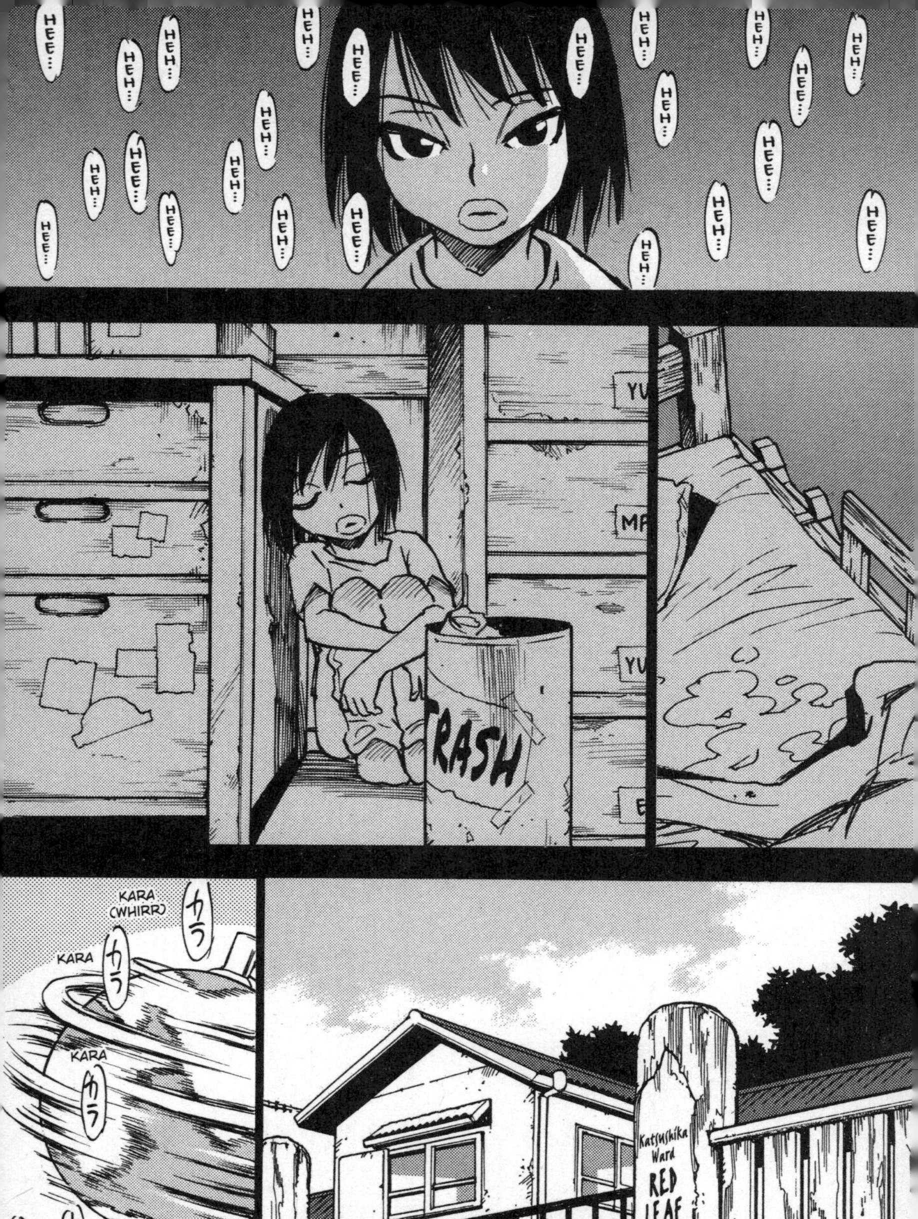
HEH…
HEE…
HEH…
HEE…
HEE…
HEH…
HEH…
HEH…
HEE…
HEH…
HEE…
HEH…
HEE…
HEH…
HEH…
HEH…
HEE…
HEH…
HEE…
HEE…
HEH…
HEE…
HEE…
TRASH
Katsushika Ward
RED LEAF GARDEN
カラ
KARA (WHIRR)
カラ
KARA
カラ
KARA
カラ
KARA
カラ
KARA

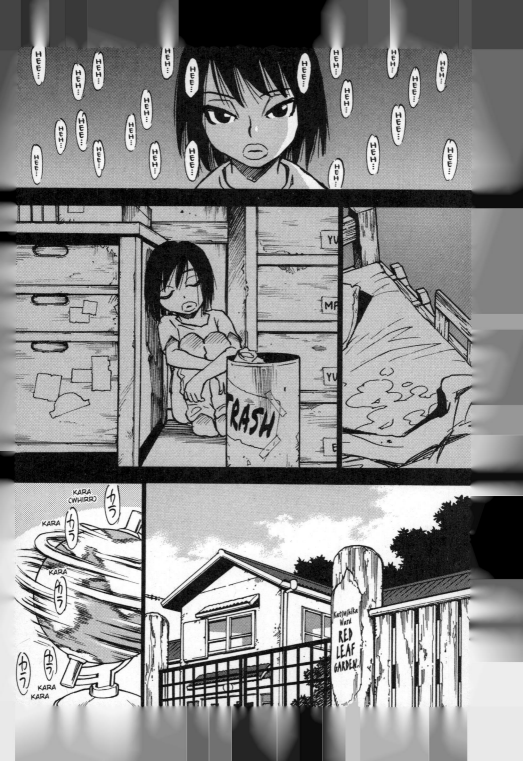

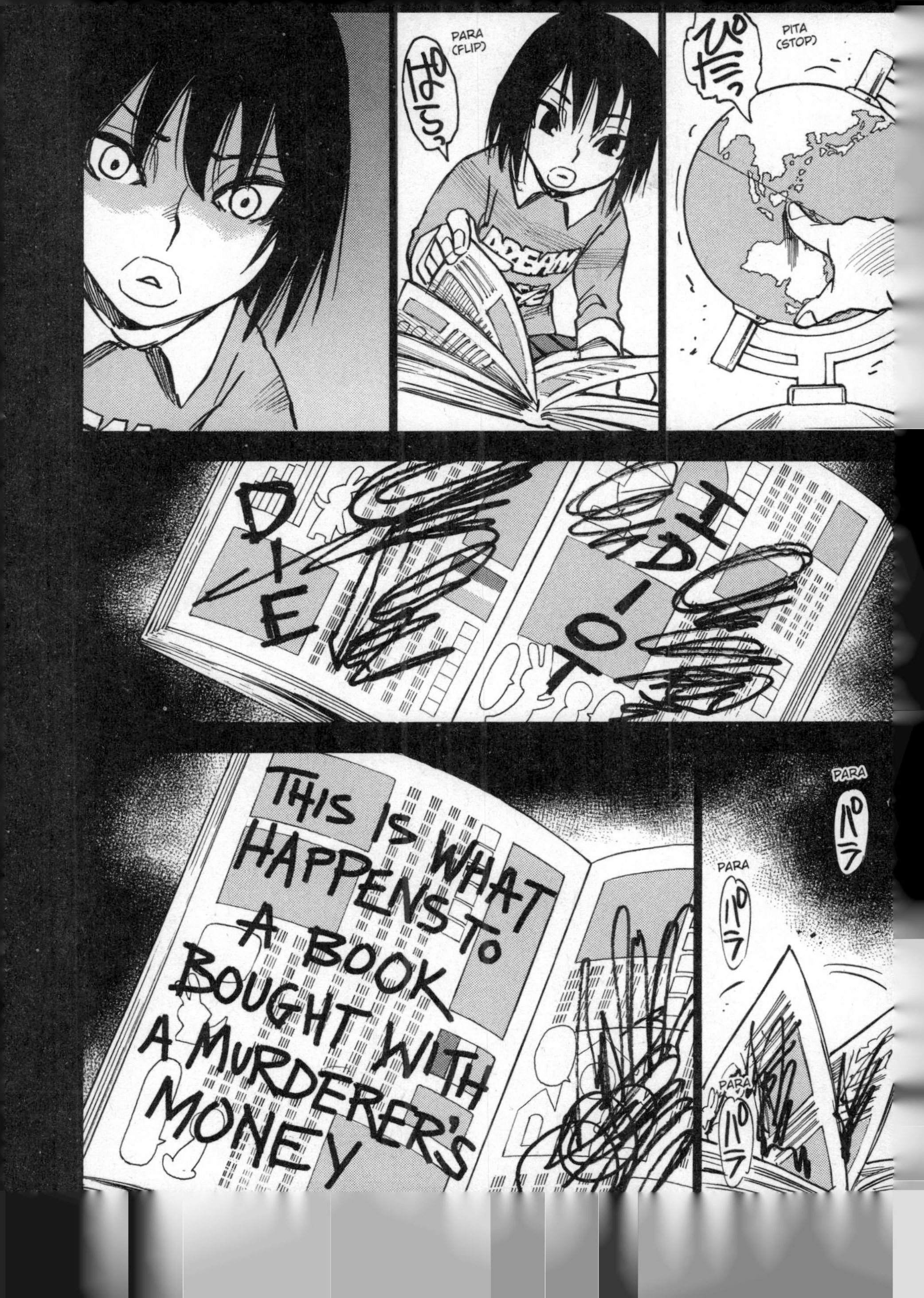

ぴたっ
PITA (STOP)
ぱらっ
PARA (FLIP)
IDIOT
DIE
PARA
パラ
PARA
パラ
PARA
パラ
THIS IS WHAT HAPPENS TO A BOOK BOUGHT WITH A MURDERER'S MONEY

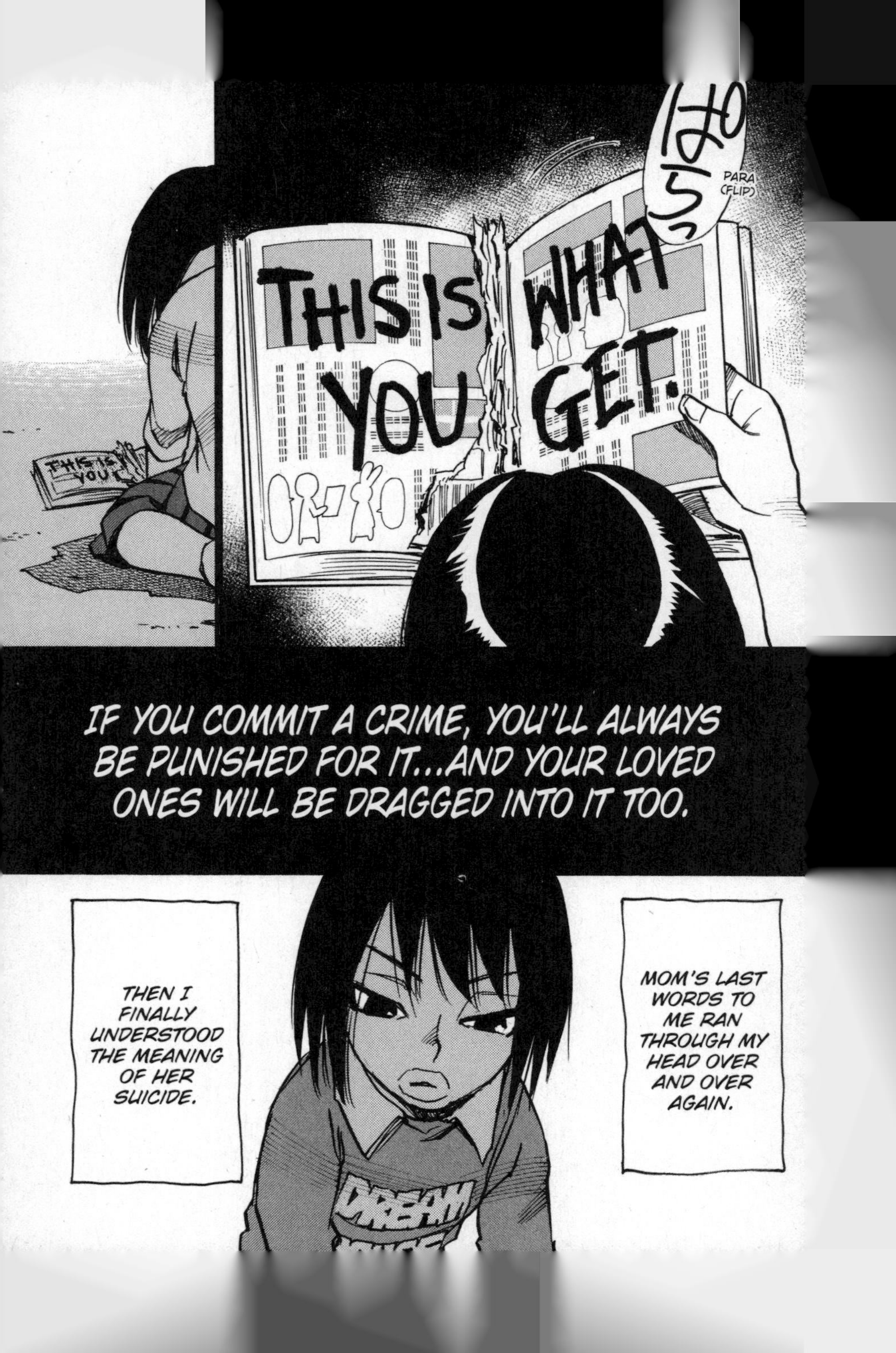
ぱらっ
PARA (FLIP)
THIS IS WHAT YOU GET.
IF YOU COMMIT A CRIME, YOU'LL ALWAYS BE PUNISHED FOR IT...AND YOUR LOVED ONES WILL BE DRAGGED INTO IT TOO.
MOM'S LAST WORDS TO ME RAN THROUGH MY HEAD OVER AND OVER AGAIN.
THEN I FINALLY UNDERSTOOD THE MEANING OF HER SUICIDE.

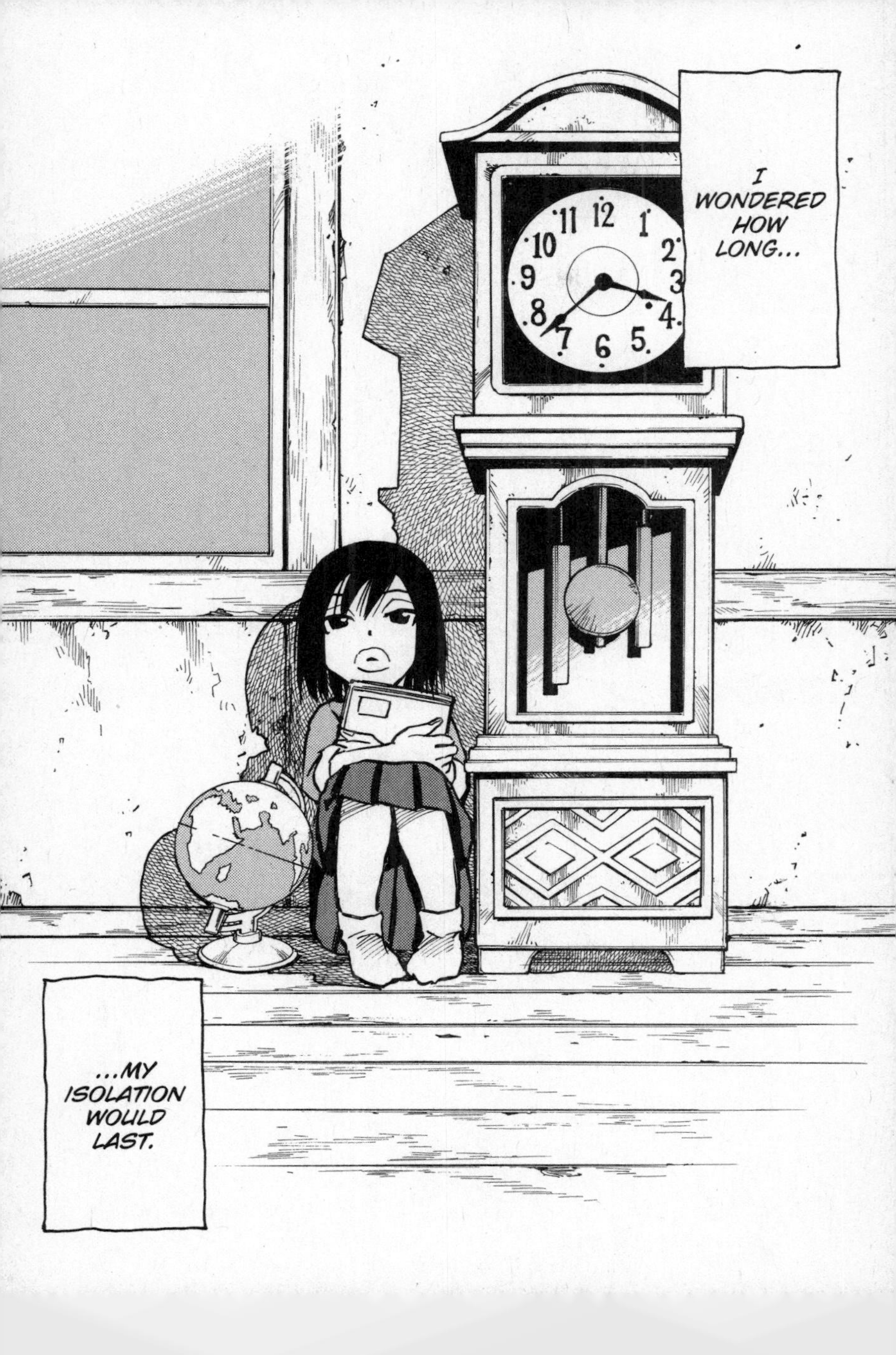
I WONDERED HOW LONG...
...MY ISOLATION WOULD LAST.

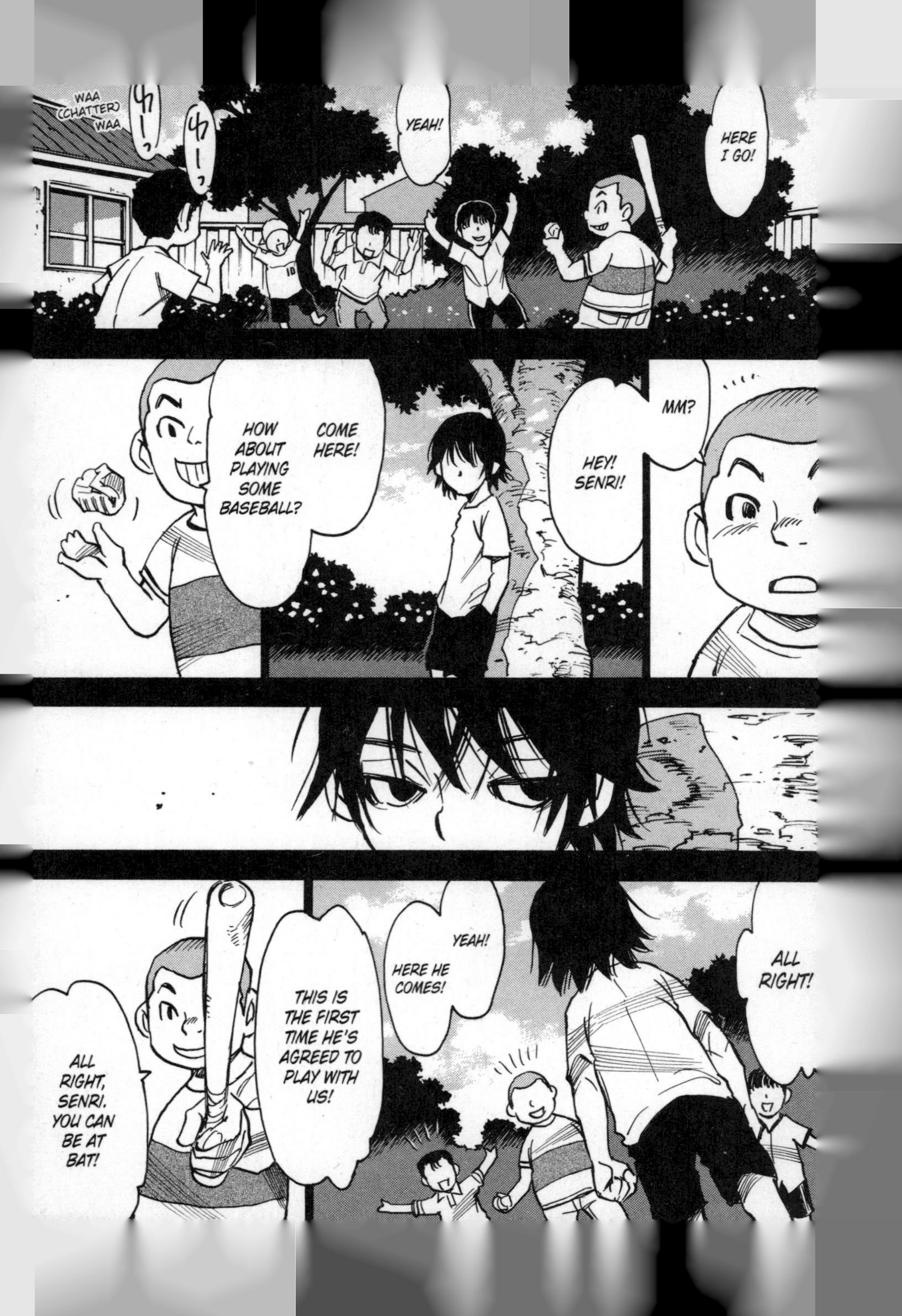
HERE I GO!
YEAH!
WAA (CHATTER) WAA
わーっ
わーっ
MM?
HEY! SENRI!
COME HERE!
HOW ABOUT PLAYING SOME BASEBALL?
ALL RIGHT!
YEAH!
HERE HE COMES!
THIS IS THE FIRST TIME HE'S AGREED TO PLAY WITH US!
ALL RIGHT, SENRI. YOU CAN BE AT BAT!

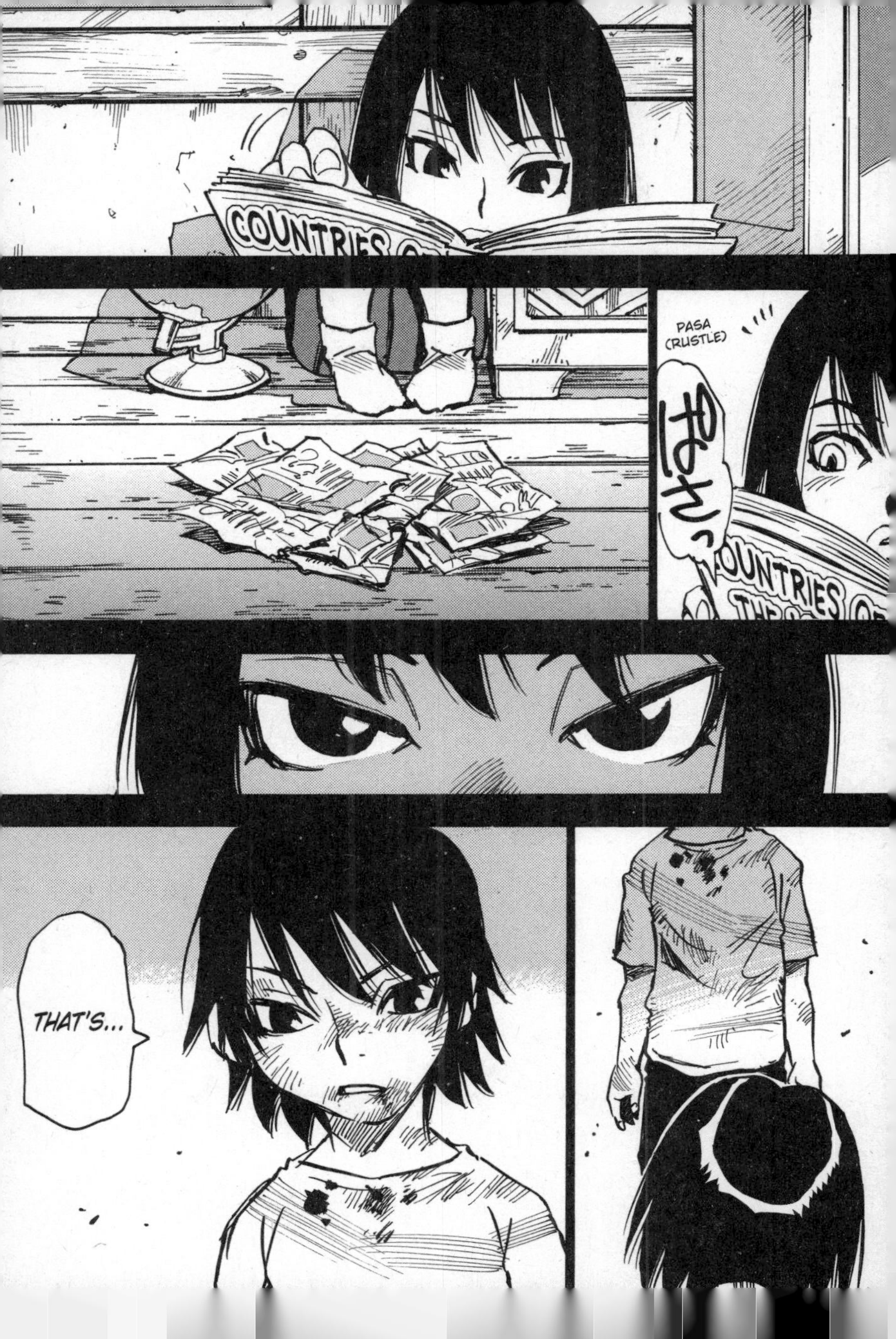
COUNTRIES
PASA (RUSTLE)
ぱさっ
COUNTRIES
THAT'S...

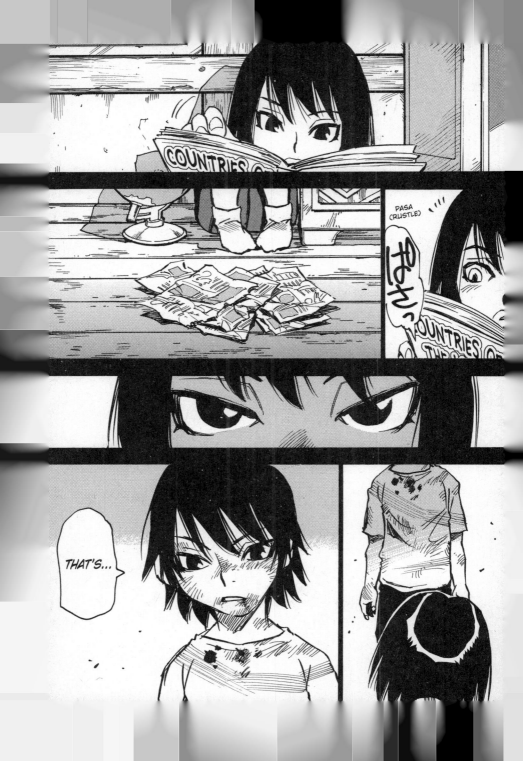

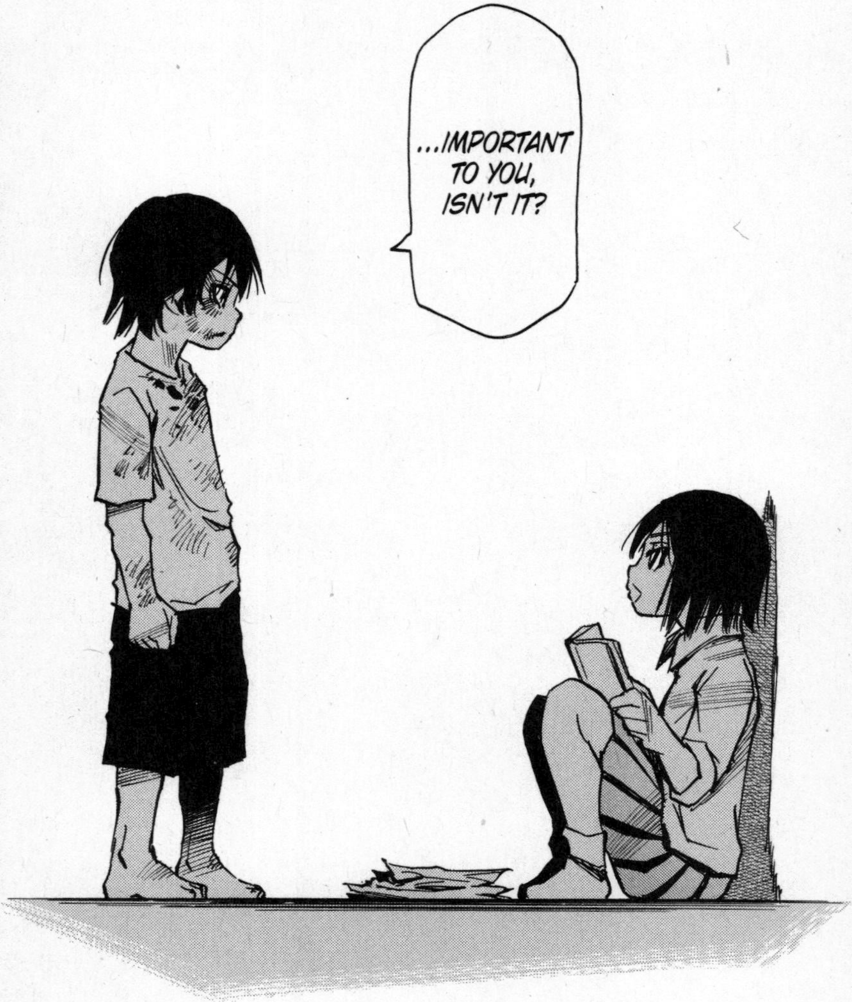
...IMPORTANT TO YOU, ISN'T IT?

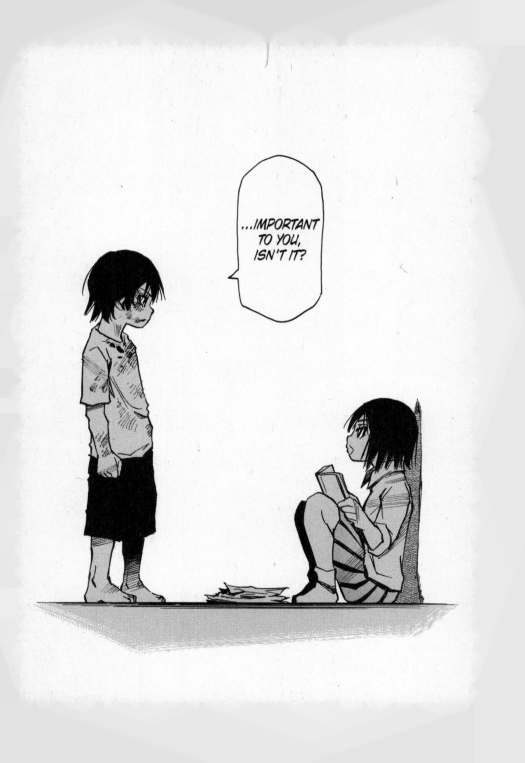

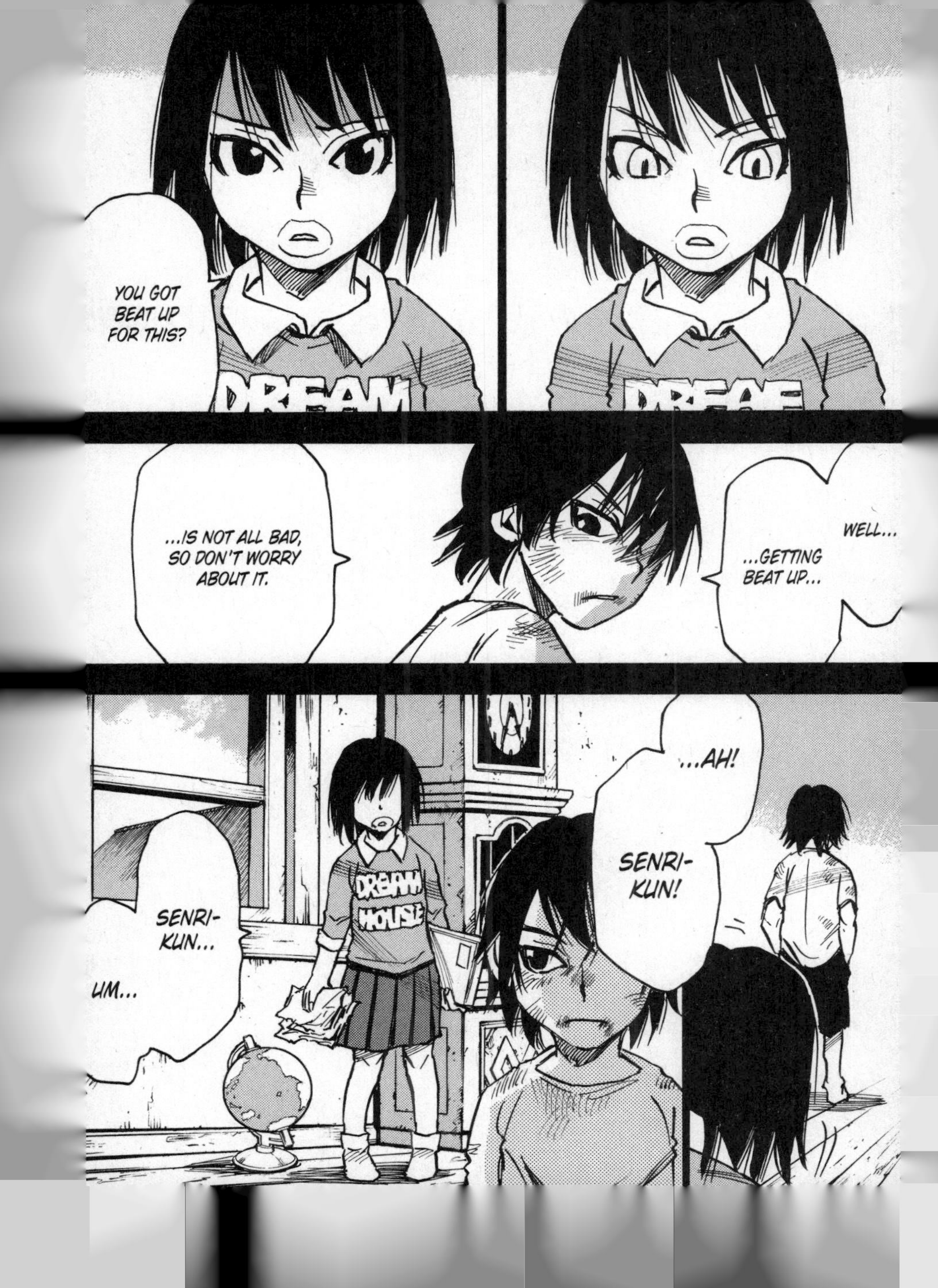
YOU GOT BEAT UP FOR THIS?
WELL...
...GETTING BEAT UP...
...IS NOT ALL BAD, SO DON'T WORRY ABOUT IT.
...AH!
SENRI-KUN!
SENRI-KUN...
UM...

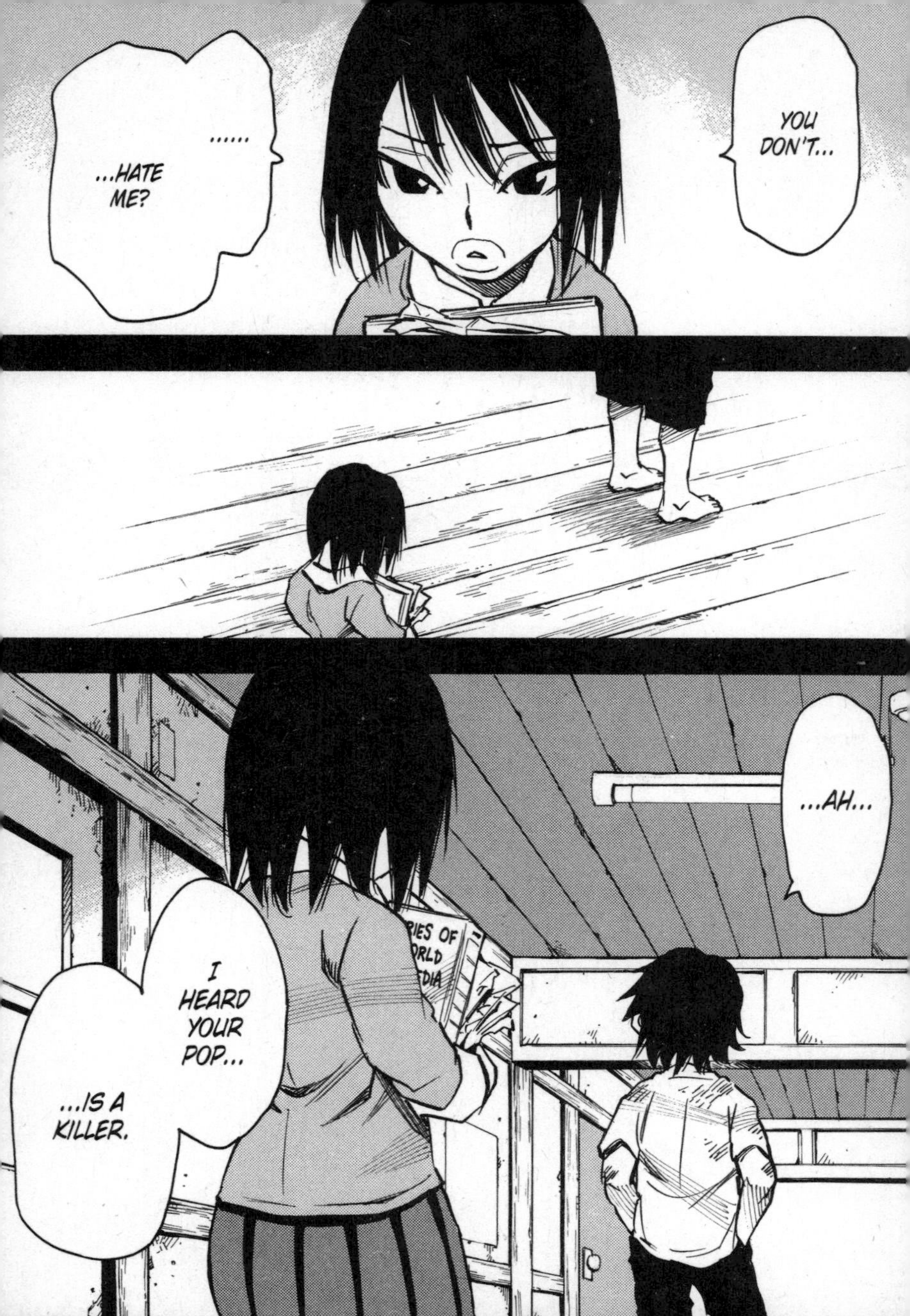
YOU DON'T...
......
...HATE ME?
...AH...
I HEARD YOUR POP...
...IS A KILLER.

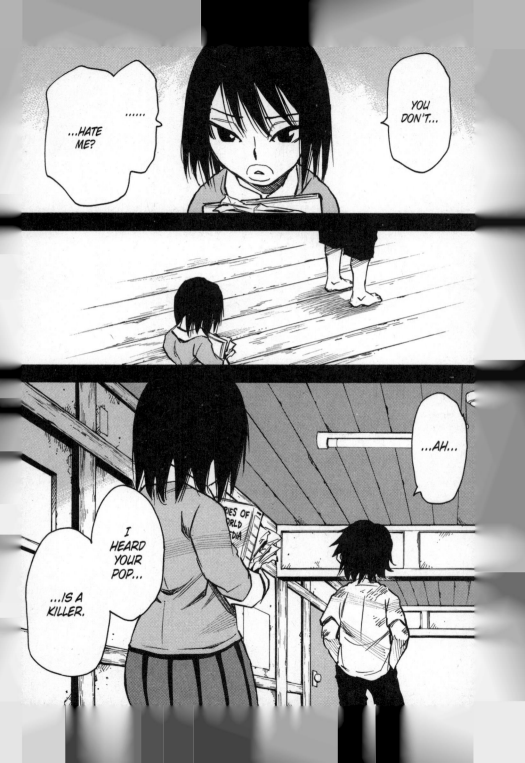

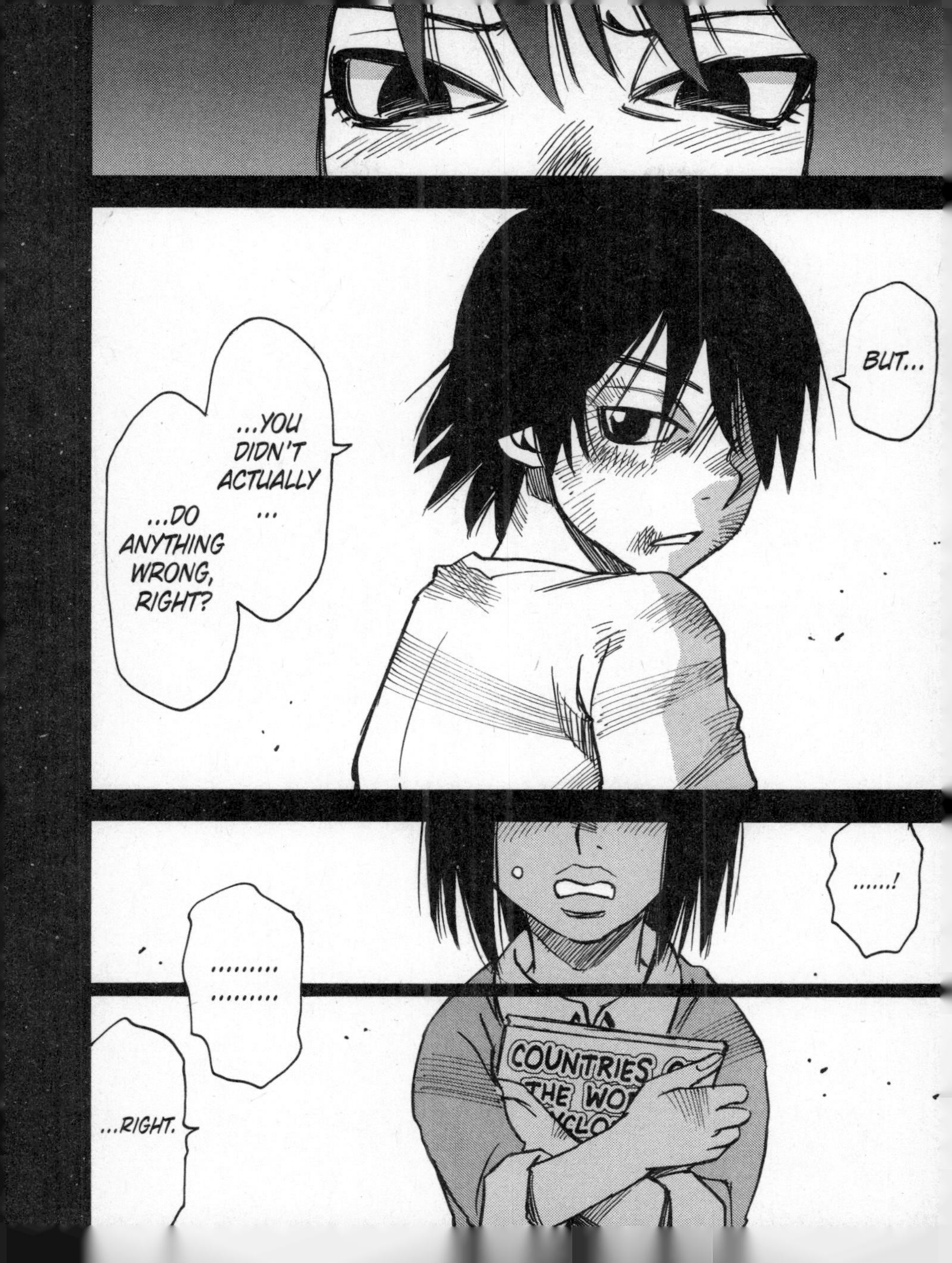
BUT...
...YOU DIDN'T ACTUALLY ... ...DO ANYTHING WRONG, RIGHT?
......!
....
COUNTRIES
...RIGHT.

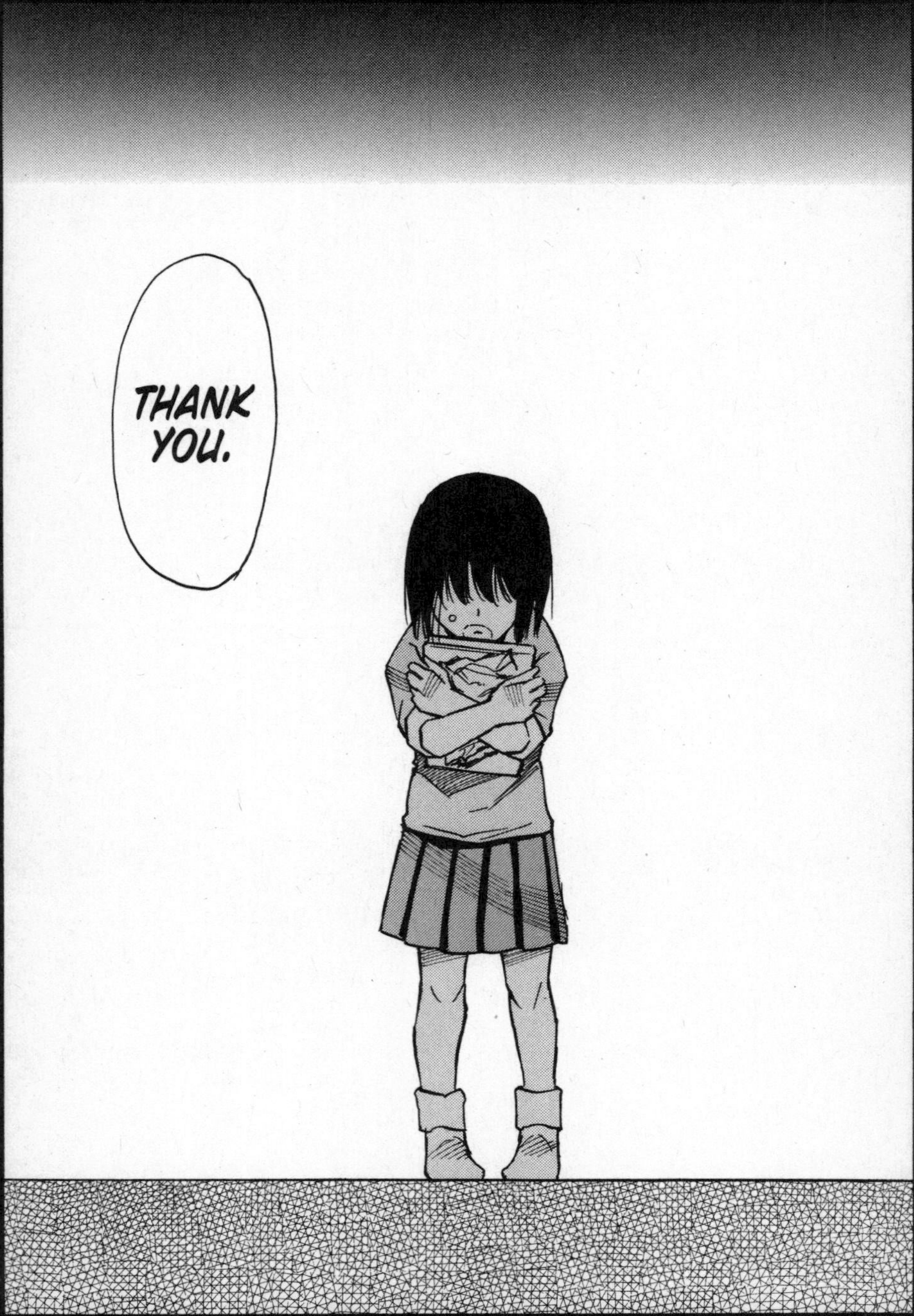
THANK YOU.

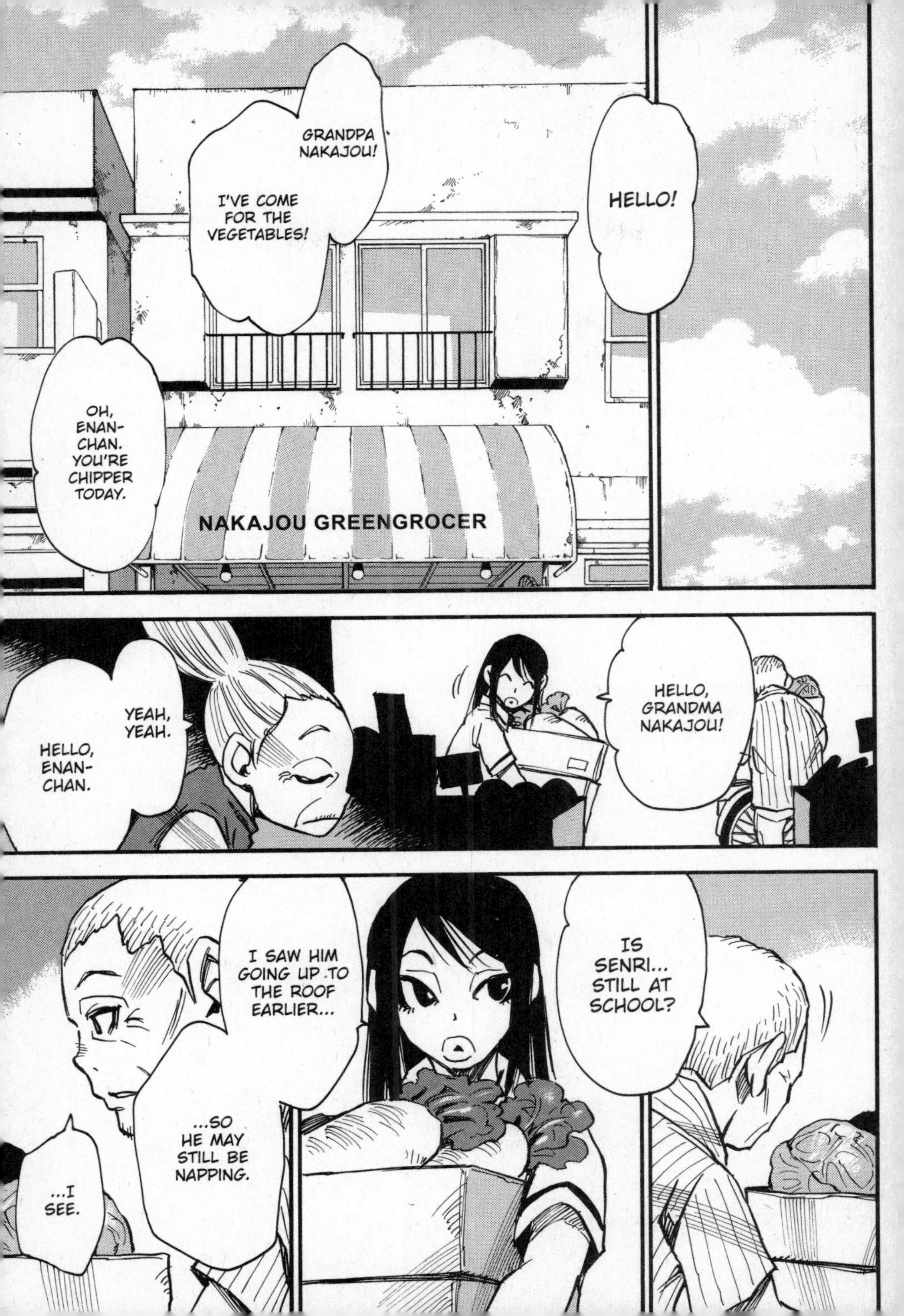
HELLO!
GRANDPA NAKAJOU!
I'VE COME FOR THE VEGETABLES!
NAKAJOU GREENGROCER
OH, ENAN-CHAN. YOU'RE CHIPPER TODAY.
HELLO, GRANDMA NAKAJOU!
YEAH, YEAH.
HELLO, ENAN-CHAN.
IS SENRI... STILL AT SCHOOL?
I SAW HIM GOING UP TO THE ROOF EARLIER...
...SO HE MAY STILL BE NAPPING.
...I SEE.

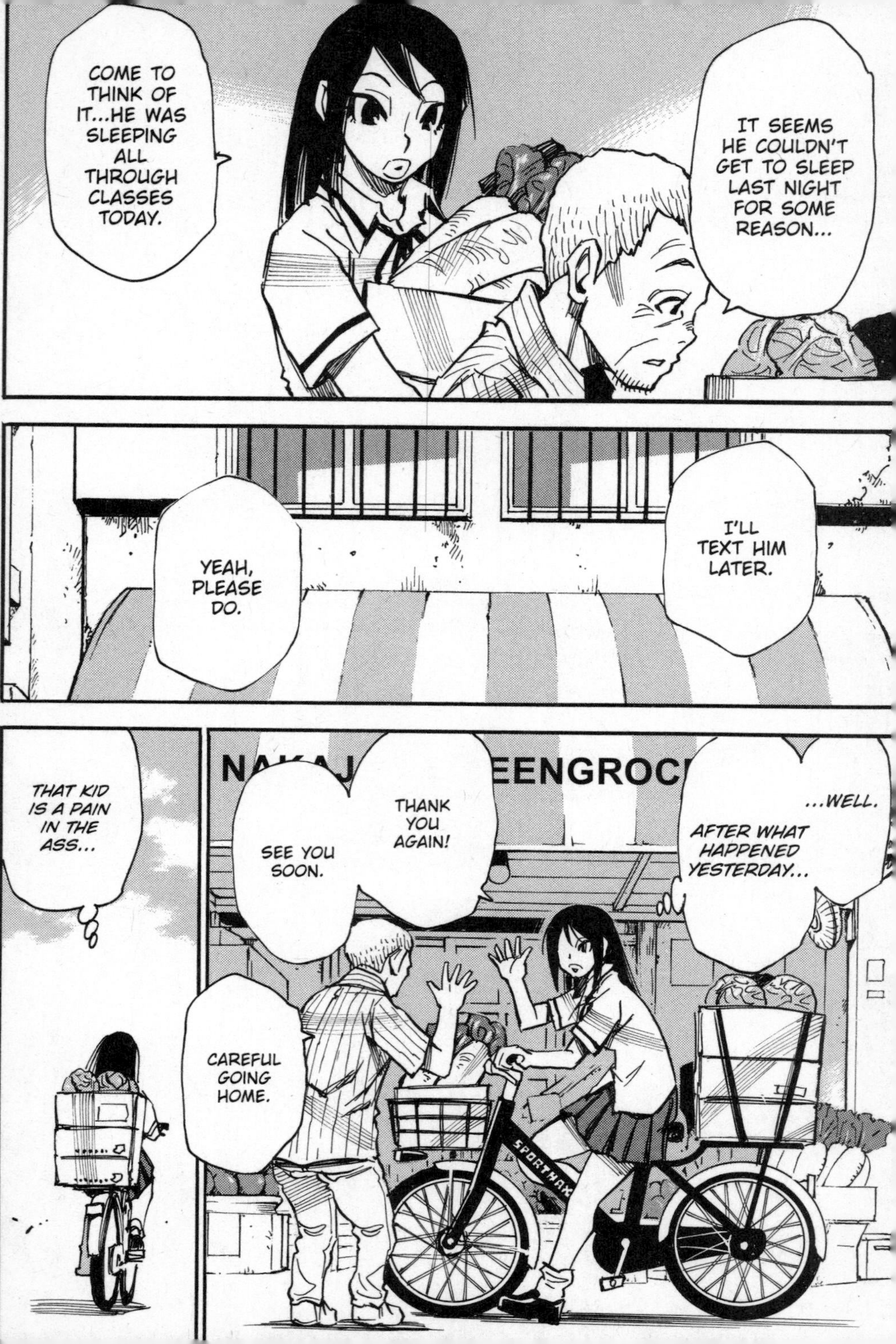
IT SEEMS HE COULDN'T GET TO SLEEP LAST NIGHT FOR SOME REASON...
COME TO THINK OF IT...HE WAS SLEEPING ALL THROUGH CLASSES TODAY.
I'LL TEXT HIM LATER.
YEAH, PLEASE DO.
...WELL. AFTER WHAT HAPPENED YESTERDAY...
THANK YOU AGAIN!
SEE YOU SOON.
CAREFUL GOING HOME.
THAT KID IS A PAIN IN THE ASS...

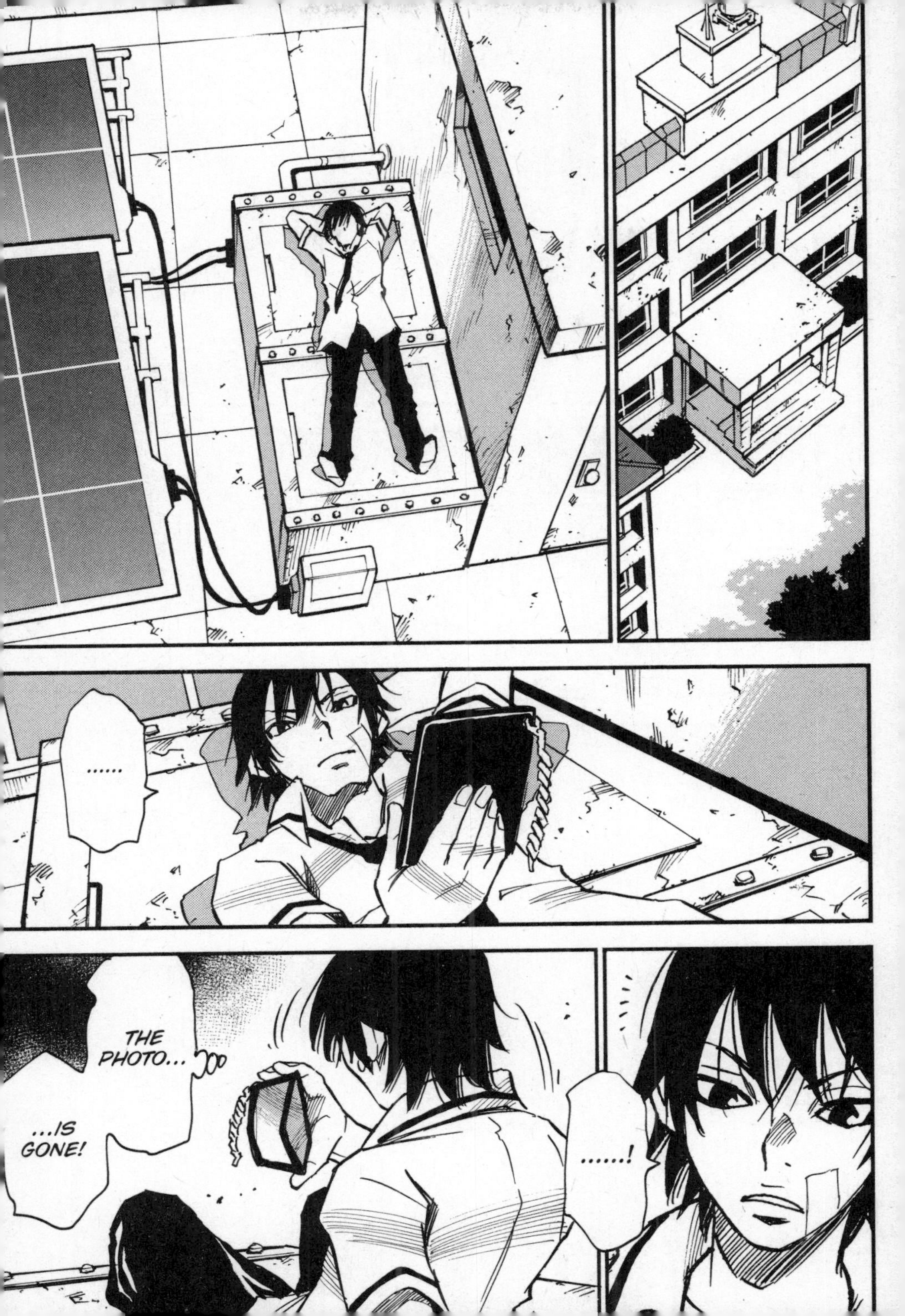
......
......!
THE PHOTO...
...IS GONE!

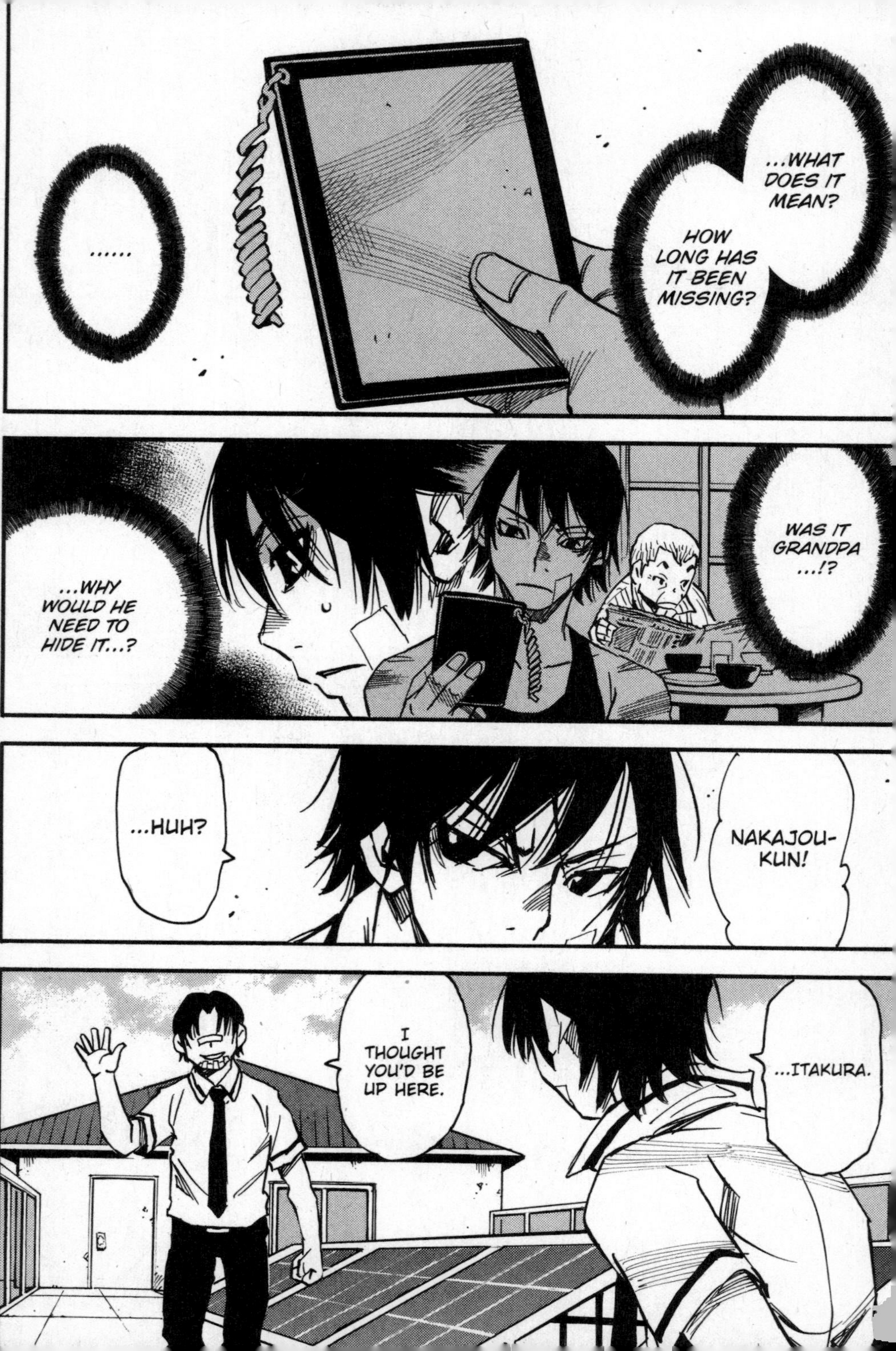
...WHAT DOES IT MEAN?
HOW LONG HAS IT BEEN MISSING?
......
WAS IT GRANDPA ...!?
...WHY WOULD HE NEED TO HIDE IT...?
NAKAJOU-KUN!
...HUH?
...ITAKURA.
I THOUGHT YOU'D BE UP HERE.

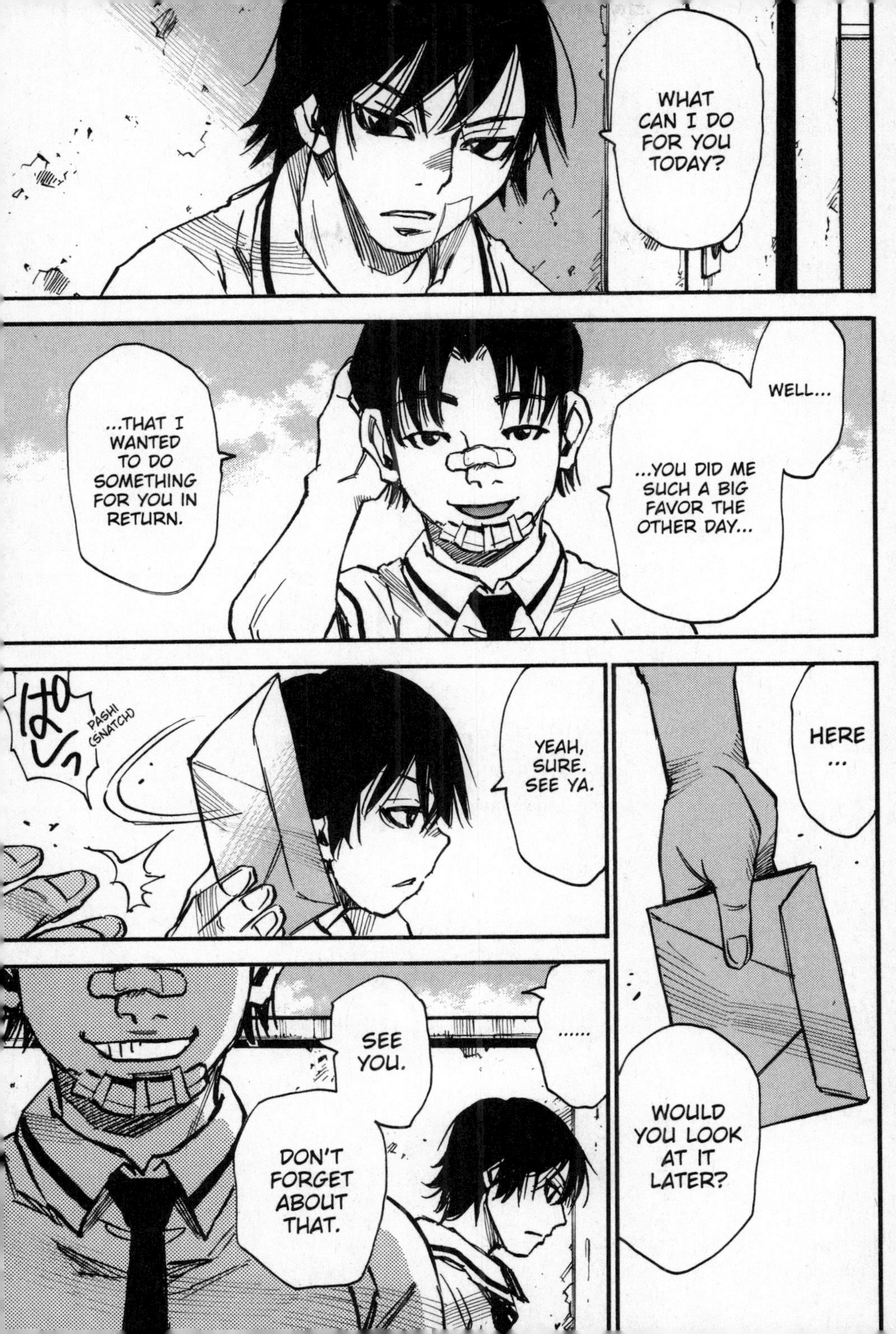
WHAT CAN I DO FOR YOU TODAY?
WELL...
...YOU DID ME SUCH A BIG FAVOR THE OTHER DAY...
...THAT I WANTED TO DO SOMETHING FOR YOU IN RETURN.
HERE...
WOULD YOU LOOK AT IT LATER?
YEAH, SURE. SEE YA.
ぱしっ
PASHI (SNATCH)
......
SEE YOU.
DON'T FORGET ABOUT THAT.

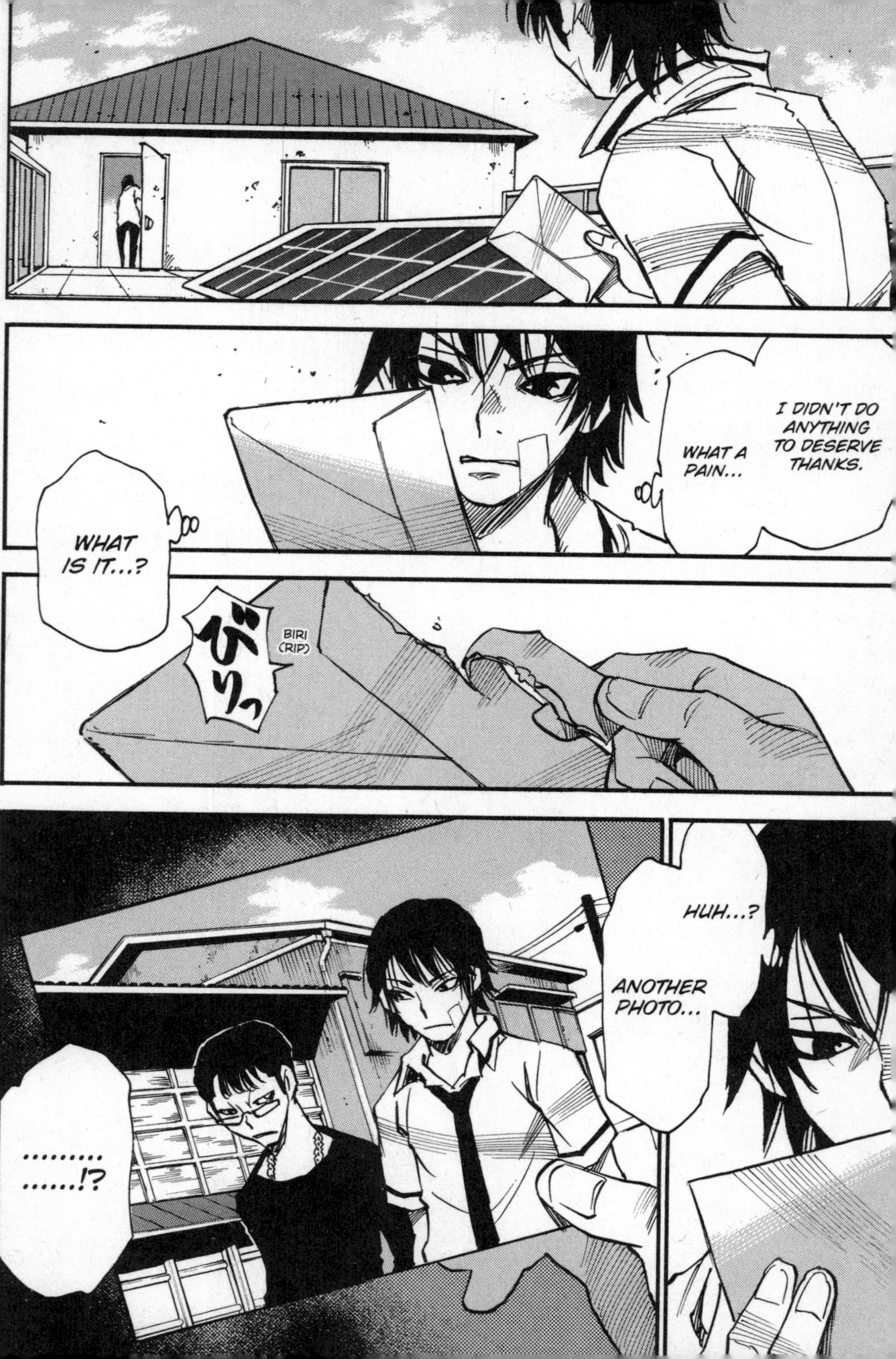
I DIDN'T DO ANYTHING TO DESERVE THANKS.
WHAT A PAIN...
WHAT IS IT...?
びりっ
BIRI (RIP)
HUH...?
ANOTHER PHOTO...
....
......!?

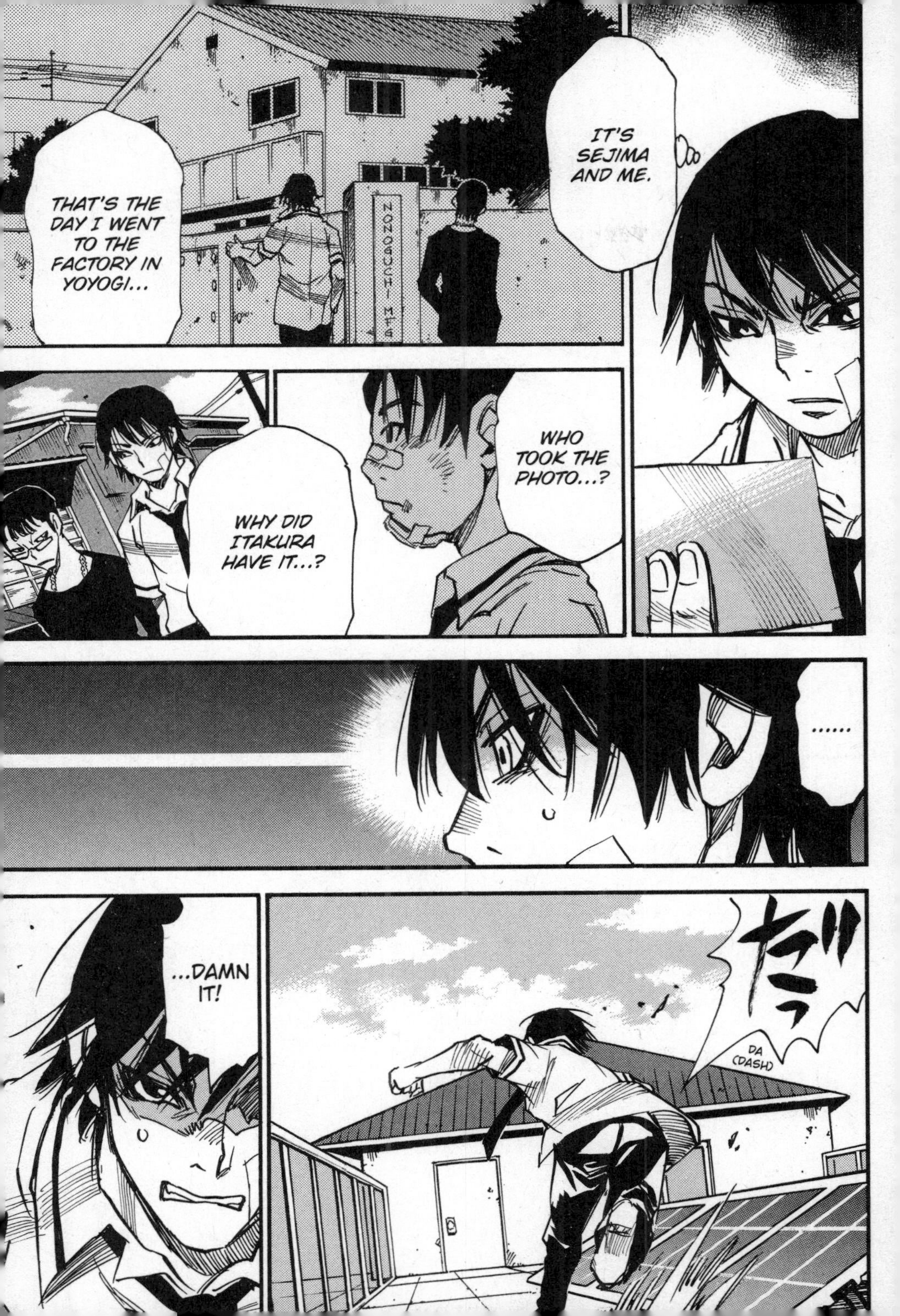
IT'S SEJIMA AND ME.
THAT'S THE DAY I WENT TO THE FACTORY IN YOYOGI...
NONOGUCHI MFG
WHO TOOK THE PHOTO...?
WHY DID ITAKURA HAVE IT...?
......
DA (DASH)
...DAMN IT!

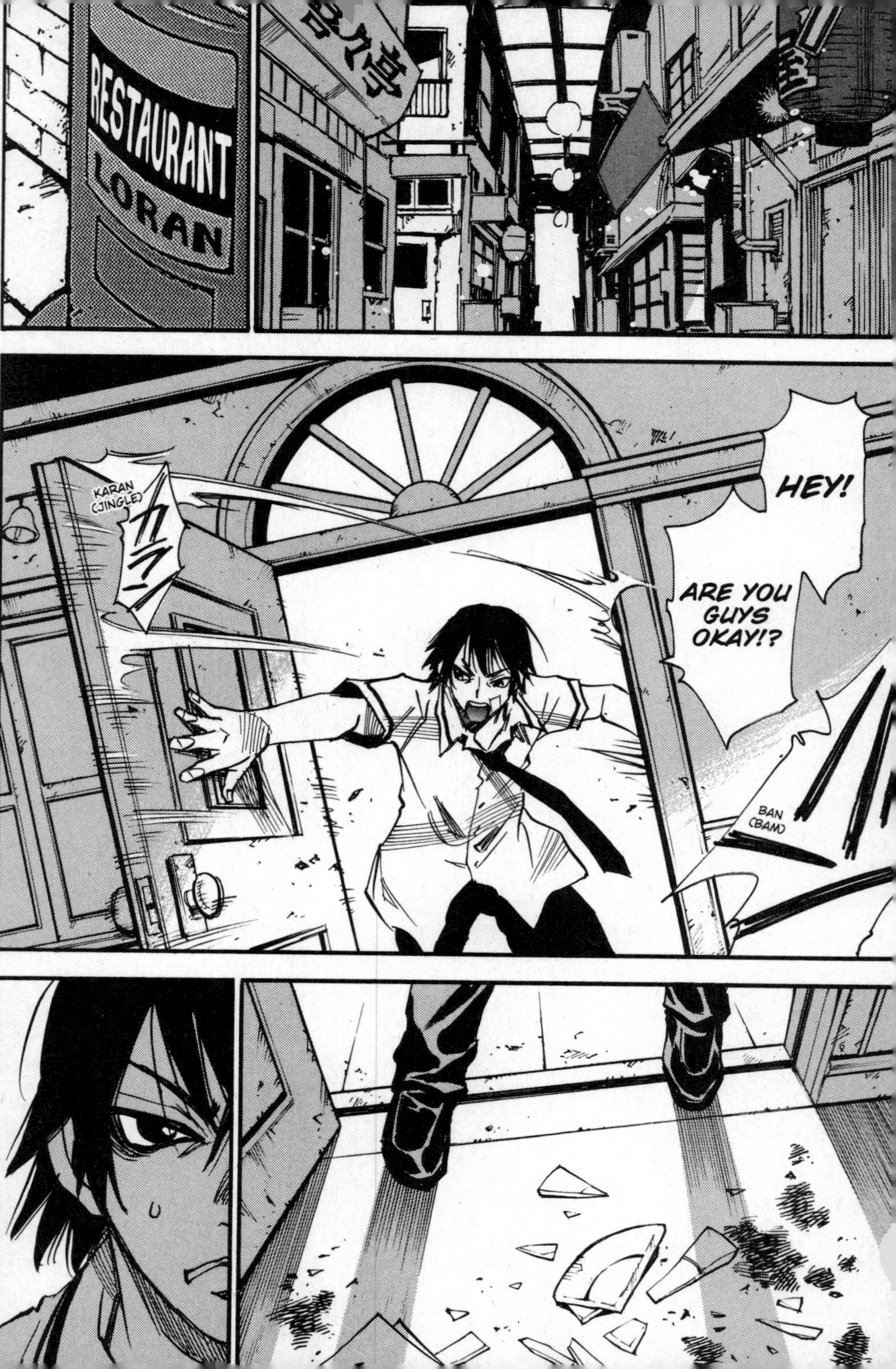
RESTAURANT
LORAN
HEY!
ARE YOU GUYS OKAY!?
KARAN (JINGLE)
BAN (BAM)

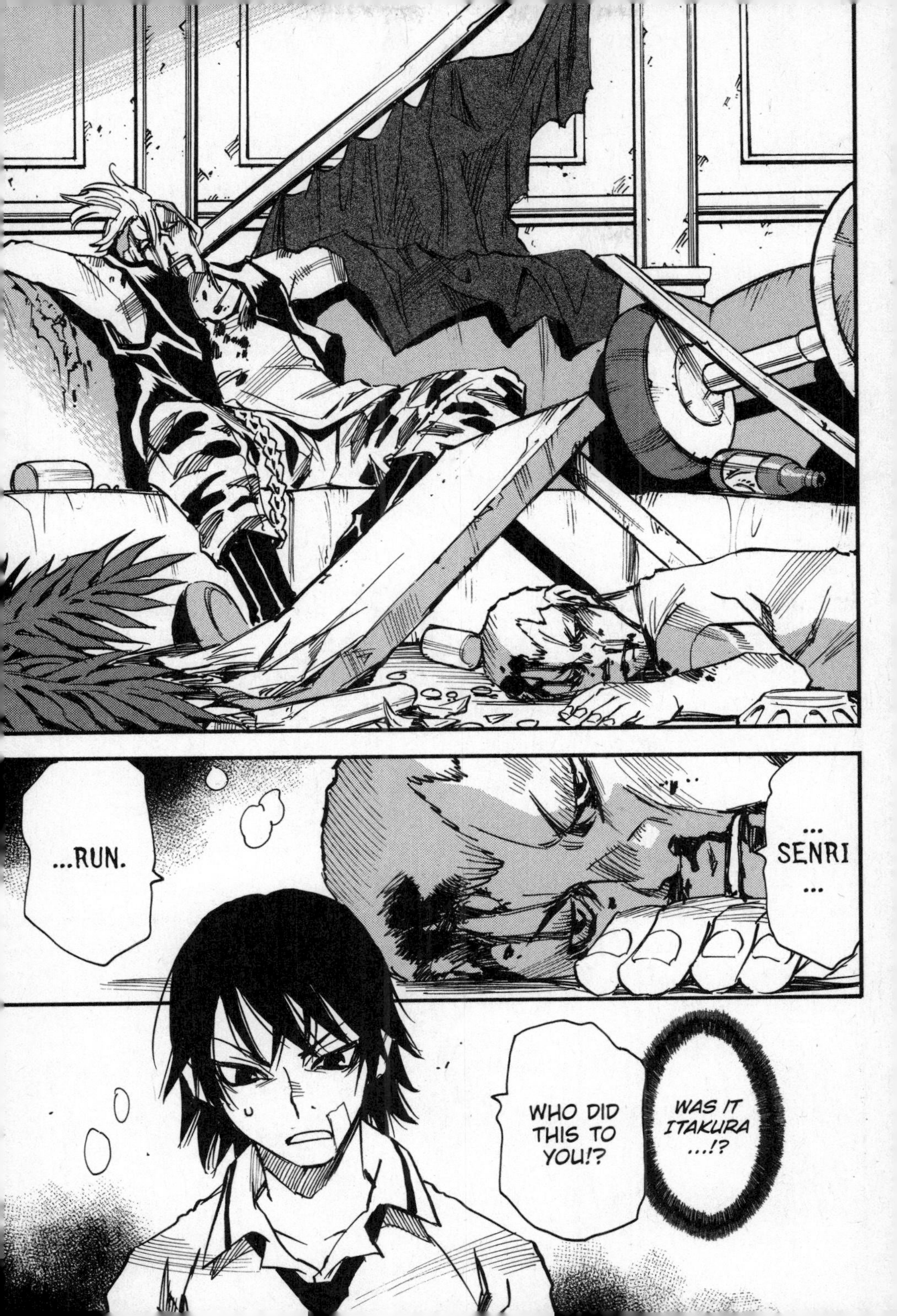
...SENRI...
...RUN.
WAS IT ITAKURA...!?
WHO DID THIS TO YOU!?

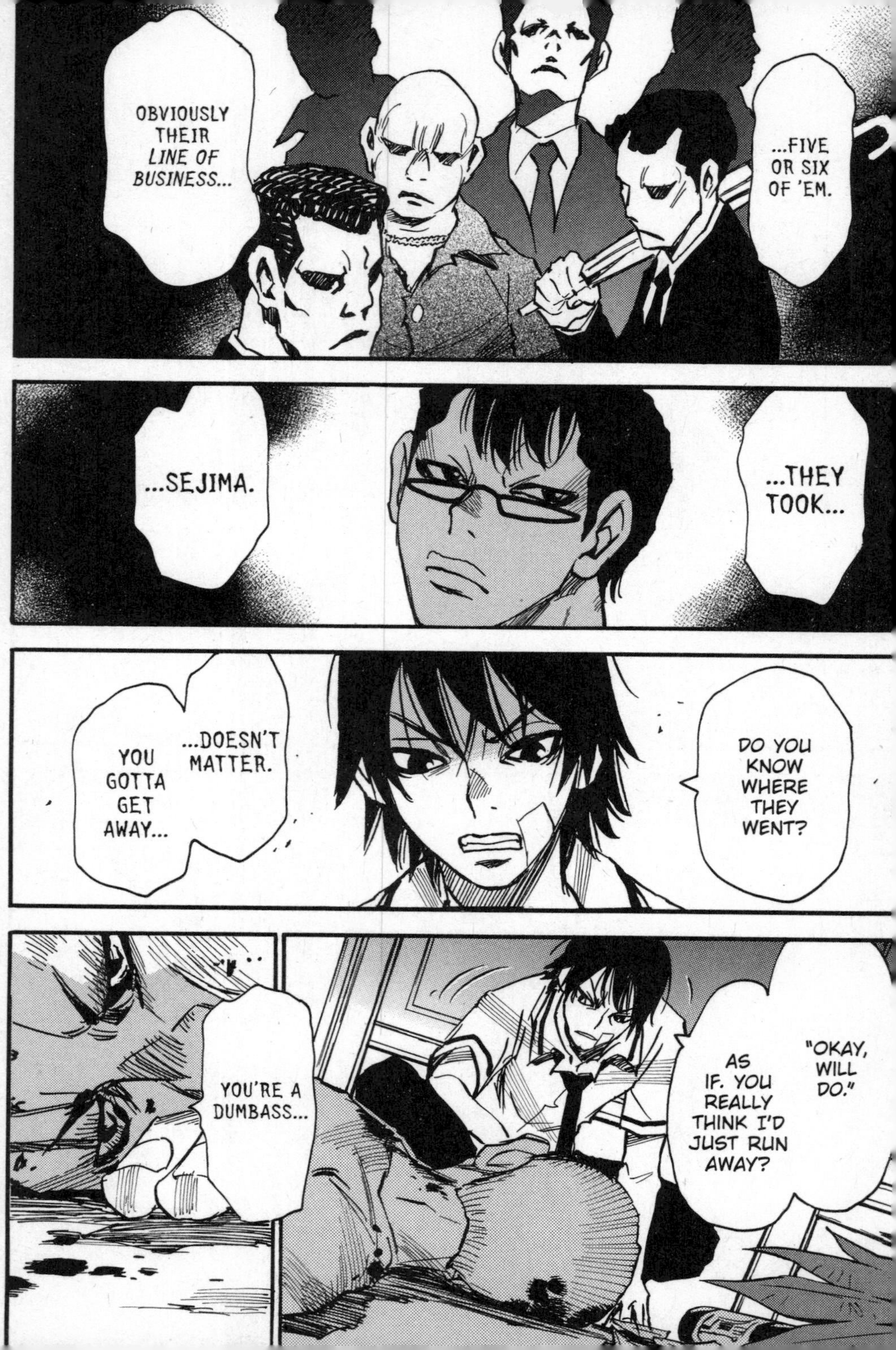
...FIVE OR SIX OF 'EM.
OBVIOUSLY THEIR *LINE OF BUSINESS*...
...THEY TOOK...
...SEJIMA.
DO YOU KNOW WHERE THEY WENT?
...DOESN'T MATTER.
YOU GOTTA GET AWAY...
"OKAY, WILL DO."
AS IF. YOU REALLY THINK I'D JUST RUN AWAY?
...
YOU'RE A DUMBASS...

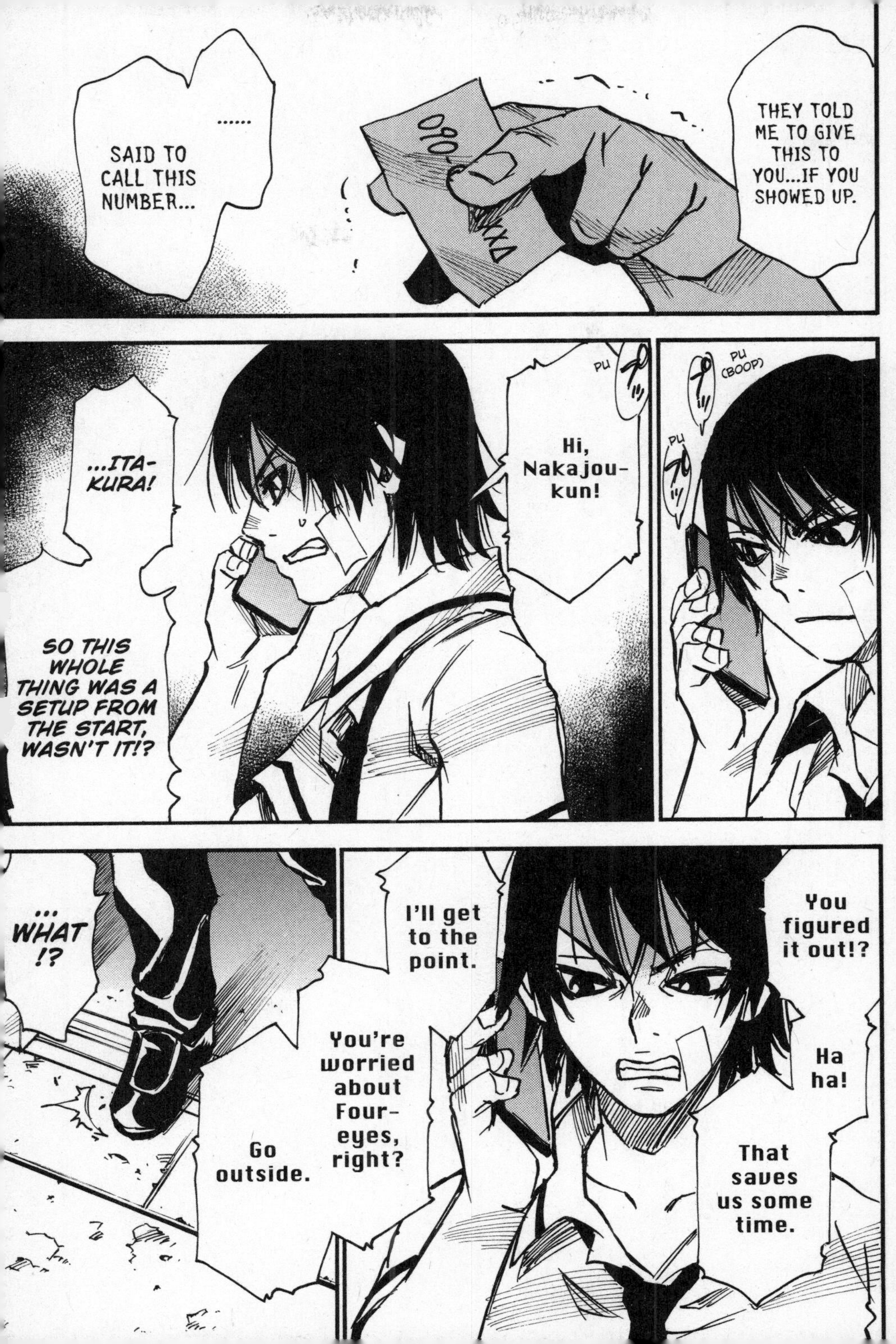
THEY TOLD ME TO GIVE THIS TO YOU...IF YOU SHOWED UP.
......
SAID TO CALL THIS NUMBER...
PU (BOOP)
PU
PU
Hi, Nakajou-kun!
...ITA-KURA!
SO THIS WHOLE THING WAS A SETUP FROM THE START, WASN'T IT!?
You figured it out!?
Ha ha!
That saves us some time.
I'll get to the point.
You're worried about Four-eyes, right?
Go outside.
...WHAT!?

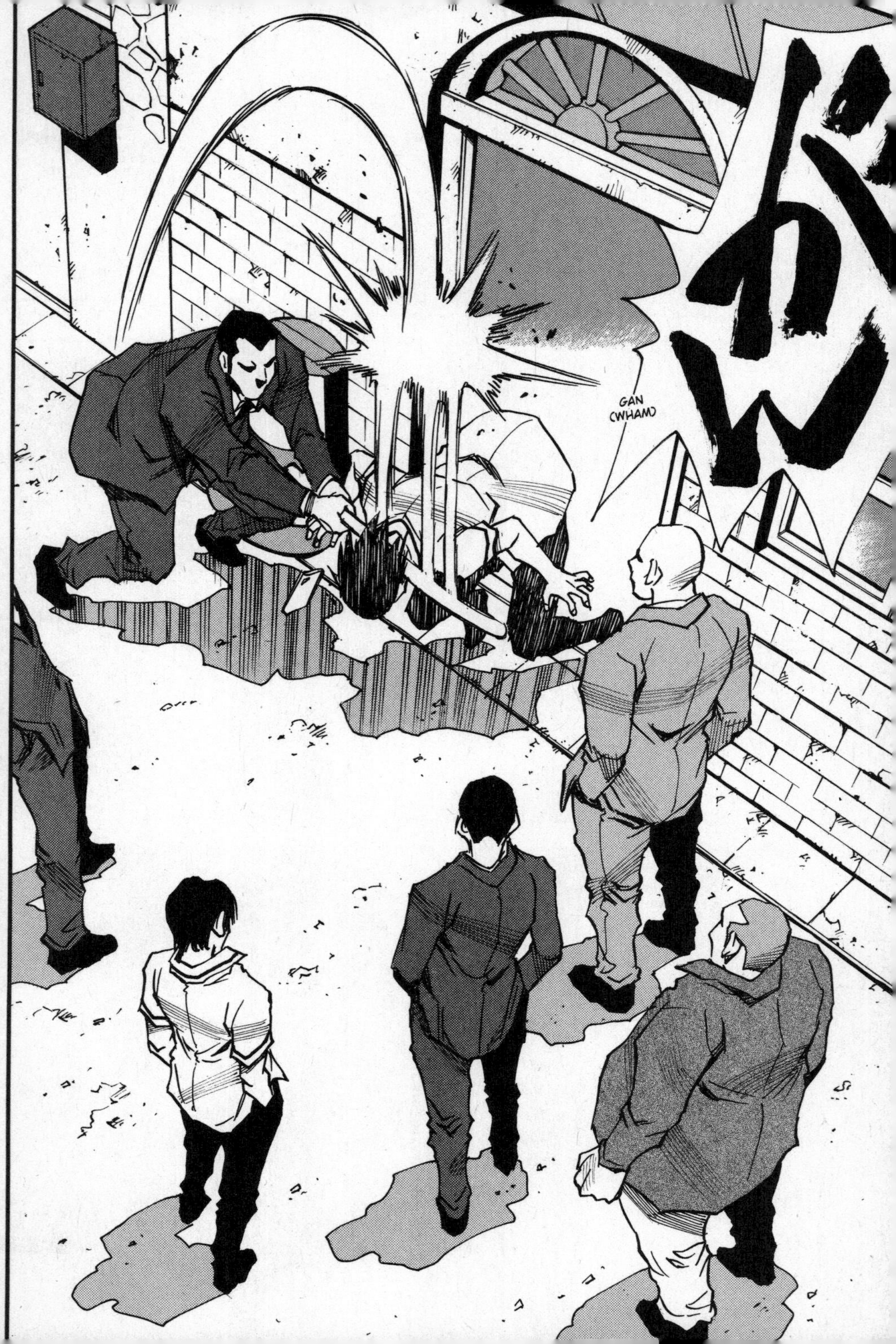
GAN
(WHAM)

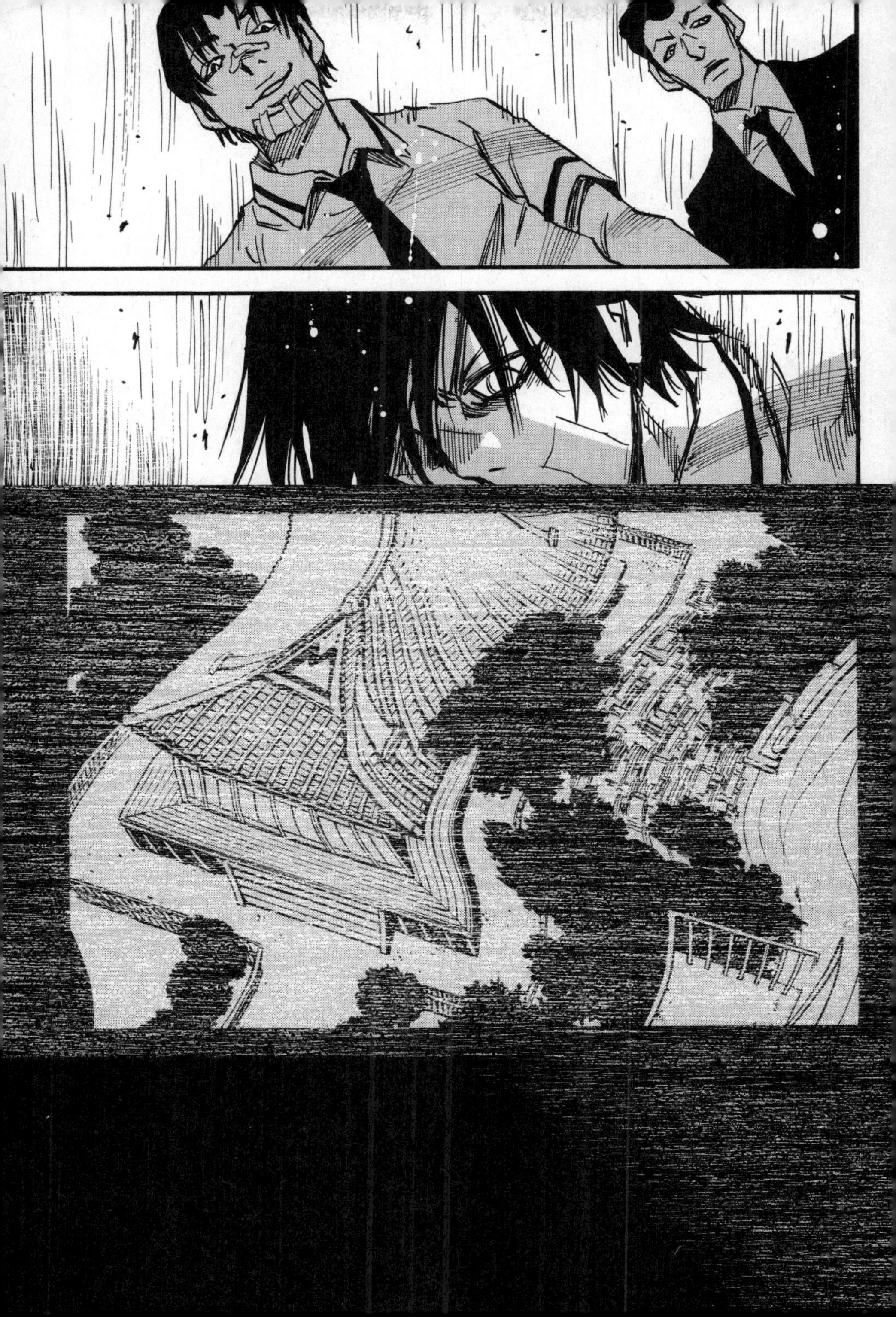

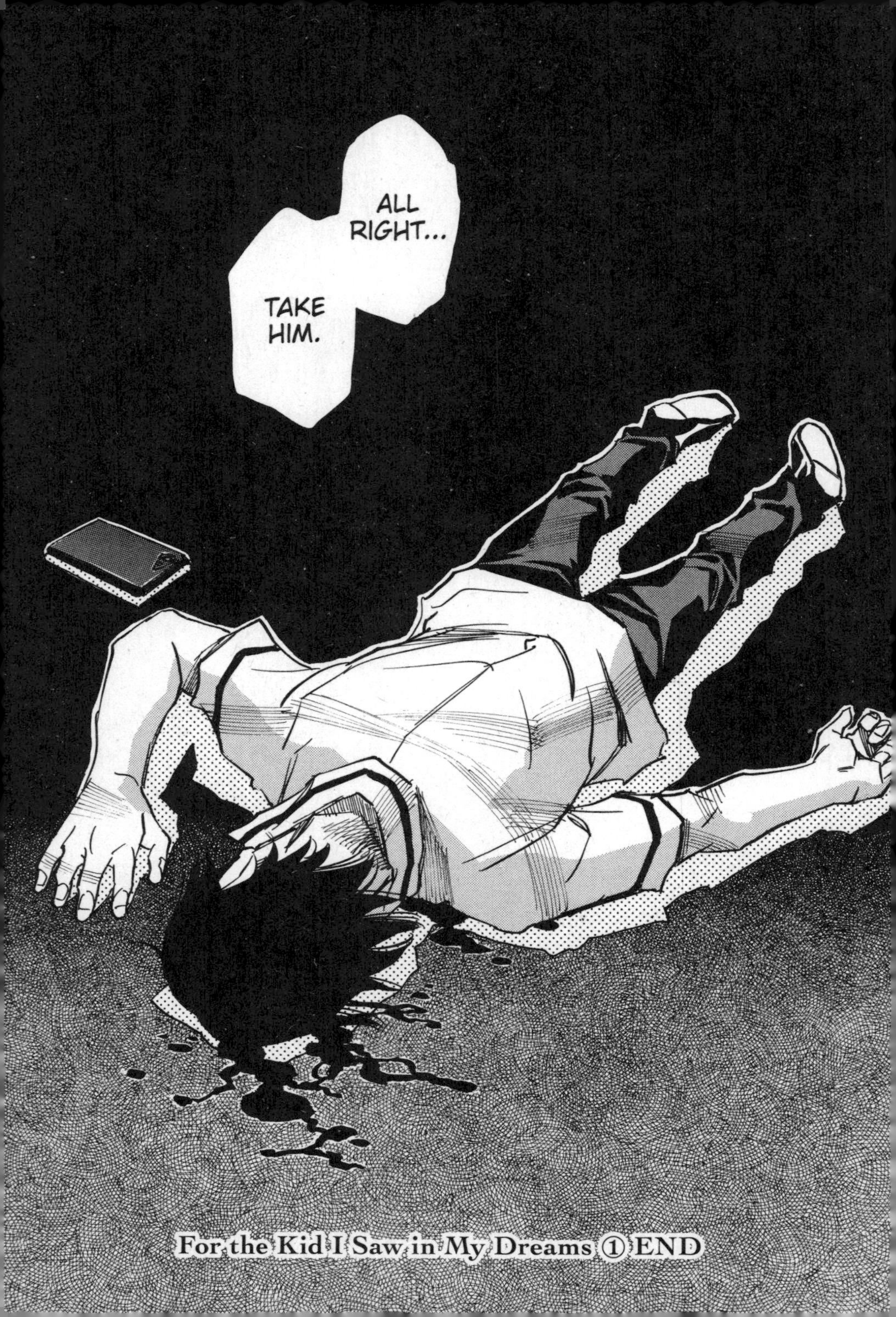
ALL RIGHT...
TAKE HIM.

For the Kid I Saw in My Dreams ① END

STAFF

Kei Sanbe

Yoichiro Tomita
Manami 18 Sai
Kouji Kikuta

Keishi Kanesada

RESEARCH/PHOTOGRAPHY
ASSISTANCE
Houwa Toda

BOOK DESIGN
Yukio Hoshino
VOLARE inc.

EDITOR
Tsunenori Matsumiya

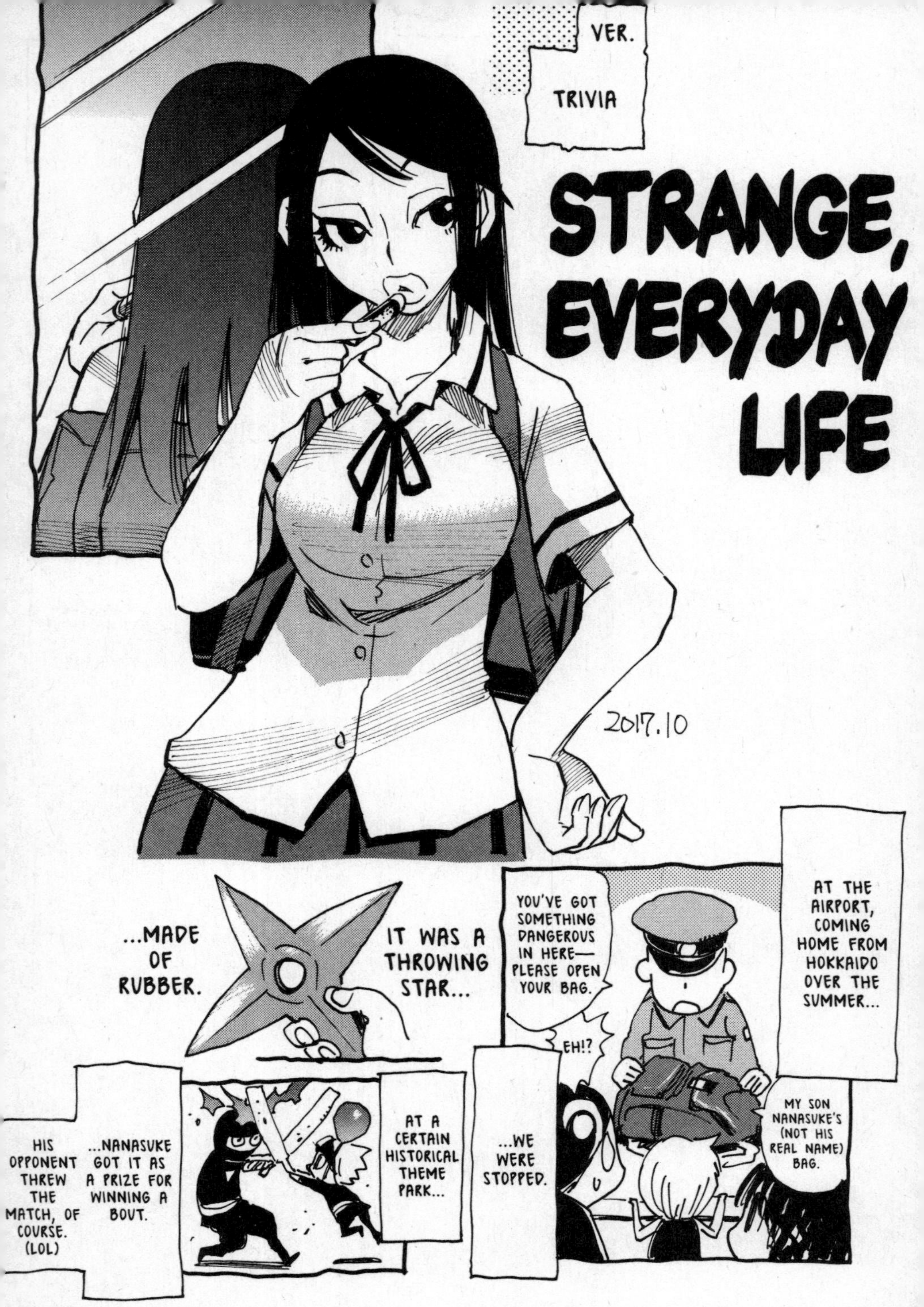
VER.
TRIVIA
STRANGE, EVERYDAY LIFE
2017.10
AT THE AIRPORT, COMING HOME FROM HOKKAIDO OVER THE SUMMER...
YOU'VE GOT SOMETHING DANGEROUS IN HERE—PLEASE OPEN YOUR BAG.
EH!?
MY SON NANASUKE'S (NOT HIS REAL NAME) BAG.
...WE WERE STOPPED.
IT WAS A THROWING STAR...
...MADE OF RUBBER.
AT A CERTAIN HISTORICAL THEME PARK...
...NANASUKE GOT IT AS A PRIZE FOR WINNING A BOUT.
HIS OPPONENT THREW THE MATCH, OF COURSE. (LOL)

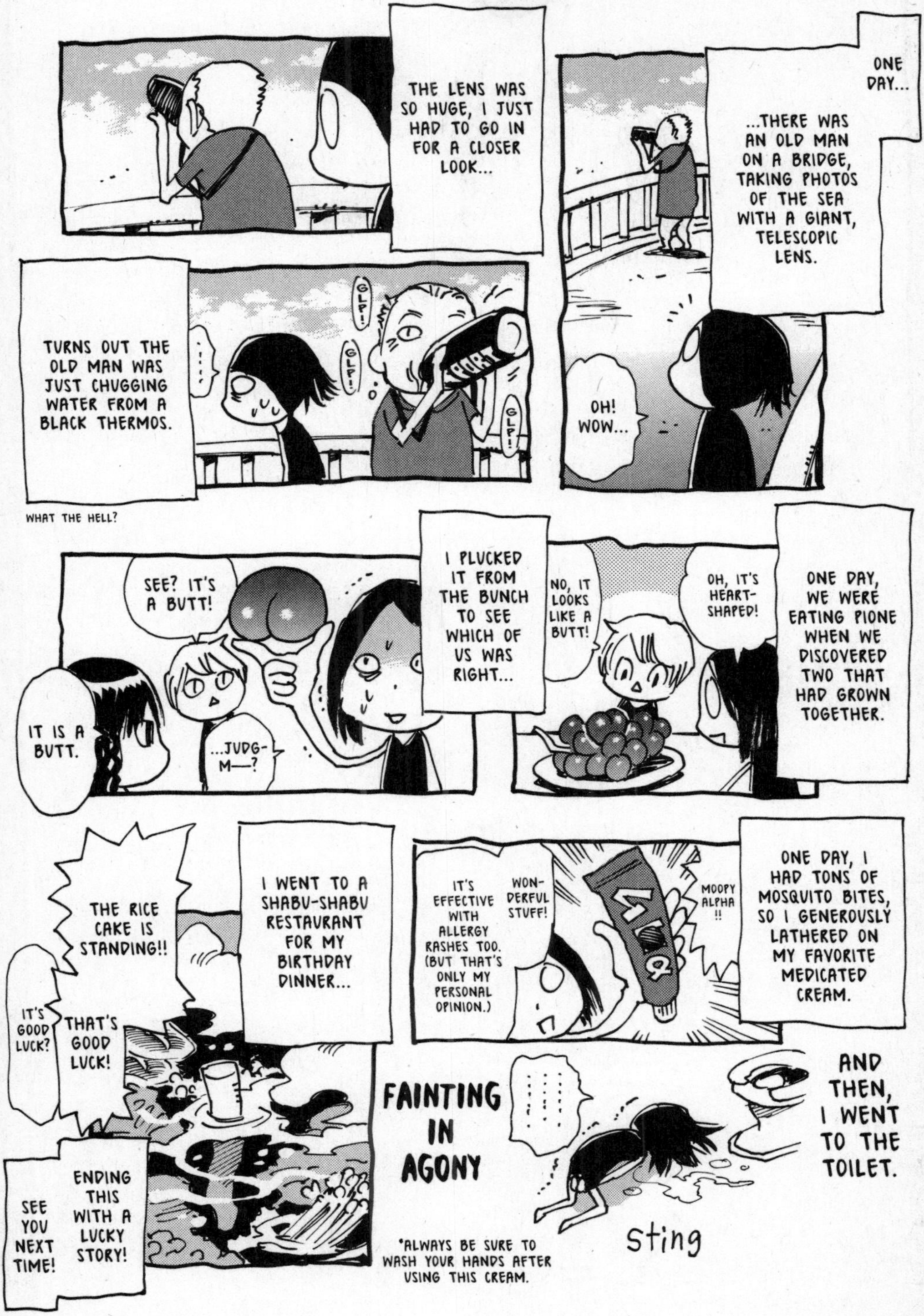
ONE DAY...
...THERE WAS AN OLD MAN ON A BRIDGE, TAKING PHOTOS OF THE SEA WITH A GIANT, TELESCOPIC LENS.
OH! WOW...
THE LENS WAS SO HUGE, I JUST HAD TO GO IN FOR A CLOSER LOOK...
TURNS OUT THE OLD MAN WAS JUST CHUGGING WATER FROM A BLACK THERMOS.
GLP!
GLP!
GLP!
WHAT THE HELL?
ONE DAY, WE WERE EATING PIONE WHEN WE DISCOVERED TWO THAT HAD GROWN TOGETHER.
OH, IT'S HEART-SHAPED!
NO, IT LOOKS LIKE A BUTT!
I PLUCKED IT FROM THE BUNCH TO SEE WHICH OF US WAS RIGHT...
SEE? IT'S A BUTT!
...JUDG-M—?
IT IS A BUTT.
ONE DAY, I HAD TONS OF MOSQUITO BITES, SO I GENEROUSLY LATHERED ON MY FAVORITE MEDICATED CREAM.
MOOPY ALPHA!!
WON-DERFUL STUFF!
IT'S EFFECTIVE WITH ALLERGY RASHES TOO. (BUT THAT'S ONLY MY PERSONAL OPINION.)
AND THEN, I WENT TO THE TOILET.
sting
FAINTING IN AGONY
*ALWAYS BE SURE TO WASH YOUR HANDS AFTER USING THIS CREAM.
I WENT TO A SHABU-SHABU RESTAURANT FOR MY BIRTHDAY DINNER...
THE RICE CAKE IS STANDING!!
THAT'S GOOD LUCK!
IT'S GOOD LUCK?
ENDING THIS WITH A LUCKY STORY!
SEE YOU NEXT TIME!

FOR THE KID I SAW IN MY Dreams 1

KEI SANBE

TRANSLATION: SHELDON DRZKA ✦ LETTERING: ABIGAIL BLACKMAN

This book is a work of fiction. Names, characters, places, and incidents are the product of the author's imagination or are used fictitiously. Any resemblance to actual events, locales, or persons, living or dead, is coincidental.

YUME DE MITA ANO KO NO TAME NI Volume 1
© Kei SANBE 2017.
First published in Japan in 2017 by KADOKAWA CORPORATION, Tokyo.
English translation rights arranged with KADOKAWA CORPORATION,
Tokyo through TUTTLE-MORI AGENCY INC., Tokyo.

English translation © 2019 by Yen Press, LLC

Yen Press, LLC supports the right to free expression and the value of copyright. The purpose of copyright is to encourage writers and artists to produce the creative works that enrich our culture.

The scanning, uploading, and distribution of this book without permission is a theft of the author's intellectual property. If you would like permission to use material from the book (other than for review purposes), please contact the publisher. Thank you for your support of the author's rights.

Yen Press
1290 Avenue of the Americas
New York, NY 10104

Visit us at yenpress.com
facebook.com/yenpress
twitter.com/yenpress
yenpress.tumblr.com
instagram.com/yenpress

First Yen Press Edition: January 2019

Yen Press is an imprint of Yen Press, LLC.
The Yen Press name and logo are trademarks of Yen Press, LLC.

The publisher is not responsible for websites (or their content) that are not owned by the publisher.

Library of Congress Control Number: 2018958636

ISBNs: 978-1-9753-2886-3 (hardcover)
        978-1-9753-2887-0 (ebook)

10 9 8 7 6 5 4 3 2 1

WOR

Printed in the United States of America

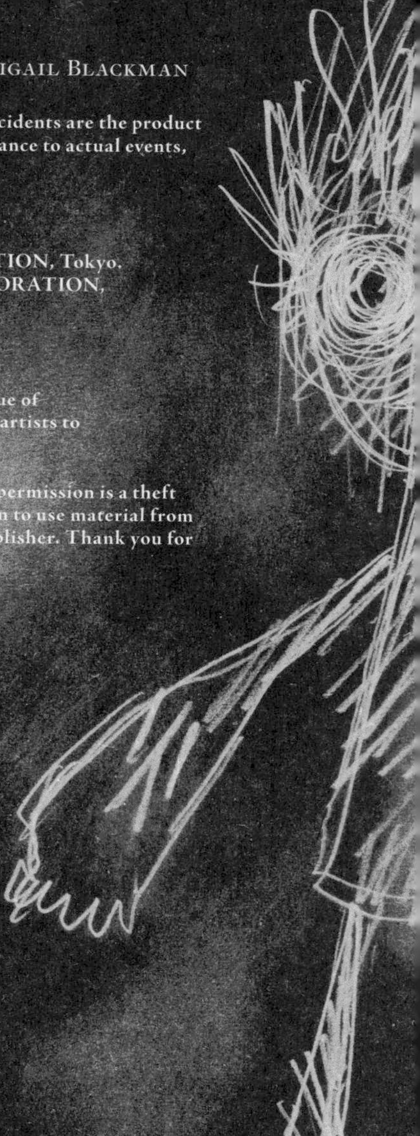